# SURVIVORS

# SURVIVORS

## Children's Lives After the Holocaust

## REBECCA CLIFFORD

YALE UNIVERSITY PRESS
NEW HAVEN AND LONDON

For information about this and other Yale University Press publications, please contact:
U.S. Office:    sales.press@yale.edu    yalebooks.com
Europe Office:    sales@yaleup.co.uk    yalebooks.co.uk

Set in Adobe Garamond Pro by IDSUK (DataConnection) Ltd
Printed in Great Britain by Gomer Press Ltd, Llandysul, Ceredigion, Wales

Library of Congress Control Number: 2020937935

A catalogue record for this book is available from the British Library.

10 9 8 7 6 5 4 3 2 1

*To my mother Julia, born in Budapest in 1944,*
*and to my children Max and Addie,*
*born in Swansea in safer times*

# CONTENTS

# ILLUSTRATIONS

1. Child survivors walk out of a children's barracks in Auschwitz-Birkenau, January 1945. United States Holocaust Memorial Museum, courtesy of Lydia Chagoll.
2. A child survivor of Bergen-Belsen concentration camp recuperates in the camp hospital, July 1945. Photo by Edgar Ainsworth/Picture Post/ Hulton Archive/Getty Images.
3. The 'Buchenwald boys' on the train to France, June 1945. United States Holocaust Memorial Museum, courtesy of Robert Waisman.
4. Joseph S. sits on the footboard of an UNRRA lorry, June 1945. Photo by Mondadori via Getty Images.
5. The 'Buchenwald boys' at their OSE care home at Taverny, 1945–7. United States Holocaust Memorial Museum, courtesy of Claude & Judith Feist Hemmendinger.
6. Joseph S. attends a memorial service in Buchenwald, c. 1946. United States Holocaust Memorial Museum.
7. Felice Z. with Juliette Patoux, who sheltered her on her farm in La Caillaudière, near Vendoeuvres, France, August 1943. United States Holocaust Memorial Museum, courtesy of Felice Zimmern Stokes.
8. Judith K. with her adopted sister Suzy Enard and another child, June 1946. United States Holocaust Memorial Museum, courtesy of Judith Koppel Steel.
9. Group portrait of children at the OSE children's home at the Château de Vaucelles in Taverny, c. 1947. United States Holocaust Memorial Museum, courtesy of Felice Zimmern Stokes.

# ABBREVIATIONS

| | |
|---|---|
| AIVG | Aide aux Israélites Victimes de la Guerre |
| AJWS | Australian Jewish Welfare Society |
| BEG | Bundesentschädigungsgesetz (Federal Compensation Law of 1956) |
| CBF | Central British Fund for German Jewry |
| CJC(A) | Canadian Jewish Congress (Archive) |
| DP | displaced person |
| DSM | *Diagnostic and Statistical Manual of Mental Disorders* |
| FVA | Fortunoff Video Archive for Holocaust Testimonies, Yale University Library |
| IRO | International Refugee Organization |
| ITS | International Tracing Service |
| JDC | American Jewish Joint Distribution Committee (the 'Joint') |
| ORT | Organization for Rehabilitation and Training |
| OSE | Oeuvre de Secours aux Enfants |
| PTSD | post-traumatic stress disorder |
| SHEK | Schweizer Hilfswerk für Emigrantenkinder |
| UJRA | United Jewish Relief Agency |
| UNRRA | United Nations Relief and Rehabilitation Administration |
| URO | United Restitution Office |
| USCOM | United States Committee for the Care of European Children |
| USHMM(A) | United States Holocaust Memorial Museum (Archive) |
| VHA | Visual History Archive |
| WLA | Wiener Library Archive |

# ACKNOWLEDGEMENTS

It is an enormous pleasure to thank the people who helped me in writing this book, and no group more so than the child survivors who shared their life stories with me through interviews. Not every story ended up in these pages – this would have required ten books – but each and every interview informed my understanding, and changed me as a person as well. My deepest gratitude to: Agnes G.-S., Andrew B., Angela S., Avigdor C., Danielle B., Dora K., Esther S., Eva M., Françoise R., Hanneke D., Harry M., Henri O., Jackie Y., Jacques F., Joan S., Joanna M., Lea R., 'Leora', Louise L.-I., Manny M., Paul Z., Peter G., Peter W., Robert T., Sylvia R., Vera S., and Zdenka H. It was an immense privilege to hear your stories.

I wish to thank the British Academy, the Leverhulme Trust, and the Sharon Abramson Research Grant scheme of the Holocaust Educational Foundation of Northwestern University for their generous financial support. The British Academy funded a six-month stay in Washington DC, where I conducted the bulk of the archival research for this book. A Leverhulme Trust Research Fellowship allowed me to have a complete break from my regular duties at Swansea University, and this not only gave me the time to write, but allowed me to clear space in my mind to experiment with writing in a new way and for a new audience. The Sharon Abramson Research Grant funded several later archive visits, and a number of interviews with child survivors. It would not have been possible to write this book without the help of these funding bodies.

I also wish to thank everyone at Yale University Press. In the midst of a global pandemic, they shepherded the manuscript through to its final form with incredible professionalism and good humour. I have rarely felt so well supported by such a remarkable team: in adverse circumstances, they performed daily miracles. I owe particular thanks to Julian Loose, my editor. Whenever I strayed too far from the voices of child survivors, he pulled me back. He helped me to keep my sights focused on the most meaningful elements of this history, and I could not have asked for a more thoughtful or more committed editor.

In carrying out archival research, I relied hugely on the expertise, wisdom and sound judgement of a number of librarians and archivists. I wish to thank in particular Megan Lewis, Ron Coleman, and Becky Erbelding of the United States Holocaust Memorial Museum, who encouraged me tirelessly over six months. I owe a particular debt to Ron, who asked me a fantastic question very early on in my research ('What would be your ideal document?'). That question helped me to figure out what I was looking for in the archives – thank you, Ron. Janice Rosen, director of the Alex Dworkin Canadian Jewish Archives in Montreal, both guided me through the collections and inspired me to think about the ethics of using child survivors' case files from new angles. The staff of the Wiener Library, London, welcomed me warmly on multiple visits; my particular thanks to Christine Schmidt for all her enthusiasm for my project. And enormous thanks are due to Isabelle Rohr of the American Jewish Joint Distribution Committee Archives in New York, who searched for a missing file for me over a period of six months – and found it! Thanks also to the staff of the Jewish Public Library of Montreal; the Library of Congress in Washington DC; the libraries at Yale University, Royal Holloway, the University of Southampton and the Hebrew University of Jerusalem; and the archives of the Imperial War Museum in London.

Many remarkable historians whose work has inspired me offered to read part or all of this book, and provided helpful critical comments. For giving so generously of their time and their thoughts, I am indebted to Martin Conway, Robert Gildea, Chris Millington, Mark Roseman, Susan Solomon, and Dan Stone. Their suggestions have made this a much stronger book, and I hope that they can each see something of themselves reflected in the final product. I owe a particular debt to Robert Gildea, who has not only gone to bat for me and my work for more than fifteen years, but who also taught me how to do oral history, even as he learned the art himself.

Other colleagues and friends have inspired me and nurtured this work. Josie McLellan urged me to experiment with new ways of writing. Boaz Cohen, Laura Hobson Faure, and Antoine Burgard shared insights from their own work on child survivors and provided me with copies of forthcoming publications; their scholarship has set a fine example. Tom Allbeson shared material that he found in his own research. I could not ask for kinder or more gracious colleagues than those I work with in the History Department at Swansea University; I owe particular thanks to David Turner, and to all the members of the Conflict, Reconstruction and Memory Research Group. I was also fortunate to work with a remarkable team of undergraduate students, who transcribed my interviews and acted as research assistants: my thanks to Chris Brent, Nathan Davies, Josh Foley, Genevieve George, Eleri Powell, Angharad Williams, and Freya Worrall.

The initial research for this book was carried out during a six-month stay in Washington DC, during which time I was a visiting fellow at Georgetown University's BMW Center for German and European Studies. I am grateful to Anna von der Goltz for welcoming me so warmly. Part of the writing was conducted during a stay at the Université Grenoble Alpes, where it was a delight to work alongside Anne Dalmasso and Anne-Marie Granet Abisset in the LARHRA research lab. Anne-Marie generously lent me her office, which has a marvellous view of the Alps. I gazed across the peaks where, during the war, members of the aid organization Oeuvre de Secours aux Enfants (OSE) smuggled Jewish children to safety in neutral Switzerland. I thought often of Marianne Cohn, a young resister who was caught by the Gestapo as she tried to shepherd a group of Jewish children across the border near Annemasse. Her bravery served as a fierce inspiration.

I wrote a good portion of this book during a time when I was ill, and being ill incurs its own particular set of debts. To my good friends Catherine, George and Lizzy: thank you for reading sections of the book and sharing your thoughts. To my mother Julia: thank you for worrying for me, so that I did not have to worry so much for myself. To my grandmother, Ibolya (but to me always Mamuka): thank you for believing that I was writing this book 'for the family'. Maybe I was. To Herschel, my partner: thank you for doing so much to nurture my spirit and body and work when I was at my weakest. It was not easy, and the debt I owe you is incalculable. You gave bountiful heaps of your own research time so that I could write uninterrupted, even when I was too tired to make much progress. You understood that when I could not do much else, being able to write – even just a paragraph or two – was transformative.

I owe the greatest debt of all to my children, Max and Ada (Addie). When illness reduced my world, they helped me to focus on what really mattered. They have been my guides in thinking about children as agents with wills and ways of their own. Watching them discover who they are is one of my life's great privileges.

# ON NAMES

Names are a fraught territory for children who survived the Holocaust. As they entered hiding places, ghettos, and internment and concentration camps, many young children lost their original names. Some were given false, non-Jewish names for their own protection, and they may have spent years answering to these, until their birth names faded entirely from their consciousness. Some were adopted shortly after the war, and took the names of their adoptive families; they may not have learned that they were born under a very different name until they were adults. Any child who could not be matched with her original name at the war's end stood little chance of ever finding any surviving parents, siblings or relatives.

The people whose stories are explored in this book understand more keenly than most the power of names to denote identity and ownership of the life story. During the course of my research, I interviewed dozens of child survivors, and listened to dozens more interviews conducted by other researchers. With only one exception, these survivors preferred to tell their stories under their own names, rather than using pseudonyms. I understand this impulse. You can lose your home, you can lose your parents and relatives, you can struggle for years to understand the most fundamental details of where you have come from and who you are – and at the end of that process, to lose your own name from your life story is a loss too far.

In my research for this book, I paired oral history interviews with archival documents. I generally started with the archives, and used the names I found there to follow child survivors into their adult lives, drawing on interviews that they had given to existing oral history projects, or tracing their current whereabouts and interviewing them myself. However, many archives allow researchers to consult material relating to individual child survivors only if the material is subsequently anonymized. This presented me with an ethical dilemma: I could interview these survivors, or use interviews that they had previously recorded, but I would have to conceal their names. I would be forced to strip their identities from their stories.

In consultation with archivists, I reached a compromise for this book: I have used child survivors' real first names and initials. This is an imperfect compromise, but it has allowed me to meet the requirements set by the archives, while ensuring that the survivors whose stories are told here are not dispossessed of this most fundamental part of their identity. In order to preserve the astounding diversity of the names of an entire generation of Jewish children from Europe (names that bore the imprint of every country and culture on the Continent), I have used survivors' childhood names as they appeared in archival documents, rather than later names altered by anglicization (or adaptations into other languages, particularly Hebrew) or by marriage. This means that a few of the people in this study appear under their adoptive names, because these were the names used in their early records.

I have used pseudonyms in only a small handful of cases: where I used archival records without a later interview (because I was unable to track down the person involved, or because he or she had subsequently died); where the archives were clear that only full anonymization would suffice; or for the one and only case where an interviewee asked me not to use her real name. For all others, I have aimed to preserve this most treasured possession as fully as possible.

# INTRODUCTION

In the summer of 1946 seven-year-old Litzi S., a survivor of Theresienstadt ghetto-camp who had been brought to England after her liberation, was approached by a man in the care home where she was living with other child survivors of the Holocaust. The man explained that he was her father, and that the woman he was with was her mother. This seemed, at the time, plausible enough: neither children nor staff in the care home, tucked away in a tranquil country village in Surrey, had a clear picture of what had happened to the children's parents. Agencies such as the Red Cross's International Tracing Service were searching for missing people across continental Europe and beyond, but these searches were slow, and those waiting for any news of their loved ones faced a long period of agonizing uncertainty. A year after the war's end, the children at the care home were in a state of continual waiting, and Litzi's family were the first to show up alive. To Litzi and to the children around her, it must have seemed a wondrous event.

Litzi went home with the family who had come to claim her, and had what was, at least on the surface, a normal childhood from that point forward. Her life before she was reunited with her family became part of a dimly remembered past. She was sometimes troubled by memories that she could make no sense of, memories of rough wooden bunk beds and large rooms filled with other children, but her parents brushed off her questions, and after a while she stopped asking. At the age of eighteen, in the midst of a family row, she screamed in anger at the man who had come to claim her eleven years before, 'I wish you weren't my father!' 'I'm not,' replied the man. He was in fact her father's brother, and like many others who cared for child survivors after the war, he had judged it better to lie about the murder of Litzi's parents than to take the precarious route forwards offered by the truth.[1]

At the same time in the same care home, staff were troubled by another of their wards, eleven-year-old Mina R.*, also a survivor of Theresienstadt. Mina's behaviour was puzzling: her language was stilted, and her emotions seemed unnatural; staff recorded that they were worried by the false smile permanently frozen on her face. One day Mina suddenly revealed to care home staff how, during the war, she had seen her mother shot through the head right in front of her. Alice Goldberger, the matron of the home, believed that speaking about the wartime past could be therapeutic for children, and she encouraged the girl to unburden herself of her painful memories. She recorded that after this dramatic and sudden revelation, Mina's behaviour improved: speaking did indeed appear to have had a therapeutic effect. Staff at the home were thus dumbfounded when, six years later, the girl's mother turned up alive, having never been shot through the head at all.[2]

Litzi's and Mina's stories attest to the strange world that child survivors of the Holocaust found themselves in during the early post-war years. It was a world in which apparent truths could be instantly, shockingly upended. Parents thought to be alive were sometimes revealed to be dead, as Litzi learned to her shock when her 'father' finally confessed to being her uncle. Parents believed to be dead, as was Mina's mother, might, in rarer cases, suddenly show up alive. The truth was often unknown, but equally often it was hidden from children. Some adults listened to children's troubling memories and questions, but far more frequently they deflected children's curiosity about their pasts.

No one at the time thought of these children as 'child Holocaust survivors'. They were called 'unaccompanied children', 'Jewish war orphans', or 'war-damaged children', among other things. More often, they were simply told that they were the lucky ones who had lived when others had died. They should consider themselves lucky to be alive, lucky to be young enough and resilient enough to be able to shed the weight of unbearable memories, lucky to be the

---

* pseudonym

objects of reconstruction efforts, rather than the subjects (who after all had to do the often demoralizing grunt work of rebuilding ruined families and communities, physically, economically, and psychologically). This was a loaded phrase. To tell a child that she was lucky to have survived, that she should put the past behind her and focus on the future, was to dismiss her efforts to make sense of her own history. As child survivors grew up, many began to push back against such stultifying assurances. They started to ask biological parents, foster parents, relatives, and care workers pointed questions about their early lives. 'What is my real name?' 'Where do I really come from?' 'Why won't you tell me about my mother?' 'Why don't you have any pictures of me as a baby?' Such questions had the potential to push individuals and whole families into an uneasy confrontation with the past.

This book seeks to uncover the post-war lives of the very youngest survivors of the Holocaust, a group that has been historically neglected by scholars.[3] It focuses on those born between 1935 and 1944, who were ten years old or younger at the moment of liberation in 1945. These young children had the slimmest chance of survival of any age group during the Holocaust (save the very elderly), but it is not this, or not this alone, that makes their stories so fascinating. Young children's experiences shed light on a question with profound repercussions: how can we make sense of our lives when we do not know where we come from? Because their pre-war memories were indistinct or even non-existent, and because there was often no living adult able or willing to fill in the key details of their earliest days and years, these child survivors often faced a decades-long struggle to assemble the tale of their origins – a simple but essential act of autobiography, fundamental to identity. If you cannot recount the story of your own family, your home town, or your formative experiences, how do you make sense of your childhood and its impacts? What work do you have to do to explain who you are? Most of us take for granted that we can make at least some sense of our childhood memories. We do not often stop to think of this as a privilege. At its core, this book explores what it means to grow up and to grow older when you do not have that advantage, and are forced by your circumstances to weave the story of your past from scraps. It is a book about the Holocaust, but more fundamentally it is a book about the history of living after, and living with, a childhood marked by chaos.

It is also fundamentally a book about memory, and in particular about early memories and their role in our lives as we age. Most people, when asked, will happily tell you about their earliest memory. Mine is of folding laundry. I guess that I was about three years old when this moment happened, as I can recall how small I was next to the furniture in the room. In this memory, I was in the front room of our house in Kingston, Ontario, the one we called the 'TV room'. In front of me was a plastic laundry basket atop a wooden chest, a chest my father made. There was a peach-coloured jumper in the basket and I reached up to pull it out, because I recognized it as mine, a gift to me from my paternal grandmother. The laundry was hot from the tumble dryer, and a wave of delicious warmth hit my hand as I reached up. When I tugged on the jumper, something amazing happened: bright sparks flew through the air. The freshly dried jumper was alive with static electricity, and the dry Canadian air of mid-winter allowed it to crackle and sing, as spark-flowers burst along my fingertips. This memory has stayed in my mind, I suppose, because it was both so surprising and so thrillingly beautiful.

But how is it that I can *understand* this memory? How do I know that the chest was made by my father, and the jumper by my grandmother? How is it that I know that I am in the TV room, that I am indeed in my own house, that my mother is nearby even though I am enjoying a moment of inquisitive solitude? It is because this memory, like all memories, is a social construction, and the adults around me have helped me to make sense of my experience. They explained who made the chest, who made the jumper, and why sparks fly through dry air in the winter. This is true not just for this one memory, but for all my early memories – and for all of yours as well. Most of us can tell the story of our lives, from the beginning through to the present, because others have helped us to build the narrative. Our parents, families and communities, the collective and social context in which we live, provide the details that we cannot remember or explain, and help us to contextualize memories that we hold in our mind's eye but might otherwise struggle to interpret.

The life stories of child survivors are fascinating in part because this social world was rent asunder for them: the parents, relatives, and communities that would normally play this crucial role were not there to do the job. In their absence, children were left with memories that they could not interpret, and stories of their early lives that were peppered with holes. As they grew, they had to piece things together for themselves, chasing down documents, photos, and living relatives flung far and wide in diaspora, all in order to be able to answer the most fundamental of questions: who am I?

This book follows a group of very young child Holocaust survivors out of the ruins of war and through their later childhoods, their adolescence, their journeys into adulthood, their marriages and their own experiences of parenthood, and finally into their old age, charting their changing relationship to their pasts over a span of seventy years. It looks at how they interacted with adults, the surviving parents and relatives, host and foster parents, humanitarian aid workers, mental health professionals, and others who tried to sculpt the parameters of their lives, who observed them, cared for them, and nurtured them – and equally at times neglected them, lied to them, and abandoned them. It explores the short- and long-term consequences of their childhood experiences on their identities, and it aims to challenge some of our fundamental assumptions about children as subjects, about the nature of trauma, and about the relationship between the self and memory.

Who were the child survivors of the Holocaust? In looking at their lives, we need to accept that there is a great deal that we will never know about them. To begin with, we will never know precisely how many children from Jewish backgrounds survived the war at all. Early post-war estimates drawn up by the American Jewish Joint Distribution Committee (hereafter the JDC) suggested that 150,000 of Europe's Jewish children survived the war, of a pre-war population of 1.5 million.[4] This is the figure that historians generally still use today, but it is not without complications and complexities.[5] It raises a number of questions, questions that have broader implications when we study children in and after conflict. Which children were visible to aid organizations such as the JDC? Which children counted as Jewish? Which children counted as survivors? Who, indeed, counted as a child at all?

The JDC based its estimates on the numbers of children who passed through the care of aid agencies after the war, but it was difficult, if not impossible, to count the ranks of those children who never received aid in the post-war period; cared for by surviving parents, relatives or host families, they passed quietly under the radar of the agencies, although they numbered in the tens of thousands.[6] We might equally consider how these post-war figures reflected Nazi definitions of who was and who was not Jewish; it is not clear, for example, if the figures included children who had one non-Jewish parent (and who might have been particularly invisible if they had little contact with Jewish organizations and communities after the war). We might ask which children qualified as 'survivors' in the eyes of the aid agencies, and indeed in the eyes of later historians. When large numbers of Jews who had survived the war in the Soviet Union began, after 1946, to flood into the camps set up for post-war refugees (then called displaced persons, or DPs) in Germany, Austria, and Italy, the JDC recorded that their original estimate had failed to account for an additional 30,000 Jewish children who had survived the war on the Soviet side. The amended figure of 180,000, however, has never been taken up by historians – which implies, of course, that these children have not traditionally been considered 'survivors' by historians themselves.[7] Finally, we might pose the question of how the very category of 'child' was defined in this context. The JDC, the United Nations Relief and Rehabilitation Administration (UNRRA), and other associated aid organizations did not always agree on where the upper boundaries of childhood lay, but most drew the line at seventeen or eighteen years of age. What is thus masked by these post-war estimates, and further obscured by the aid agencies' use of images of babies, toddlers and young children in their fundraising literature, is the fact that the majority of child survivors were adolescents (just as is true for most child refugees today).[8] For all these reasons, we should bear in mind that post-war statistics on child survivors mask a number of larger questions about the boundaries of childhood and the nature of survival. We should therefore accept that, as a demographic group, there is much about child survivors that we will never know.

Beyond numbers, however, it is clear that child survivors were the remnant of an entire generation of European Jewry, and as such they were the focus of much adult attention and anxiety in the early years after the war. It is ironic, then, that as a group they have received scant attention from historians until very recently. In a broad sense, children and their experiences have traditionally been on the margins of historical scholarship, and in many ways that is where they remain. Historians looking at children have tended to focus on constructions of childhood, rather than on children themselves, examining what adults thought of children in the past, rather than what children thought of their own lives and worlds, or how they might have acted as valuable witnesses to adult behaviour. This has been particularly true where historians study war and conflict. Even though children found themselves to be the targets of violence in the wars of the twentieth century as never before, war can appear to be the most adult of topics. We struggle to fit children into our understanding of conflict, tending to see them almost exclusively as part of the massed ranks of the victims, and it is challenging to move beyond their victimhood. But children, even very small children, were actors and agents in their own right in the history of war. Jewish children caught in the net of genocidal Nazi policies during the Second World War were extremely vulnerable, but if we see them exclusively as victims, we miss the fact that they could also be creative evaders, negotiators, manipulators, and even perpetrators of retributive violence. After the war, when they found themselves the objects of a massive humanitarian campaign to care for and repatriate Europe's 'unaccompanied children', they could and did work to stymy, subvert, and reject the well-intentioned plans of adults for their futures. They forged their own paths in the aftermath of conflict, and we do children an enormous disservice when we view them simply as victims.

Historians have perhaps been more comfortable in examining the adults who helped child survivors after the war, rather than the children themselves. The concerns and the visions of these adults have been the subject of a recent wave of historical scholarship, including books such as Tara Zahra's *The Lost Children* and Daniella Doron's *Jewish Youth and Identity in Postwar France*. Adults' fears and hopes for children are fascinating historical topics, but we must resist the temptation to see this as a window onto children themselves, as human beings with their own agendas. Since we have all at one point been children, we all know that the desires of adults with authority, and the desires of children with little authority, can sometimes rather spectacularly part ways. This book takes the approach that children are not simply on the receiving end of power: adults may often regard them as objects, but they are subjects nonetheless. An examination of children in the web of their relations with family or other carers, with agencies and institutions, and between these institutions and civil society, suggests that we need to seek new avenues for inserting children's history into our broader understanding of the past.[9]

How might children have asserted themselves as subjects in their own right? One simple way was by asking questions about their own pasts, and probing adults for answers, but here they often ran up against difficulties. Adult carers, whether surviving family members or aid organization workers, often did not have much information themselves in the long, uncertain period of limbo that stretched through the early post-war years. As Litzi's and Mina's stories reveal, this was a period when it was rarely clear who was alive and who was not. Moreover, many adults did not want to burden young minds with such knowledge as was available. Care workers were divided on the question of whether it was helpful or harmful for children to talk about their wartime experiences, but even where carers encouraged children to speak about the recent past, the imagined goal was to help a child to let go of recent losses and move on. In this, adults were aided by the assumption that children's psyches were malleable and resilient. In the words of one French journalist, commenting on child survivors of Bergen Belsen concentration camp in August 1945, 'happily memory is short at this age, and the need to live is intense. Do they feel simply that they have lived through a vague nightmare, the memory of which has already begun to fade?' Adult insistence that children would soon forget (and the assumption that this was in the child's best interests) silenced many children's curious questioning about the immediate past. There were certainly environments in which the wartime past was openly discussed, but it was a rare environment indeed where a child's war experiences were given any sort of moral equivalence to those of an adult.

This assumption that children could and would forget the past and focus on the future, that they were 'lucky' and that this luck would be enough to silence memory, took a long time to fade. It was child survivors themselves who eventually challenged it, but it was a challenge that took decades to mature. We see this in the story of Felice Z. In 1983, Felice was only beginning to learn who she was. The year before, at the age of forty-two, she had finally received confirmation that her parents had been killed in Auschwitz. The family – Felice's parents, David and Lydia, her older sister Beate, then aged three, and Felice, then one year old – had been deported from the little town of Walldürn in the Baden area of Germany to the internment camp of Gurs in the south of France. The two small girls had been rescued from the camp by the Red Cross, and hidden with French Catholic families until the Liberation. Felice's parents were deported and murdered.[10] Felice had been trying, since her early twenties, to trace the details of her own early years and of her parents' lives and deaths, but there were still holes in her understanding. She struck up the courage to attend the first American Gathering of Jewish Holocaust Survivors, the largest meeting of Holocaust survivors ever held, which took place in April 1983 in Washington DC. Hoping to meet others with similar stories, but uncertain where her own story fitted in the broader context of 'surviving the Holocaust', Felice braved the criticism of older survivors, who told her: 'You were a child, so what do you know? You don't remember.' Speaking with a volunteer who recorded a short interview with her at the Gathering, Felice's frustration exploded:

People don't understand, and it's very hard for me to talk about it. I don't belong, I didn't go to a camp, I didn't suffer in that way. There was nothing to show for it. [. . .] I felt that I'm not a survivor, but then I thought: I am a survivor, in my own way. My parents died, my whole family died, and besides my sister and myself everyone else is gone.[11]

Around the same time, across the ocean, Denny M. was having a similarly disheartening experience. He had tried to participate in some of the early support groups for Holocaust survivors in Britain, but found himself running up against the incredulity and even hostility of older survivors. Born in November 1940, Denny had been sent to Theresienstadt as an infant, and had no memory of his murdered father and mother. When he arrived in Britain after the war's end, he was not yet five years old. He was aware that his experience in Theresienstadt was different from that of an adult survivor of a camp such as Auschwitz or Buchenwald, but he was shocked by the stark belittling of his experience that he encountered in the survivors' support groups: he recalled that older survivors suggested that he had effectively spent the war years 'in a sort of Butlin's holiday camp'. Denny, Felice, and countless other child survivors confronted this same barrier again and again: older witnesses to the war, including many older survivors, were unwilling to admit children's experiences into the ranks of what 'counted' as survival.[12]

Felice's and Denny's stories provide a further clue as to why the history of child Holocaust survivors has remained marginal for so long. Their toxic encounters with older survivors and their sense of not belonging suggest the contours of an exclusionary politics of memory surrounding the very concept of a 'survivor'. We now take a broad view of what constituted survival in the Holocaust, and who might call themselves a survivor, but the accepted definitions were once far narrower. For many decades after the war, a 'survivor' was understood primarily to mean a concentration camp survivor, a category that excluded the majority of child survivors (and many adult survivors as well). The figure of the camp survivor had a cultural power that was reinforced by public opinion, but was also policed by camp survivors themselves, who were not eager to see those they imagined had suffered less dilute the potency of this notion of survival.

Child survivors had to fight not only against the external criticism of older survivors, but also an internal voice that suggested that they were not really survivors but merely fortunate kids, that their war experiences were in some way less authentic than those of camp survivors. Nicole D., who in 1991 organized the first international meeting of children who had been hidden during the Holocaust, has observed that 'one can never break into the hierarchy of suffering'.[13] It is only recently that child survivors have taken on some of the roles that not long ago were the preserve of older survivors. They often speak to school students. They volunteer at Holocaust museums and exhibits. They give talks for Holocaust Memorial Day. Seventy-five years after the end of the war, they have finally been recognized as survivors, and there is a clear rationale behind the shift: they are the only ones left.

The story of these youngest child survivors is a profoundly transnational one. At the war's end, they could be found in every country in Europe, and some could even be found beyond the continent, having managed to escape during the war. Some had spent at least a portion of the war years on the run across and between different countries. Many were then flung into a global diaspora at the war's end, leaving continental Europe for the Anglo-American world, for Palestine, or for other destinations. Their collective story cannot be told from any one regional or national perspective. In this book, to capture this almost overwhelming diversity of experience, I started by examining the stories of a hundred individual children, and I mapped out a few fairly loose criteria to narrow down the choice. First of all, given that at its core this book concerns how a person can make sense of her life when she cannot tell her own early story, I chose those who were ten years old or less in 1945: I wanted to find children who had been alive and present in Europe during the war years, but who did not necessarily have clear memories of the experience.[14] Second, given that this book seeks to unpick the ways in which people remember and make sense of their childhoods at different moments in time and over the course of decades, I favoured those individuals whose stories I could reconstruct *both* through archival sources and through later oral testimony. When I found a child's name in the archives, I searched to find if she had later given an interview (or multiple interviews) describing her experiences, and I also conducted interviews myself. This meant that I could dig into the ways in which the past held very different meanings for individuals through changing historical contexts and phases of life, and I could weigh up some of the long-term repercussions of short-term decisions, something that is difficult to do with archival material alone. Finally, I favoured the stories of those children – the majority – who left Europe after the war. As I was interested primarily in how people make sense of their childhoods over time, I started from the assumption that this process was all the more complex when a child had lost language and culture in addition to home and community. The double dislocation of war and emigration made for a particularly compelling, collective, transnational story: children born in Antwerp, Riga, or Salonika ended up in East London, Seattle, or Winnipeg; and yet despite the vast reaches of space (and time) that stretched between their communities of origin and the places where they later lived, despite the different cultures that they came from and ended up in, their stories share common elements that are surprisingly rich and deep.

To tell these stories, this book draws on a remarkable collection of archival material – documents originating from nearly a dozen different countries, including care agency files, records from care homes, indemnity claims, psychiatric reports, letters, photographs, and unpublished memoirs: a paper trail on child survivors that takes us across the globe. Yet despite this rich documentation, the voices of child survivors themselves are elusive in the archives. Adults created nearly all of the documentation that discussed these children in the years after the war, and it is difficult to uncover what the children themselves thought and felt in the past. In my archival research, I occasionally turned up letters, short essays, and poems written by young child survivors after the war, and there are a few rare collections of drawings by children dotted in archives here and there. But for the most part archives choose to save documents considered valuable, and children's work is rarely valued in this way. Even where young children do leave documents, we can question the extent to which these reflect a child's own emotions and opinions. Children are often told what to write, and what to draw. They also tend to choose their subject matter to please the adults who care for them. It is thus challenging to tease meaning out of these rare letters and drawings that turn up in the archives, although equally exciting to try.[15]

Even the most compelling archival sources are insufficient to follow children into and through their adulthood to look at the long-term consequences of ruptured childhoods. This book thus draws on interviews with grown child survivors, conducted over a span of time from the late 1970s (when a number of pioneering Holocaust-centred oral history projects began) through to the present, interviews that allow us to glimpse experiences that we could never see from the archives alone. The story of Litzi S. is an interesting case in point. The archival records of her care home duly note that Litzi 'left us and lives now with her uncle and aunt in London'.[16] Without her later interview, we would never know that Litzi would then spend the next dozen years believing that her uncle and aunt were actually her father and mother, and we would certainly never be able to unpick the consequences of such an experience.

Oral history gives us, of course, the grown child's adult perspective on the past, from a vantage point at the end of a long process of reflection and reconsideration. It tells us less about what children thought or felt in the past, and more about impacts and consequences, about how individuals have made meaning out of their childhoods and made their pasts a part of their present identity. As psychologists recognize, the interests and goals of children rarely correspond to those of adults. When we remember our childhood selves, we map our adult understandings of what is important and relevant onto our narratives, and in the process we change the story.[17] Interviews with child survivors thus tell us as much about the journey to make sense of childhood as they do about childhood itself.

As the book weaves stories of war-torn childhoods into the arc of human lives, we see that many of these lives became wonderfully ordinary over time. But I want to guard against the impulse to equate 'ordinary' with 'easily knowable'. Every chapter of this book explores issues and outcomes that I, as a historian with two decades' experience thinking, reading, and writing about the Holocaust, found not only unexpected, but shocking. The choices that both children and adults made, their assumptions about and relations with each other, upended everything that I thought I knew about family and community after the Holocaust. The insistent, unpredictable role of childhood memories in a human life, as revealed in these child survivors' life histories, has caused me to rethink profoundly my understanding of the nature of memory itself. All these unexpected elements serve a vital purpose: they point out just how far, in many ways, we still do not understand the Holocaust and its aftermath – and indeed, in a broader sense, how limited is our understanding of how human beings live with, confront, deny, obscure, and make sense of ruptured childhoods over the course of a lifetime.

# ONE
## ANOTHER WAR BEGINS

Zilla C. was born in Mannheim, Germany, in June 1940. At the age of six months she was deported to the internment camp at Gurs, in the south of France, along with her parents, her toddler brother Eric, and most of the other Jews of Baden and the Palatinate region in the south of Germany. She passed her first birthday in the camp. Her parents were then transferred to another French camp at Rivesaltes before being deported to Auschwitz, while Zilla and her brother were among the children rescued from Gurs by the Oeuvre de Secours aux Enfants (OSE), an aid organization that rescued an estimated 5,000 Jewish children trapped in Vichy France.[1] She was taken to an OSE-run care home for infants, the Pouponnière, in Limoges. When the OSE was forced to close its wartime care homes after the fall of unoccupied France to the Nazis in November 1942, Zilla was smuggled into the countryside and hidden with an eighteen-year-old French girl. Later – towards the war's end – she was moved to the home of the Apard family in Oulches (Indre), who hid her under the assumed name Cécile Apard.[2] After the liberation, the OSE took Zilla back into their care, placing her first in a care home at Montintin, and then in August 1945 in a home at Draveil, where she was reunited with Eric, a brother she could not remember. She was five years old, and she had experienced seven different 'homes': her birth home, an internment camp, two host families, and three institutional care homes. The war had passed, the liberation had come and gone, but still Zilla's peripatetic existence seemed to continue: the constant transfer of attachments to different places and people was the only life that she had ever known.[3]

When psychoanalyst Judith Kestenberg interviewed Zilla in 1987, Zilla explained that, although she was then forty-seven years old, she still struggled to make any sense of these early years. The war's end had not brought with it a sense of closure; rather, it had marked the beginning of a decades-long effort to try to piece together the story of her life when she had only meagre scraps of information to work with, few family members who could help, and no pre-war existence that could be resurrected:

> *Judith Kestenberg:* Where do you belong?
> *Zilla C.:* I don't belong anywhere, you see. I don't belong anywhere. [. . .] For most survivors who are not young child survivors, there was a before, you see. There was a before. There was a time when their life was normal, then there was this horrible interruption, and then to whatever degree they could, they continued. There was a base in family, there was a base in religion, there was . . . they had some normalcy. With me, I've never been normal, you see. [. . .] When the war ended, there was no base for me to go back to.[4]

For young child survivors, another war began after the fighting ceased on the European continent. Adult survivors, and even older children and adolescents, had memories of pre-war life and a pre-war identity: this identity may not have been re-attainable, it may have had to be abandoned after the war was over, but it was there. What makes the lives and experiences of very young child survivors distinctly different from those of adults and children in or on the cusp of their teenage years is that there was no pre-war self that could be remembered, no identity that could be revisited and re-assumed or set aside. Rather than a descent into madness, the war years were these young children's earliest years of simply being alive. Children are adept at treating the exceptional as normal, and because they had no other life to compare it with, the years of persecution did not necessarily feel dangerous, fraught or chaotic to young survivors. For a great number of them the true moment of disorientation and shock was not the period of the war, but the months and years immediately afterwards.

The 'liberation' had a dark emotional heart. It brought with it a great deal of insecurity (physical, financial, geographical, existential), and the first tentative confrontations with unfathomable loss. It was a moment that demanded that children, even children who were barely more than toddlers like Zilla C., fundamentally recraft their identities – but equally a moment when adults could provide few tools to help with this process. The adults involved in caring for children after the war, whether surviving parents and relatives or aid agencies' care staff, hoped to 'reconstruct' children's identities, but where children could not remember their early lives, such claims to be facilitating a return to an authentic pre-war self made no sense. After all, children who survived had often done so by deliberately concealing their origins, their Jewishness, their native languages, their very names. New names and new identities had been part of the fabric of their childhoods in the war years, woven into their notion of who they were, where they belonged, and what daily life was like. The end of the war turned these constructions upside down.

During the war, the scope of adults' plans for children's survival (and children's plans for their own survival) was focused overwhelmingly on the present. Their decisions reflected the hope to survive a day, a week, or a month, because the long-term future could not be predicted. After the war, survivors had to begin to make provisions for the future, both immediate and long-term, but the future had collapsed. It no longer appeared to belong to them. Adult and child survivors alike had spent months and years removed from their communities of origin. Virtually all extended families had been ruptured, and no Jewish community was unaffected by the murder of its members. Homes and possessions were gone and could not be reclaimed. Both adults and children were forced to work towards the realization that loved ones would not return, a realization that took years and even decades to reach its full, terrible maturity. Thus survivors faced decisions after the war that seemed to offer no real path forwards. They were forced to consider how to proceed with their lives in the absence of any means, whether material or emotional, with which to do so.[5]

Although this book places its emphasis on child survivors' *post-war* lives, we can only make sense of their post-war emotions, experiences, and decisions if we understand how and why they lived through the war. There were countless ways in which children managed, against enormous odds, to survive the Holocaust, but here we will look at four of the key routes that defined children's wartime experiences: survival in hiding, in flight to a neutral country or Allied territory, in ghettos and transit camps, and in concentration camps. Each of these four scenarios was of course very different (and the boundary between them is artificial: many children experienced more than one), but what is striking is just how similar were children's emotional pathways out of them. The war's end was a moment when a pronounced period of uncertainty began for most child survivors. This was the point at which a rift opened between a child's history and his or her ability to make sense of the past, for as children were asked quickly to set aside wartime identities and don 'reconstructed' ones in their place, a child's war experiences no longer seemed to fit into her own story. Where adults refused to talk about the past with a child, encouraged forgetting, or avoided a child's questions, they further tore the social fabric of her memory. In exploring the question of how we can tell the story of our lives when we do not know where we have come from, we see that for many child survivors, the 'liberation' was the moment during which the life story fell apart. For some, it was also the starting point of the decades-long process of piecing it back together.

Felice Z., whom we met in the introduction, was born in October 1939 in the little village of Walldürn in the Baden area of Germany, and like Zilla C., she was deported with the other Jews of Baden and the Palatinate to Gurs in October 1940. She had just passed her first birthday.[6] In early 1941 an aid worker asked Felice's parents, David and Lydia, if they would agree to release Felice and her older sister Beate into the OSE's care, and Felice was taken to the same care home in Limoges that housed Zilla.[7] When the Pouponnière was closed, Felice was separated from her sister and placed with Gaston and Juliette Patoux, peasant farmers who lived in a tiny house in the village of La Caillaudière, near Vendoeuvres. Decades later, Felice recalled that:

Madame Patoux was a very simple lady. She was maybe in her sixties when
I came there, a very warm and caring lady, and so was her husband. All they

were interested in was taking care of me. She basically saved my life. She was always ready to run. She hid all her jewellery under the earth, and she never went to sleep in her nightgown, she always wore a slip, because she knew how very dangerous it was [to keep a Jewish child]. I took it for granted that she was my mother, I called her mémé (nana) and it was really the first close relationship I had with a human being. I became very attached to them. Very.[8]

Although she was separated from her family, Felice spent the war years in a safe and loving environment in the home of the Patoux family. She had been separated from her parents at such a young age that she had no memory of them. She did not know that the Patouxs were not her biological family, that she was Jewish, that she had a sister, or even that she was in hiding. Her earliest memories, which date to the time she spent with the Patouxs during the war, were tranquil and happy. It was the end of the war that brought unsettling developments.

As the Allied landings brought the war to an end in France in the summer of 1944, the thousands of Jewish children hidden in France began to come out of hiding, and Felice recalled the jarring experience of re-encountering the sister that she had forgotten: 'I saw this little girl coming up the walk, holding a pear, and I didn't like the way she looked; she looked too much like me. I didn't know that I had a sister.' The reunion of the siblings was disorienting, rather than joyful, and raised questions about where they belonged, and to whom. It was the start of a process that was, for Felice, far more upsetting than anything she could recall from the war years. Soon after the sudden reappearance of her sister, Felice was removed from the Patoux family:

The OSE said that we had to leave, and I didn't understand that. They didn't explain it to me. I think they might have said 'you can't stay here because [the Patoux family] are not Jewish. You have to start being Jewish.' But I couldn't understand what being Jewish meant. There was nothing we could do, and we had to leave. It was very traumatic. The war was over, and they said we had to leave.[9]

19

Throughout her time with the Patoux family, Felice had remained a ward of the OSE, and it was the OSE's policy to return hidden children to Jewish environments as quickly as possible after the war. For Felice and Beate, this meant a transfer to an OSE children's home at Draveil (where Zilla and her brother Eric were also placed), and then a second transfer to another OSE children's home at Taverny. Felice eventually adapted to this change, but 'the separation from this couple [the Patoux] affected me so much that it took me a long while to recover'. She emphasized that 'I don't remember anything for two years [after the war]. It was such a painful separation between this couple and I.'[10]

In hiding, children could find themselves with one or both parents, with siblings, or (most frequently) alone.[11] They were smuggled out of ghettos and internment camps, or placed directly with host families by parents who were about to flee.[12] They may have found themselves with families they knew, or with complete strangers, some of whom were paid to conceal the children; others did so not for financial gain but might have had other reasons beyond the purely altruistic for taking in a Jewish child. Children were taken in by all manner of people: single women (and occasionally single men), childless couples, and families from across the social strata. The children were more likely to be placed with peasant families in the countryside than with well-off families in urban areas, because they were more likely to escape detection in remote rural areas. They were also hidden in institutions, particularly in convents.[13]

As might be expected, children's experiences in hiding ranged from the overwhelmingly positive to the terrifyingly negative. While in hiding, they were vulnerable to physical, sexual, and emotional abuse, but more common was the experience of simply being frightened or lonely. Children absorbed the fears of their wartime host families, and of parents and older siblings if they were hiding together, taking to heart injunctions to keep inside, be quiet, or stay in lofts or cellars lest they be caught. In addition to being frightened, many also experienced cold, hunger, and an isolation which sometimes bordered on the extreme. At a time when little children need social contact to develop their linguistic and cognitive skills, many hidden children found that they spent most or all of their waking hours by themselves.

Yet for all the deprivation and loneliness that many children experienced in hiding, it was also a time that could be relatively stable and secure. This helps to explain why so many hidden children remember the period immediately after the war, not during it, as the moment when the conflict really entered their lives. Some had formed deep bonds with their host families, who had sometimes cared for them for years. In a considerable number of cases these hosts were the only parents a child could remember. The end of the war, however, brought with it the end of the need for protection from the Nazis and their collaborators, and thus the end of the very need for host families. Some children continued to live with their host families after the war,[14] but for the most part children were removed (in certain cases with physical force) from their familiar situations, and returned to surviving parents or relatives whom they might not have remembered (and with whom they often no longer shared a common language); or they were placed in Jewish care homes when no relatives able or willing to take them could be found. It was a moment of rupture that punctured the quiet routines of life in hiding, and thrust children into a new world filled with uncertainty. As Maurits C., who had spent the war in hiding in the Netherlands, recalled in an interview with the historian Debórah Dwork four decades after the war's end:

> During the war, I was a child and I was engaged with everyday living. The very impact of the consequences of the war I experienced after the war ended. My war began in 1945, and not in 1940. When I learned that my father and mother would not come back, and my brothers, then the war started.[15]

A small but still significant number of Jewish children survived the war by flight to safer spaces in Europe's neutral nations (especially Switzerland, but to a lesser degree Spain, Portugal, and Sweden), or into Soviet territory. Francoist Spain had fairly porous borders for Jewish refugees throughout the war, but the government refused to issue permanent residence permits, which meant that while more than 100,000 Jewish refugees entered Spain during the war, most were forced to move on fairly quickly.[16] Some continued on to Portugal, which tolerated longer stays. A handful of rescue agencies, in particular the US-based Quaker organization American Friends' Service Committee, attempted to shepherd Jewish children out of Vichy France and into Spain and Portugal, from where they hoped to bring the children to the United States; however, only 200 children were rescued from wartime Europe in this way.[17] Spain and Portugal were also comparatively difficult to reach: refugees generally came in via routes through the Pyrenees mountains, which meant that flight to Spain was an avenue open only to those who were already in unoccupied France. Sweden was similarly difficult to reach. Although it famously aided in the rescue of Jews from Norway and Denmark, and was the only neutral state to forge an active policy of rescue during the war, it proved nearly impossible for Jews outside the small Scandinavian Jewish community to make the journey there.[18] Tens of thousands of Polish Jews fled into Soviet territory following the opening of the Eastern Front in the spring and summer of 1941, but Russia was a perilous haven: Jewish refugees faced onward deportation into Siberia and Central Asia, where they experienced malnutrition and starvation, and where typhus and other diseases were rife. An estimated 30,000 Jewish children returned from Russia after the war, but it is not known how many died there.[19]

For those children who survived the war by escape to a neutral country, the most important destination was Switzerland. It was not, however, a welcoming haven. The Swiss government had little interest in aiding Jewish refugees, and this included children. In the early years of the war, the Swiss government repeatedly vetoed proposals to bring Jewish children into Switzerland, brushing aside pleas from the Swiss Red Cross – Children's Relief to help the children in the care homes they ran across the border in Vichy France, who were in danger after the autumn of 1942. This meant that the majority of Jewish children who entered Switzerland did so illegally. Between September 1939 and May 1945, 51,129 Jewish and non-Jewish civilian refugees entered Switzerland without a valid visa, predominantly from Italy and France. Of these, over 10,000 were children.[20]

The border crossing was a dangerous undertaking. Both Swiss and Nazi (or Nazi-allied) police guarded the border. As many as 24,500 refugees were caught and refused entry, often handed over to German police who then interned them in transit camps such as Drancy, near Paris, before they were deported further to Auschwitz and other camps in the East. The success of illegal crossings depended on many factors. A *passeur* had to be found, someone familiar with local conditions who acted as a guide through the mountains. In engaging local help, refugees made themselves vulnerable to theft, blackmail, and the risk of being abandoned. As well, the Swiss authorities had created a 12-kilometre-wide zone along the border in which anyone caught was at risk of being turned over to the Germans. However, loopholes in the regulations concerning refugees meant that, from the beginning of 1943 onwards, children under sixteen who made it across the border could be recognized as 'hardship cases', which meant that they would not be turned away. As a consequence, rescue organizations such as the OSE began to move children illegally across the French border from the spring of 1943. An estimated 2,000 children entered Switzerland this way, with the help of the OSE's sophisticated escape network, but it was a perilous undertaking both for the children and for their rescuers. It is worth noting that this rescue network was run predominantly by a brave group of adolescents and young adults, mostly female, who repeatedly risked their own lives to bring children over the Alps into Switzerland. When twenty-one-year-old Marianne Cohn was arrested with a group of Jewish children near Annemasse, in the French Alps, in May 1943, the Gestapo imprisoned her and eventually beat her to death with a shovel. Her remains were found by her friends from the rescue network after the liberation.[21]

The OSE children entered Switzerland without their families, but other children arrived with their parents or other relatives. Those families who were admitted to the country after illegal border crossings found that they were not allowed to stay together, and faced a long journey through a string of internment camps. They were held at police-run assembly centres near the border until they could be billeted elsewhere, and then families were systematically divided: fathers were sent to work camps, mothers were often compelled to act as domestic servants in private households, and children were placed with Swiss foster parents.[22] The separation of children from their parents was encouraged not only by state authorities but also by the Schweizer Hilfswerk für Emigrantenkinder (Swiss Committee for Aid to Children of Emigrés, SHEK), the main aid agency that helped Jewish refugee children, where it was believed that children would benefit more from the 'normal' environment in foster care than they would from staying with their parents or relatives in internment and work camps.[23]

Cecile H. was one of these children. She was born in November 1937 in Brussels to Eastern European parents who had immigrated to Belgium in the 1920s. She spent her early years in Antwerp. When the Nazis invaded Belgium in May 1940, the family tried to get to England via France, but they were turned back and returned to their home in Antwerp, unsure of what to do next. Cecile recalled that her parents were terribly tense during this time, and the family took to hiding in the cellar to avoid night arrests. In 1942 her father was caught on the street, and sent to the transit camp at Malignes; from there he was sent to Auschwitz, and then to a labour camp. Cecile and her mother became afraid to leave the house, and Cecile remembered the 'exceedingly nervous' atmosphere at home, and the fact that she slept all the time from the boredom of being constantly inside with her frightened mother. One day not long after her father's arrest, her uncle's maid showed up with a truck in the middle of the night. The young woman, fond of the family, had concocted a plan with her boyfriend to help Cecile and her mother escape. They were taken to the boyfriend's parents' potato farm in Boom, where they were hidden for a year and a half. Cecile remembers the farm as a warm and loving environment, but by 1944 there were concerns that their presence might be putting the farm's family in danger, and the woman of the household made contact with the Belgian underground in order to find Cecile and her mother a new hiding place.[24]

The Belgian resistance network La Brigade Blanche sought to exploit the directive concerning 'hardship cases' as far as they could. In February and March 1944 the network secreted several groups of Jews from Belgium to Switzerland via France, Cecile and her mother among them. The network had developed an elaborate system to make the best possible use of the police directive: they created fictitious families. Adults with no children 'borrowed' a child from another family, parents falsified their children's birth dates, and single men and pregnant women presented themselves as couples.[25] Cecile remembered this deception from the border crossing, although she did not understand it as a child: 'There were about thirty people trying to cross together, and we had to "adopt" a man. [. . .] I kept telling him, "you're not my father, I can't call you papa." He said "just pretend".'[26] Like everyone else in the group, Cecile and her mother entered Switzerland under false papers, presenting themselves as 'Esther and Cecile Reisler'. The Swiss police files note that Cecile's false identity was not uncovered until she had been in Switzerland for two months, by which point the military police had launched a broad investigation into the activities of the Brigade Blanche.[27]

Cecile and her mother were taken first to a border-area internment camp, where they stayed for a month, then to another holding camp, where they remained for a second month until the Swiss authorities decided what to do with them. By this point, the investigation into the Brigade Blanche was uncovering the extent of the network's use of false identity papers, and the Swiss police decided to place the Belgian refugees in prison camps. Cecile's mother was sent to a camp on the outskirts of Geneva, and Cecile was taken to a separate camp in Bremgarten in the canton of Aargau, more than 250 kilometres away.[28] From there, Cecile was placed in a foster home in the remote village of Vordemwald: 'One day they lined us all up and the Swiss Red Cross came in. I remember that they had brushed our hair. An elderly couple came over to me and said "we'll take that one".' It was August 1944. Cecile had no choice but to go home with this couple, and she later recalled that her elderly foster father was a 'very sick man. [. . .] You know, I adored the woman, I called her "maman", and he wanted me to call him "papa" and I didn't. I couldn't stand him.' The six-year-old Cecile quickly observed that her foster father seemed to relish tormenting her:

He threatened me several times, but [one incident] scared me the most. He left me in the woods all by myself, and it got dark, and I heard animals and thought it was a wolf. A woodsman found me, and he said 'you're a naughty child, papa was looking for you', and when we got back to the house [my foster father] warned me that if I told his wife, he would chop off my head.

One day, without warning, he simply returned her to the Red Cross.[29]

The Red Cross placed Cecile with another family, who were kind towards her despite the fact that she 'kicked them and cried' when they were first introduced. By this point the war was already drawing to a close. Cecile's mother was released from her prison camp, and they left Switzerland together in July 1945. But the war's end propelled the then seven-year-old into a new conflict, one where the battleground was the family and the issue was just how far, in that intimate sphere, parents and children could discuss what they had lived through during the previous five years. Cecile's father survived his internment in a concentration camp, but when he returned to the family Cecile recalls that he was 'eighty-five pounds, and had holes in his lungs from the malnutrition and the beatings'. They no longer had a common language, as by that point Cecile only knew how to speak Swiss German. The chasm that the war had opened up between the two only grew wider as Cecile had a shocking confrontation with her father's war experiences:

Father had found photos in the barracks or SS lockers when he was liberated, and had taken some because he was worried that no one would believe him. He hid these pictures in the house on top of a closet, and once I took those pictures and lay them all out on the floor, and I'll see those pictures until my dying day. They were the worst, horrible. Trenches, bodies half burned, funeral pyres, mutilated bodies, half burned, hands, legs, the worst, just the worst. My father knew that I had seen them. I kept having nightmares after that, and he burned them. He said, 'I'm never going to talk about that again.' It was a difficult time for us, after the war.[30]

Like many other child survivors who were returned to survivor parents after the war, Cecile had been through much on her own, but there was no space in her reunited household to discuss her own war story, nor any way to ask questions about her parents' experiences. Her parents hoped to close the door on the past, but for Cecile, insistent and troubling questions punctured the safety of the newly reconstituted family.

⟋⟋ ✳ ⟍⟍

Although it might strike us as unbelievable, daily life in a Nazi camp could be relatively stable for a small child. This was particularly true in the Theresienstadt ghetto-camp, though it was run in a way that was notably different from other Nazi places of internment. Litzi S., whom we met in the introduction, was deported to Theresienstadt with her parents as a three-year-old toddler, along with her older brother Herschel, then five. She survived; he did not. At the time, however, Litzi was not yet aware of her losses. Her memories of the camp were 'just images and impressions', but she recalled her arrival:

> We came to this place where we were shown into a room where 'wood' was the predominant feeling that I have, wood that you could splinter your hand on. We were greeted by this angry type of lady, and we were ordered to go in. I had to control myself and not cry. I had a feeling that we had to do what we were told. [. . .] I don't think I was aware of what it was, where we were, what we were doing. I just was. It was all I knew.[31]

Denny M., whom we also met in the introduction, was sent to Theresienstadt at the age of two. Like Litzi, his time in the camp was 'a jumble of memories, of things which now don't make very much sense', but he recalled 'living in group circumstances with lots of other children and other carers. There were lots of large rooms, with lots of beds, and I was simply in these rooms with lots of other children.'[32]

Theresienstadt was unlike any other camp in the Nazi *univers concentrationnaire*. It was, as the historian Tara Zahra has noted, the site of 'one of the most ambitious child-welfare schemes behind ghetto walls in Nazi-occupied Europe',

27

a programme that was not only daring but by many measures highly successful. The camp was built in the Bohemian town of Terezin, a former garrison north of Prague, which was commandeered and cleared of its residents to become the Theresienstadt ghetto-camp at the end of 1941. Reinhard Heydrich, head of the Nazi Sicherheitsdienst (SD) Security Service, planned to use Theresienstadt to funnel Jews out of the Reich Protectorate of Bohemia and Moravia. He initially intended it to be little more than a transit camp for Jews and political prisoners, a way station on the road to the concentration and death camps of the East. However, the camp developed a second, ad hoc function as a smokescreen intended to mask the reality of the genocide of Europe's Jews. Heydrich realized that the camp could be used to quiet criticism about what was happening to Jews in deportation, especially those such as the elderly who could not conceivably be sent east to work. The first Czech Jews arrived at the camp in November 1941; by the autumn of 1942, some 43,000 German, Czech, and Austrian Jews had been sent to Theresienstadt, and the majority of these were elderly.[33] Indeed, Nazi authorities promoted the camp as a spa town where, in exchange for all their property, elderly Jews could live out the rest of their years in peace. This deception might have been short-lived were it not for the fact that in December 1942 twelve Allied governments protested against the Nazi treatment of the Jews, and Nazi leaders sought to allay this criticism. In the spring of 1943 the Nazis set in motion a campaign to 'beautify' Theresienstadt in order to show the 'model ghetto' off to the outside world, a project that culminated in the carefully managed visit of Red Cross delegates to the camp in June 1944. Like some of the other youngest survivors of Theresienstadt, Denny M. remembers walking around in a circle, naked, in one of the courtyards on a sunny day – an unknowing participant in the camp 'beautification' project, as the guards attempted to expose the children to some sunshine to make them appear healthier for the Red Cross.[34]

This beautification project was, of course, entirely cynical. From January 1942 transports took the inmates of Theresienstadt onwards to the firing squads of the SS Einsatzgruppen, and from July of that year directly to the gas chambers of the eastern concentration and death camps. From the time of the first transports to Theresienstadt through to its liberation in May 1945, 141,184 people were deported there, of whom 88,202 were subsequently deported onwards to Auschwitz-Birkenau, where the majority were murdered upon arrival. Some 33,456 people – mostly elderly – died in the camp of disease and privation. At the time of the liberation, 16,832 prisoners remained in the camp alive.

The notion that Theresienstadt was a 'model' camp was a lie, and yet it was the SS's decision to put resources into the camp that enabled Jacob Edelstein, the German-appointed Elder of the Jews, and his Council to take child welfare seriously. The Jewish Council in the camp created a Youth Welfare Department, which ensured that children received privileged rations (indeed, the elderly in the camp were systematically starved so that extra food could be provided for the children). The Council tried to keep children off the transport lists, although they were often unable to halt the onward deportation of children. Most importantly, they worked to construct a unique system of children's homes in the camp, the Kinderheim, where boys and girls over four years old were in some ways insulated from the reality of starvation and disease that was taking root elsewhere in the camp. They also created an infants' home for those under four years old, which made it comparatively safe for a very young child to be in Theresienstadt without parents. While the numbers of children in the camp fluctuated, there were between 2,700 and 3,875 under the age of fifteen in the camp at a time, and about half of these lived in the children's homes.[35]

In September–October 1944 the children's homes were liquidated, and the majority of their residents sent to the gas chambers of Auschwitz-Birkenau. While only 819 children remained in the camp after these mass deportations, large numbers of children from other camps soon began to arrive. In April 1945, three weeks before liberation, 300 children arrived from Bergen-Belsen and Dachau, bringing with them spotted typhus.[36] By this point Theresienstadt was one of the few camps still under German rule, and it was quickly becoming a dumping ground for prisoners on death marches from other camps, 15,000 of whom had arrived by the end of April. When Czech health workers entered the camp on 4 May to try to stop the spread of typhus, German troops were still present, but the following day the last of the SS men left, along with the camp commandant, Karl Rahm.[37] Theresienstadt was free.

Of the 12,000 children who had passed through the camp, 1,600 were liberated, and of the thousands of children under fifteen sent eastwards, a mere 142 survived.[38] Yet despite this, many child survivors of Theresienstadt recall the liberation and its aftermath as the most disorienting moment of their war experiences, and not the chaotic final months of the camp.

Peter B. was one of the rare child survivors of Theresienstadt whose mother was also in the camp at the moment of liberation. Peter was born in July 1936 in Berlin, and his family quickly began to disintegrate under the strain of anti-Jewish measures; his father fled Germany to Shanghai in 1938 when Peter was two years old. Peter's mother had no choice but to go out to work every day, leaving Peter alone in their Berlin apartment. In 1943, when he was seven, he was home by himself when the Gestapo knocked on the door; he sat with the Gestapo officers in his silent apartment, waiting for his mother to come home so both could be arrested. He and his mother were sent together to Theresienstadt, where he was separated from her and placed in one of the children's homes. He recalled that he saw his mother 'every other weekend, or every weekend. Those visits were uneventful. I don't really remember seeing her a lot during that time. [. . .] I was primarily on my own.'[39] Like Litzi, Denny, and many other of the youngest survivors of Theresienstadt, Peter had only indistinct memories of daily life in the camp. It was the end of the war, and not the war itself, that fixed in his mind. He recalled the strange, liminal moment of the camp's liberation:

I woke up one night, a couple of days before we left, and it was the middle of the night and there was a lot of commotion and noise outside. I looked out the window and there was a bonfire with maybe twenty or twenty-five survivors around it, with pitchforks and sticks and brooms, trying to force a German soldier into the fire. He was not fortunate enough to get away. Every time he tried to run out of the fire, they kept beating him back. So he finally fell down in the fire and he expired. That was my goodbye to that camp.[40]

At the liberation, Peter, who was still with his mother (and her new husband, a man she had met in Theresienstadt who had arrived at the camp, towards the end of the war, from Buchenwald), was in a precarious position. The family had nowhere to go, and no resources to draw on. They returned to Berlin, where they had to scavenge just to eat: 'we were just trying to stay alive. We would follow [the American] soldiers around and they would drop their cigarette butts there, and we would take all the cigarette butts and take them home to our parents, and bits of food.' When the soldiers made coffee, 'we would go to the trash cans and very carefully scoop out some of those hot coffee grounds before they hit any of the other trash, as much as we could, and take them home. You'd be surprised, [my family] would make coffee four or five times from those grounds.' Without jobs or possessions, and hoping to immigrate to the United States, Peter's family entered a DP camp at Deckendorf, where he daily encountered a level of anti-Semitic violence that he had never experienced in Theresienstadt:

> [My mother] sent me to an outside school. I don't know what was in her mind. I'm sure I wasn't there ten minutes when they knew I came from the barracks, and I was a Jew. And I'll tell you something, I experienced anti-Semitism like I never had in my life during that six or seven months in school there. I was in three fights a day. And it wasn't one on one, it was five against one. I used to go home, if you can call it home, with clothes torn, bloody nose. And my mother was blind to all this. [. . .] That's about all I remember from that DP camp, and we were there for about two and a half years.[41]

Like Cecile, Peter was back with his family after the war, but the reconstructed family home was not an environment in which he felt comfortable or even safe. The post-war period brought with it daily forms of violence that seemed to him more severe than any he had witnessed in the camp. His mother and stepfather were distracted by their own emotional turmoil, and thus Peter retreated, with his jumble of memories, his questions and his fears, into himself.

The children whose stories we have examined up to this point all came from, and stayed in, Central and Western Europe. Zilla and Felice were deported from Germany to France. Cecile fled Belgium for Switzerland. Peter was sent from Germany to Czechoslovakia. We should not be surprised to find that a larger percentage of children survived the war in Western Europe than they did in the East, for the nature of the war and the genocide was dramatically different in the two areas. If roughly 11 per cent of Europe's Jewish children survived the war in total, this figure is closer to 3 per cent in countries such as Poland. In the West, the Nazis made efforts to conceal the persecution and internment of Jews from the rest of the population: transit camps such as Gurs, and the 'model ghetto' of Theresiestadt, were tucked away in the countryside, out of sight of too many eyes that might protest against scenes of deportation.[42] In contrast, the ghettos of Eastern Europe existed in plain sight. In Poland, and later in the Baltic countries and in the occupied zones of the Soviet Union, ghettos were to be found in the heart of the urban areas where large numbers of Jews were living. In the eyes of the occupiers, there was no need, in the East, to put into place the legal system that first stripped Jews of their possessions, and then isolated them in remote, marginal camps out of sight of their fellow citizens: the colonial approach to occupation that the Nazis used in Eastern Europe left no room for such measures.[43]

The ghettos of Eastern Europe were a dangerous and deadly world for children, although this was not always clear to ghetto inhabitants at the outset. Unlike those in the transit camps of the West, Jews in the ghettos of Warsaw, Łódź, Vilna, Radom, and elsewhere found themselves in familiar places, many having previously lived freely in the very streets where they were now imprisoned. Families remained together, and because adults were forced to work in the ghettos, children could find that they gained a modicum of new freedom behind closed ghetto walls. For those who entered the ghettos early in the war, living conditions were crowded and food was insufficient, but families with children maintained a degree of normality in urban areas that were at least familiar. Things did not stay this way, however. From mid-1942 onwards the SS stepped up drives to expunge ghettos of their 'useless', non-working inhabitants, including the elderly, the chronically ill, and young children. Deportations from the ghettos became more frequent. In these conditions, children who were too young to work had to become invisible, or (as happened in earnest after mass deportations began) to escape the ghetto altogether and undertake the perilous work of trying to live in hiding on the 'Aryan' side. In the Warsaw ghetto, mass deportations which began on 22 July 1942 aimed to remove the 'unproductive elements' from the ghetto, including children, who were rounded up in orphanages, in hospitals, and in their homes. This 'great deportation' continued through to September. Of the 51,458 children under the age of ten in the ghetto, only 498 remained after the wave of deportations was complete.[44] In the same month, the head of the Jewish Council in the Łódź ghetto, Chaim Rumkowski, asked ghetto residents to turn their children over for deportation voluntarily, in exchange for an SS promise to protect 100,000 working ghetto inmates. No one volunteered.[45]

Sybil H. was born on 6 November 1940 in Kraków, but was sent with her parents and her mother's sister to the Radom ghetto when she was only one year old. She stayed there until she was three. In the ghetto her mother Ester worked in an embroidery factory, but her aunt had the good fortune to find employment in the ghetto hospital, which gave her access to the sleeping pills that ultimately played a huge role in Sybil's survival. If children in the ghetto had to become invisible in order to survive, it was easier to hide a sedated three-year-old than an energetic one, and Sybil later recalled that 'I was drugged a lot of the time'. Despite her family's privileged access to medication, however, Sybil's father Elazar died of pneumonia in the ghetto. Sybil remembered seeing him lying in bed when he was dying, and her mother 'was crying and I went over to her and I asked her not to cry. I told her that if she cried I would also cry, so she stopped crying.'[46]

After her father's death, Sybil's mother, aunt and uncle were sent to a forced labour camp at Bliżyn, twenty-five miles southwest of Radom, along with other prisoners from Radom and several other ghettos. They arrived at Bliżyn in the summer of 1943. Towards the end of that year or early in 1944 most of the children in Bliżyn were removed from the camp and murdered, but Sybil was not among them; her mother and aunt may have drugged her and concealed her, as they had before. As the fighting on the Eastern Front began to approach the labour camp in mid-summer 1944, the remaining prisoners were transferred to Auschwitz. The contingent that arrived from Bliżyn on 31 July 1944 included 715 women and girls admitted to Auschwitz-Birkenau and tattooed with prisoner serial numbers. Sybil's mother Ester received the number A15212, and three-year-old Sybil was tattooed with A15213.[47]

Of the hundreds of thousands of Jewish children brought from every corner of Europe to Auschwitz, the vast majority were murdered upon arrival, and mothers with small children in tow were routinely sent straight to their deaths in the gas chambers. Sybil's history is exceptional because her unlikely trajectory differed from the fate that awaited most children deported to Auschwitz. Yet there were children in Auschwitz, as there were in all the large Nazi concentration camps. Thousands of them were registered as prisoners at Auschwitz, most of them adolescents or on the cusp of adolescence, and most of them used as slave labour, subject to the same hardships that adults were: hunger, abuse, roll calls, and backbreaking work. Children were not exempt from SS beatings, nor from official punishments like the penal work details.[48] The number of children at Auschwitz waxed and waned over time: the chances of a child under fourteen being admitted to the camp were virtually non-existent in 1942, but increased to a peak in 1944, when some documents record as many as 18,000 children and adolescents under the age of seventeen in the camp (although most of these children were not Jewish).[49]

Sybil arrived at the camp in the summer of 1944, the peak moment in terms of children's numbers there. The reasons for this increase in child numbers were manifold. As the war on the Eastern Front expanded and the demand for slave labour grew, some transports to Auschwitz were registered in their entirety, including children (however, most of these children went on to die in the camp).[50] There was also a political rationale. The so-called 'family camp' in Auschwitz-Birkenau was set up after the arrival of two transports from Theresienstadt in September 1943, carrying 5,000 Czech Jews, including 760 children between the ages of two months and fourteen years.[51] The relative privilege of the family camp, in which there was only partial segregation of the sexes, where children could sometimes stay with parents, where inmates could keep their own hair and wear civilian clothing, and where rations were somewhat better than elsewhere in the Auschwitz camp system, stemmed from a deliberate SS design. The family camp's inmates did not know it, but the Red Cross was scheduled to inspect Theresienstadt, and the inspectors had also been invited to inspect the Birkenau family camp. The camp was thus part of an elaborate ruse to conceal the genocide, a deception that drew a direct line between the 'model ghetto' at Theresienstadt and the sham of acceptable family living quarters in Auschwitz. The Red Cross visit to Birkenau never materialized, and after the threat of this international scrutiny was past, the family camp was destroyed on 11 and 12 July 1944, with 3,200 of its inmates selected for slave labour, and the remaining prisoners – nearly 7,000 children, women and men – murdered in the gas chambers.[52] The destruction of the family camp meant death for most of the young children living there, but a handful managed to survive, passing themselves off as fit for labour, lying low in the hospital wing, or taking advantage of the fact that some of the SS guards were drunk during the selection process.[53]

Sybil was briefly together with her mother in Auschwitz, but then her mother – young and still healthy – was sent to the Kratzau forced labour camp, a satellite of Gross Rosen concentration camp. Sybil now found herself alone in the children's barracks, although her aunt was still nearby, working in the Birkenau hospital block. Sybil's memories of Auschwitz-Birkenau had 'no particular emotional association'; she did not remember being hungry, although she did remember that 'for some reason, I wouldn't eat'; she did not remember being afraid of the death that surrounded her, although she knew that children in her barracks would die in their bunks in the night. Yet the moment of the camp's liberation brought with it an uncertainty that lodged in her memory. As the Red Army pressed closer to Auschwitz in the winter of 1944–5, many of the remaining prisoners were forced to leave the camp and move westwards. Sybil's mother was sent to Kratzau in November 1944. Her aunt and uncle were sent west on the death marches of January 1945, along with roughly half of the 130,000 prisoners in Auschwitz and its subsidiary camps.[54] In Birkenau, after the last of these evacuation transports had left, the remaining survivors were assembled in the cold and snow by some of the medical staff from the hospital block. Notes made by these medical personnel record that on the day before the liberation of Auschwitz, 26 January 1945, there were 435 boys and girls under fourteen present at this assembly. Among them was Sybil.[55]

In the chaos of the period during the liberation of Auschwitz, Sybil recalled that:

> I went to the storage room; everybody was doing it. I got a loaf of rye bread and some jam. And then I didn't know what to do with it because it was a whole loaf. I went over to this woman who I knew, a Polish woman who had worked with my aunt and who I knew well, and I asked her to help me with the bread. [. . .] And anyhow, that woman took me with her. [She took me] to Tarnow. She had a farm.[56]

The woman who picked Sybil up and walked out of Birkenau with her was Wala D., a Polish Catholic woman sent to Auschwitz for her resistance activities.[57] Wala had worked alongside Sybil's aunt in the hospital block, and knew the child from her visits there.[58] When the Red Army liberated the camp, Wala left with Sybil, and returned to her home in Tarnow, Poland. Sybil lived there with Wala and her family from January to May 1945. It was not a long time, but it was long enough for the child to become attached, and also to come to see her own birth family in a different light: Sybil picked up a deep suspicion of Jews during the months she spent with Wala's Catholic family. Sybil's mother managed to track the child down in May 1945, and Sybil recalled that 'Wala didn't want to give me up, and I didn't want to go.' Her mother was physically changed from starvation and over-work, and Sybil recalled that 'I must have known she was my mother. I must have recognised her, but in a way I didn't. I denied it. I was upset that she was Jewish. I had become an anti-Semite by then.'[59]

Throughout the dangers of the ghetto, the forced labour camp and the concentration camp, Sybil had lived with an awareness of the possibility of her own destruction, which had come to seem so normal as to be unremarkable.

Now the world was suddenly filled with a different set of dangers. Given a brief chance to escape her Jewishness and the certainty of destruction that went with it, the sudden and unexpected appearance of the emaciated woman who claimed to be her mother was a step too far: it seemed to rob her of the safety of shedding her Jewish self. Moreover, it was not at all clear that this new, post-liberation world was any safer for Jews in Poland. Sybil recalled that her mother took her back to Kraków, where there was the threat of a pogrom. The family – Sybil, her mother, her aunt and her uncle – subsequently fled Poland illegally, briefly staying in Austria before landing in a DP camp in Stuttgart, where they remained for two years. To make the illegal journey across the border to Western Europe, Sybil's mother and aunt drugged the four-year-old, one last time.

The months and years following the war's end were until recently rather neglected by historians of the Holocaust. Scholars still have a tendency to treat this period as a parenthesis, a liminal interlude that bracketed the horrors of the war and the re-establishment of lives after it. The problem with this way of seeing the post-war moment is that it suggests it was ultimately unimportant, or had few lasting consequences for people's lives. This, however, is manifestly untrue for child survivors of the Holocaust – and indeed, I suspect, for many other children whose lives were affected by the conflict. As one war wound down, another one began for children, one that was fought in the intimate sphere of families, of households and of private living spaces, and for which the battleground would be a child's very sense of who she was and who she was expected to be. Nor was this conflict confined to the fleeting months after VE Day. For many, it would stretch on for decades. It would shape the very ways in which children understood their pasts throughout the rest of their child-hoods, and well into their adult years.

# TWO

# THE ADULT GAZE

On 11 April 1945 American troops liberated Buchenwald concentration camp. There they discovered a children's barracks, Kinderblock 66, that housed more than a thousand starving Jewish children. Most of these children had endured deportation to and imprisonment in Auschwitz, and then, after the Red Army drew close in January 1945, they were evacuated westwards on a forced march that brought them to Buchenwald. The shocked American military staff had not expected to find children in the camp, and were unsure what to do with them. Two army chaplains attached to the unit, Rabbi Herschel Schacter and Rabbi Robert Marcus, contacted the head offices of the OSE in Geneva. Some of its representatives soon arrived and began to make arrangements for the children to be sent to France, Switzerland, and England. Four hundred and thirty of the children, ranging in age from eight to eighteen, were chosen for transport to an OSE-run reception centre at Écouis in Normandy, there to begin a new life.[1]

However, the adults who accompanied the 'Buchenwald boys' on their trip to France began very quickly to have doubts about the children's psychological state. A physician who travelled with the group stated emphatically that the children were hooligans. Every time that the train stopped, the boys jumped from the windows and wreaked havoc. Their chaperones reported that they destroyed property, stole, and assaulted civilians; there is some evidence that they raped German girls as an act of revenge.[2] The train journey lasted for four days, during which time the accompanying adults despaired of their charges. Nor did it seem that the children would be welcomed in France. Wearing purloined Hitler Youth uniforms, the 'wild' boys were greeted icily by the civilians they encountered at the first French train stations through which they passed, because the French thought they were captured Germans. It was difficult to see how the boys could once again find a place in the civilian world. What could the future possibly hold for them? At Metz, someone had the presence of mind to scrawl 'orphelins de KZ Buchenwald' (Buchenwald concentration camp orphans) in large chalk letters on the side of the train. This at least went some way towards preventing bystanders from hounding the children as the train rolled through the French countryside, but did not ease the worries of their guardians. Orphans or not, the boys seemed to evoke more fear than pity.[3]

When they arrived in Écouis, the Buchenwald children were examined by the OSE's chief psychiatrist, Eugène Minkowski. He recorded that the children appeared as a 'homogeneous mass, with no hair, faces swollen from hunger and uniform clothes; a group with an apathetic, unconcerned and indifferent attitude, with no laughter or even a smile, and a marked aggressiveness towards the personnel; mistrust and suspicion.'[4] The boys seemed numb and devoid of emotions. Minkowski labelled this state 'affective anaesthesia', and argued that this loss of emotions had developed as a defence against the dangers that the boys had experienced in the concentration camps. The psychiatrist also noticed that the boys' troubled emotional state was manifest in guarded, aggressive behaviour: they were wary of adults, hoarded food, and fought violently with one another. The director of the Écouis reception centre was terrified of them. He argued that the boys were psychopaths, and probably always had been. Indeed, he suggested that the whole reason they had survived where others had died was because their very insensitivity and indifference had allowed them to do whatever had been necessary to ensure their own survival in the camps, even if this came at others' expense. He quit his job in frustration, concluding that the Buchenwald children were beyond saving.

But not everyone gave up on the Buchenwald boys. Judith Hemmendinger, an OSE social worker who took over the boys' care when they moved to a new home in the village of Taverny, northwest of Paris, thought that the boys simply needed a different sort of help to return to normal. She agreed with Dr Minkowski that upon arrival, the children appeared 'closed off, insensitive, expressionless, and suspicious and aggressive toward the staff and the outside world', but she did not see them as beyond repair. At twenty-two, Hemmendinger was only a few years older than the oldest of the boys, and she shared with them the experience of having been persecuted during the war: a German Jew living in France, she had fled with her mother and siblings to Switzerland, but the family was caught by Swiss border guards and interned. Hemmendinger's father had been caught by French police and imprisoned at Gurs internment camp before being deported to Auschwitz, where he was murdered on arrival. At Taverny, Hemmendinger decided to organize a care home that would be the opposite of what the boys had experienced in the camps: a 'therapeutic community' where the boys could set some of their own rules, where structures would be kept informal, and where warm and permissive maternal figures would replace the male authority figures that had dominated the boys' lives in the camps. The children were welcomed and encouraged to speak about their war experiences. They were invited to reorganize their dormitories in a manner of their choosing, and they opted to group themselves according to their home towns. Hemmendinger and her colleagues went so far as to arrange special transport for the boys into the nearby town of Vendôme so they could visit a photographer and have their portraits taken. 'They often looked at these pictures,' she wrote years later. 'It was proof to them that they were alive.'[5]

As the care workers involved with the Buchenwald boys argued over whether or not they could be helped, across Europe aid workers, reporters, psychiatrists, and policymakers were observing child survivors with exactly the same set of concerns in mind. They feared that the children's bodies could be restored, but not their psyches. Whether they worried that child survivors were permanently psychologically damaged by their war experiences, or hoped that these children would prove to be resilient, they were generally united in the assumption that the war had rendered children abnormal, morally, psychically, and emotionally. The adults who worked most closely with child survivors thus questioned how (or indeed whether) these children could again be rendered normal, debated what approaches might best help with this process of re-normalization, and argued about the very parameters of 'normality' itself.

If we are to understand the environments that shaped the early post-war lives of child survivors of the Holocaust, then understanding the adults who managed this world is an essential step. Their vision of children was built as much on prejudices and anxieties as it was on the realities of children's lived experience either during the war or in its immediate aftermath. When adult carers looked at survivor children, their gaze reflected a host of assumptions about what had happened in the ghettos, concentration camps and killing fields of Europe during the war. It is easy to forget, from a twenty-first-century vantage point where Holocaust survivors are seen as precious witnesses to be honoured, that those who lived through the genocide conjured up very different images in the public mind in the early post-war years. The assumption that an individual must have done something immoral, something corrupt and damning to have survived, clung to adult survivors, but it attached itself to children too (as in the case of the Buchenwald boys). Adult survivors were sometimes cast as beyond hope of rehabilitation, and care workers wrung their hands over whether children, too, were beyond hope. Adult survivors were imagined to have lost their moral compass, and thus observers gazed on child survivors and wondered whether their undeveloped moral sense could possibly be restored. Adult visions of children in these early years after the war tell us as much about the nature of public consciousness of the genocide, and about hopes and fears around the process of rebuilding, as they do about all-too-real children trying to find their feet in the post-war moment – a moment, as we have seen, that could be more disorienting for children than the war itself.

At the liberation, the massive logistical problem of how to care for the tens of thousands of 'unaccompanied children' (both Jewish and not) who had survived the war consumed the energies of military authorities and humanitarian aid workers alike. As the historian Tara Zahra has written, the 'lost children' of the Second World War developed a powerful hold on the post-war imagination that went well beyond the challenge of administering care for huge numbers of orphans. The state of children in Europe at the war's end 'spawned dystopian fears of European civilization in disarray', but equally seemed to suggest a link between the reconstruction of the bodies and minds of Europe's children and the rebuilding of the ruined continent in a more expansive sense.[6] It was a moment in which children's very minds took on enormous symbolic import: here seemed to lie evidence both of the extent of the war's destructive powers, but also – for optimistic observers – of the potential for post-war renewal. If Europe's children as a whole seemed to embody both the destructive forces of the war and the regenerative potential of the moment of liberation, this appeared to be all the more true for Jewish children, whose experiences of persecution had been the most extreme. And while many adult witnesses hoped that these children could be rescued from ruin, they nurtured fears that this might in fact be a task beyond hope.[7]

The very language adults used to describe child survivors reflected a sense that the war itself had removed the children from the spheres of acceptable human behaviour and emotions. Social workers and psychiatrists commenting on 'war orphans', and specifically on 'Jewish war orphans', described them as 'abnormal', 'maladjusted', 'war-damaged' or 'war-handicapped'. Some of the more optimistic commentators preferred the term 'de-normalized', which at least suggested the possibility of a return to normality. Such language reflected an underlying assumption that war had corrupted survivor children in a fundamental way, although many of the recognized experts on the condition of these children disagreed as to just where this corruption lay. Were the children likely to be 'mentally sick', or rather was their chief problem likely to be emotional disturbance? Could they – in the quasi-religious and distinctly non-Jewish terminology of the time – be 'redeemed': not simply cured of their abnormality, but saved in a more existential sense? Could they, as one writer put it, 'reclaim their human heritage?'[8] The assumption that children's minds had retained lasting damage fit well into a wider discourse of ruination, and just as commentators were not in agreement about the best way to reconstruct Europe's damaged buildings, communities, cities, infrastructure, and institutions, so they disagreed about the reconstruction of the damaged post-war mind, for adults as well as for children.

However, if survivor children had been corrupted by the war and needed to be restored to normality, what was the 'normal' state to which they should be returned? It was not just that experts disagreed on whether or not children could be returned to normal: they did not agree on what a 'normal' childhood looked like. The very notions of a 'normal' child and what constituted acceptable behaviour for children were in a state of flux in the early post-war period. Definitions of normative behaviour and emotions were greatly influenced by new developments in the field of child psychoanalysis, which was entering a period of growth in the early post-war moment. Child psychoanalysts, concerned with the mother-child relationship, the development of the individual ego, and the concept of emotional health, were among the chief architects of new definitions as to what constituted a 'normal' and a 'healthy' childhood. Thus if child survivors had been 'de-normalized' by the war, their return to normality did not mean a return to a pre-war understanding of what was good or bad for children; rather, their reconstruction was expected to conform to rather radical new notions of psychological and emotional health. These psychoanalytically informed notions of normative behaviour were not the only ones on offer in the post-war period, and child survivors did not experience homogeneous approaches to their care as they came into the orbit of aid workers (many of whom owed a greater intellectual debt to the pedagogical theories of the educational reform movement, which flourished in the earlier part of the twentieth century). Yet the 'psychological' approach to children's rehabilitation had a long reach, and we can observe aid workers turning to developing theories of the child's psyche in reception centres and care homes across the Continent.[9]

In this sense, the history of child survivors in the early post-war period is deeply entangled with the history of the rise of a new class of experts on children: the aid workers, social workers, psychologists, and child psychoanalysts who debated how best to care for Europe's 'war orphans'. Often female, armed with the psychoanalytic theories and social work practices that dominated in North America and Britain, funded by the JDC or UNRRA, they saw themselves as having a professional approach to humanitarian aid that was scientific, modern, and apolitical. These new experts communicated across national lines, publishing reports and guidelines, predominantly in English and French, that circulated widely and helped to establish a shared approach towards the treatment of unaccompanied children in Europe. They also benefited from a close relationship with the printed press in the anglophone world and in Western Europe, which widely and sympathetically reported on their efforts, publicizing the links which these experts themselves saw between the work of rebuilding the damaged psyches of Europe's future citizens and the re-establishment of European stability, democracy, and peace. It was a world of adult voices that set out how child survivors would be cared for, weighed in on what their physical and psychological rehabilitation should look like, and shaped the choices and trajectories that were open to them.[10]

This is not to say, of course, that child survivors of the Holocaust were not in a troubled psychological state at the war's end. Nor is it to say that they did not behave strangely, experience loss of emotion, or in some cases exhibit pronounced signs of traumatic stress. As we have seen, the war's end propelled many children into new, unknown environments with unfamiliar expectations. They had often developed a deep suspicion of adult motivations and behaviour. They had evolved coping mechanisms that seemed odd and disturbing to adult observers; or, in contrast, their coping mechanisms utterly gave way when the war finally ended, leaving them to collapse. In addition, their physical condition was precarious: their bodies were malnourished, many suffered from illnesses linked to vitamin deficiency, and diseases such as tuberculosis sometimes hindered their chances of a swift physical recovery. Thus the adult observer's view of the survivor child as damaged was not out of place. Yet the experience of total war, and the extent of the destruction wrought by the war on the European continent, made it difficult for adults to see these children as normal human beings who had lived through abnormal events. To understand what happened to those children as they took their first steps in the post-war world, to make sense of the obstacles they faced and the choices they made, we need to map out the boundaries of an adult gaze that was strung between the binary poles of pity and fear.

In 1948 a journalist for the British weekly newspaper *John Bull* wrote a report on the physical and mental state of a group of young child concentration camp survivors who had come to Britain in the summer of 1945. Buoyed by the calm and the fresh air of the British countryside, he wrote, the children were now thriving, and were scarcely recognizable as the same children who had arrived three years before. He described for readers how the new arrivals had once become hysterical at the sight of a postal van:

> One afternoon, three years ago, a country postman drove his van into the grounds of a manor house at Lingfield, Surrey. A group of cowed-looking children with cropped heads, whom he had never seen before, were huddled on the drive. At the sight of his lorry they stampeded, shrieking with fright. Some threw themselves on the ground and burst into sobs. The postman put his van into reverse and backed out.
>
> The children were Jewish boys and girls who had survived Hitler's concentration camps and had been brought to England in a terrible physical and mental state. They had identified the post van with those used in concentration camps to carry people off to death.[11]

The postal van story was compelling, but it was not true. The child survivors of Theresienstadt who arrived at the Weir Courtney care home in Lingfield, Surrey, in December 1945 had already spent six months recuperating at a reception centre at Windermere in the Lake District. They no longer had cropped hair. They had had ample time to adjust to postal vans; indeed, while their carers did remark that they remained afraid of dogs, they reported that the children were fascinated by all manner of motor vehicles, vans included.[12] The story of the van did not reflect the truth, but it did reflect a mode of reporting on child survivors that had emerged quickly in the wake of the war, one that allowed readers to view, voyeuristically, the supposed abnormality of these children, the better to savour the wonder of their recovery.

The reporters and the readers of the print press in Western Europe and the Anglo-American sphere were fascinated with the plight of 'war orphans' in the early post-war period, but the picture of child survivors that circulated in the press was a fiction shot through with assumptions about the very nature of survival. And for every story that suggested a happy ending for children who had survived, there was another that painted a dystopian picture. The Irish-American writer Alice Bailey was certainly not alone in pandering to audiences' worst fears when she wrote about 'those peculiar and wild children of Europe and of China to whom the name "wolf children" has been given. They have known no parental authority; they run in packs like wolves; they lack all moral sense and have no civilized values and know no sexual restrictions; they know no laws save the laws of self-preservation.'[13]

Concern in the press over survivor children's physical state was quickly superseded by assumptions regarding their moral condition. Having witnessed the photos of emaciated corpses that circulated in the print press in the spring of 1945, having seen newsreel footage or heard the first emotional wireless broadcasts from liberated Buchenwald and Bergen-Belsen, reporters and readers alike wondered if children who had lived through such horrors would be able to learn the difference between right and wrong. Many commentators in the press questioned whether such children could possibly be re-civilized. Much of this reportage bordered on the titillating, and was punctuated by a morbid fascination with the debased physical and moral conditions of Europe's concentration camps. The considerable public appetite for stories about 'war-damaged children' betrays just how far children stood as convenient symbols, both of the destruction of European civilization and of the fear that rebuilding efforts might not be sufficient to snuff out the destructive impulse wrought by the war.[14]

Adults working with child survivors had an influence in the media, but equally they themselves were influenced by it. Indeed, those care workers coming from outside Europe used the print media and newsreels as key sources to prepare themselves for work with survivor children. Thus while media representations of Europe's 'war orphans' were peppered with inaccuracies and tinged with more than a hint of voyeurism, they nonetheless had a powerful influence on the very adults who would be the first point of contact for many child survivors in the immediate post-war period. Margot Hicklin was a psychiatric social worker who, in July 1945, was among a group of thirty educators and social workers at the Windermere reception centre in the Lake District. The centre had been refitted to welcome 300 child survivors of Theresienstadt, the first children to arrive on a programme intended to bring 1,000 'camp survivor orphans' to Britain.[15] Hicklin recalled that the Windermere staff had few resources to hand to help them understand what the Theresienstadt children had experienced during the war, beyond the images from liberated Buchenwald and Bergen-Belsen that had appeared in the press in the spring of 1945.[16] These images seemed to suggest that an impossible task lay ahead. '[The children] have been described by many observers in such discouraging terms that many interested people are feeling a kind of despair at ever being able to make an appreciable contribution to the recovery of this generation,' she wrote. 'The films and photographs which were made available in the spring of 1945 created the impression of irremediable doom awaiting the apparently sub-human victims.'[17]

Hicklin recalled that her team felt convinced, before the children's arrival, that all their combined expertise and training would be of no use: they would surely not be able to help such deeply damaged children. But when the children finally arrived:

> One glance at them assured us that they were human. Our surprise was not over. They also showed no signs of starvation or illness. They looked well-fed, they smiled! They made themselves understood in German and Yiddish. They co-operated in every arrangement that was made for them, as soon as they understood it. [. . .] Surely, these were not the children whose pictures we had seen in the papers and films, three months ago?[18]

The experiences of the Windermere staff were repeated in homes, hostels, and reception centres for children across Europe, as adult care workers struggled to understand what child survivors had been through during the war, drew on the terrifying images and stories that circulated in the press after the liberation of the camps, and concluded that children who had witnessed such scenes with their own eyes were bound to develop psychoses.[19] When, as in the Windermere example, it became clear that the children had not in fact been rendered psychotic by their war experiences, care professionals began to think more expansively about where the children's psychological damage might lie. Many began to locate it in the realm of the emotions.

In early 1946 the JDC commissioned a comprehensive study of the psychological health of survivor children in the DP camps. The study's lead author was Dr Paul Friedman, a New York-based psychiatrist and psychoanalyst who had been born in Lublin and had done his medical training in Switzerland, and who spoke German, French, and Yiddish. The JDC originally agreed to fund Friedman on a three-month tour of the DP camps, where he could meet with the leaders of JDC-funded care homes and children's colonies, and interview children themselves.[20] In the end, however, Friedman spent six months in the DP camps in the German zone, and his report – the first and only major study of the mental health of child survivors conducted during the early post-war period – was published to considerable media fanfare in February 1947.[21] As with Margot Hicklin and others before him, Friedman imagined the worst in preparing for his trip to Europe, recalling that 'it was all too easy, especially for the psychiatrist, to think of Europe as a huge, unattended hospital for neurotics, psychotics, and the hopelessly insane'. Instead, what he found was a world in which survivors were not 'mentally sick', but rather suffered from problems of the emotions:

> When I was appointed by the Joint Distribution Committee to undertake the task of making a psychological survey of the surviving adults and children, with a view to a program of therapy and guidance, I was filled with dread at what I might discover in Europe. But when I met the DP's in their camps and the children in the camp centers and foster homes, I was delighted to find that my forebodings had been decidedly exaggerated. When I talked to the survivors – the adults and children who had been in the concentration camps or had hidden in the forests – I was amazed to see how quickly they had recovered. They all gave evidence of an incredible physical and psychological resilience. [. . .] Here were no monsters, no savages, no psychotics. But I soon discovered that these children had serious emotional problems, usually of a neurotic nature. They would have been distinctly abnormal not to have had them. To have lived, as these children had, in Hitler's Europe,

was to have inhabited a world where all the accepted modes of human intercourse had been destroyed and all moral standards subverted.[22]

Friedman argued that all DPs, adults and children alike, suffered from 'emotional numbness', but that this was particularly troubling in the case of the children. Citing Eugène Minkowski's concept of 'affective anesthesia', he argued that the shutting off of emotions had developed as a defence against the dangers and anxieties that children had to negotiate whether they were in camps or in hiding, a defence that could fall apart when the danger was passed and children 'then, at the end of their resources, permitted the long-repressed anxieties to break through in manifest symptoms'.[23]

If, as Friedman and his colleagues assumed, the children were not mentally ill but rather emotionally broken, the solution seemed to be to restore them to a normative set of feelings, both about the world they had come from, and about the one they were entering. But the boundaries of what a 'normal' child should feel were themselves in flux in the period following the war, part of a broader trend among psychoanalytically informed child experts to redefine the role of emotions and emotional control in child development. Leading child psychoanalysts, and particularly those based in Britain (Anna Freud, Melanie Klein, Donald Winnicott, John Bowlby, and others), were in the process of developing new approaches and theories in the wake of the war, with an emphasis on the ties between emotions, citizenship, and democracy. As historian Michal Shapira has written, total war profoundly affected how British child psychoanalysts viewed children, who 'came to be seen, on the one had, as vulnerable and in need of protection; on the other hand, as anxious, aggressive subjects requiring control'.[24] Moreover, these psychoanalysts increasingly linked the proper control of emotions to the successful growth of social democracy. With a hand in post-war government policy and the regular presence of leading child psychoanalysts on the BBC, the ideas of London-based psychoanalysts reached a large audience and enjoyed a moment of significant influence. They began to argue that any future cooperation between citizens, and thus the very future of democracy, had to build upon the successful control of emotions such as anxiety and aggression, and emotional control had to be learned, and indeed taught, in childhood. Emotions were thus increasingly seen not simply as an issue for individuals, but as a problem for the state.[25]

This was a new development. Dominant models of child-rearing in the interwar years had focused on behaviour and hygiene, privileging children's bodies over their feelings. The earlier generation of 'hygienist' experts were unlikely to emphasize the mother-child bond, and were suspicious of too much tenderness between children and their parents. Instead, they saw the backbone of a sound moral character for adults in strict childhood routines surrounding toilet training, sleeping, feeding, fresh air, and cold baths. The post-war psychoanalytical shift towards foregrounding children's emotions and psyches was thus a direct refutation of earlier hygienist models, and one that found a broad public audience in the wake of a devastating war.[26] Thus Paul Friedman looked to survivor children's emotions and saw there the worrying signs not of an individual problem of potential mental illness, but of a collective problem of potentially unfit future citizens.[27]

There was clearly a disjuncture between what mental health experts feared and what children themselves actually felt. This is not to say that some children did not experience muted or even deadened emotions after the war. However, it is challenging to unpick a genuine loss of the ability to feel from something rather different: a disconnect between what children after the war felt and what their adult carers expected them to feel. Even very small children tended to be only too aware of adult expectations regarding emotions and behaviour, which could easily mean that feelings that did not fit these expectations became subversive, and had to be concealed. Evidence of this crops up frequently in the archives. Notes kept by volunteers working at an institution housing 300 survivor children reveal just how wide the disjuncture could be between the feelings of a child and the expectations of an adult carer:

The children were very excitable. A child started crying in the playground. I forbade this. It [*sic*] replied, 'Where should I cry? At home, I cannot, because of the landlady, and in school not, because of the teacher.' Therefore, I allowed him five minutes for crying, and after this time it became quiet.[28]

Thus while some children may have experienced muted emotions in response to the trauma of their war experiences, others had not lost the ability to feel as much as the capacity to tap into a certain expected set of feelings. The experts' discussion about an assumed emotional anaesthetization was as much about defining the boundaries of a 'normal' child's emotional landscape, and nudging child survivors towards this ideal, as it was about anything else.

For many experts, nothing seemed to indicate the depths of the damage to survivor children's emotional health more than the issue of play. Child experts fixated on the idea that survivor children had forgotten how to play, and the notion was picked up by the print press, fascinated as journalists and readers alike were with the assumed abnormality of these children.[29] Toby Shafter, a welfare officer working with an UNRRA team as a field representative of the JDC in the US zone of occupation in Germany, wrote in 1948 about her experience of watching children play in the DP camps of the region. Shafter observed that, months and even years after the end of the war, Jewish DP children still tended to act out scenes from their war experiences in their play:

> Most DP children, far from wanting to forget the experiences in the concentration camp or brushes with German authority, were continuously re-enacting scenes of horror – sometimes with the most cold-blooded equanimity. [. . .] Living constantly in the shadow of the gas chamber or the crematorium, the children came to regard them almost as a part of every-day living. Still, it is difficult to reconcile so-called normal recreation patterns with the sight of a small boy scampering about with a large cardboard bearing a convict number and joyously excusing himself from the daily rest period because 'all the children who are in the concentration camp have a rehearsal'.[30]

Shafter added that even children who had not been in concentration camps incorporated 'death and imprisonment' into their play in a manner that was clearly disturbing to the adults charged with their care, if satisfying to the children. 'The recreation of the youngest children presented a most signal and distressing example of how greatly the lives of these children had been "denormalized",' she wrote. Dolls were not popular with the children. Doll carriages were not used as adults intended them to be used, but rather were commandeered by the children as vehicles for pushing things down hills – rocks, dirt, other children. The separation between how survivor children played and how adults expected them to play thus mirrored the larger issue of how the children felt, and how their carers expected them to feel. Children's disturbing play seemed to indicate the extent of their disturbed emotions, at least to the adult care workers. They believed that learning to play in ways typical of 'normal' children would aid them in their return to the realm of 'normal' feelings.[31]

If adults worried that children sometimes acted out their war experiences in their post-war play, they equally fretted that children seemed to cling to some of their wartime behaviour patterns after the liberation. Interestingly, care workers seemed just as troubled by good behaviour as they were by bad. Concerns about 'delinquent' behaviour were part of a broader post-war trend that stretched far beyond the care of Jewish orphans, and reflected widespread concerns that the war had robbed an entire generation of European young people of moral training.[32] But those adults caring for Jewish children worried in particular that some of the activities that these children had engaged in during the war out of necessity, such as stealing, lying, and hoarding food, would lead to delinquency in peacetime if not quickly rooted out. A full ten years after the liberation, the leaders of the British branch of the World Jewish Congress argued that the entire cohort of child survivors of the genocide had only been 'rescued from delinquency' thanks to the intervention of the JDC. The care that children had received in JDC-funded homes and hostels had, these leaders argued, weaned them away from their 'restless cruelty' and their 'aggressive and destructive' impulses.[33]

It is not surprising, given the pervasive image of the 'wolf child' that circulated in the press in the early post-war years, that adults feared survivor children would unleash a wave of delinquency, and it is also unsurprising that these adults were happy to take the credit when this wave of delinquency failed to materialize. More interesting, perhaps, is how worried adults were about certain types of overly good behaviour in their young charges. Toby Shafter noted that the DP children she observed failed to exhibit the 'mischievous, high-spirited and imaginative' gestures that adults expected from normal children. The children that caused their care workers the greatest concern, she argued, were not those who stole small objects or hoarded food, but rather those who were too obedient, who went to bed too readily when told to do so, and who did not cry when they fell and scraped their knees. Their war experiences, she reasoned, had left these children too willing to obey adult demands: their 'egos had been crushed'.[34] She was not alone in arguing that the solution was to build a sense of individualism in the children. Sir Leonard Montefiore, one of the architects of the Central British Fund's scheme to bring 1,000 Jewish war orphans to Britain, wrote in 1947 that a return to a sense of individualism was one of the strongest signs that child camp survivors were on the mend, mentally and emotionally, because it demonstrated that they had moved past the world view learned in the camps. ' "Gleichshaltung" is a word of evil memory which means the extinction of the individual, and in the camps meant the suppression of every instinct except that of self-preservation,' he wrote. The fact that the children 'have once more become individuals' was, in his mind, the clearest evidence of the success of the agency's efforts to rescue and redeem them.[35]

Thus the borders of what constituted 'normal' behaviour for children, in the early years after the war, rested somewhere between outright delinquency and obsequious cooperation with adult demands. This made sense in the post-war context, as the recent experience of the rise and fall of fascism suggested that there were profound social and political repercussions where emotions and behaviours such as aggression and blind obedience were allowed to develop unchecked. The war clearly gave the question of how to confront such emotions in child-rearing practices a novel political dimension, and one that seemed all the more relevant as the Cold War began to develop. The post-war fascination with individualism was, of course, very much a Western preoccupation (as Tara Zahra reminds us, collectivist approaches to children's rehabilitation were far more standard currency in the countries of Eastern Europe), but it was one which many child survivors in diaspora encountered as they journeyed westwards.[36] If both too much aggression and too much obedience were tainted by association with fascism (and communism), then future citizens of a healthy social democracy had to walk a line between the two. The earlier hygienist model of child-rearing that stressed strict routines and behaviour seemed entirely too 'Prussian' in this context, and an emotions-based psychoanalytic model widely came to take its place. A return to individualism thus appeared, to adults anxious about these children, to be a healthy sign of a child's release from the grip of wartime behaviours.

This is not to say that adults' fears about survivor children were without foundation. Some children did manifest their inner turmoil through behaviour that was violent and aggressive; others chose to protect themselves and keep their heads down with studied good behaviour; many were highly suspicious of adults and adult motives, with good reason. However, the adults who cared for these children were not operating in a vacuum. They were influenced by a host of factors: the waning of hygienist models of children's behaviour and the rise of psychoanalytic ones; the rise of the 'expert' care worker, trained in new techniques such as the 'casework' model; the growing sense of a connection between psychological health and citizenship; the representations of survivors and survival that circulated in the media; and, in general, the idea that there were parallels between the reconstruction of European civilization and the reconstruction of its future citizens. In this sense, adult observers interpreted the feelings and actions of child survivors through a lens that was very much a product of the immediate post-war climate.

In reflecting on the power that adult care workers and child experts had in defining what constituted normal behaviour and feelings for children in this period, we should be attuned to the possibility that children may equally have acted, in their own ways, to subvert and manipulate adult agendas around psychological reconstruction. They were much more than simply the objects of these anxiety-fuelled attentions. Understanding the perspective of adult carers tells us a great deal about the environment in which child survivors found themselves after the war, and about the scope children had for cutting their own paths through this environment. However, adults' reflections on children sometimes revealed children's own awareness, and in some cases clever exploitation, of adult goals for their psychological and emotional renewal.

In the summer of 1947 the JDC invited Paul Friedman to write a report on the psychological health of adults and children detained in the nine internment camps in Cyprus, where the British military held more than 18,000 DPs who had illegally tried to enter Palestine.[37] Friedman observed that many of the psychological and emotional problems that he had witnessed in the European DP camps were evident in Cyprus as well, and were further exacerbated by the frustration felt by adults and children alike in finding themselves back behind barbed wire two years after the war's end. Friedman described the case of a girl in the children's camp in Dekhelia, who came to the camp doctor when she lost her voice and could only speak in a whisper. The girl had survived the war in hiding, and was an orphan. Her mother and two siblings had been deported to their deaths, and she had seen her father forced to dig his own grave. Friedman's psychiatric team were concerned about the girl, noting that she 'manifested a rather indifferent attitude', in addition to having lost her voice. But they recorded with satisfaction that when the girl was placed on the list of those recommended for early departure to Palestine, her voice returned within a few days. 'We do not mean to say,' Friedman recorded, 'that the only factor that cured her of her condition was the assurance that she will leave Cyprus and go to Palestine, but certainly it is not a mere coincidence that she suddenly gave up her symptom when her name appeared on the list.'[38]

Friedman's own choice of words here – the girl 'suddenly gave up her symptom' – indicates that he himself was quite aware that children could employ troubling behaviour to achieve certain ends. They could equally return to 'normal' when the situation seemed to merit such a response. Children were adept not only at negotiating adult priorities in the early years after the war, but also at manipulating them. While adults staked out the boundaries of what were acceptable feelings for a child to have, children became skilled at nurturing their less than acceptable emotions in private, while polishing the correct ones for adult consumption. We come across evidence of this in both the archival record and in later memoirs and oral history. Fritz Friedmann was six years old at the war's end, and was one of the children brought to the Weir Courtney care home in Surrey. He recalled in his 2009 memoir that, in the home, he had been bullied by the two older boys who shared his dormitory room. When the matron came to tuck the boys in at night, 'sometimes I was crying. I told her I was thinking about my mother. I wasn't.'[39] If he was afraid to reveal to staff the real cause of his misery, he nonetheless knew well how to render his sadness acceptable and accessible to the adults observing his behaviour.

However, while adult views of survivor children were built on the assumptions, prejudices, and understandings of the early post-war moment, this does not mean that their methods were unhelpful. Of course, the care that children received after the war was uneven. The adults whose fears and hopes have been described here were committed to their work, believed in its efficacy, and desperately wanted to help their wards, but not all children found themselves cared for by such sympathetic and generous women and men. Nonetheless, child survivors often remember their care workers with great fondness and respect. They acknowledge, as adults looking back on their childhood experiences, that they may have baulked at some of the methods the care workers used, but they were nevertheless greatly helped by their care. Returning to the Buchenwald boys, who troubled and terrorized so many of the adults that first tried to help them, it is worth noting that they escaped the curse of the head of the Écouis reception centre who branded them psychopaths. Many went on to achieve remarkable things. One, Elie Wiesel, grew up to write what is now one of the best-known works in Holocaust literature, the autobiographical *Night*, which describes his experiences in Auschwitz and Buchenwald. Wiesel won the Nobel Peace Prize in 1986. Around the same time he wrote to his former carer Judith Hemmendinger. In his letter he recalled that, after the boys were brought to France, 'we didn't want any of your help, or your understanding, or your psychological tests, or your charity'. He also acknowledged, however, that the OSE care workers had rescued and transformed the boys: although the children had resented some of their efforts, the OSE workers had done immense good. 'In a short time,' he wrote, 'we managed to find ourselves on the same side. To what do we owe that miracle? How can we explain it? To our religious sensibilities? To yours? The fact is that all of those children could have turned to violence or opted for nihilism: you knew how to lead them towards trust and reconciliation.'[40]

# THREE

# CLAIMING CHILDREN

No one wanted to take Robert B.

Robert was born in Budapest in August 1936, the only child of working-class parents. His experience during the war years was similar to that of other Jewish children who found themselves in the Hungarian capital, for the Holocaust came to Budapest late, but with an exceptional fury. Around 1941 or 1942 his father was taken away to the forced labour battalions, and Robert never saw him again.[1] In the summer of 1944, Robert and his mother were forced to move into one of the state-designated 'yellow star' houses, in an apartment complex not far from his own home, although he had no memories of this event. His earliest memories began when his mother secreted him within a safe house under the protection of the Swedish diplomat Raoul Wallenberg, and left him there alone.[2] There were lots of other children in the safe house who were for the most part without their families. Robert's mother managed to visit him every Sunday, but then, he recalled, 'one Sunday she didn't come':

> There were always a lot of kids who were crying, they were younger. I don't know if I did, but I remember being sad when my mother didn't show up, the feeling of being let down, the loneliness. I sat and sat in the window and I watched [for her], I remember the cold. It was becoming fall. I touched it, the window.[3]

On an autumn day pouring with rain, soldiers showed up at the safe house. They screamed at the children to get out fast and line up in the street. The

58

children stood in the rain for a long time, getting wet, and were then marched to and interned in the Budapest ghetto. In the ghetto, Robert was left without adult care. He has no memory of how he escaped; he only remembers suddenly being out on the street, tearing the yellow star off his jacket. He managed to find a woman who knew his family and was able to take him to where his mother's sister was hiding under false papers. He went into hiding with this aunt and her children. It was not long until Budapest was liberated by the Red Army. Robert was eight years old.

The liberation only brought more uncertainty. He moved from his aunt's care to that of another aunt, and then quickly on to a third. His aunts asked anyone and everyone for news of Robert's mother. A former neighbour who had returned from Bergen-Belsen believed that his mother had been there, but this was never confirmed. Robert recalled that he was a difficult child to manage; he would run away from home, he could not control his emotions, and he would lash out violently at his cousins. In 1946 his aunts placed him in a care home.

Robert liked the home, which was run as a kibbutz by Zionists who hoped to prepare the children for onward migration to Palestine. He was excited to play with other children, thrilled by the luxury of a swimming pool, and curious to learn that he was Jewish. 'This is where I really began realising that I was Jewish,' he remembered. 'I never realised that I was being picked on because I was Jewish.' The staff gave the children Hebrew lessons, and tried to inculcate enthusiasm about moving on to Palestine, but 'I didn't pay too much attention to that. My big focus was on the swimming pool or climbing trees.'

One day, without warning, the staff informed him that he would not be going to Palestine after all, but instead to North America. Care workers from the Hungarian branch of the JDC had selected him for inclusion in a Canadian scheme to bring 1,000 'Jewish war orphans' to Canada. He later recalled overhearing some uncomfortable conversations around his aunt's dinner table, as his aunts wondered aloud what it meant to give up their sister's only child, and pondered who should inherit his parents' furniture. He was nonetheless bundled onto a train for France, where he awaited transport to Canada.[4] What struck Robert as he waited in France was that he belonged nowhere:

[I had] this feeling, that I belonged nowhere, that I didn't belong to anyone special. It manifested itself in my behaviour. There was this wildness, this uncontrollable behaviour, and it kept on showing up. Probably if I had been a quiet child, one of my aunts would have kept me. I was always getting into trouble. They couldn't deal with me.

In late December 1948 Robert sailed to Canada. He landed in Halifax, and was then taken by train to Calgary, Alberta. He was placed with a foster family, but they found him difficult and asked that he be moved. His second foster family reached the same conclusions. The Canadian Jewish Congress (CJC), which was responsible for the care of the orphans on the scheme, agreed to move him to Winnipeg, where there was a larger Jewish community, and, they hoped, a more suitable foster home could be found. He moved to Winnipeg in February 1949, then twelve years old, and quickly went through three different foster homes. As with his aunts in Budapest, no adults could deal with Robert. His case notes record that he was intelligent, 'attractive', and in desperate need of affection, but also 'highly emotional and volatile, and almost every aspect of his behaviour indicates the fact that he is greatly disturbed'.[5] In addition to his outbursts, Robert had a physical symptom of emotional distress: he wet the bed. In this, he shared a great deal in common with many other child survivors. Enuresis (bed-wetting) was frequently recorded in children's case files, and while psychoanalytically informed care staff generally saw it as a symptom of psychological trauma, not all carers took such an enlightened view.[6] If Robert had been placed in a larger city, his care workers might have seen his troubled physical and emotional behaviour as part of a larger pattern among child survivors. But there were not many child survivors in Winnipeg, and it is clear that the local agency, Jewish Family Service, simply did not know what to do with Robert. They lamented in their notes that there were 'no resources for adequate psychiatric guidance' in Winnipeg, and finally in desperation they placed him in a home for delinquent boys.[7]

From the time he had run away from the Budapest ghetto at the age of eight, no adult had wanted to care for Robert, although some had wanted to claim him. His Zionist care home had claimed him for Palestine, and the Canadian Jewish Congress had claimed him for their orphans' scheme. His Canadian foster families may well have wanted to claim him as an adoptive son, but they were ill-equipped to deal with the psychological needs of a child who had experienced such extreme events. In 1952, however, a childless Jewish couple in their forties approached the Winnipeg agency to ask about adoption. They agreed to foster Robert. Within six months his enuresis stopped. 'Very significant changes took place in my behaviour. I seemed to settle down. The obvious thing was that I felt that I belonged somewhere, that I was part of a family situation.' At the age of sixteen, in a new country with a new language and family, Robert B.'s post-war dislocation finally came to an end.

As Robert's story shows, in the early post-war years child survivors found themselves occupying a strange place in adult attentions. Adults could see these children as precious remnants, but equally as damaged objects. Wartime host families, surviving relatives, local Jewish agencies, overseas agencies, and potential adoptive families might all stake a claim to a survivor child, at least in theory, but sometimes this nonetheless meant that no adult wanted to take on the burden of caring for a troubled child in practice.

The children whose stories are explored in this chapter were all 'unaccompanied', to use the term favoured by post-war humanitarian aid agencies: they found themselves alone after the war, although this did not necessarily mean that they were without surviving family members, even parents. 'Unaccompanied children' occupied considerable space in the post-war adult imagination, and the anxieties over who could and should claim them reveal a great deal about adult views of child survivors in symbolic, political, and ideological terms. Such 'unaccompanied children' did not constitute the majority of child survivors: there were many children who stayed with parents or relatives throughout the war, and many more who found their way quickly back to surviving family members afterwards (their stories will be explored in the next chapter). In the years after the war, the JDC estimated that of the 180,000 children who had survived the genocide, 120,000 received JDC aid: 32,000 in more than 350 JDC-funded care homes, and 85,000 through their families.[8] Yet 'unaccompanied' child survivors could find themselves pushed and pulled, in the early post-war moment, by a baffling array of competing demands for their bodies, minds, and souls. Wartime host families were sometimes reluctant to give up the children they had cared for over many years. Local Jewish agencies sought to reclaim children to ensure the rebuilding of local or national Jewish communities, and saw the children's value both in demographic and symbolic terms, as emblems of the community's very future presence. Surviving relatives could have complex reasons for claiming children, ranging from genuine affection to a sense of duty to murdered loved ones, or an urge to keep the children in the fold because they were among the only family members left. Jewish aid agencies outside Europe sought to claim children not only for humanitarian reasons, but because the community members who financed their operations wanted Jewish children to adopt. Children were thus caught between competing nations, families, and religions, and the process of reclaiming them required a significant investment of emotional, material, and communal energy. Caught in the middle of these competing interests were the children themselves, who quickly figured out that there could be a wide gulf between claiming children as remnants and symbols, and genuinely wanting children to raise as individuals and human beings.

Survivor children's very bodies were seen by many of the adults involved as sites of meaning and memory, as objects of pity, as vulnerable and innocent, as redeemable, and as the building blocks for a Jewish future in Europe and beyond. In claiming children, it was often this symbolic body that adults had in mind, the one that would repopulate decimated Jewish communities, act as a tangible reminder of (and memorial to) the bitter recent past, and rebuild the next generation of a Jewish family. The real body, however, where emotional distress was often laid bare through 'difficult behaviour' such as bed-wetting, stuttering, or speechlessness, could fit uncomfortably with such idealized notions. Thus some children found themselves in the strange and distressing position of having multiple claims on their corporeal selves, and yet no one who truly wished to raise them.

If adults hoped to claim children's bodies, they were often equally interested in their souls. This was most true where children had been hidden with Christian rescue families during the war. The fear that Christian families would not return Jewish children post-war, a fear fed by a handful of well-publicized court cases where this was precisely what had happened, consumed the attentions of Jewish aid agencies in the early months and years after the war's end. These agencies consistently overestimated the number of children that they hoped to find hidden away in Christian homes and institutions, fearing coordinated efforts to baptize Jewish children en masse, and failing to understand that most of these children had, in fact, 'been lost to the gas chambers and not to Christianity'.[9] Such fears are understandable in the light of demographic losses, a sense of duty towards murdered community members, and Jewish communal leaders' own uncertainty concerning their communities' place in the body politic after the war. But attempts to return children to Judaism met with complex emotional responses in the children themselves, as we have seen. Young children had had years in which they learned only too well that being Jewish was a dangerous thing to be. They had practised hiding their Jewish roots. Some had forgotten entirely that they had ever been Jewish; the very youngest had never known it to begin with. Moreover, in the tussle over children's souls, although adults might have been concerned with religious and ethnic belonging, children were generally more anxious about holding onto the security of familiar environments.

These competing claims fed into an environment that, as we have seen, was one of rapid transitions, enormous instability, and fleeting emotional attachments. Children moved (or were moved forcibly) in an overwhelming number of directions after the war. Those hidden with host families were claimed by Jewish aid agencies, or by surviving parents or relatives. Some aid agencies were local or national, some were transnational (such as UNRRA and the JDC), and some were based overseas. These overseas agencies, in turn, sometimes hoped to place children with adoptive Jewish families in their own countries. Thus a child could find that, in a short period of time, she might move from the home of a host family to a Jewish care home run by a local aid agency, from the care home to an UNRRA- or JDC-run reception centre, from the reception centre to a ship leaving Europe, and very quickly she was in a new country with a new adoptive or foster family, trying to convey her feelings in a language she did not speak. Surviving relatives might have stepped into or out of this turbulent process at any point. These claims on children restructured their post-war worlds in every conceivable way, and cast them into a global diaspora. Not all survivor children left Europe after the war, but the majority did, and thus the process of claiming children and the event of their global migration were tightly bound together.[10]

A number of factors shaped how adults regarded children in this fraught process of claiming, and equally how children themselves negotiated the process. A child's age mattered, for in a moment of vigorous competition between so many parties there was a hierarchy of adult desire that placed the youngest children at the top. Very young children, many adults assumed, were the most adaptable, resilient, and malleable, capable of being reshaped according to adult wishes. It equally mattered whether or not a child was in good physical and mental health, for children who were physically ill or deeply emotionally troubled were not accepted onto emigration schemes, and had difficulty in finding foster families (or, indeed, in being cared for by their own surviving family members). It also mattered whether or not a child was a full orphan, or at least if she was adept at pretending to be one at the right moments, as some funding schemes and care homes were earmarked for orphans, and most immigration schemes would only accept orphaned children. Surviving parents, as we shall see, at times only complicated a child's journey through this world of competing claims.

A child's gender could matter, as potential adoptive or foster families tended to request girls from the agencies. Social class also mattered, sometimes greatly. A child who was known to come from an affluent or educated background stood a better chance of being prepared for eventual adoption by local or overseas aid agencies, and was more likely to be placed with an affluent family if she was adopted. At the same time, however, her surviving family members might have found themselves too poor after the war to be able to take her back. The 'children's colonies' and care homes throughout Europe in the post-war period were filled with children who had surviving family members, but their families lacked the material (and often emotional) resources to reclaim them. We do not often talk about social class and the Holocaust, but a family's means (or lack of means) after the war could make a lifelong difference to the trajectories of its youngest members.

Finally, a child's own resourcefulness and willingness to perform the roles set by adult demands naturally shaped her experience as well, and in this, children had far more agency than it might at first appear. Children could find themselves caught in the whirlwind of competing claims, but they were also quite capable of navigating these to their own ends. They had learned a great deal during the war about crafting and re-crafting their identities, and presenting parts of themselves for adult consumption while hiding others from sight. If they were buffeted by the forces that tried to remake them in the post-war moment, they were also skilled at using this very competition to carve a path for themselves.

Few issues preoccupied post-war Jewish aid organizations as relentlessly as the question of how to reclaim children who had been hidden by Christian families during the war. This preoccupation was out of all proportion to the scale of the situation, for most wartime host families turned children over to local and national Jewish aid organizations without a struggle, if many nevertheless did so with regret. In most European countries where children had been hidden in large numbers during the war, Jewish aid agencies took responsibility for the emotionally fraught process of reclaiming children from host families and either returning them to surviving family members or bringing them to live in Jewish care homes.[11] In so doing, their driving goal was to repopulate the ranks of regional and national Jewish communities: they acted so that the children would not 'be lost to us'.[12] And although this was generally a non-confrontational process, these agencies were not above using judicial procedures, kidnappings, and the payment of ransom to bring every possible child back into the Jewish fold. As the historian Daniella Doron has argued, aid workers and community leaders believed that after the population losses of the war, 'the future of the Jewish people hinged on reclaiming every last Jewish child'.[13]

Linked to this sense that every hidden child needed to be reclaimed, Jewish community leaders persisted in believing – despite evidence to the contrary – that large numbers of 'lost children' remained hidden in Christian homes after the liberation. In 1947 writers for London's *Jewish Chronicle* painted a bleak picture of the search for these children:

> The saving of these children from forced apostasy is a paramount religious obligation. Their spiritual safeguarding, after the martyrdom of their parents, must be a first charge upon the conscience of Jewry. [. . .] Every obstacle is put in the way of the restoration of these Jewish orphans to their ancestral faith. Upon the remnant of Israel's children who have escaped massacre are centred our fondest hopes and prayers. No people holding themselves at some worth spiritually would agree to the rending away of their future 'capital', and we Jews, who believe we still have a moral destiny in this world, cannot admit to the right of others to snatch away our children from us. Yet there are Church dignitaries who do not scruple to take advantage of these orphans' cruel plight, in order to prevent the restitution to them of their own spiritual heritage.[14]

Such hyperbolic language reflected a genuine unease on the part of post-war Jewish aid organizations. French Jewish agencies believed that there were 3,000 such 'lost children', British agencies posited 5,000, and American agencies suggested a baffling 20,000 children were secreted away in Christian homes and institutions across Europe.[15] Yet despite enormous efforts and investment of resources, the masses of children that Jewish agencies expected to find in Christian homes were never found – not because their return was blocked by an intransigent Church, but because they did not exist. The vast majority of children who had hidden with Christian families during the war years were reclaimed without incident. In Belgium, for example, of the 1,816 children placed with Christian families during the war, only 87 had not yet been returned to the Jewish aid agency Aide aux Israélites Victimes de la Guerre (AIVG) by December 1946.[16] In 1948 the Comité Supérieur de l'Enfance Juive began searching for 'lost children' in France, using young adults hired to comb the countryside during the summer holidays. They searched until May 1949, but found only fifty-nine certain cases of Jewish children still living with their host families.[17] The state of near panic that surrounded the issue of children hidden in Christian homes after the war is telling, not because it reflected reality, but because it sheds light on just how far Jewish leaders and organizations feared that the coordinated attempts to destroy Jewish life in Europe had not ceased with the war's end. Children, as the community's 'future "capital"',￼ were the battleground over which this coda of the war was fought.[18]

This panic was fed by a string of high-profile legal battles. The best known of these was the court case concerning the Finaly children, two boys whose Austrian Jewish parents took refuge in Grenoble during the war before being deported to their deaths. The boys had ended up in the care of Antoinette Brun, the director of a Catholic crèche, and Brun refused to return the boys to their surviving aunts after the war, prompting a legal battle for their custody that stretched until 1953.[19] But the Finaly affair was only one of many similar cases, and the Jewish press worldwide reported on each one in detail. There was the case of five-year-old Ruth Heller, who had been living with her Christian host family in the Netherlands since the age of one. The child's surviving aunt and uncles took the host family to court to press for her to be sent to them in Palestine, but lost.[20] Cilla Bernstein, born in 1936 in Antwerp, had fled to Paris with her mother and was eventually hidden with an elderly couple in Paris, the Boyers. Her entire family was murdered, save one aunt on her mother's side, who managed to trace Cilla after the war, only to find that the girl had become a devout Catholic. The case went to a Paris courthouse, where the aunt insisted that Cilla 'belonged to her next of kin', but the court deferred judgement, allowing Cilla to stay with the Boyers.[21] The orphaned Anna Cymbler, left to fend for herself when her parents were deported from France to the east, found a form of shelter on a farm near Dijon, but her host family effectively used her for slave labour. In 1949 she set fire to some of the farm buildings and was sentenced to five years' imprisonment, a decision that prompted global outrage. 'Anna's is not an isolated case,' wrote a reporter for the *New York Times*. 'Although Jewish organizations have rescued thousands of children from monasteries, convents, and homes, hundreds more are known to be living on farms throughout the country, at the mercy of brutal foster-parents.'[22] Such press coverage left readers with the impression that there was a vast conspiracy to keep Jewish children in Christian hands.[23]

These legal battles had the effect of justifying, to Jewish organizations, the use of any means necessary to wrench children back from Christian host families and institutions. This meant legal action in some cases, but far more frequently it meant the swift, forced removal of children from their rescuers. Paulette S. was born in Paris to Polish Jewish parents in March 1938. She and her older siblings were hidden in the countryside by the OSE; her parents were deported to their deaths. The OSE provided Paulette with false papers and a fake surname, Sabatier, and she was moved with her sister several times during the war years. The girls were finally brought to Châtillon-sur-Indre, a village near Châteauroux, where they were sheltered by a woman named Henriette Gateault. 'This was the happiest period for me throughout the war years,' Paulette wrote decades later. 'We had food and warmth, and I felt loved and cared for. She asked me to call her Maman Gateault.' Mme Gateault protected the two girls through the final months of the war. When the Germans retreated through the village in the summer of 1944, they shot residents and committed atrocities, including beating Mme Gateault's partner Pierre Doliveux so badly that he later died in hospital of his injuries. Paulette, however, does not recall feeling frightened; on the contrary, Mme Gateault's household was the first place where she remembered feeling wholly safe and wanted.[24]

By September 1944 the region had been liberated. The two girls simply continued living with Mme Gateault after the liberation, and Paulette did not recall any discussion of an alternative. It was more than a full year later when, without warning, Paulette and her sister were removed by the OSE:

In November 1945, we were returning from visiting [Mme Gateault's daughter Lucienne] in the hospital. She had just given birth to a baby boy. It was a sunny, peaceful afternoon and we were strolling home. I was lagging behind Maman Gateault and my sister, picking flowers from the footpath. Suddenly a black car stopped and two men in dark suits and hats ran out and grabbed us. They said, 'Don't be scared, we are Jewish. We are taking you back.' I could hear Maman Gateault screaming, 'They are my children, don't take them away.' I heard those words for so many years to come. She loved me. She was good to me and I was so happy with her.

I hated those two men for so many years. What they did seemed so brutal at the time. I didn't want to go with them, I didn't want to be Jewish. Later I discovered that some families who had harboured children refused to part with them. Some did so because they had grown to love them, others because they had baptised them and wanted to 'save their souls'. Some even held them to ransom, demanding a large monetary reward. Maman Gateault did not fit any of those categories. We should have been given a chance to say goodbye properly.[25]

Agencies such as the OSE employed force in wresting children from their rescuers precisely because they knew that they faced a still larger challenge in bringing children's hearts and minds back to Judaism. After all, children in hiding had had to bury their Jewishness deep. They had taken on Christian names and Christian identities, and had constructed Christian pasts for themselves. Some had picked up anti-Semitic thinking from their hosts. As memories of Judaism had faded – and the very youngest may have had no such memories at all – it began to seem like a toxic association. If the Jews were being persecuted, some children mused, they must surely have done something to deserve it. Why would one choose to be Jewish if there was an alternative? The very fact of their host family's non-Jewishness is what gave children security and protection, and children were only too aware that to let slip evidence of a Jewish past was to bid adieu to this security. Some hidden children, like Paulette, never had significant encounters with religion in their rescue homes, but others developed an intense attraction to Catholicism. In their efforts to hustle children back towards a 'normal' state of Jewishness after the war, local Jewish agencies such as the OSE removed children from wartime host families and placed them in institutional Jewish care homes, where they encountered environments that could be 'Jewish' in a range of ways. Some of these homes were religiously observant, some encouraged the children to learn or relearn Yiddish or Hebrew, some had a Zionist outlook and sought to prepare the children for eventual immigration to Palestine. However, this could simply drive children to conceal their ongoing connection to Catholicism – and hidden children, of course, were well versed in secreting away aspects of their identities. In the European DP camps, Paul Friedman encountered Zionist youth leaders who sought to return children to the Jewish fold through sheer force of will:

> At the beginning the children had offered great resistance to [their youth leader] and wanted to return to their Gentile foster-parents, though these no longer had a place for them. [The youth leader] told us that she was often compelled to lock the doors to prevent them from running away. She believed, however, that all the children's conflicts had been solved and that she had been successful in bringing them back to a faith in Judaism. When I pointed out that the children still kept crosses and prayer books under-neath their pillows, she brushed this aside as an innocuous addiction to souvenirs. Unfortunately, after having discussed this particular problem with many of these children, I found it impossible to be as optimistic. Many of them had deep conflicts concerning their Jewishness, which for years had been a secret whose betrayal might mean death.[26]

Friedman, of course, was concerned about the psychological and emotional consequences of such demands. From the perspective of the children involved, however, holding onto crosses and rosaries was an assertion of will, a determi-nation to maintain elements of the wartime self in the face of adult demands to cast that self aside.

The early post-war months and years were a moment of profound geographical instability for many child survivors, in addition to a time of emotional and material uncertainty. Decisions sometimes made in haste in this period could have lifelong repercussions, thrusting children into a diaspora that fanned out across the entire planet and was shaped by the emerging geopolitics of the Cold War.[27] Children caught in custody battles faced the issue of being taken from homes where they may have wanted to remain, but far more children confronted a very different alternative: they had no home at all. At the war's end, children were found not only in hiding with families, but in forced labour and concentration camps, in ghettos, in neutral and Allied countries, in hiding in the forests, living with partisan brigades, and in many other situations. There were numerous pathways out of such scenarios, but few of these led a child back to the town or region of her birth. Rather, after the war tens of thousands of Jewish children found themselves on the move, en route not only towards new homes and new families, but also to new citizenships.[28]

In this process of transnational dislocation, many children passed through the DP camps that were erected in occupied Germany, Austria, and Italy after the war's end. By the summer of 1947 there were 250,000 surviving Jews in the European DP camps, and roughly 182,000 Jewish DPs in occupied Germany alone – a significant number, although small compared to the estimated 10 million people uprooted and displaced by the war.[29] Occupied Germany thus became a key locus of convergence for deracinated Jews after the war, both adults and children.

As children passed through the DP camps, they came into contact with the care workers of transnational humanitarian aid organizations such as UNRRA and the JDC. Created in November 1943, UNRRA was the body charged, at the war's end, with administering the DP camps. It was financed principally by the United States, Britain, and Canada, and the bulk of its staff were American and British.[30] UNRRA worked in close coordination with the JDC, an American aid organization that provided funding not only for Jewish DPs, but equally for the local and national Jewish organizations that helped survivors in countries across Europe.[31] Both UNRRA and the JDC worked to establish a 'scientific' approach to children's aid, drawing on the casework model to establish where a child had come from, where her parents might have ended up, whether she had living family or not, and what her particular individual needs were. They set up and maintained the network of children's homes and assembly centres that welcomed survivor children; Jewish children made up 60 per cent of the 'unaccompanied children' in these facilities. The humanitarian aid organizations also considered where a child might go when she left the DP camps.[32]

This was a thorny political question, as well as a complex ideological one. While the majority of Jewish children in the DP camps had come from Eastern Europe, they did not necessarily want to return there. From late 1945 waves of refugees began to arrive in the DP camps of the Western zones of occupation in Germany and Austria, the so-called 'infiltrees'. These were Jewish survivors who, facing continuing anti-Semitic violence in Poland and elsewhere, were brought to the DP camps as part of a semi-organized underground movement called the Bricha, or 'flight'. Those who fled Eastern Europe with the Bricha had not necessarily survived the war in occupied Europe. A large share had fled to the bleak refuge of the Soviet Union, where they had sometimes been further deported into Siberia or Central Asia. Following a repatriation agreement in 1946, scores of refugees returned from the far reaches of the Soviet Union to Poland, and finding no one and nothing left there for them, they joined the ranks of those fleeing, illegally, towards the Western DP camps. An estimated 200,000 Jews fled Eastern Europe in this way, and around 7,000 unaccompanied Jewish children fled Poland alone.[33]

To the consternation of UNRRA and other aid agencies helping children in the camps, many 'infiltree' children came alone, but they were not without families: surviving relatives sometimes sent children with the Bricha in the hopes of getting them to Palestine, or at least out of those regions of Eastern Europe where anti-Semitic pogroms continued after the war. According to an autumn 1946 UNRRA report, 20,000 'infiltree children' had arrived in the American zone of Germany; 6,000 of these were unaccompanied, but UNRRA estimated that most in fact had family either elsewhere in the DP camp network or back in their countries of origin. Bricha leaders had advised the children not to reveal their family ties, in case it lessened their chances of getting into Palestine.[34] The infiltrees posed a particularly thorny problem for UNRRA, because the organization did not want DPs to linger in the camps. At the Yalta conference in

February 1945, UNRRA had agreed to repatriate DPs to their countries of origin, and in the spring of that year more than 80,000 people were repatriated each day.[35] However, repatriation was not an option that the infiltrees could accept, and their numbers continued to swell through 1946 and 1947.[36]

The leaders of the Bricha had only one final destination in mind for the infiltrees: Palestine. However, Palestine under the British Mandate remained inaccessible to the majority of Jewish DPs who hoped to immigrate there. The MacDonald White Paper of 1939 had limited legal entry to Palestine to 1,500 visas per month. Those caught trying to enter illegally were sent back to Europe, or interned in camps first at Atlit, and later on Cyprus.[37] Bricha leaders, and the leaders of other Zionist organizations (growing in strength inside the DP camps), saw in the increasing numbers of Jewish DPs an opportunity to put pressure on the British government to lift the quota system. Thus while UNRRA and the JDC worried about the psychological state of children confined to the DP camps, and hoped to move them swiftly on to more stable homes, Zionist groups in the camps were reluctant to agree to any solution for displaced children other than immigration to Palestine, even though this remained out of reach. Children thus found themselves caught between the competing views of aid organizations such as UNRRA, which wanted to see them leave the camps swiftly, and the Zionist organizations which wanted them to stay.[38] In this tense climate, UNRRA records from the time occasionally marked entire lists of children as 'disappeared', indicating that the Bricha had illegally taken them towards Palestine. Many of these children ended up interned on Cyprus.[39]

It was an unsustainable situation, and one further complicated by the intervention of a number of overseas Jewish aid organizations that proposed their own programmes to bring children out of the DP camps and into safe homes abroad. Four countries – Britain, Canada, Australia, and South Africa – created dedicated 'war orphan' schemes intended to bring orphaned Jewish children to live abroad, financed by local Jewish communities in these countries. In addition, the United States eased its immigration visa system to allow children to enter on 'corporate affidavits' under the sponsorship of an aid agency. At their core these programmes all subscribed to the assumption that emigration would be healing for psychologically troubled children who had witnessed the destruction of their families, homes, and communities. However, they also scrambled to secure the healthiest, most capable, and youngest children. Children with physical disabilities (either congenital or resulting from wartime injuries) were generally rejected from these migration schemes, as were any children showing signs of extreme psychological distress. Older children could also find themselves disqualified. Definitions of where childhood ended, and of who qualified as a child, varied from scheme to scheme: UNRRA defined a child as anyone up to the age of seventeen, and the Canadian and British 'war orphan' schemes accepted adolescent children as old as eighteen, but the South African scheme drew the line at twelve years of age.[40]

Thus although the overseas agencies couched their work in terms of humanitarian aid and 'saving' Jewish children trapped in insalubrious conditions in the DP camps, their workers were looking for some rather specific traits as they scoured the camps for potential 'war orphans': they wanted adaptability, and in some cases adoptability. They wanted children who were young and healthy enough, in body and mind, to become productive future citizens, and possibly also young enough to be readily adopted by foster families in the home countries. The 'war orphans' programmes were funded entirely by donations from Jewish communities in the countries that offered these schemes, and in some cases these communities were motivated not merely by the idea of rescue, but also by the desire to expand their own ranks by adopting children assumed to be small enough to shed their pasts and take on a new cultural and national identity. In this, the organizers of these schemes found themselves frustrated when they began searching the camps for potential young candidates, for there were very few young children available for migration schemes. The agencies reported back to their supporters that this was because almost no young children had survived, but the reality was more complex: very few young children had survived without adult protection and attachments, and this made it difficult to determine which children were truly 'unaccompanied'.

This meant that there was a ferocious competition, between the various agencies and organizations operating in the DP camps and beyond, over the youngest and healthiest survivor children. Some local and national aid agencies, such as the OSE and the Belgian AIVG, clung to their wards. The AIVG argued that only adults should be allowed to choose a step as drastic as emigration, and the OSE showed a reluctance to part from 'its' children.[41] These organizations found themselves in the position of relying heavily on JDC funds to run their care programmes for children, but they clearly resented this extra- territorial interference.[42] It also became increasingly difficult, as the Cold War began to take shape, to remove children from the Soviet satellite countries. In addition to these complexities, the overseas agencies were in direct competition with each other. As a Canadian Jewish Congress observer complained, by the time the Canadians arrived in the DP camps, 'representatives of Australian and South African Jewry had already been dispatched to Europe and were actively bidding for their quota of youngsters'.[43]

There was additional pressure from Zionist organizations in the camps and from the Jewish Agency for Palestine, which used children and young families as key symbolic and strategic elements of their political strategy, because children in particular reinforced the idea that survivors were a community unfairly trapped in the land of their oppressors. As such, Zionist organizations both within the camps and transnationally staked a claim to 'most of the young children available in Europe'.[44] The files of the overseas agencies are filled with evidence that their caseworkers found this Zionist policy to be obstructionist: aid workers for the Central British Fund sent word to the organization's head office in Bloomsbury House, London, in November 1945 that 'there was a great deal of unrest' on the ground in occupied Germany, with 'the Zionists in the Camps endeavouring to prevent the children leaving, attempting to influence them by stories of non-Jewish homes in England'.[45] The head of the Australian Jewish Welfare Society (AJWS) similarly unleashed his frustration on JDC leaders, writing that:

I cannot understand why certain organisations are adversed [sic] to handing over a couple of hundred children so that they can be taken immediately from the horrors of Europe and given succour in a democratic Jewish community. I have always maintained that irrespective from [*sic*] what the outcome of Palestine will be, Jewish Communities elsewhere must be built up so that they can always help to finance the needs of Palestine.[46]

With all these competing claims on children, it may seem miraculous that any young child survivors managed to emigrate out of Europe at all – and yet, in the end, the majority did. This was because the situation in Europe was very much in flux, and this instability brought with it certain opportunities. One was the pressure created by the rapid growth in the number of Jewish 'infiltrees' flooding into the DP camps of the American zone of occupied Germany through 1946–8, particularly in the face of continuing anti-Semitic violence in Poland.[47] By 1948 approximately 250,000 Jews from Eastern Europe had entered Germany illegally, including many orphans, and these survivors were getting impatient. The borders of Palestine were closed to them, and the creation of the state of Israel in 1948 brought with it further warfare.[48] With mounting demographic pressure in Germany, but with Palestine/Israel an unreachable and increasingly unattractive final destination, both adult and child Holocaust survivors began to search for alternative migration routes, and this gave the overseas agencies increased leverage to claim 'unaccompanied' children.[49]

The second factor was the changing nature of the Cold War, and its effect on the aid bodies that were helping children in the DP camps and beyond. UNRRA was slowly dissolved after 1946 and replaced by the International Refugee Organization (IRO), a change that effectively confirmed the divorce between East and West on the matter of humanitarian aid.[50] The IRO was largely financed by the United States, and the Soviets refused to participate. This meant that UNRRA's policy of repatriation had to be dropped, and the IRO instead increasingly explored the option of onward migration from Europe for DPs. At the same moment, the large transnational aid agencies began to cut their budgets. From the autumn of 1947, the JDC dramatically clawed back its operating budget, which in turn affected the budgets of national aid organizations such as the OSE. In this climate the OSE became more willing to relinquish the orphans in its care to international migration schemes. Following the JDC's budget cuts, and in light of the continuing difficulties in reaching Palestine, the OSE began making arrangements with the overseas agencies to allow 'their' children to leave. Children were given a choice concerning where they would like to go, with efforts taken to place children in countries where they had relatives, even if those countries were very distant.[51]

These changes over time help to explain why some of the Anglo-American 'war orphan' schemes were more successful than others. In the spring of 1945 the Central British Fund (CBF) secured an agreement from the Home Office to allow 1,000 orphaned Jewish children 'from the camps' to come to Britain, and the first 300 children arrived on this scheme in August 1945.[52] However, the CBF never fulfilled its post-war quota of 1,000 orphaned Jewish children, and this was largely due to timing. In November 1945 the aid worker Ruth Fellner was sending gushing telegrams back to London promising that 'there were more than 1,000 [children] and that more were going into the British and American Zones each day', but less than a month later these hopes were dashed by the 'tense' situation with the Zionists, who made it clear that 'there was no prospect of children desiring to go to Palestine coming from the Continent'.[53] CBF workers explained the situation to their constituents by stating that there were too few children left alive in the liberated concentration camps, but this was not true: what they meant was that there were very few children available for immigration who had not already been spoken for by others.

However, other 'war orphan' schemes had the accidental advantage of arriving on the scene rather late. This was partly because, throughout the Anglo-American world and beyond, immigration was severely restricted in the immediate post-war period. The 'war orphan' schemes marked the first tangible signs of a slow easing of these restrictive immigration policies, but as such they took enormous time and effort to negotiate. In the Australian case, the AJWS had managed, during the war itself, to broker an agreement with the government to bring in 300 refugee children, but due to restrictions on transport not a single child managed the journey during the war. After the war, however, the government extended the wartime agreement, and a total of 317 children arrived by the close of the scheme in 1950. The Canadian scheme, discussed in detail below, launched only in 1947.

It had an initial quota of 1,000 children, but it had brought over more than 1,115 by 1952.[54] Other countries had no specific scheme for unaccompanied Jewish children, but agencies in these countries nonetheless managed to push for the easing of restrictions on post-war immigration to allow some DPs to come. In this way, child survivors immigrated to Argentina, Brazil, New Zealand, Kenya, and elsewhere, but most significantly to the United States. In the wake of Earl Harrison's scathing 1945 report on conditions in the DP camps, President Truman issued a directive, on 22 December 1945, that allowed aid agencies to provide corporate affidavits for immigrants, which eliminated the need for a prospective immigrant to have a relative sponsor an affidavit as required by US law. For children, this meant that those with no known relatives in the United States could enter on the corporate affidavit of an agency such as the United States Committee for the Care of European Children (USCOM), although strict national quotas were still in force. By December 1947, USCOM had brought 1,170 orphaned 'young citizens-to-be' from Europe to the United States using its corporate affidavit, although the majority of these children were not Jewish. The passage of the first DP Act in July 1948 further loosened US immigration policy, allowing 110,000 Jewish refugees to enter between 1948 and 1952, an unknown number of whom were children.[55]

All these policies and practices suggest the contours of a high-stakes competition over children in the period from 1945 to the early 1950s, one in which children could easily find themselves the objects of adult tussles staked out along demographic, geographic, symbolic, and political lines. But as the case files of the aid agencies show, even very young children could prove remarkably adept at playing these adult concerns off against each other to cut their own pathway out of Europe and into new homes in new countries. To explore how children could act as historical agents in this process, we will now turn to the case of the Canadian Jewish Congress's 'War Orphans' Program', which was the most expansive of the war orphans schemes – but nonetheless fraught with some interesting problems that revealed how far the emotional triangle between children, aid agencies, and potential new families was one roomy enough to accommodate children's own agendas.

The Canadian Jewish Congress (CJC), which represented the Jewish communities of Canada in administering its scheme, began pressing the Canadian federal government during the war itself to allow 1,000 child refugees to be brought to Canada from Vichy France. However, although the immigration-wary federal government agreed, this wartime rescue scheme became impossible after the Allied invasion of North Africa prompted the Nazis to occupy Vichy France in November 1942. After the war ended, the CJC saw an opportunity to renew this earlier agreement. The process ran up against the thinly veiled anti-Semitism of certain key decision-makers in the federal government, who hoped to keep the borders closed to Jewish DPs, but by 1947 the quota of 1,000 children had been reinstated.[56] The 1947 order-in-council that authorized the programme stated that 1,000 'Jewish orphan children under the age of eighteen years' could be brought to Canada, provided that they were 'bereaved of both parents', and that they could meet the standard immigration requirements of physical and mental fitness. The government further stipulated that the CJC had to assume all financial responsibility for the scheme.[57]

It seemed at first an easy enough task to bring Canada's Jewish community on board to support the scheme materially and financially, for there was great enthusiasm over the idea of 'rescuing' small children who could then be adopted into Canadian Jewish homes. The CJC archives contain scores of letters from couples, often childless, who hoped to be able to adopt a young child via the scheme. Manfred Saalheimer, a CJC officer and one of the chief organizers of the programme, feared that there would not be enough orphans to meet with the demand from prospective families. He wrote to one such couple in May 1948 that there were far more 'suitable homes for adoption' in Canada's Jewish communities than there were orphans for placement.[58] But potential adoptive families had a rather narrow view of what sort of orphan they hoped to have. Families requested 'a girl as young as possible', or 'a Jewish girl of about 6 to 7 years', or 'a little girl who must be under 8 years of age', or occasionally 'a boy under the age of five'.[59] Such requests – and the fact that the CJC did not dissuade them, at least at first – reveal how both the agency and the community behind it wanted to claim children young enough to be absorbed and recraft them in their own image. In the words of one commentator in the local press, the children would be 'potentially the best immigrants' because 'a child who is brought to this country before it is in its 'teens will grow up as a Canadian, speak our language as its own, and have almost no recollection of any other homeland'.[60]

In its emphasis on migration for the purposes of adoption, Canada's war orphans scheme was something of an outlier. Both the British and the Australian schemes placed children predominantly in specially prepared care homes and hostels, rather than in private homes. In the British case, this was partly because adoption of a foreign-born child was not legal until the mid-1950s, but also because the British agencies had had ample experience of using a foster family system for the nearly 10,000 Jewish children who had come to Britain in 1938–9 on the Kindertransport scheme; they knew that private homes were often a very poor match for children who had been forced to flee their homes and families of birth, and who had continuing loyalties to their parents. But officers in the Canadian scheme hoped that such ongoing loyalties would not complicate their programme. On the ground in Europe, they gathered potential candidates at UNRRA-run children's centres in the American occupation zone in Germany. There the children would be observed for some months, while staff used the central registry of the International Tracing Service to try to locate their parents or relatives. The children would be sent on to Canada only if staff could confirm that they were truly orphans.[61]

Children themselves, however, were quite aware of this stipulation, and took their own steps to navigate it. Sometimes children claiming to be orphans would be discovered to be receiving mail from parents while at UNRRA reception centres. In these cases the children were generally returned to where they had been found. Notes written in pencil at the top of the case files of children rejected from the CJC scheme make clear that the chief reason why they were not accepted was the agency worker's suspicion that a child was not truly an orphan, citing 'not unaccompanied: mother living in Poland' or 'rejected: has parents in Roumania'.[62] The CJC worker Ethel Ostry noted in a report that she rejected children where there was even a suspicion of a living parent:

> It is interesting to note that in one interview where a girl and a boy were commended to me by one of the centres and presented as cousins, I refused to accept the girl because there were strong rumours that she had a mother living. I later discovered they were not cousins, but brother and sister, and therefore declared them both ineligible.[63]

The CJC was not alone in insisting that child migrants on its scheme should be orphans: the British, Australian, and South African programmes did the same. This stipulation generally came at the behest of national governments, who were reluctant enough to allow DP children to immigrate, and had no interest in admitting their parents. However, the CJC's dream of adoptable children complicated its insistence on orphans, and it was on these lines that the scheme nearly failed. Of the more than 1,115 children brought to Canada on the programme between 1947 and 1952, the vast majority were between fifteen and seventeen years of age, and boys outnumbered girls by two to one.[64] This meant that the CJC's initial optimism about more adoptive homes in Canada than children who needed homes quickly had to be abandoned, for the families that had dreamed of rescuing a girl under eight from the chaos of the DP camps were considerably less enthusiastic about sheltering an adolescent boy. Offers of adoptive homes for the orphans quickly dried up, and the CJC promptly switched its strategy from adoption to fostering, believing that an 'intimate family environment' would be better for the psychological health of the children than would an orphanage, and hoping that foster care might be an acceptable stop-gap solution.[65]

This policy proved to be endlessly frustrating, not only for the CJC but for the children themselves, and for the foster families who were rarely well equipped to deal with the psychological needs of child survivors. There were never enough foster homes to accommodate the children, so many ended up in 'reception centres', regardless of the CJC's bias against institutional care for the orphans. Here additional, unexpected problems arose. In order to raise funds for the project, the CJC had used every means at their disposal to publicize their work. The unintended consequence of this was that the orphans became objects of curiosity. In order to try to move the children out of the reception centres and into homes, the agency encouraged the local community to come and visit, but this meant that 'large numbers of the idle curious with little intention of offering shelter' began to spend time at the reception centres.[66] Local teenagers took to using the reception centres as a place to hang out, sometimes outnumbering the orphans.[67]

The youngest children on the scheme were particularly squeezed by this tension between adoption, foster care, and the reception centres, for the CJC still held out great hope that they would be adopted. Partly with this in mind, the agency set up a hierarchical system with 'free' foster homes (where foster families assumed the costs of caring for a child), and 'paid' homes (where the agency covered the child's room and board), with the former clearly deemed the better, and reserved for younger, more 'adoptable' children, and children with 'an unmistakable aptitude for academic study'.[68] The 'free' homes could come saddled with enormous expectations on the part of foster parents who hoped to adopt a child. It quickly became apparent that the weight of such expectations caused many of these relationships to break down. In the early 1950s CJC workers undertook two follow-up studies of the children placed in 'free' homes, one in Toronto and one in Montreal. They found that the majority of the 'free' home placements broke down, and children moved on to 'paid' foster care, which came with fewer expectations and obligations.[69]

The CJC's insistence on using foster care rather than group homes failed to take into account the emotional dimensions of the fostering relationship. Many of the CJC's 'orphans' reacted negatively to the pressure created by a home environment in which the parents expected the child to be absorbed into the family, emotionally and legally. Part of the problem was the fact that the adults involved often struggled to see past their own assumptions about the children, assumptions built from media reports on 'Europe's lost children' and images of the liberated concentration camps. These adults expected 'a group of docile, wan, exhausted young martyrs',[70] who would be only too happy to receive a loving home, and were surprised to find children who had their own ideas, their own memories of earlier homes that they wanted to preserve, and their own reasons to chafe at the expectation that they would simply be absorbed into new families in a new country.

Relatives could insert themselves forcefully into the triangle that existed between children, the agency and the foster families, preventing any future claims on a child by making it clear that they would stand in the way of a formal adoption. We find frequent examples of this both in the Canadian case and elsewhere where war orphan immigration schemes existed. Relatives were often unable or unwilling to take survivor children in themselves, yet they insisted that the children could not be adopted by unrelated families. It is not difficult, perhaps, to understand the motivations behind such refusals: surviving relatives often found themselves struggling, financially and emotionally, to re-establish their own lives after the war, and with entire families decimated, they did not want to lose another family member to adoption. However, from the perspective of the agency and of the foster families (and of some children themselves), this could appear to be a form of obstructionism, preventing a child from being placed in a secure family environment.

Freda Z., born in 1937 in Komanc, Poland, was brought to Canada on the CJC scheme in November 1949, a month after her twelfth birthday. She was placed with a family who were eager to adopt a child, but Freda's situation was complex: she had an older sister and two older brothers in the United States, and the foster family quickly realized that her allegiances were torn. Her siblings, for their part, desperately wanted her to join them in the US, but there was little chance of her immigrating on the oversubscribed Polish quota. The agency hoped that the siblings would 'decide eventually to allow Freda to be adopted', but such assurances did not come quickly enough to prevent the girl's foster family from breaking off their fledgling relationship. '[Her foster mother] is anxious to adopt a child', Freda's CJC caseworker noted. 'She asked the agency to place Freda in another home.'[71] Within a year Freda had moved through two more foster families, discovering as she travelled through these homes that no foster family wanted a child who could not be adopted. Thus Freda found herself unable to be reunited with her older siblings in the United States, but equally unable to find a stable home in Canada. There were a large number of similar cases among the CJC 'war orphans', and occasionally caseworkers gave voice to their frustration over this situation in children's case file notes. Caseworkers for Tomas R., born in 1937 in Trnava, Czechoslovakia, wrote of their frustration that the charming boy, who gave the 'impression of being a perfectly happy child', would be difficult to place since 'anyone taking him would want to adopt him', but his uncle in Pittsburgh and his surviving relatives in Czechoslovakia forbade this.[72]

Nothing muddied the waters of the fostering and adoption process quite like the sudden appearance of a living parent. Marcel J.* was born in 1935 in Warsaw. His case history records that he was with his parents and his older sister Sabina in the Warsaw ghetto until 1943, then was smuggled out of the ghetto and hidden with a Catholic farmer, who had him work on the farm. After this point, however, the history that Marcel gave to CJC officer Ethel Ostry and head of Aglasterhausen children's centre Rachel Rottersman became rather vague:

*1943–1945:* He worked until liberation then he left with his sister and friend. They went to Lodz and after they went together to Germany.
*1946:* Fromberg, Germany: He lived private [sic] with his sister and friends.
*1947:* Stuttgart, Germany: He lived with his friends until he was transferred to our Children's Center.[73]

Ostry and Rottersman wondered how Marcel and his sister had managed for such a long time on their own after the war, moving illegally from Poland to occupied West Germany, but staff had run the usual checks on the children, and opted to admit them to the scheme. The two children were brought to Calgary in June 1948, and placed in a 'free' foster home. The agency clearly

---

* pseudonym

had a high regard for the foster family, describing them as having 'a fine family life in which love and affection mean a great deal'. They were pleased that Marcel was proving to be a 'lovable, cooperative child', but there were hints that something was amiss. His older sister was secretive, and it was 'difficult to distinguish truth from untruth in her stories of their past'. As a consequence, the foster family had a hesitant relationship with the sister, but it seemed clear to the agency that they adored Marcel.[74]

This situation came to a sudden halt in the autumn of 1949, when Marcel accidentally let slip that his mother was alive, and that he had known this all along. His case notes recorded the shock of both his foster family and CJC officers at the news:

The children often received mail from Germany written in Polish, the contents of which they never disclosed to the R's [the foster family]. On one occasion in Oct. 1948, Marcel unthinkingly mentioned a letter to Mrs. R. which they had received from their Mother. At no time previously, had Congress here, nor the R's, had any idea that their mother existed. Naturally the R's were pleased that the mother lived, but were greatly upset that the children had lived a lie for so many months. [. . .] It was the mother's plan to have the children register as orphans. She changed her name so that the children would not be identified as being hers. She assured the children that she would be able to follow them to Canada within a month.[75]

It thus became clear that the children, in collaboration with their mother, had put together a complex series of lies to ensure that Marcel and Sabina could immigrate to Canada under the scheme. Their mother had gone so far as to change her name to disguise their connection, but the children had also been willing collaborators in the process. The truth destroyed the relationship between the children and their foster parents. Sabina was quickly moved to another city, where she began working as a waitress and moved out of foster care altogether. Marcel, on the other hand, wanted to stay with his foster family, but they were no longer sure that they wanted him. The children's caseworker wrote that by May 1950, Marcel's foster father was calling her office asking that Marcel be moved to a new home. Relations between his wife and Marcel had broken down. Marcel was 'still very much attached to Mr. R.', but 'at this point Mrs. R. is anxious to be relieved of all the responsibility'. In July 1950 Marcel left his foster home 'at the request of his foster parents'.[76]

If Marcel's situation ultimately slipped beyond his control, others among the youngest of the 'war orphans' managed more successfully to assert their will. Dorota J.* was born in the then Polish town of Borislaw in 1938. According to her case notes, she had been with her parents in Borislaw until 1943, when they placed her in hiding with Gentile friends. The child spent the war years in a string of different homes until she was located by her aunt in 1948. The aunt was planning to immigrate to Canada on a special scheme for tailors,[77] and was 'willing to take care of the child' once she had settled, so IRO caseworkers ran checks to verify Dorota's orphan status and admitted her to the CJC scheme. Her caseworker noted that she was an 'attractive and likeable child' who, because she had come originally from a well-to-do family and her father had been an engineer, should be 'placed in a cultured home' and encouraged to continue her education.[78]

The CJC knew that Dorota's aunt would soon arrive in Canada, and that she intended to care for the child. Yet the situation quickly grew complicated, because the agency placed Dorota in a 'free' foster home, and the child and foster family became attached to each other. Dorota's case file shows that she arrived in Montreal in October 1948, and that she was immediately placed with the foster family in the wealthy, English-speaking Westmount area of Montreal. Her aunt arrived only a few weeks later. She was surprised to find her niece in a foster home, but agreed that it was a 'very nice and wealthy home with pleasant people, who had their own boy of 7. At the very beginning Dorota told me that she would like to stay in this home and she is happy there.' The foster family clearly wanted to keep Dorota, and the foster father told the aunt that 'it was a love from the first sight'.[79] The aunt, herself barely

* pseudonym

an adult, planned to continue on to Vancouver, to stay with a friend when she arrived, and to look for work. She had no financial security, and no means to care for a girl on the cusp of adolescence, so she left Dorota with her foster family and went on alone to the west coast.

However, both Dorota and her aunt knew something that the agency and the foster family did not: Dorota's father was still alive, and was living in Israel, impoverished and without employment. It is not clear, from the notes in the case file, just how this secret slipped out in June 1949, but there were swift and angry reactions from the foster family, from the agency, and from Dorota herself. By this point the foster family hoped very much to adopt Dorota, but Quebec law stipulated that no formal adoption could take place in such circumstances. Dorota's social worker observed that the agency might try to secure a document from the father consenting to allow Dorota to stay indefinitely with the foster family, but that this would be 'worthless from the legal point of view'.[80] This development seemed to be all too much both for the foster family and for Dorota herself. Her foster father wrote to the aunt in a rage:

> We are sick of being regarded as criminals. It seems you withheld the truth somewhere. You knew our intentions from the beginning. We have no proof that the father exists: let him furnish legal documents as to existence and his right to her. This must be done at once before we make any decision, or we will start legal proceedings of our own shortly; we will not permit further mental torture of the child.[81]

Contemporary readers may well wince at the thought of a wealthy and secure foster family demanding that a Holocaust survivor utterly without means furnish legal documents to prove both his very existence and his 'right' to his own daughter. Dorota, however, was very much on their side, and was willing to take action to ensure that she was not returned to a parent whom she had not seen in six years. Dorota began to write 'the most undiplomatic letters' to her family, in the hopes of driving off their claim on her. The CJC, for its part, supported Dorota in her fight to stay with her foster family. In the end, she does not appear ever to have returned to live with her family of origin.[82]

What is fascinating in Dorota's story is not only the significance of her own role in determining the outcome of the situation, but also the ways in which social class factored into the decisions made. The CJC placed Dorota with a wealthy family precisely because she had come from a wealthy background. Her birth family's former social standing, however, gave them no advantage in their efforts to reclaim the child, for after the war they found themselves with nothing. The agency judged that a child from a well-off background deserved to continue living in affluence, even if this meant that she was not returned to her own family.

In this, Dorota's family were certainly not alone. Whether they had been poor before the war or well off, adult survivors who were struggling materially after the war, who lacked housing or a steady job, who were hospitalized or too weak to rebuild their homes, faced a sometimes insurmountable task in attempting to reclaim their children (or nieces, nephews, young cousins, or grandchildren). These parents and relatives sometimes felt that a child's life chances would be better if she stayed in the care of an aid agency, and aid agencies often agreed. Where surviving parents and relatives lacked the means to reconstruct the family home, the fraught process of claiming children became deeply shaped by who had money, with lifelong repercussions for the families involved.

From the perspective of the children themselves, however, what cases like Dorota's and Marcel's reveal is just how flexible children could be in re-scripting their pasts to fit their present needs and desires. Caught between the competing claims of adults, children proved remarkably adept at publicly re-casting their histories – even to the point of concealing knowledge of a surviving mother or father. Amidst the push and pull of adult agendas, children asserted their own wills by hiding information and emotions, refusing to give up established loyalties, and in some cases deliberately doctoring their own histories. The question remains as to how far these fictional pasts, forged out of necessity, might later have become so tangled in their life stories that the children themselves lost sight of where the boundaries of the fiction lay.

# FOUR

# FAMILY REUNIONS

In 1948 officers of the Canadian Jewish Congress found two orphaned children in the DP camp at Feldafing, Bavaria, who were interested in immigrating to Canada. Isak B., born in Pułtusk, Poland, and thirteen at the time, was with his older sister Michla* in the camp, but the pair had not been able to find any other relatives beyond an aunt in the United States who was neither willing nor able to help them. They had been searching for three years. The Child Search Branch of the IRO had assisted: they had enquired with the Polish Red Cross, had checked the International Tracing Service's master index of people searching for missing relatives, and had put out a call for the children's families via a regular Radio Geneva broadcast that listed the names of survivors searching for missing loved ones. None of these attempts had yielded a response, so the children were deemed eligible for the Canadian immigration scheme. In preparation for their move overseas, Isak and his sister were brought to the International Children's Centre at Prien, in the American zone of occupied West Germany, which served as one of the key collection points for children joining the Canadian war orphans scheme. There the children told their story to CJC officers, who duly recorded it in their personal case files:

> 1943 the children were placed by their parents with a Polish family. Few months later [the parents] were killed in Ghetto in Pultusk. The children stayed with the Polish family until liberation in Dec. 1944. Short time after liberation they were taken to a Jewish Children's Center in Lodz where they

---

* pseudonyms

remained until Aug. 1946. At that time they were sent with a Jewish children's transport to Germany. Arrived in D. P. Camp Feldafing Dec. 1946.[1]

Isak and his sister were sure that their parents were dead. They left for Canada in September 1948, and upon arrival were placed in a foster home, with a 'middle-aged widow who is very attentive to them, but not very stimulating for them'.[2] What they thought of their new home remains unrecorded.

The children had gone through a dizzying series of changes in the years both during and after the war, and indeed, the agency only knew a part of their story. For reasons known only to the children themselves, Isak and Michla had concealed the truth about their wartime experiences from CJC officers. They had not, in fact, been hidden with a Polish family during the war. Their parents had never entered the ghetto in Pułtusk. Instead, the children's father had been forcibly conscripted into the Polish Army, and had never been heard from again. The children had fled with their mother to Russian-occupied Poland, and from there had been sent to Siberia, and then farther again into Central Asia after the opening of the Eastern Front in the summer of 1941. They made it as far as Stalinabad, the Tajik capital (now Dushanbe), where living conditions were grim. Typhus and malaria were rampant, and it was here that the children's mother became very ill, entered the hospital, and disappeared. After the war, the children returned to Poland, stayed briefly in Łódź, and – as they had reported to CJC officers – were then brought to Feldafing as part of a transport organized by the Bricha. Here they had stayed until the agency found them. It is not clear why the children had felt the need to lie about their wartime experiences, as orphaned Jewish children who had spent the war years in the distant reaches of the Soviet Union were allowed to join the Canadian programme. Whatever the reasons for their choice, they opted to place their trust in the CJC, bend the truth of their war experiences into an easily recognizable 'unaccompanied children' story, and board a ship bound for Halifax, Nova Scotia.[3]

The children had no sooner begun to settle, however, than something remarkable happened. The Polish Red Cross reported that their mother had

been found alive. The children were incredulous. 'These children were definitely not aware that their Mother is alive,' their caseworker wrote in February
1949:

> I might say, in fact, that they had become so accustomed to thinking of her
> as dead, that the news was so unbelievable to them. They are in fact
> wondering whether there is not some error and whether it might be some
> other person, perhaps a relative, who is looking for them. I gave them the
> address in your letter but I doubt whether they will initiate the correspon-
> dence. They asked that their Mother, in writing them, recall some events
> which they would all remember and also send a picture.[4]

Isak and Michla were right to be wary. A document in the children's file in the
archives of the International Tracing Service – the final mention that I could
find of these two children in any archives – noted the following in April 1949:

> We wrote to the Polish Red Cross Delegation for Germany requesting
> them to check on the address of the mother, as a letter to her had been
> returned marked 'unknown'. As soon as we receive a reply from them, we
> will communicate with you again.[5]

No further letters ever followed. The children's mother, who had remained so
elusive for so long, had disappeared once again, and this time she did not
resurface.

Isak and Michla's story was not all that unusual. As we have already seen, the early
years after the war's end were an agonizing period of uncertainty for child survivors, as they braced themselves to learn of the death of their parents, but equally
held out hope that they might still be alive. Those living in care homes knew only
too well that living parents could resurface months after the liberation, and even

many years later; missing parents arrived at care homes to claim lost children right through the late 1940s, and well into the 1950s. Children in these environments thus knew that they had to prepare themselves both for the possibility that their parents were dead, and also for the chance that they were alive – and they had to maintain this conflicted emotional state for years. The scepticism of the B. children when confronted with the possibility that their mother was alive was a natural response to this protracted period of uncertainty: she had disappeared in Tajikistan in 1942, so how could she possibly turn up alive in Poland seven years later?

Here we look at reunions between child survivors and their families after the war, whether they found themselves with both parents alive at the war's end, with one parent alive, or with neither parent alive but reunited with relatives. In a book full of emotive topics, there is probably none more emotive than this one, and our own assumptions intercede strongly when we think about family reunification after the war. As the historian Rebecca Jinks has observed, the trope of 'cathartic scenes of joy as families are reunited', frequently found in film and literature concerning the Holocaust, is so familiar to us that we struggle to set it aside and look more closely at a darker picture.[6] We are seduced by the presumption that the reunion of survivor children with their families marked a positive outcome for a child, especially as so many children found themselves with no known living relatives at the war's end. Children in this situation were frequently reminded of how lucky they were. Yet Isak and Michla B. clearly did not respond to the news of their mother's appearance with joy, and in this they were not alone. Family reunions could be among the most difficult and distressing experiences that children went through after the war. The reunified Jewish family was intensely fragile, and it is not difficult to understand why. As we have seen, parents and children had often been apart for years, and the war had changed them. They frequently had no common language anymore, and children might also have had new names, new religious and national identities, and strong attachments to their wartime host families. The youngest children might have no memory of their parents or relatives at all, and were effectively returned to strangers.

Surviving parents and adult relatives had changed too. They had been in concentration camps, in forced and slave labour situations, in hiding or living a dangerous existence by trying to pass as Aryan, and many were in a state of physical and emotional exhaustion by the liberation. As we saw in the last chapter, adults faced staggering poverty and non-existent or ungenerous resti-tution policies after the war, and children sometimes returned to families that lacked housing, clothing, and food. The additional burden of caring for a child could push families in these circumstances to the brink of collapse. Economic instability and emotional fragility combined in many reunited families to ensure that family reunions were fraught, even disastrous. Not one child in this study who was returned to his or her family found this process easy or joyful.[7] Those children who ended up in care homes after the war generally describe happier and more settled post-war childhoods than those 'lucky' enough to be returned to their families. If we find this fact uncomfortable to accept, it only exposes how powerful is the assumption that family reunions naturally marked happy endings for survivor children.[8]

The issue of family reunification forces us to see how far the conflict continued to rage in the intimate sphere of the home long after the war was over. Nor was this a small or isolated problem. Of the 120,000 survivor chil-dren who received financial support from the JDC after the war, a sizeable majority of 85,000 lived with surviving parents (most frequently with a surviving mother) or relatives. The reunion of damaged families in precarious circumstances was, of course, not solely a Jewish problem. The writer Dorothy Macardle, drawing on Red Cross figures, estimated in 1949 that as many as 13 million European children lost at least one parent during the war. Across the continent, then, broken families were limping towards their post-war lives, and it is not surprising to find that many of these parents – Jewish or not – lacked not only the means to care for their children, but also the desire.[9]

Of course, families were not alone in the reunification process: the aid agen-cies oversaw and policed family reunions. This is thus a story that takes place in the private sphere of the household, but equally in the administrative world of aid institutions and organizations. These organizations brought their own value judgements to the table, and played a significant role in dictating what the post-Holocaust family could and should look like. This was an intimate process, a practical one, and a political one, shaped by emergent ideological visions of the place of the family in post-war democracies. This was, after all, a moment marked by the ascendency of the concept of the 'nuclear family', the term itself revealing its Cold War origins. In the West, the nuclear family increasingly came to be seen as a potential barrier against the collectivist impulses both of fascism and (as the Cold War evolved) of communism. As the historian Tara Zahra has argued, there was a strong perception in post-war Western states that if Nazism had sought to destroy the family, then its restoration would be Europe's salvation. Thus the process of family reunification was linked, in the minds of many of those who managed the grand humanitarian aid projects of the post-war moment, with the broader process of post-war reconstruction. Nor was this simply a return to pre-war norms, for as Zahra reminds us, this was also a moment in which the very concept of what a family is and should be were being re-imagined.[10] A new vision of the family as one of the basic building blocks of renewed Western democracies was constructed and championed by a number of different actors: states, institutions, and particularly by a new world of experts – the social workers, psychologists, psychiatrists, and youth workers who represented aid agencies such as UNRRA and the JDC. They not only assumed that the nuclear family needed to be restored and protected, they equally sought to control and professionalize the process.[11]

As we have seen, these experts often saw themselves as working at the intersection between mental health, emotions, and citizenship, and their embrace of the nuclear family lay within this remit. In this sense, aid agencies had a pressing ideological need to insist, as did the British Home Office in its dealings with survivor children, that only a 'good family home' could provide children with the 'security and steady background of support and affection' that they required.[12] Much public-facing aid agency literature, where it discussed family reunification, set out stories of smooth transitions from destruction to renewal. Thus the United States Committee for the Care of European Children (USCOM), in its quarterly report of December 1947, related the story of Germinal L., a boy it had rescued in 1942. Germinal's parents had been located in South America, and 'a joyous, long-awaited family reunion will mark his arrival at the new home those parents now have established in South America'. A thoughtful reader, however, might have wondered how a boy who had not seen his parents in five years, and who no longer shared a common language with them, might have experienced this 'joyous reunion'.[13]

Part of the reason why agencies sang the praises of family reconstruction was because of the influence of new developments in psychoanalysis on their practice, for child psychoanalysts were also fascinated by the nuclear family in the post-war moment. Social workers at the time spoke of the 'well-established ground that an intimate family environment is indispensable to the growth and personality development of an individual', but this concept was in fact quite new.[14] Anna Freud and Dorothy Burlingham's war-era work on evacuated children in Britain was ground-breaking in this regard, and was well known to the general public. Freud and Burlingham asserted that separating children from their families, and particularly from their mothers, was more harmful than the risk of being bombed, arguing that 'all of the improvements in the child's life [brought about by evacuation] may dwindle down to nothing when weighed against the fact that it has to leave the family to get them'.[15] This idea – that separating children from their parents was intrinsically harmful to their mental and emotional health – was novel, and had a profound impact on both professional and popular visions of how an ideal family should function.[16] Nor were Freud and Burlingham the only psychological experts making the case for keeping families together at all costs. The child psychoanalysts working in Britain in the early post-war period, a circle that included Freud, Melanie Klein, Donald Winnicott, and others, all espoused this vision of the importance of the mother-child bond to some degree. This was most true for John Bowlby, whose work was likewise well known to the general public, and who argued even more forcefully that separating children from their parents 'is one of the outstanding causes of the development of a criminal character'. In a 1950 report for the World Health Organization, Bowlby linked 'maternal deprivation' in early childhood to a host of psychic maladies, ranging from delinquency and depression to retardation. In extreme cases, he argued, maternal deprivation transformed children into 'affectionless characters' doomed to a lifetime of crippled emotional relationships.[17]

In their private correspondence and reports, however, aid agencies acknowledged that they walked a precarious line between advocating the reconstruction of the family as an ideal and confronting its messy reality in practice. One of their key concerns was with survivor parents themselves: agency workers wondered whether survivor parents (or survivor relatives) were mentally fit to resume or take up the role of caring for children. Here the widespread post-war prejudice against survivors, and particularly against camp survivors, shaped their vision. As we have seen, in the early post-war popular imagination, adult survivors were often depicted as morally compromised by their time in internment and concentration camps, and as fundamentally damaged by Nazism.[18] Aid workers worried that survivor parents would not be fit to rebuild families, and that survivor mothers in particular had lost their 'maternal instincts'.[19] These doubts about the mental and moral fitness of parents to reclaim their children meant that the agencies were in a difficult position: they both advocated family reunification as an ideal, and knew that it often failed in practice. The director of the British Movement for the Care of Children from the Camps opined that it was 'our saddest time when children "went home" to be miserably unhappy', but her organization nonetheless espoused a policy of reunion even where children clearly suffered.[20]

Agencies were aware that practical issues could also put family reunifications under strain. Despite the fact that organizations such as the JDC gave material support to tens of thousands of Jewish families after the war, aid workers also recognized that many children would struggle with economic hardship if returned to their parents, and some parents (and indeed some children) shared this concern. In rare cases the agencies favoured preventing children from being reunited with a parent based on economic concerns, as we saw with the case of Dorota in the last chapter. In addition, as we have seen, because some immigration schemes were open only to fully orphaned children, some parents and some children thought it politic to hide the fact of the parents' survival so that the children might leave Europe quickly. The agencies were aware that many 'orphans' were not in fact truly orphaned, but in some rare cases they sided with the children in maintaining the outcomes of this subterfuge.

This reminds us that while children could find themselves caught between the different visions and fears of aid organizations and of surviving adult family members, they had their own agency in the process of family reunifications as well. We should ask not only what sort of outcomes awaited children who were returned to live with surviving parents or family members, but also how this felt to children, what it meant to them, and how they might have fought to establish their own ground in reinstated families. The memory of the recent past was an area in which children particularly asserted their agency, but if memory was a battleground in these households, it was a battle in which children rarely had the upper hand.

Some 'reunited' families quickly broke apart again. There were considerable numbers of parents who managed to survive the Holocaust, located their surviving children after the war, fought to reclaim them from wartime host families – and then subsequently placed them in care homes. This was not an uncommon trajectory, and given what we have seen regarding the material and emotional fragility of survivor families, it should not surprise us. As JDC-funded care homes, kibbutzim, and children's centres opened across Europe to take in 'unaccompanied children', surviving parents saw in these institutions an opportunity for their children to have better care than they would receive in the family home, and children themselves sometimes agreed. These arrangements were often meant to be temporary, but the belief that placing a child in institutional care was in his or her best interests meant that such placements could easily become a long-term solution, or even a permanent one. For some families, the decision to place children temporarily in institutional care while surviving mothers and fathers tried to forge their place in the post-war world simply extended the period in which parents and children grew stranger to each other, until too long a time had gone by for the relationship to be restored.

It is impossible to know exactly how many children in post-war care homes had surviving parents, but we can venture some estimates. As of September

1946, the OSE had 1,207 children in its care, but only a quarter were full orphans. Statistics were not dissimilar in Poland: among the 866 children living in the care homes of the Central Committee of Polish Jews, only 228 were full orphans.[21] If these figures reflect broader trends, we can posit that as many as three-quarters of survivor children who ended up in care homes after the war had at least one living parent. We can also map out how children might have experienced the decision to place them in care. We have already seen, in the cases of Marcel and Dorota, that some children understood their time in agency-managed care as a temporary arrangement, necessary to get something they needed and wanted (in their case, emigration out of Europe). We have also seen in these two cases that children could collude in these schemes, either to ensure that these temporary arrangements led to the eventual reunification of the family abroad, or – as in Dorota's case – that they in fact never led a child back to her family. More frequently, however, families drifted into the situation of agency-led care without clear ideas of where this choice might lead in the future. Indeed, as agencies began to move their wards around the globe, some families lost track altogether of children who had been placed 'temporarily' in care.

Erwin B. was a child who ended up in just this situation. Unlike most children whose parents placed them in care homes after the war, Erwin had in fact stayed with his mother Rosa throughout the entire war; they were only separated afterwards. Born in May 1937 in Liptovský Svätý Mikuláš, Slovakia, Erwin's earliest memory was of seeing his father taken away to a labour camp:

> My mother took me to the train station and I saw him, how the Jerries took him away, took away everything he had, and put him in a wagon for cows. [. . .] I always see that in front of my eyes. It follows me since I can remember, and I was age four. I saw them take away his razor and things, and then they took the clothes off my father. Then my mother took me away.[22]

Soon afterwards, his mother went into hiding with Erwin, living in temporary shelters and in the woods. Rosa had a valuable skill: as a young woman she had participated in an exchange run by the Alliance Israelite Universelle, and had learned to speak German fluently. As they wandered from hiding place to hiding place, Rosa protected them by speaking to her son in German, a language he did not understand at all. This continued until 1945, by which time Erwin's stomach was distended from hunger, and Rosa's legs were so swollen that she could not walk. They managed to return to her home town, Kežmarok, on a horse-drawn carriage, but by the time they arrived Rosa had to be taken to a hospital. Erwin was found by his aunt, walking behind the carriage; she took him home and cared for him for a few months, but eventually placed him in a local JDC care home for child survivors.

Here is where Erwin's period in care began, and like many such decisions, it was meant to be temporary. His mother was so physically exhausted that she could not care for him, at least at first. However, even after her physical recovery she did not take him back, for by that time a new set of pressing concerns had entered her horizons. It was clear to the few survivors from Erwin's extended family that there was no future for them in Slovakia, and they began planning to leave. Agents from the Bricha offered Rosa the opportunity to travel illegally to Palestine, but without her son. She decided to take the chance, partly because the JDC home where Erwin was living was a kibbutz in which the children were meant, eventually, to be brought to Palestine. Rosa arrived in Palestine in 1946, was caught attempting to enter illegally, and was placed by British troops first in the internment camp at Atlit, and then on Cyprus. At the very same moment, for reasons that are not entirely clear, the head of Erwin's care home selected the boy for immigration to England. In the spring of 1946 he was sent to the Weir Courtney care home in Lingfield, Surrey. No one in Erwin's family was aware that he had been sent to England, least of all his mother, who was then incarcerated at Atlit.[23]

Up to this point, circumstances had conspired to keep Erwin and his mother apart. When the opportunity arose for them to be reunited, however, the years that had passed made Erwin's return to his family difficult. By late 1948, Erwin's aunt had managed to trace the boy in England, and his uncle requested that he be sent to Israel, which was by then an independent state.

Erwin duly made the journey to Israel, arriving in August 1949 at the age of twelve, but no family waited to greet him. He was taken not to his mother's home but to a transit camp in Kiryat Shmuel near Haifa, where he stayed in a tent in the sand. Rosa eventually arranged for Erwin to be transferred to a Youth Aliyah care home at Ramat Hadassah. She herself had remarried, and was living in Ramat Gan with her second husband, his four children, and his sister. They did not have room for Erwin, or at least this was the argument presented to him: the issue was clearly more complex. 'I couldn't talk with my mother,' Erwin recalled in later interviews. 'I talked English. I had forgotten everything else. I didn't know Hebrew at all.'[24] Rosa's new husband had to translate everything that Erwin said, and it was clear to Erwin that his presence was an imposition in this reconstituted family.

Erwin stayed at the Youth Aliyah care home for a year, and then was moved to Kibbutz Givat Chayim, where he had his bar mitzvah. At a certain point the kibbutz asked his mother to take him back. He later recalled:

> This teacher said, 'No, I'm sorry, you take him back. If your son doesn't live with his mother, he's going to be a criminal. If your husband has four, then he can have five children. His place is in your home, not here. Because all the other children who are here don't have parents. He has a mother, so how can you think about not keeping him in your own home?' [. . .] My mother then went to the Jewish Agency and begged them to take me. I was put with a family in the south, and from there I came to [Kibbutz] Ein Harod. [. . .] I wanted to be with my mother. Every child wants to be with his mother.[25]

Erwin never returned to live with his mother again. He remained in Ein Harod until his death in 2017. He saw his mother occasionally, but she moved to Canada with her second husband in 1956. He later stated that among the most painful elements of this journey that had taken him away from his mother was the fact that the rupture of the family took with it the bulk of his child-hood memories, leaving him struggling to piece together the details of his early years from the handful of documents he had in his possession:

One of the most painful things for me today is that almost all of my child-hood memories have been erased. Even the Slovak language, my mother tongue until the age of seven, I completely do not remember – nothing. I do not remember my dad, either, nor the years I spent with my mother. [. . .] Even many years after the war, my mother refused to talk about this period, and so did my other family members who survived. We never talked about this period.[26]

When Erwin died, his friends and colleagues in the kibbutz recorded in his obituary that Erwin had kept a drawer in his home dedicated to the little handful of official documents that told the story of his early life, and his journey to Israel. 'They were little pieces of a puzzle for him', they wrote, 'and he completed the story of his life around them.'[27]

If it is difficult to discern how many survivor children who ended up living in care homes actually had a surviving parent, it is equally challenging to gauge how many were returned to live with a surviving parent after the war. The sociologist Diane Wolf, in her study of child survivors in the Netherlands, interviewed seventy child survivors and found that a third went back to live with their parents at the war's end. It is impossible to know whether this statistic might apply more broadly, although of the hundred children whose stories make up the fabric of this book, about a quarter were returned to one or both parents after the war.[28] Children in these reunited households faced a particular challenge at the war's end, for they were both survivors in their own right, and the children of survivors. They were often told that they were fortunate to have seen their nuclear families survive fully or partially intact, and yet few of these reunited families had a smooth transition out of the war.[29]

Children who could remember their parents were often shocked by how the war had altered them. Some parents no longer physically resembled the mothers and fathers their children had last seen, and weakened parents suffering from malnutrition, exhaustion, or physical wounds could seem inadequate protectors in a world that still appeared dangerous to children. The literary scholar Shoshana Felman describes the story of Menachem S., whose parents smuggled him out of the Płaszów concentration camp when he was four years old. His parents both survived, against incredible odds, but the people who returned from the camp, 'dressed in prison garb, emaciated and disfigured', seemed so alien to the child that he could not bring himself to call them 'mum' and 'dad', but rather insisted upon the formality of 'Mrs' and 'Mr'.[30] This was not an uncommon response. Parents were not only altered physically, but emotionally as well. Like their children, some had learned the skill of emotionally distancing themselves from events in order to survive. It was a skill that, in some cases, could not be unlearned. A notable minority of children returned to parents who had become physically violent; more common, however, was an emotional distance that marked a different type of violence in the reunified household.

Some children struggled to trust their parents, wondering how to put their faith in people who they felt had left them. They were angry at their parents for abandoning them, even if they were old enough to understand rationally that their parents had had no choice, and many felt further anger when their parents removed them from wartime host families where they felt comfortable and loved. The return to parents gave children an opportunity to vent these frustrations. They had had to be obedient, quiet and good to stay safe during the war, whether they were in hiding, in ghettos or in camps. Now they could rebel.[31] They withdrew emotionally from parents, refusing to touch them, voicing their anger, abstaining from eating, and in some cases letting their parents know that they found them – with their broken bodies, their strange accents, their Jewishness – embarrassing. Henri O., who was hidden in the Netherlands during the war, saw both his parents survive, but recalled the terrible discomfort of their post-war reunion, when he was only five years old:

When they turned up, I recognized my mother, and I said, 'You stayed away a very long time.' Yeah, two and a half years, half my life. Okay. And then somebody says, 'Why don't you want to sit on your daddy's lap?' So I sat on my daddy's lap. But it wasn't quite the same.[32]

Because parents and children were all survivors in these households, each had stories of survival – and yet there was little space for children's stories to be voiced or heard. There were many reasons why children found that they could not tell their war stories, nor ask the questions that they sometimes longed to ask, in reunited families. Some children felt that they had to steady themselves to take on the role of caring for their emotionally fragile mothers and fathers. Some parents assumed that children would quickly forget their war experiences (or in any case, this is what they told their children). Some parents were jealous of a child's relationship with his or her wartime host family, and avoided these difficult emotions by shutting down any discussion of the period in hiding.[33] Many parents clearly felt that their own war experiences had been marked by real suffering in a way that their children's had not, and thus set out, implicitly or overtly, a hierarchy of pain in which children's stories did not really count.[34]

Yet for all parents' attempts to quell a child's discussion of the recent past in the family, memory punctuated every aspect of life in these homes, awkwardly and unpredictably. Some parents busied themselves as much as possible to avoid discussing the past, and encouraged their children to do the same. This deliberate whirl of activity, however, was continually punctured by news about the fate of loved ones, and each time a new piece of news was received, it was followed by crying, or a stony silence, or whispering behind closed doors, or in some cases spells of madness. And while it was rare that a child found a sympathetic ear for her stories in these 'lucky' families, some parents spoke continually and without control about their own war experiences, weaving their distress into the everyday fabric of the household. Saul A., born in 1937 in Kraków, was in the Kraków ghetto and then in Theresienstadt with his mother. After the liberation, the two managed to locate Saul's father, who had survived a string of concentration camps. When a psychologist interviewed Saul in 1985, he recalled that his father had spoken continually of his time in these camps. Saul defended himself against this onslaught of information by forgetting everything that his father had told him:

*Saul A.:* One of the burdens I'm carrying is that I do not recall the camps that my father was in. I feel I ought to know. I didn't give myself the opportunity. I did know at one time, but I don't recall. [. . .] He was in some of the real bad [camps], but I don't know where or what they were.

*Interviewer:* Did he have numbers tattooed on his arm?

*S.A.:* No, he never got to Auschwitz, that I know.

*Int.:* You may have those memories in time. If you say you once knew, it may be with time . . . you know, it's been many years since you made the decision to forget.

*S.A.:* Oh, I knew. I gave this knowledge, past the point of consent to get, because my father used to tell me stories, and I was just blocking them out.

*Int.:* Also, you are an only child, and your mother and father tried very hard to protect you.

*S.A.:* Not my father. He was very open about these stories in my presence.

*Int.:* How would you feel when he would tell these stories?

*S.A.:* I wanted to run.

*Int.:* Did you?

*S.A.:* I don't know.[35]

Some parents could not stop talking about the wartime past; others would not talk at all. It is difficult to say which situation was more challenging for children. As early as 1968, psychologists and psychiatrists studying mental and emotional disorders in the children of survivor parents (children who were generally not survivors themselves, having been born after the war, but who did share many things in common with child survivors in reunited households) found that 'in the healthier patients, the parents rarely talk about the war', but that those patients who faced the most challenging problems had parents who used their children 'as the audience in the relentless recounting of their terrifying memories'.[36]

The situation could be even more complicated for a child survivor where only one of her parents survived. In households run by a single survivor parent, the absence of the dead parent was very marked, but rarely discussed. It was palpable in the home, a tangible space of loss that was spiked with dangers for children, particularly when they wanted to ask questions about a missing parent whom they could not remember, but which the surviving parent was unwilling or unable to answer. This set up a tense dynamic between child and parent: children compared their (surely ideal) dead parent to their (clearly damaged) living one, pressed for any information that would help them to better fix the missing father or mother in their minds, and continually had their questions rebuffed.

Zilla and Eric C. (we met Zilla in chapter 1) learned shortly after their placement in an OSE children's home after the war that their father had survived Auschwitz, and had returned to his home town in Germany. The children were sent to live with him in September 1946. They had no memory of him, as they had last seen him when Zilla was a baby and Eric was a toddler. They returned to a stranger who seemed harsh and distant. Eric later recalled that:

> In terms of how I remember him from the beginning, he was a very cold person at that point. Having grown up now as an adult, I try to give him the benefit of the doubt in terms of why he was the way he was, and of course his experiences in Auschwitz had to have been horrendous. But there was no warmth, there was no love, no affection, and for whatever reason he really could not give us what I would have liked to have at that time.[37]

For Eric, the family home was heavy with a silence in which the absence of his mother was conspicuous. He recalls resenting that his father would not tell the children anything about their mother, and that he did not have a single picture of her in the house, so that the children could not know what she had looked like, or visualize her in their longing for a warmer parental figure. Their father equally refused to speak of his time in Auschwitz, and refused to ask about or listen to the children's own stories of their years in hiding. 'There was no discussion about it,' Eric recalled. 'What I'd been through wasn't important enough to talk about.' The relationship between survivor parent and survivor children broke down after a few years. In 1950 their father sent Eric and Zilla to live with their maternal grandparents in the United States, and effectively terminated their relationship. Eric only saw his father once again, during a brief business trip to Germany when he was in his early thirties and the father of little children himself. He and his wife spent a few hours talking to his father 'about mundane sorts of things, things that you would talk about with a business associate but not with your father. I wound up getting a very bad headache, and we left.'

Judith K. was born in February 1938 in East Berlin. In May 1939 her family tried to escape Europe on the ill-fated *St Louis*, a German ocean liner carrying more than 900 Jewish refugees that was turned away successively from Cuba, the United States, and Canada. After protracted negotiations, the UK, France, Belgium, and the Netherlands each agreed to take some of the passengers; the ship returned to Europe, and Judith's family found themselves in the village of Nay in the south of France. In late summer 1942, French police caught Judith and her parents and took them to Gurs, but Judith was then taken out of the camp by the OSE. She vividly recalls the moment when her father turned her over to the OSE workers:

> It was dark, and [my father] took my hand, and we walked until we came to a place where there was a room, some people; don't ask me where or what, I was only four years old. The next thing I know, I'm holding my father's hand, and he says, 'Look over there, Judy!' And he let go of my hand, and I was still looking, and my hand was picked up again, and all of a sudden I turned around and looked, and it wasn't my father. He was gone. I never saw them again – they were taken away. When I realized that my father was gone, I went into complete hysterics.[38]

The Enards, a French Catholic family who had known Judith's family in Nay, agreed to hide Judith, and she stayed with them until the end of the war. Mrs

Enard became 'Maman' to Judith, and the Enard children became like siblings. Judith recalled that 'it was the greatest love affair of my life, being with this lady', and she passed the rest of the war period in peace and tranquillity in the Enards' home, where she felt that she was 'very loved'. At the liberation, however, an uncle and aunt of Judith's living in the United States contacted the OSE and said that they would be willing to take her in. Judith remembered that:

> I was told that I had to leave, that my family in America wanted me, and that I was going to go away from France. It was hard to understand this. This had been my home – it was all I knew. Maman took me to Paris, and in Paris I was brought to the OSE office, where Maman just let me go, just like my father let me go in Gurs. I remember screaming and crying and carrying on, because she was going away, just like my father had gone away.

Judith was taken to an OSE-run reception centre at Les Glycines, and then put on a ship to New York City in August 1946.[39] Although she eventually came to call her uncle and aunt 'father' and 'mother', she found the transition into their home difficult. She no longer spoke German, and knew no English, but her relatives did not speak French. They kept an Orthodox home, but Judith had been attending church with the Enards, and resented being 'told that it was wrong'. But the most painful aspect of her transfer across the ocean to a new and very foreign home was her uncle and aunt's insistence that she sever her connection to the past:

> I was told that I had to stop writing to my Maman, and for me that was the most difficult part. My new parents meant well, of course. They just said, 'Well, that was then and now is now, so drop it! Forget the past and start again!' But that's kind of impossible to do.

Although she found the move to her uncle's home difficult, and was angry that her relatives seemed to expect her to put her past aside and forge a new identity without it, Judith had a comparatively good and stable experience in her relatives' care. As a whole, however, the group of children who were returned to live with relatives after the war had a more challenging experience than any other group: more than those who went back to one or both parents, more than those who spent the remainder of their childhoods in institutional care, and more than those who ended up in adoptive and foster homes. To understand why this was the case, we need to consider what motivated relatives – mostly surviving aunts, uncles, and grandparents – to take children in. There was naturally a spectrum of reasons that underpinned this decision, but many relatives acted predominantly out of a sense of duty to the dead, and out of a desire to keep children in the family and ensure that they continued to bear their family's name. This is understandable in the face of intolerable loss, but it was not necessarily a recipe for a warm home environment. The relatives who were best positioned to care for survivor children were often those who had emigrated from Europe before the war and who had established themselves in other countries, and thus, like Judith, many children found themselves shuffled across oceans in order to be with relatives they had never met, or whom they had not seen since before the war. If a sense of duty motivated the initial decision to take in children, this sometimes drifted over time towards resentment and even anger that the beloved sister, brother, son, or daughter had been killed, and their child remained instead. Children in these households often recalled feeling like unwanted stepchildren who were never quite accepted.[40]

Like Judith, many children who ended up in relatives' households chafed at the demand, stated baldly or implied covertly, that they set their pasts aside. As we have seen, this also happened in households where children lived together with their surviving parents, but attempts at forced forgetting could take on different and uniquely unpleasant tones in households where children lived with aunts and uncles. Daisy L., born in 1939 in Czechoslovakia, spent the war years in hiding and was taken forcefully from her hiding place by her two aunts after the war. Her aunts were her father's sisters. They had lost their husbands during the war, and had no children of their own. Daisy later recalled that while her aunts felt a strong duty to raise their dead brother's child, their resentment towards Daisy's mother – and by extension towards Daisy herself

– frequently boiled over. 'They never talked kindly about my mother, never,' she recalled. Through their constant petty remarks and criticism, her aunts blocked Daisy from the knowledge she most wanted in the world: the details that would fill in the fading memories of the mother she had loved.[41]

The issue of how memory was approached in reunited families runs through all the stories in this chapter. It was sometimes the fault line along which relationships broke down. The pioneering sociologist Maurice Halbwachs, who first theorized the concept of collective memory in the 1920s (and who died in Buchenwald in 1945), argued that all memory is socially constructed, and that the family is the original collective in which our early memories are shaped. Our families feed back to us, again and again, the stories of our early selves that become the basic components of our autobiographies. They help us to arrange events chronologically, digest their significance, and bestow them with meaning. As we remember together, we set out the story of who we are, as a family and as individuals. The family's collective memory strongly shapes the individual's view of the past.[42]

In survivor families, however, memory often took a different route. Where survivor parents and relatives tried to block discussion of the past, survivor children sometimes pushed back against this, and relationships splintered along the lines of what could and could not be openly remembered in the household. We will see in upcoming chapters that this does not mean that child survivors had no opportunities to discuss their pasts after the war – in some care homes and institutions, they were strongly encouraged to speak of their war experiences – but few families made room for these conversations. And if the issue sometimes simmered in the background through children's pre-adolescent years, we will see that the desire to know the past and assert a right to it was, for some, a force that could no longer be contained as child survivors moved towards adulthood.

# FIVE

# CHILDREN OF THE CHÂTEAU

In 1948 there were roughly fifty children at the OSE care home in the beautiful Château de Vaucelles, in the village of Taverny, thirty kilometres from Paris. The château had previously housed some of the 'Buchenwald boys' under the care of OSE social workers Judith Hemmendinger and Gabi 'Niny' Wolff, but by 1947 the boys, mostly adolescents, had moved on. The château at Taverny then became a care home for child survivors between the ages of six and fourteen, run as an Orthodox institution by director Erich Hausmann. 'My chief ambition,' recalled Hausmann in later years, 'was to create a joyous and warm Jewish home for the children who had been placed in my care.' By all accounts, he succeeded. Many of the 'children of the château', as the Taverny villagers referred to the young survivors under Hausmann's care, remembered the home as 'a very loving place', and recalled that they 'felt a kinship' with the director, referring to him – then thirty-seven years old and not yet a father himself – as 'Papa Hausmann'.[1]

One of these children was Felice Z., whom we encountered in chapter 1. Felice came to Taverny from another OSE care home at Draveil, where she had not been happy. 'I don't remember about Draveil,' she later recalled, 'because I was in such pain from [being separated from my wartime host family] the Patoux, who were in essence at that point my parents.'[2] If Felice's time at Draveil had been marked by a painful adjustment to a new post-war reality, however, her years at Taverny were different: here she remembered being comfortable and happy, feeling a sense of belonging, and feeling loved. This was due in large part to the kindness and compassion of the staff. As part of his work to make Taverny feel like a home, Erich Hausmann organized the children into little groups, each headed by a counsellor. The counsellors were themselves barely out of their adolescent years, young adults who had spent time in concentration camps or in hiding during the war. Like the children under their care, they had lost their families and were in need of homes, and of something to ground their uprooted lives. Felice's counsellor, Hélène Ekhajser (born Chaja Ekhajser in Warsaw in 1927), had been deported to Auschwitz at the age of sixteen in February 1944, and was barely into her twenties when she took charge of her little clutch of survivor children in the château. Felice recalled following her like a puppy. Hélène called her 'mon petit chat' with a warmth that helped the eight-year-old Felice to move past the shock and stupor that had gripped her in Draveil.

The bond between counsellor and children was forged, at least in part, through the warm intimacy of storytelling. Hélène's group would snuggle around her for bedtime stories. 'We used to sit by her side,' Felice recalled, 'I used to sit by Hélène's feet, and she'd tell us stories about the war.' But these were stories with a twist. '[She] had gone through the camps, [and she] used to tell us unbelievable horrific stories, but we loved it,' Felice remembered. The children would ask Hélène to tell one story in particular, the story of what she had witnessed on a death march from Auschwitz to Ravensbrück in January 1945:

[In the story] everybody was walking in the snow, and this little girl wanted to . . . she couldn't walk any more, so they asked the Germans if she could ride in the truck. And they said sure. So [the Germans] took her up in the truck, and then they killed her. And we thought – wow! That's a wonderful story![3]

When we approach the Holocaust, we do not generally do so from the angle of the bedtime story. We should thus ask why this story carried such a powerful significance for this little group of children, gathered around their counsellor in the falling dusk in a manor house in the French countryside, three years after the war's end. Why would the children have begged Hélène to tell this terrifying story? Why would a grown child, decades later, remember the telling of this story as a moment of particular warmth and affection?

Interestingly, in a later interview Hélène herself recalled the cosy bedtime discussions she had with her group of children at Taverny, remembering that she often told them the story of the Auschwitz death march to instil in them the sense that 'you have to fight to live'.[4] This might have been the message she hoped to impart, but is it the one that the children received? Felice's own later accounts suggest a very different reading. In a 1992 interview she remembered that the story of the death march was 'an exciting story for us. These children were all in the same boat.' Six years later, in 1998, she gave a similar account: 'It was an amazing story. We were a close-knit group, and it was wonderful. It was a really warm-feeling house.'[5] In other words, what made the story precious and desirable for that little group of children gathered around their counsellor was not its content but its implications. The listeners, all child survivors, the speaker, herself a child survivor, and the murdered girl in the story all shared a common bond. They had all been threatened with death by the Nazis, and they had all seen their homes and families torn apart and thrown into chaos. Their shared histories drew them together. The story was a fable, based on Hélène's all-too-real experience, in which there were clear villains, clear victims, and a delicious sense of synergy between the speaker and the assembled listeners. Through such stories, children could begin to understand the murderous wave of violence that had consumed their parents, but the past sat somewhere in that realm between fantasy and reality that is part of the lives of all young children, whether they are survivors of genocide or not.

We have seen how difficult it could be for children to be returned to survivor parents or relatives after the war, and how a child's own war story never quite had the same moral equivalence, in reunited households, as that of a parent. If the shared experience of survival strained the bonds of biological families in the years after the war, why then did it sometimes have the opposite effect in the care home environment? Of the children whose stories I consulted in writing this book, most of those who spent time in post-war care homes remembered these institutions warmly. Indeed, several of those who were subsequently returned to live with their families wished in hindsight that they could have stayed in the care home instead. I initially found this shocking, for it so powerfully goes

against our deepest assumptions about the value of the nuclear family: it is difficult for us to imagine that a care home could be a more loving and more
supportive environment for a child than a family home. However, we might
better understand this if we take a closer look at the nature of care homes for
survivor children after the war, because the care homes of the post-war moment
were in many ways unique. As survivor communities, the wartime past lay close
to the surface of communal life in these homes, even if it was not openly discussed
– and its presence in the background of daily existence fed a sense of mission, for
both staff and children, that was a rarity in post-war years marked by despair,
shock, and grieving for so many surviving Jews.

If we step back from 'Papa' Hausmann's Taverny and cast an eye across Europe,
what might we see in the care homes of the post-war period? While there were
doubtless a good number of post-war children's homes run by unenlightened
staff to poor standards, the moment was marked by some remarkable innovations in terms of how communal living for children was conceived of and
managed. It was in many ways a golden age for those institutions that had once
been called orphanages – for the women and men who ran many of these homes
deliberately rejected that term. They called their communities care homes, children's colonies, children's villages, or simply 'foyers' (homes), terms that reveal
just how far this was not merely a practical response to the pressing need to
provide for children without families after the war, but in fact a utopian experiment, pedagogically and ideologically. It was an opportunity for adults who
had themselves often lost so much to explore new models for mending the tears
in the European social fabric, informed by progressive values and child-centred
practices. As historian Daniella Doron writes, children's homes in this period
'operated as experimental laboratories where child welfare experts could harness
progressive pedagogy as well as Jewish learning to cast the children into the ideal
members, if not leaders, of European and Jewish society'.[6] In children uprooted
and separated from their families, care home leaders saw potential: the potential

to find out whether a progressive pedagogical upbringing would create democratically minded citizens, the potential to address children's psychological rehabilitation through communal living, and the potential – for adults who themselves had lost everything – to discover if caring for 'war-damaged children' might rehabilitate their own broken lives.

The emotional needs of the adults involved were thus in some ways as significant as those of the children. We see examples when we look at the histories of some of the care home directors of the early post-war period. Syma Klok was a young woman of twenty-four when she began working for UNRRA after the war. Born in Vilna, she and her husband Marcus had managed to flee Poland for Japan during the war, but the trials of their years in flight destroyed their marriage. At the war's end, Klok discovered that while her brother had survived the war in hiding in Belgium, both of her sisters had been murdered along with their husbands and children. She was young and healthy, but also alone and bereft. Drawing on her earlier training in teaching and child development, she launched herself into UNRRA's mission, working as a Child Search Branch officer and travelling through the countryside requisitioning buildings and resources to shelter abandoned children. In 1948 she founded an IRO children's home at Bad Schallerbach, in the American zone of Austria. It housed an average of sixty-five children, both Jewish and non-Jewish, and was staffed primarily by DP volunteers, with one member of staff for every four children. The staff shared in Klok's vision for Bad Schallerbach, seeing the home as a place where, in her words, they would help the children 'to accept the tragedies they had, [and] release their feelings of hostility and confusion about these, as best they could'.[7] The staff at Bad Schallerbach thus saw the institution as much more than a collection site for children separated from their families by the war: it was, in their eyes, the physical locus in which staff could carry out a broad mission of psychological rehabilitation.[8]

The tools that Klok and her team planned to use to help the children on this journey were love, permissiveness, and understanding. As the staff had had similar wartime experiences to the children, 'they too welcomed the opportunity of having a consistent stable atmosphere in which they could feel needed and useful and secure'. Since the children had known only restrictions and dangers during the war, the staff allowed them to choose their activities freely. As they had had little chance for a sympathetic adult's ear, Klok and her staff made a point of going to each child at bedtime to say goodnight, give them a hug and a kiss, and listen to their concerns, as 'it was at this time many of the children were able to talk of the things which bothered them most'. Klok was convinced that her approach was transformative, and four years later, when she was undertaking social work training in the United States, she could not resist poking fun at the 'scientific' social welfare methods so fervently espoused by her American colleagues. 'As [psychoanalyst Bruno] Bettelheim phrases it, "Love is not enough",' she wrote in an essay, 'but in our specific situation LOVE was there and it served a lot, for you see when there is no love, warmth and understanding, nothing is enough – not even CASEWORK.'[9]

Lena Kuchler similarly found herself bereft at the war's end, and ready to channel her anger and despair into something useful. Like Klok, she was Polish, she had trained as a teacher, and she had separated from her husband. Unlike Klok, she had not managed to escape Europe during the war: she had instead watched her infant daughter die of starvation, had lost her parents, and survived by passing as Aryan and working as a nanny in a remote village. Her beloved sister Fela, who joined the partisans, was denounced and murdered only days before the liberation. Kuchler was thirty-four years old, and she later recalled that 'after the war I was broken and crushed, with nothing to live for. The children saved me – by helping them I redeemed myself.'[10] Kuchler threw herself into the task of securing food and shelter for a group of survivor children in Kraków, who were milling about the Jewish Committee buildings with only minimal organized care. Because no one else seemed to be doing it, and because she herself had nowhere else to go, Kuchler undertook the task of setting up a home for the children in Zakopane, a resort in the Tatra mountains. After the home was repeatedly attacked by paramilitary Polish Nationalist forces who hoped to drive the few remaining Jewish survivors out of Poland, Kuchler illegally escaped with her staff and all the children under cover of night, and refounded the home in France, before ultimately decamping with her wards to Israel in 1949.[11]

Kuchler was among the Holocaust survivors interviewed by the Lithuanian-American academic David P. Boder in 1946. Standing with her wards in their reconstituted home in Bellevue, a suburb of Paris, Kuchler emphasized that 'this is not an institution. This is one family. [. . .] I would like . . . to remain with them forever. I would like to see them get married, and to already have my own "grandchildren". I do not have a family of my own. I have nobody here.'[12] Like Klok, Kuchler had gathered round her a staff who had lost their own partners and children during the war, and showed a ferocious dedication to Kuchler's project of rehabilitating the children through warmth and permissiveness. Like Klok's care home, Kuchler's home was a child-centred world: staff and children regularly had group meetings, formed a children's secretariat and a cultural committee, and even had a children's court to deal with minor disputes and disciplinary issues – a practice first set out by Janusz Korczak before the war, and widely adopted in other post-war children's homes.[13] The staff sought to help the children re-establish their social skills by practising self-management, engaging in open discussions, and taking on a measure of responsibility for the community as a whole.

This approach to running a children's home came to fruition after the war, but it had been developing in the minds of its advocates for some time, as the scale of the 'unaccompanied children' problem began to reveal itself during the conflict. Austrian Ernst Papanek, a trained Adlerian psychologist and supporter of the Free School movement who was referred to by his colleagues in the OSE (sometimes fondly, sometimes in irritation) as 'the Goy', directed a home for Jewish refugee children at Montmorency in France during the war. He recognized that the children under his care, most of whom had fled Nazi Germany, had been wrenched from their communities and needed to be returned to a sense of social belonging. 'We were a community of very special children with very special problems,' he later wrote. 'They had come to us, strangers and afraid, and we had to make them happy again. Not merely by creating a well-ordered home. Not with parties or songs. When I speak of making them happy, I am not talking in terms of amusing them. Our task was to create an atmosphere in which they could develop and bloom.'[14] In a similar vein, anticipating the enormous task that would face care workers after the war, the Swiss journalist Walter Robert Corti proposed in 1944 that children orphaned by the war be cared for in dedicated 'children's villages' where they would be 'treated as individuals and looked after in small living groups, rather than seen as a homogenous mass of inhabitants as in a traditional institution or orphanage'. Structures of self-governance would ensure the children developed a sense of community. For children deprived of communities, Corti argued, this was more than a means of re-establishing their social networks: it was a pathway back to democratic living.[15]

If the American, British, and Canadian care workers who joined UNRRA and the JDC soon after the war's end were generally schooled in social work and child psychology, European-trained staff were often motivated by a different set of influences. Many saw themselves as professional pedagogues, inspired by the educational reform movement of the early twentieth century, and privileging the theories and approaches of such radical pedagogical thinkers as Maria Montessori, Johann Pestalozzi, Janusz Korczak, Anton Makarenko, and Henri Wallon (who in fact trained some of the prominent OSE leaders of the post-war period directly in the theory and practice of *éducation nouvelle*).[16] They were, in many ways, a profoundly European group: they had both come from and ended up in every corner of the continent, they drew their inspiration from earlier pan-European intellectual movements, and they tapped into a deeply held European faith in children 'as critical players in reconstructing national boundaries and rejuvenating post-war societies'.[17] They saw themselves as experts with a mission: to use progressive pedagogical techniques to help children in the first instance to recover their psychological strength, and in the long term to train them as future leaders who might work towards strengthened Jewish communities and more just societies.

This was clearly an ambitious project, and it had to face off against the demands posed by ideological visions of the nuclear family. As we have seen, aid agencies in the early post-war period, informed by the arguments of psychoanalysts such as Anna Freud and Melanie Klein, regarded the return of survivor children to the environment of the nuclear family as ideal, and were prepared to argue their case vociferously. Debates over whether institutional living situations could meet children's psychological needs raged across Europe, and the question found its way to the heart of policy and practice for most of the aid agencies that cared for children after the Holocaust. Tara Zahra has suggested that aid workers found themselves on different sides of this debate as much by geographical ties as by ideological bent, setting the 'individualist ideals of Western humanitarian workers' against the 'collectivist visions of East European and Jewish refugees and policymakers'.[18] In fact, however, there were no neat geographical boundaries to a debate that burned at the heart of the question of how best to care for orphaned or abandoned Jewish children. In France and England just as in Poland, in the DP camps of Germany, Italy, and Austria, in the homes run by UNRRA, by the JDC, and by local Jewish organizations, adults argued over whether children's best interests could be served by group living, and how institutions born of necessity might in fact be harnessed to repair not only children's psychological needs, but the broader needs of recovering societies.[19] Even those who argued most persuasively and influentially that the nuclear family was the key to a child's healthy psychological development sometimes embraced collective living where the circumstances were right: Anna Freud, for example, had a direct hand in the running of the Weir Courtney care home in Surrey, where the values of collective living were embraced, and where few of the children were put up for fostering. Indeed, only the youngest of the Weir Courtney children ended up in foster homes – which may have been in part because they were too young to speak out clearly against it.[20]

While child psychologists and psychoanalysts might have sung the praises of the nuclear family in theory, in practice the Jewish family was greatly weakened by the war. Assumptions about the family's strength, stability, and even value were difficult to maintain in light of the overwhelming evidence that survivor families were struggling in the post-war period. This situation is thrown into sharp relief if we look at the status of children under the OSE's care in France after the war. The OSE publicly stated that family reunification was their 'most important and most urgent task', but this advocacy on behalf of the nuclear family was largely theoretical.[21] Approximately 40 per cent of the children in the OSE's twenty-five post-war care homes had two living parents, and an additional 34 per cent had one living parent. This put true orphans in the minority, and illustrated just how far reunion was an unrealizable ideal for many families. This situation, moreover, grew more pronounced over time: by 1949–50, 90 per cent of the children placed in OSE homes had living parents.[22] OSE leaders worried that this evidence suggested the post-war Jewish family was not all that salubrious an environment for children. 'The Jewish family,' wrote Vivette Samuel, who had organized the OSE's clandestine wing in Chambéry during the war, 'was once known as a family that holds onto its children, that wants to keep them, that never wants to abandon them. Now, we see – and not only in France but else-where – families that give up their children more easily than ever to organiza-tions.'[23] Samuel was not alone among the OSE's leaders in fearing that France's Jewish families were no longer fit to act as the cradle of a reinvigorated post-war Judaism, and in private they did not hesitate to criticize survivor mothers and fathers for neglecting their children, even if they understood that abject poverty was often the cause, in combination with poor physical and mental health.[24] Indeed, it took some time for OSE staff to realize the extent to which mental illness stood in the way of family reunifications. It was only in the 1950s, after some children had been forcibly removed from their families through civil litiga-tion and brought to the agency, that OSE staff publicly stated, 'we unfortunately have a large majority of parents who are either insane or unbalanced'.[25]

If families appeared unable to play the role that the agencies envisaged for them, then the agencies began to consider how care homes might fill this void – and they quickly came to see collective living not only as a practical alternative to failing families, but one with utopian potential. Although the agencies sometimes worried that survivor staff could have psychological prob-lems that might affect the treatment of the children in their care, in practice it is clear that, for many of the staff involved, caring for children gave their lives meaning and focused their resolve at a moment when they were coping with enormous loss. This had a great deal of value for both staff and children. In families, a parent's emotional and psychological struggles were compounded by the need to reclaim homes, recover possessions, and find employment. The daily battle of facing these practical issues made the care of children an extra burden, and very often a burden too many. The staff of care homes, on the other hand, had none of these daunting material issues to face, and often saw the children in their care not as a burden but as a mission. Of course, not all care homes for survivor children employed staff who were also survivors, but those that did formed unique communities of survivors in which the bond of shared experience was one of the building blocks of a collective identity. Insulated from post-war austerity, surrounded by peers who had been through similar war experiences, both children and staff often thrived in the environment of the care home. 'It is hardly surprising,' writes Daniella Doron, 'that children who struggled to understand their family's poverty, to reconcile themselves to a new step-parent or to contend with emotionally distant parents welcomed collective environments.'[26]

Care homes were also, however, artificially created environments that eventually dissolved. Whether they closed due to funding restrictions or simply because their wards aged out of them, most post-war care homes were temporary communities that ultimately ceased to exist once they had lost their primary function. For the children who had spent part of their childhoods there, this could lead to a terrible hunger, in later years, for the care home 'family' that had dissolved away and could not be revisited. Whether they left the care home through return to a biological family, adoption or fostering, immigration to a new country, or simply ageing out of the care system, many children found it more difficult to transition out of care homes than into them, and mourned the loss of their care home 'family' for many years. To examine this in more detail, let us turn back to the château at Taverny.

Unlike many other directors of children's homes in this period, Erich Hausmann was not a survivor. Born in Basel in October 1915, he had pre-war connections to some of the leaders of the OSE via the transnational Jewish youth movements of the interwar period, but he had spent the war years in relative safety in his native Switzerland.[27] He did, however, have many years of experience working with Jewish children displaced first by anti-Jewish restrictions and later by the conflict. Only months after acquiring his teaching diploma in 1938, he found himself head of a Swiss recovery camp for Jewish children who had fled Frankfurt-am-Main after Kristallnacht. He then worked with the Schweizer Hilfswerk für Emigrantenkinder (SHEK) to set up a home for Jewish refugee children that operated throughout the war years (first in Buus, and then in Langenbruck). At the war's end, OSE leaders invited him to head one of their new care homes, and he worked first as director of the Fontenay-aux-Roses home from 1945 to 1947, and then, in the summer of 1947, he welcomed fifty-six children between the ages of six and fourteen to the Château de Vaucelles at Taverny.[28]

The staff that Hausmann gathered around him, however, had had a range of harrowing wartime experiences. The young counsellors, whom Hausmann called his 'educators' (although most had no pedagogical training), were barely out of their adolescence when they joined him at Taverny. For many of them it was a welcome interlude in which they could recuperate after a period of hiding, deportation, and internment. Hélène Ekhajser, Felice Z.'s counsellor, had herself been a ward of the OSE when she first returned to France from the concentration camps of the East in May 1945, since at seventeen she was still a child according to the OSE's criteria.[29] Régine Rabner, another of the 'educators', had also been a ward of the OSE after fleeing from Germany to France as a refugee child, and spending much of her childhood in OSE homes before, during, and after the war. Binem Wrzonski, one of the few with pedagogical training, had come to France as one of the Buchenwald boys. These three were among a staff of seventeen adults who worked to care for the children and to manage the practical aspects of life in the château, a group that included a bursar, an accountant, a full-time cook and her helper, two housekeepers, a washerwoman, a gardener, a handyman, a nurse, and the OSE child psychiatrist Dr Irène Opolon, who made weekly visits to the home.[30]

We have seen that most of the children cared for in OSE homes in fact had one or both parents still alive, and this was true at Taverny as it was elsewhere.

Erich Hausmann's later account of his time as director offers a fascinating glimpse into the families that existed in the background of his young wards' lives. According to Hausmann, the parents of one child, Albert T., were both alive, but his mother was too ill to care for him. The mother of another, Jean-Paul K., had also survived, but she lived in precarious circumstances with a violent man who beat her. A sibling group of three children had initially had both their parents with them, but the family was living in a shack in the woods trying to make ends meet by growing vegetables and keeping chickens; when the father was arrested, the mother placed the children with the OSE. 'They were wild and had never bathed,' Hausmann later wrote. A sibling group of six children, the M. children, had seen their father deported to his death, and their survivor mother end up in a psychiatric hospital. For Michel and Denise R., their father and sister had been deported to their deaths, and their mother found herself alone with three remaining children. She made the difficult decision to keep the oldest child with her, but place the younger two with the OSE. One of the youngest of the Buchenwald boys, Isio R., found himself alone at the war's end, but was convinced that his mother and sisters were alive and living in a German DP camp – which turned out to be correct. He stayed at Taverny until his mother was able to move to Paris, and took him to live with her again.[31]

All this meant that the children of Taverny found themselves in some ways suspended between the private world of the family and the institutional world of the care home, alive to the possibility that someone might come and claim them (which was not necessarily what they wanted). On every second Sunday relatives were invited to spend the afternoon at Taverny, and children were allowed to leave the château to visit relatives who lived locally. Among those who visited was a woman who professed to be the mother of Doudou P., another of the youngest of the Buchenwald boys. Doudou, however, insisted that the woman was not his mother, and equally that he would not accept her as an adoptive mother. She turned out to be a close friend of Doudou's biological family. She continued to visit the boy, and he continued to reject her, until she eventually immigrated to the United States.[32]

122

For those who had no relatives to visit, Sundays were a strange time, a reminder of a world that had been lost. Paulette S., whom we met in chapter 3, later recalled that:

> On Sundays, nearly all of the children would get picked up, and disappear. The whole château would become deserted and I had the place to myself. [. . .] I dreaded those lonely weekends. Why was everyone being taken away to have a good time, but not me? I didn't understand. I was as good a child as the others, so what had I done to deserve being left behind? When the children came back, they never talked of what they did. Maybe they didn't want to make me jealous, or maybe they were upset to come back. It was like two worlds, the children's home being one, and the weekends away, another.[33]

For children who traversed these two worlds, it was clear to many of them that the château, with its dedicated staff, warm and welcoming environment, wide grounds, and beautifully decorated Sabbath dining tables redolent with favourite foods, was the preferable one. Impoverished families struggling with financial and psychological burdens did not generally present an attractive alternative. And while the material plenty of the château was certainly appealing, what won the hearts and minds of many of the children was the staff's desire to nurture their independence by placing trust in them. Paulette S. recalled that at Taverny:

> Slowly I started acting like a normal child. I began to interact with others and stopped wetting my bed. [. . .] Everything we did was designed to make us feel like a family. We older ones were shown how to help look after the younger children. We chose one child every day to help dress in the morning and prepare for bed at night. I loved feeling trusted and useful.[34]

She remembered with particular joy how Hausmann would take the children in little groups of two or three and bless them under his *tallit* (prayer shawl) on Friday evenings before the Sabbath meal. 'As the benediction finished, I always felt a wave of ease and happiness enveloping me.'[35]

123

The children, the young counsellors, and Hausmann did not necessarily discuss what the children had gone through during the war, yet many later recalled that part of what made the social world of Taverny so attractive was the unspoken knowledge of shared loss. Jacques F., born in 1938, whose parents were both murdered in Auschwitz, recalled that 'everyone was in the same situation; we all had a sense of what had happened'.[36] Beate Z., whose parents were also killed in Auschwitz, remembered that this knowledge of the fate of murdered parents was quietly in the background, and that there was a solidarity in this sense of a shared past:

*Interviewer:* Did you know what happened to your parents?

*Beate Z.:* Oh yes, yes, I knew.

*Int.:* Who told you?

*B.Z.:* I don't remember specifically. I don't even remember asking. It was just known; we were all the same.[37]

In considering the nature of Holocaust 'memory' during the early post-war period, we might reflect on how shared knowledge in a collective environment could be a powerful form of remembrance, one that gave children a sense of belonging to a very particular community. It was often this, more than the loss of the material plenty or the attentions of dedicated adults, that made it so difficult for so many of the children when they had to leave Taverny. In leaving, they lost an environment where awareness of the wartime past was always close, always alive, the very fundament of what united the group – and they moved into environments where, in many cases, no one shared this history, and no one understood its implications.

The OSE received a large part of its funding from the Jewish Joint Distribution Committee, but after 1947 this funding began to shrink year on year. In 1947 the JDC covered 70 per cent of the OSE's operating budget, but this fell to 46

per cent in 1948, and continued to fall further thereafter.[38] The JDC was particularly concerned that children with living parents were spending years in the agency's care, and the budget cuts placed pressure on staff to return children to their parents, whether or not this was what children (or parents) wanted.[39] For those who had no parents or other relatives to return to, the OSE began to explore the possibility of adoption.

The issue of adoption brought with it questions of social class. We have seen that surviving relatives, care staff, and even children themselves were anxious about both material resources and social position. In the case of Dorota J., who had been born into a wealthy and educated family, we saw that the agency favoured placing the girl with a wealthy foster family in Canada, and equally that when Dorota's father turned up alive but impoverished in Israel, the child worked together with her foster family and the agency to ensure that she was not returned to him. We can see similar trends when we look at adoption at Taverny. Erich Hausmann and other OSE staff took the approach that the wealthier an adoptive family was, the greater a right they had to claim a child of the château. Sometimes, indeed, a wealthy adoptive family's claim to a child trumped that of an existing biological family. The care home had a *parrainage* (foster parent) scheme with two Parisian synagogues, and some of these relationships ended in the adoption of a child. In his memoir, Hausmann writes of a child, 'little Fred', whose parents were alive but were extremely poor. They lived deep in the countryside and received social assistance to be able to visit little Fred occasionally in the care home. The child was paired, in the *parrainage* scheme, with a wealthy, childless couple from the synagogue, who eventually began inviting little Fred to stay at their home. 'The child could not help but notice the stark contrast between the wealth and comfort of this couple, and the home of his parents,' Hausmann later wrote. Little Fred struggled with the situation, but in the end he went to live with the wealthy couple, who formally adopted him. 'To add to the joy of the situation', Hausmann wrote, 'the adoptive parents were then blessed with the birth of a son.' One can only suppose that the situation was far less joyous for little Fred's birth parents, who lost their child to a couple with greater financial resources.[40]

It was not only local wealthy couples that came to Taverny looking to adopt. The care home was also a site at which international adoptions were brokered, particularly for American couples. As funds leaked out of the OSE system, such well-off adopters seemed to solve a basic problem for the OSE – but for children, it meant that adoption was sometimes presented as a 'prize' to be won by the most likable, intelligent, or physically beautiful among them. In 1949 a number of American individuals and couples visited Taverny in the hopes of adopting a child. The children put on a show to impress the visitors, dressing in their best clothes, dancing, and generally seeking to please. OSE staff, however, worried that the charm act would not be enough for potential adopters who were 'wealthy and for the most part quite cultured'; they fretted that the children were physically attractive, but not 'destined for an intellectual career'.[41] Such performances in the space of the care home, where survivor children were put on display and where their ability to please (or their failure to do so) could so dramatically change the course of their futures, exposed the extent to which the collective living experiment was beholden to American funding, whether this came from the JDC or from private families. It also unmasked just how deeply children's lives could be shaped by the post-war power imbalance between European and American Jews.[42]

Adults' celebratory rhetoric around adoption also veiled a truth that was rarely discussed openly: leaving the care home was terrifying for children. Most of the children at Taverny recalled feeling happy there, surrounded by a circle of peers and 'educators' who shared their past and their present. Leaving might have been accompanied by vague adult promises of a positive future, but the children themselves often experienced it as a forcible rupture with a beloved world that stripped them of any semblance of control over their own destinies. The spectre of leaving was part of the very fabric of the institution, for eventually every one of the children had to leave it, whether they left to join (or re-join) a family, or simply grew too old to stay any longer. Nonetheless, the moment of leaving often came as a shock. In June 1949, when she was eleven years old, Paulette S. was called to Hausmann's office. Her older brother Joseph, whom she had not seen in a long time, was there. He spoke to her, but she later could not remember what he said:

I felt that familiar numb feeling that had been absent for a long time. I didn't open my mouth. Then the headmaster came back into the room and my brother left. It took me some time to understand that he was going to Australia, which meant nothing to me, except that change was threatening my life again. Why Australia, where we knew nobody? I found out later that the boys in Joseph's hostel were given the choice of migrating to Australia or Canada. Since they knew nothing about either place, one boy stood in front of a map of the world, shut his eyes and pointed with his finger. It landed closer to Australia than Canada and that is why forty young men ended up in this country. This almost careless decision decided my fate as well. [. . .] Leaving Taverny and all the people I loved there must have been very painful, because I have blocked out every memory of it.[43]

OSE staff tried to prepare the shocked girl for her move around the globe by suggesting that it would be an opportunity to forget her past. 'Just think it never happened,' they urged, 'and you will start a fresh new life.' This was not what Paulette as a child on the brink of adolescence wanted or needed, and as an adult she often contemplated just how thoughtless was the implication that her past was a burden to be cast aside, rather than a core aspect of who she felt herself to be. Fifty years later, she titled her memoirs *Just Think It Never Happened*, underscoring both the impossibility of abandoning the past and the harm caused by the assumption that forgetting was in a child's best interests.

For Felice Z., the moment of rupture with the Taverny community came in 1951 when her uncle, who lived in New York, asked the OSE to send Felice and her older sister Beate to the United States. The girls experienced a double devastation, for not only did they have to leave an environment that they loved, but upon arriving at Newark harbour they discovered that the uncle who had secured their affidavits and demanded their emigration had no intention of actually caring for them. When the boat landed:

There was no aunt and uncle, there were just two social workers who didn't speak French, and we knew no English. They said, 'You won't be able to live with your aunt and uncle, they can't take you in.' We were just devastated, Bea started to cry, and I saw her so then I started to cry, I mean it was just terrible. That was one of the worst days.[44]

Decades later, in an interview, Felice recalled the consequences of her forced emigration. 'It was almost as if I broke,' she recalled, using her hand to make a gesture that implied *to break off* or *to break away.* 'I repressed everything. I forgot about my life in France.' She lost contact not only with the Taverny community, but also with the Patoux family, the wartime hosts who she had loved like her own parents. With a child's aplomb and blithe unawareness of what lay ahead, she had written one final letter to Mme Patoux only a week before she boarded the *Washington* ocean liner to sail to Newark:

> I hope that you are well. We are well. We can't come to see you this year, because we leave for America on the 23rd of January on the 'Wochingtown'. Last Thursday we went to the pool, and that was really good. [Mr Hausmann] put some films on for us to see: *Aladdin and the Magic Lamp, The Little Negro*, and *The Seine and the Loire*.[45]

Unlike Paulette, Felice, and Beate, Regine P. had a surviving parent: her mother, who lived in Paris and whom she visited twice a month. Yet when Regine eventually had to leave Taverny, it was not to return to her mother, but simply to move into the care home for the 'grandes' (the adolescent children) at Versailles. Regine then moved to Israel in 1959 as a young woman, married in 1960, had two children, established a career, and divorced in the late 1970s – and around the same time, she began to reflect on her past. She longed to get in touch with both Hausmann and with the other children of Taverny, for there had been no way to maintain contact with them as she grew up: the community dissipated for children from the moment that they left it. As she approached her fortieth birthday, the need to find Taverny again became insistent. Regine spent two months in France trying to trace the children of the château. She found many former wards, but no one seemed to know how to locate Hausmann. She telephoned Taverny, which was still an OSE care home (as it remains to this day), but its director refused to give her Hausmann's address. In the summer of 1981 she finally tracked down someone who knew the Hausmann family, and after telephoning Hausmann's grown daughter, she was able to re-establish contact with him for the first time since 1955. In writing to him, she summed up the emotions of many of the former children of the château, who became aware with the passing of time of all they had lost when they had to leave Taverny:

You can't have forgotten that we, we were your children before your own children. When I think of Taverny, of you, Papa Hausmann, it is as if I think of my real home, more real than that of my mother, where I used to go for visits twice a month. I searched for [the former Taverny children] as I needed to see them again, and to my great surprise they had missed me too. They had all felt the need to go back, to connect with the past; I wasn't alone in longing to take that path again. It's as if we were looking to attach ourselves to something strong, something good, in lives marked by the sense of having lost something very important.[46]

# SIX

# METAMORPHOSIS

Jackie Y. was born in Vienna in December 1941, but he did not know this. He had tried, at certain points in his childhood, to ask his parents where he had been born, but they had answered vaguely that it was somewhere in Hertfordshire, and quickly changed the topic. He had memories of which he could not make sense: he remembered, for example, a day when, at about the age of five, he had been playing with a group of other children. Someone had taken him away from the group and ushered him towards a young couple. They wanted to take him for a drive in the country. He was then informed that he was to go alone and stay with them for a few days. He ended up living with them and calling them 'mum' and 'dad', but never quite had sufficient information to begin to unpick what this strange memory meant. He also had a series of recurring dreams that both troubled and intrigued him. One involved a big house, with sprawling grounds filled with tall trees that swept down to a horse-racing track; another, frightening one involved towering waves coming towards him and water everywhere. His mother told him that everyone had dreams like that.[1]

In 1951, when Jackie was ten years old, a boy at his school told him that he was adopted. He went home and confronted his parents, who were speechless at first, but then confirmed that it was indeed true. Seeing them upset made him upset in turn, and he hugged them and promised them that it made no difference to him: they were his parents and he loved them. This new knowledge, however, did in fact make a difference, for Jackie was on the cusp of adolescence, and he soon began to long to know more. He tried gently to question his parents. Where had he really been born? Who were his real parents? They avoided his questions, and he started to become increasingly frustrated. One day a few years

130

later he went to visit his father's mother, and she confessed to him that he was originally from Austria. This was wholly surprising news: although he had accepted that the couple he called 'mum' and 'dad' were not his birth parents, he had not entertained the prospect that he himself might be anything other than a 'North London Jewish kid'. 'That's when the stuff hit the fan with my mum and dad,' he later recalled, for while his parents were furious and tried to avoid the topic, Jackie was now desperate to learn more, and could not let it rest.[2] He began to feel an enormous resentment that his adoptive parents 'often recalled their past memories, and yet I was supposed to drop the first five years of my life and forget about it'.[3] At the very moment when he was beginning to wonder what direction he should take in life, his sense of self had been undermined, and he had little information to piece together who he might in fact actually be. His parents doted on him with material things, but ferociously avoided his past. If he tried to ask his father about where he had come from, '[my father] would walk out, and my mother would say, "you're hurting him"'.[4]

As he struggled to learn about his past, so Jackie struggled to determine his future. He left school at fifteen and tried a variety of occupations – hairdressing, work in an electrical retail shop and a menswear shop, bookmaking – but settled on none. In his late teens, he met a young woman at a dance, and soon fell in love. He asked her to marry him, she said yes, and they found themselves attending the offices of the Jewish Board of Deputies to receive permission to be married in the synagogue. With them were Jackie's adoptive mother and his fiancée's mother. In the Jewish religion, it is necessary to demonstrate that you are Jewish before you can be married in a religious ceremony, and the simplest way to demonstrate this is to prove that your mother is also Jewish. This, however, was not a straightforward matter in Jackie's case. The secretary asked to see proof that Jackie's birth mother had in fact been Jewish:

My adopted mother assured him that she was, and that the document was in the safe deposit box and couldn't he take her word for it? 'Certainly not,' he said, 'you will have to go and get it.' [. . .] We all went to the safe deposit and

I just could not wait to get my hands on those papers. I wanted to see what my mother was trying to hide. I begged her to let me look at them, but crying and shouting she held onto them. On returning to the office, [. . .] I snatched the papers away as [the secretary] handed them back to my mother and to my utter astonishment, I saw that I had been in a concentration camp. My real name was Jona Jakob Spiegel. [. . .] We all stood there dumbfounded, and I was hysterical. I had heard about these terrible places and couldn't accept that I was involved. My mother kept repeating that it was a very long time ago and that I was only a baby. I shouted at her 'Why couldn't you tell me before? I always find out from other people!'[5]

That evening, shocked and angry, Jackie asked his father where he had been adopted from. His father reluctantly admitted that Jackie had come from a care home for orphans located in the village of Lingfield in Surrey. On a sunny afternoon soon after, Jackie and his fiancée drove down to Lingfield. After making enquiries at the local police station, they found themselves standing at the gates of a big house, with sprawling grounds filled with tall trees that swept down to a horse-racing track – the former Weir Courtney care home for child survivors of the Holocaust. Jackie Y. had walked straight into his own childhood dream.

The oldest children in this study were born in 1935, and the youngest in 1944. This means that, as a group, they began to enter their adolescence in the late 1940s, and to leave it in the early 1960s, if we understand adolescence to be a life stage that begins around the physical milestone of puberty, and ends around the cultural milestone of reaching the age of majority. Thus far, we have focused on these children in the immediate aftermath of the war, as they entered new homes and new families (or old families, greatly changed) and spread out across Europe and the globe. Here we begin to examine their lives going forwards, starting with their teen years, a period during which many became increasingly curious about their own stories. Adolescence is an insistent moment with regards to the question of 'Who am I?', and if it is also a rebellious moment, the particular rebellion of many child survivors was to push on the doors to the past. In so doing, they began to glimpse, sometimes for the first time, not only missing parents and siblings, but entire annihilated worlds, worlds that should have been theirs. It was a life stage that called for a different relationship with the past: as bodies and minds matured, many child survivors began to feel that they were old enough to know the truth about their early childhoods. They began to push against the barriers that their carers had constructed to protect them from the facts, even as the adults around them sometimes doubled down, insisting that the sanitized versions of the past were the only ones.

All this happened in a very particular historical context, for while the 1950s were not the period of silence on the Holocaust that historians once supposed them to have been, nor were they a period in which information on the destruction of Europe's Jews during the war was readily available. Jackie recalled that he was shocked to learn he had been in a concentration camp because he had 'heard about these terrible places', and if hearsay was Jackie's only source of information about the camps, he was no different in this from most of the other North London Jews in his community. If he had wanted to go to his local library, or even the nearby British Library, and read more about the murderous process that had led to his mother's deportation and death, he would have found very little literature that could help him make sense of this family history. Before the publication of Raul Hilberg's landmark study *The Destruction of the European Jews* in 1961, there was only a tiny handful of book-length works on what would later come to be known as the Holocaust. Those works that did appear in the early 1950s came out in small print runs, and were generally read only by a limited circle of academics.[6] Other sorts of literature that might have helped to answer the questions posed by curious children were equally difficult to access. The yizkor (memorial) books that were written in this period by survivors' associations contained precious information about the destruction of Eastern European Jewish communities, but they were intended for the semi-private use of the associations that made them, and were often written in Yiddish – a language that was part of the cultural heritage lost forever to many child survivors.[7] Some recalled a clandestine search, in their teens and early twenties, through libraries and bookshops for information on the genocide, but few remembered finding any material that helped them answer the questions that had begun to trouble them.

It is difficult from today's perspective, in which the academic literature on the Holocaust is so vast that no individual scholar could ever know it in its entirety, to appreciate the scarcity of information in the early post-war decades. This does not mean that the 1950s was a period of silence on the genocide; as scholars such as Hasia Diner and Laura Jockusch have shown, Jewish communities commemorated the dead in this period, and an early network of historians laboured to create research institutes and preserve archival documents.[8] The information that existed, however, was challenging to access, and 'knowledge' of the fate of Europe's Jews was informed by suppositions, prejudices, and stigmas, and fed at times by a voyeuristic fascination. It was a historical moment in which growing survivor children faced a great challenge when they sought to piece together the details of their own pasts.

Nor did they receive a great deal of help from those closest to them. Although we need to add nuance to the notion that the 1950s was a broadly conformist era, it was a period in which survivor families generally wanted (and were expected) to fit into the communities and countries where they had settled. In the late 1940s and early 1950s large numbers of survivor families left Europe for other countries, especially after the founding of Israel in 1948 and the passage of the Displaced Persons Act in the United States in the same year.[9] Many child survivors thus found that their entry into their teen years coincided with a shuffle around the globe, bringing with it the need to learn a new language and a new culture. If adapting was difficult for budding adolescents, it was all the more so for their parents, who were in many cases keen to bury evidence of their histories as they worked to adjust to life in cultures and countries that had not directly experienced the Holocaust. Having survived the war, endured the DP camps, and emigrated into a global diaspora, parents were aware that their new host communities expected them to settle down and return to normal life – and they often wanted this for themselves as well. Nor were things all that different for adoptive and foster parents, such as Jackie's, who hoped to shelter their adoptive children and themselves from scrutiny and questioning. They generally opted to turn away from the past as well. It is not surprising, therefore, to see that uncomfortable clashes developed between adults who were bent on quietly fitting in and teenaged children who wanted to probe their family's very point of difference.

All families have an origin story, and all children, perhaps, prod at these stories as they grow up. As Jackie Y.'s story reveals, however, an adolescent survivor's insistence on picking at the holes in the family narrative could have explosive results for children and parents alike. As we have seen, acting on the assumption that their children would not remember their early childhoods, many parents (biological, foster, and adoptive) chose to avoid talking about the past. They did so for many reasons. Some feared feeding childhood nightmares or robbing children of a sense of security. Some – adoptive parents in particular – hoped to encourage their children to construct new identities to fit with new families. Where parents were themselves survivors, attempts to curtain off the past were sometimes driven by a parent's own psychological needs. By the time child survivors were in their teens, parents had often expended considerable emotional resources over many years blocking aspects of the past from entry into the family home. When adolescent children challenged these narratives, the very foundations of a family's sense of itself, carefully built around certain admissible versions of the past, could begin to unravel.

Adoptive and foster parents sometimes had different motivations for their silence. Jackie's parents, for example, may have hoped to protect their son from the knowledge that he had been in a concentration camp, but equally they did not want him to know that he was adopted at all. Their family story was constructed around a central mistruth (that Jackie was their own birth child), and his adoptive mother and father were heavily invested in maintaining this story. Nor were they alone in this, for in the 1940s and 1950s adoption was still a matter treated with secrecy, and carried with it two parallel stigmas:

infertility and illegitimacy. Adoptive parents, especiallye mothers, generally judged it wise to hide the fact of an adoption both from their children and from their communities. In this way they concealed their private fertility problems, and protected their children from the bullying and taunting that could follow the suggestion of an illegitimate birth.[10] By hiding the truth from him, Jackie's parents were simply following the cultural norms of the era.[11]

Where children learned that they were in fact adopted, the truth could have a destructive influence not just on a child's sense of self, but on the mother's and father's as well. In addition, if these parents were not themselves survivors, they might have had scant knowledge to draw on to answer the questions of curious children. They likely did not know what had happened to a child's birth parents. They might have known very little indeed about the Holocaust, and as we have seen, there were few sources to turn to for those who wanted to learn more. Many adoptive and foster parents, lacking an intimate and first-hand knowledge of the Holocaust, reflected back to children a broader collective discomfort with the question of what had happened to Europe's Jews during the war. They did not, moreover, relish revealing their own ignorance, but over time this gulf in understanding between what children wanted to know and what adoptive and foster parents were able to tell could prove incendiary.

Children in care homes sometimes managed to sidestep these issues, at least temporarily. As we have seen, memories of the wartime past played a different role in care homes than they did in private family homes. Even if adults in the care home environment said little about the war and its consequences to children, the children had each other: they might not have spoken frequently about the past, but they had the comforting knowledge that they shared a common history. Children living with families were far more likely to feel isolated. As they entered adolescence, children in care homes often found themselves in social circles primarily made up of other survivor children; such circles were not easily accessible to children outside institutional environments.

How did it feel for children to learn the truth about their past where this had been kept hidden from them, and what events forced these confrontations? For many children, the onset of puberty proved to be a decisive moment, for physical maturity brought with it a new set of emotional expectations between children and their parents. Children felt that they were growing towards adulthood, and no longer needed to be protected from their own histories; for parents, however, the well-learned habit of guarding children from their past could be difficult to set aside. In many cases this set children and parents up for a period of conflict, as children argued that they were now old enough to know the truth, and parents hesitated. In a few cases, parents pre-emptively chose to reveal something of the hidden past to a child entering puberty, in the hopes that this might then dampen future conflicts around the issue. Gittel H., born in Berlin in 1942, lived with her grandmother after the war. They had survived Theresienstadt together, and had immigrated together to the United States in 1951. Gittel's grandmother chose to tell the girl what had happened to her parents on the day after she had her first period. Gittel later recalled that:

> When I was thirteen, she finally decided to sit me down. She told me about the menstrual period, and the next day I started. You know, I saw blood and I didn't know what it was, and I showed it to her and she said, 'It can't be that' and right away I knew what she meant. It was just a coincidence that the next day I started. And then she sat me down and started to tell me about what happened to my parents.[12]

The news, however, did not come as a shock, for Gittel already knew how her parents had been killed. Her grandmother had never told her directly, but had told other people in her presence:

> My grandmother told me very little. She was always protecting me. I'm a survivor and I'm a grandchild of a survivor. You instinctively learn not to ask questions, because it's painful. [. . .] She used to tell me that my mother was in America. So if somebody would ask me, 'Where is your mother?' I would say 'She's in America.' I don't know what she told me once we came here [to the US] [. . .] But throughout my life, my grandmother would tell the story

[of what happened to Gittel's parents] to everybody that she met. I can remember standing at a bus stop and my grandmother would tell whoever was with us about what had happened and she didn't think that I heard her or understood her. [. . .] She must have thought that kids don't have ears.

The fact that her grandmother had kept the truth from her while telling so many others ultimately caused their relationship to fall apart, and Gittel recalled that 'I was very unhappy growing up with her.'

The links between puberty and the growth of conflict in the family were not always as explicit as in Gittel's case, but they were common nonetheless. As children developed adult bodies and responsibilities, they argued that they deserved an adult's access to the past. Where parents could not or would not comply, in some cases they became violent. Peter B., whom we met in the first chapter and who survived Theresienstadt with his mother, encountered this. He had immigrated to the United States with his mother, stepfather, and a baby sister in 1947. His mother had struggled emotionally after the war, but things took a grave turn for the worse after the family arrived in the US, and she proved unable to 'settle back down into a normal life'. Peter had just turned eleven when they arrived, and as he went through puberty his relationship with his mother deteriorated:

It was just intolerable for me to be at home. By the time I was fourteen, I had probably run away from home about half a dozen times. I was truly an abused child. I mean physically abused. Once a day at least, most of the times twice a day, by my mother. [. . .] There was a lot going on in her [. . .] and she just didn't know how to handle it. And when we came to the United States, instead of embracing that, she got worse. Maybe it all welled up in her at that time, maybe she finally had a chance at that time to let it all hang out. And she just took it all out on me. Absolutely. So I left home when I was fourteen, and I have never been back since.[13]

For children living with foster parents, the tension that welled up as they entered adolescence took on different forms. After spending most of his childhood in a care home, Denny M. went to live with a string of foster families in the later part of his teenage years. He recalled that the uncomfortable relationships he had with his foster parents – he passed quickly through a succession of four different foster homes – grew out of the fact that the foster families knew nothing of the Holocaust:

> A lot of Anglo-Jewry were not really affected by the Holocaust, and when they took somebody in they were not really in tune with the situation. It reminds me of the short story by Franz Kafka called 'Metamorphosis', where a member of the family suddenly becomes an insect, and at first the family is terribly concerned about him, but eventually they destroy him. [. . .] Moving in you would bring out something of their feeling of guilt, and of something that they perhaps resent within themselves, and that then becomes projected onto the person who like myself moves into the family, and the situation becomes impossible.[14]

Tension in the family could have grave practical implications for child survivors, implications that stretched far beyond the emotional politics of their households. Instability at home meant that many struggled to focus on or complete their educations. Denny, who became a music teacher after having worked as a clerk in a music shop, wondered whether he would have had better career prospects if he had not been forced to endure such a difficult period in foster care right at the very moment when he had to choose a future career path. 'There wouldn't have been all of these emotional obstacles, and emotional obstacles affect achievement,' he recalled. 'And living with families who have been hostile doesn't enhance emotional stability.'[15] Many of his peers shared this sentiment. Education was an encounter with the expectations that the world had for adolescent child survivors, and it brought some face to face with the realization that the adults around them no longer quite thought of them as the 'precious remnants'. As small children, many had found themselves the objects of charitable and humanitarian interest, but as they entered their teens this dynamic changed. Those in care homes and in foster care were particularly vulnerable to this change, as sources of funding dried up and care homes closed. This was the point at which agencies began to fret about how survivor children could be ushered towards economic independence neatly and speedily. Thus even exceptionally bright children often felt compelled to put intellectual pursuits aside and train for blue-collar professions. This could happen at the behest of an aid agency, but it might equally have been the free choice of a child eager to be 'good' by moving as quickly as possible out of a dependent relationship. Encounters with the educational system (and the decision to leave it) left some child survivors unsure of their worth, and mourning the idea of a lost self that might have attained more under better conditions.[16]

Adult carers encouraged children to work towards a swift independence and at the same time worried about the repercussions of such choices. At the OSE's care homes, for example, staff sought to give children a 'solid professional training', but this almost always meant in a trade. Only a tiny minority of the OSE's wards completed their secondary education at a *lycée* (an academic secondary school), and this minority grew even smaller after October 1947, when the JDC cut the stipend it had provided for children bright enough to have won a scholarship for secondary education.[17] At the same time OSE educators worried that the children themselves did not seem to care about the loss of educational opportunities. OSE staff remarked that the children lacked motivation for their studies and often hoped to end their training as quickly as possible in order to become financially independent. Staff also observed that many of their wards had great difficulty in concentrating. If they were aware that the children's inability to focus had its origins in the pain of the past, they were nonetheless unable to do anything about it.[18]

What was the connection between memory of the past, crises in the family, and educational attainment? Jackie, destabilized by his parents' refusal to tell him where he came from, left school at fifteen and moved uncertainly through apprenticeships and a variety of unskilled jobs, until he got engaged and came under pressure to settle on a profession quickly (he chose taxi driving, which he did until he retired).[19] When he could no longer stand his mother's violence, Peter ran away from home at the age of fourteen, leaving school in the process. He recalled, 'I survived. I was on my own for so many years, all alone, that it was nothing for me to move to Texas and get a job on a ranch. I got various jobs and kept bumming around.'[20] Emigration also complicated survivor children's educational chances, for it brought with it new languages, new cultures, new educational systems, and new gender expectations. Felice Z. and her sister Beate were sent from the OSE home at Taverny to the United States at the behest of their uncle, but were placed in a care home in New Jersey when the uncle declined to take them in. They stayed in this care home until it closed down, and were then placed in a series of foster homes. Felice recalled that when she started at a New Jersey secondary school at the age of fourteen, after having struggled so hard to adapt to a new culture, a new language, and a new (and unexpected) living situation, the school guidance counsellor made it clear that her different past had foreclosed upon any scholarly future:

> That was another problem. I went and the school counsellor said to me, 'Oh, English is not your first language, so you can't study on the college prep courses. We're going to put you in the secretarial division.' So I said okay. I mean at that point, I was still very docile. Fine, all right. So that's what I did. Most of my friends were not Jewish, because the Jewish children were going to go to college, so they took college prep courses.[21]

Given the confluence of challenges that child survivors faced in their teen years, it is not surprising to discover that some found the years of continuous destabilization too much to bear. Suzanne N. was born in January 1939 in Paris, the youngest of three siblings. During the war she was hidden in a convent, and then with a family in the countryside whom she remembers only as having been abusive to her.[22] After the war, she and her two older brothers were taken to the OSE orphanage at Fontainebleau, and in 1948 an uncle who was willing to take the three children was found in Canada. The three subsequently immigrated to Toronto in May 1948 on the CJC's war orphan scheme. Suzanne's first CJC case file report noted optimistically that 'Susan [*sic*] fitted very well into [her uncle and aunt's] home and . . . became an integral part of the family', but in fact she and her brothers found the transfer to Canada a gruelling experience.[23] The uncle and aunt spoke no French, and the children spoke no English – and once the problem of language was overcome, other issues followed. Suzanne's relatives had little understanding of what she and her brothers had been through, and the relationship between the three children and the adults became strained. Suzanne's brothers refused to talk to her about the parents that they remembered but she could not, and they left home when she was in her mid-teens. Suzanne had been happy in the OSE care home in Fontainebleau, where she had been surrounded by children who had shared similar pasts, but in Toronto she felt utterly alone.

As she entered adolescence, the spectre of the unknown past suddenly began to rear up unbidden in her daily life in the strange, safe world of late 1950s Canada. Suzanne recalled attending a B'nai B'rith summer camp in her early teens:

> We were getting ready to go to bed, and there was a mosquito on my arm, and I said to the girl next to me 'Don't kill it.' But I guess she didn't want it to bite me, so she just tapped it. You know, when you kill a mosquito, there's a little bit of blood that comes out. So I looked at my arm, I looked at the blood, and I didn't really see the girls and the camp and everything: all I saw was destruction and dead bodies around me, and I became very hysterical, and the counsellor had to run after me and hug me and settle me down.[24]

It was not that Suzanne was remembering what she had seen as a child; rather, she was imagining a world that she had never seen, the unknown world of her parents' murder, a realm that asserted itself so forcefully in part because she could find no one who could tell her anything about it. Her present life, so safe and yet so punctuated by terrors, became unbearable. At the age of thirteen, before her brothers had fled her uncle and aunt's home, Suzanne made her first attempt at suicide:

> I was unconscious, and my brothers came upstairs to see why I wasn't coming down to dinner. I was lying there. [My middle brother] just shook me from the shoulders and slapped my face a few times, and he said to [my older brother], 'you know, I didn't really realize that she needs parents, and we have to protect her'.

Suzanne had nightmares that she was being chased by Nazis. She started running away from home. When she was sixteen, she had a hallucinatory episode in which she imagined 'that there were bees all over, bees on the ceiling, bees on the walls, and I just went berserk. I couldn't touch anything.' After this event, Suzanne's uncle and aunt decided that they could no longer look after her, and they threatened to have her committed to a mental hospital. She recalled:

> There must have been a very small part of my psyche that didn't want to be completely destroyed. I called a doctor [. . .] and I started intensive psycho-analytic therapy. [. . .] I think he saved my life. I was really bent on destroying myself. For whatever twisted reason, I blamed myself for my parents' deaths. Why did I live, and everybody else died? I tried to commit suicide quite a few times. I had very, very deep depressions, where I thought I would never come out and there was no light at the end of the tunnel. It took about sixteen years until I finally got things into some kind of order.

We have seen, in previous chapters, that psychoanalysts and psychiatrists turned to opining about child survivors' psyches and emotions very quickly after the war's end. However, few child survivors received therapy in their pre-adolescent years; more did so in their teens, although they were never the majority. Some, such as Suzanne, were unquestionably helped by therapists, but the relationship between child survivors and the mental health professions was a complicated one. As some adolescent survivors entered psychoanalysis, they encountered analysts ill-equipped to understand and respond to the particular issues faced by growing children who had lived through the genocide. In 1963 a Hungarian-Jewish analyst in Anna Freud's circle, Edith Ludowyk Gyomroi, published a paper on her work with 'Elizabeth', a child survivor of Auschwitz who had come to England at the age of 'about four'. Elizabeth had asked her carers to let her try analysis at the age of seventeen, because, in Gyomroi's words, 'with entry into adolescence Elizabeth increasingly became aware of her inability to be a person in her own right, to believe in her own capacities, and to pursue her own wishes'.[25] Gyomroi's analysis of the case revealed just how difficult it was for therapists, drawing on the psychoanalytic theory and practice of the time, to understand the particular issues that child survivors faced, or indeed even to credit that their memories, patchy and fragmented as they were, might in fact reflect their real, lived wartime experience.

Memory became a contentious issue for Gyomroi and her young patient, because Gyomroi was convinced that Elizabeth had repressed her memories of her time in Auschwitz, and replaced them with fantasies. It is important to note here that the understanding of how very young children remember – and why they forget – was poorly developed in the 1950s and 1960s, and is still not fully understood today. No matter what conditions we have been raised in, we tend to have discontinuous memories of our early childhood, and to have no memories at all of our lives before the age of three. This phenomenon, which Sigmund Freud labelled 'infantile amnesia', is now generally understood to be tied to a host of cognitive developmental factors, among which language acquisition and the ability to shape an autobiographical narrative are central.[26] However, Freudian analysts of the era, such as Gyomroi, understood the phenomenon as 'the result of repression set up against retaining in conscious-ness the primitive infantile drive experiences against which the child has turned' – a defence against the humiliation and disappointment that followed when a child had to repudiate her earliest aggressive and sexual impulses. Gyomroi believed, moreover, that Elizabeth's particular repression of the past differed from 'the usual type of infantile amnesia', because her early years had been 'a bewildering kaleidoscope of figures, short-lived relationships, passing images, experiences, and even language'.[27] The analyst's conviction that her patient's blotting out of the past went deeper than usual meant that Gyomroi largely dismissed as fantasy the fragmentary memories that Elizabeth brought to their therapy sessions. When Elizabeth recalled that she had once slept on 'wooden bunks' and 'on a table' along with other children, Gyomroi specu-lated that this was little more than a 'cover image' that allowed the girl to organize her imaginings. It was not until the late 1980s that the girl (by then a woman in her forties) would learn more about her own early years via archival documents, discovering that she had been in Theresienstadt for some time before being deported to Auschwitz, and that those rough wooden bunks that she and so many other children recalled from the camp had indeed been a central part of her early childhood. At a time in adolescence when so many child survivors were so desperately trying to learn more about their pasts, it is not difficult to imagine the intense frustration of a young woman who brought her few thin memories to her therapist, only to have the therapist suggest that these were mere fantasy, and that the genuine past had been so completely blocked off as to be permanently inaccessible.[28]

In searching for concrete information about their pasts, child survivors were often let down by their parents, their carers, and even their therapists. Nor did scholars offer much help, for any child with the resources and energy to comb their local libraries and booksellers for information about the genocide would have found little that set out what had happened to their families and commu-nities of origin. Yet at the same time, in the mid- to late 1950s many came into contact with a legal process that demanded they know a great deal about their pasts, more than they possibly could. This was West Germany's new indemnifi-cation scheme for victims of Nazi persecution: an initiative peppered with obstacles for child survivors, one that forced applicants to delve into their memories and to probe the holes they found there. It was a system that generally demanded the sort of clear, logical, and complete synopsis of the war experience that lay beyond the reach of child survivors, particularly those who were orphaned. At the same time it was a scheme that occasionally provided child survivors with precious scraps of information that could be secured through no other route.

The Federal Indemnification Law of 1953 (the Bundesergänzungsgesetz – replaced by the Bundesentschädigungsgesetz, or BEG, in 1956) was the first codified indemnification law in history. In theory it opened the way for those who had lost their families, livelihoods, and health to Nazi persecution to receive some minimal financial compensation from West Germany. In practice, however, it could be a grinding, degrading, soul-crushing process for child survivors to access the scheme, because an applicant needed to obtain documentary proof of their persecution. This was challenging enough for adult claimants to provide, but often impossible for those who had been children during the war. They may have had no official documents in their possession, not even a birth certificate. Many did not know their parents' names, or their dates or places of birth, or the date on which they were deported; some were not even sure of their own birth names. Where child survivors (and adult survivors) needed help in navigating the restitution process, most turned to the services of the United Restitution Office (URO), a legal aid body founded in 1948 to help survivors who lived outside Germany and Israel negotiate the smaller, regional indemnification schemes that had pre-dated the BEG.[29] Once the BEG was launched, the URO became the chief organization that survivors turned to for counsel, because it acted as an intermediary between individual survivors and the German authorities.[30] The URO had branch offices throughout the world, and claimants were expected to use the office closest to where they were then living. The local office would liaise with other offices to track down necessary documents that an applicant could not provide, such as birth certificates, proof of residency, or evidence of deportation and internment. In securing these documents, the URO worked with archives across Europe, including Jewish community archives, municipal record offices, and most importantly the archives of the Red Cross International Tracing Service, which had millions of documents stored underground at the small German resort town of Bad Arolsen. The URO and the network of archivists and researchers it worked with did not have unlimited access to the necessary documents, for the Cold War ensured that any archival material stored on the Eastern side of the Iron Curtain remained inaccessible. It nonetheless could broker contact with archives and their precious documents in a way that no individual (and certainly no individual adolescent without means) could ever do alone.[31]

Applicants to the restitution scheme could claim for loss of life of close kin, loss of health (although not ongoing mental health issues, as we shall see in the next chapter), loss of property or possessions, and loss of vocational or economic pursuits where their working capacity had been permanently impaired. One can see, from this list, that children were at an immediate disadvantage in the process: they might claim for their parents' lost lives (if they were able to prove that their parents were indeed dead), but they could not claim for property or possessions that they had never owned, and they could not argue that their persecution had robbed them of their vocation. Neither was it straightforward for children to claim for 'loss of liberty', because to qualify they had to prove that their living conditions had been 'inhumane' – and a life in hiding was not considered 'inhumane' by the authorities. Theresa E., who spent her early years in the Warsaw ghetto before being smuggled out and placed in hiding with a Polish family near Warsaw, found that she could claim for 'loss of liberty' during the period when she was in the ghetto, but not for the period afterwards. The URO London office wrote to her legal guardian in 1959 that:

We claimed indemnification for the period from November 1940 until December 1944. The starting date – enclosure of the Ghetto – is not quite certain. It might be that January 15th, 1941, and not November 1940, is the crucial date from which onward the indemnification for detention in the Ghetto can be claimed. The period after January 1943 is 'illegal life'. Theresa was taken out from the Ghetto and hidden with a Polish family in Jozefow near Warsaw. For this period the Authorities request evidence that Theresa had to live under 'subhuman conditions'. It will be difficult to provide this evidence.[32]

This excerpt sheds light on two important issues. First, it makes clear that children – who so often survived the war in hiding – were from the outset disadvantaged in the restitution process, for no matter how terrifying their experiences in hiding may have been, and no matter how great their loss of freedom, security, and health, the German authorities would not recognize their experiences as worthy of indemnification. Second, it reminds us that while the authorities would only accept a claim where indisputable proof of persecution could be provided, they themselves were operating with sparse information. The authorities requested that claims be submitted by 1958. This was a period in which, as we have seen, there existed very little historical scholarship on the genocide. Even basic dates and facts, such as the sealing off of the Warsaw ghetto in November 1940, were still unclear to the very authorities who were ready to deny claims based on incorrect facts.[33] Further examples demonstrate just how arbitrary, unfair, and upsetting the authorities' judgement could be where child survivors were concerned. Mirjam S., born in Czechoslovakia in August 1937, spent the war years in hiding with a peasant family. The family confined her to a room in the upstairs part of the house; downstairs, German soldiers were sometimes billeted. She later recalled that:

> I ate up there all the time. They never saw me. I wasn't supposed to but I would always sit by the window, and I would stare at the rats in the garbage pile across the way for hours. [. . .] [The mother of the house] would tell me all kinds of things because she wanted me not to do anything to endanger them. Like she'd say, 'This will happen to you if you do this.' When somebody came I was supposed to hide under the bed.[34]

Mirjam's older sister was deported to Ravensbrück concentration camp, but survived; her father died in Sachsenhausen, her mother in Sered', and her older brother was killed in an unknown location.[35] Nonetheless, the legal adviser in her local URO office was doubtful that she could be compensated, writing that 'this claim can only be granted if it can be proved that the illegal life she lived was inhuman. Anyone in hiding living under a false name and separated from their family does not constitute a claim. [. . .] With regards to claim on father, proof needed that he lost his life in Sachsenhausen.'[36]

As time went by, more and more regulations were invoked to delay or refuse claims, and more and more claims were rejected because they contained factual errors, despite the authorities' own uncertainty about the facts. In entering the restitution process, often with the expectation of genuine good will on the part of the West German state, many applicants were horrified to find themselves caught in a sickeningly familiar relationship of power in which German authorities judged Jews to be liars and cheats, echoing well-established Nazi anti-Semitic stereotypes.[37] The restitution process was bewildering for child survivors, then in their teens. Adult applicants knew whether or not they were telling the truth as far as they could know it, but children often simply did not know where the parameters of the truth lay.

Janek E.*, born in 1936 in Poland, had suffered a singularly terrifying trajectory during the war. In 1940 all the Jews living in his home town of Kraśnik were rounded up and taken to forced labour camps. His mother was sent to one camp, and he, his father, and his siblings were sent to another camp at Budzyń. His brother and sisters were shot in the camp. He was then sent, with his father, to a number of forced labour and concentration camps, passing through the salt mines at Wieliczka before ending up in Flossenbürg. His father died shortly after liberation, from brain injuries sustained when a camp guard in Flossenbürg beat him so badly that he lay unconscious in the barracks for three weeks. With the death of his father, Janek was the last member of his family alive, completely alone at the age of ten in a DP camp in Salzheim. In 1949 Janek immigrated to the United States with the help of an uncle, and while he was a secondary school student in Los Angeles he submitted a claim to the local URO office for loss of liberty.[38] His URO case file does not preserve the statement of his experience that he (and all applicants) would have had to write up in order to make a claim, but it does include his legal adviser's sceptical response to the statement:

* pseudonym

We have to inform you that it is impossible that you had been wearing the Jewish star since December 1939. At this time you were only three years old and according to the law children had to wear the Jewish star only after they had reached the 10th year [*sic*]. Since you were mistaken in this case, we are afraid that you were also mistaken concerning the Ghetto of Budzyn. According to the decision which is based on official documents Budzyn became a concentration camp only in October 1942, and was before never a closed Ghetto.[39]

Janek was thus in a terrible position. He had no one left alive who could help him to piece together the chaotic events that he had lived through from the ages of three through ten. He did his best to set out the story of his life for the legal advisers of the URO Los Angeles office, only to be informed that his memories were 'impossible' and he was 'mistaken'. In the end the authorities granted him a small single payment for 'loss of liberty'. A few years later Janek submitted another claim, this time for the loss of his father's life. In this case his URO file has preserved his statement. He wrote:

My father was severely mistreated in Flossenbürg. He was beaten with whips over his head, so that he collapsed covered in blood. He later had a large scar on his forehead. In 1946, we came to the DP camp at Salzheim near Frankfurt. My father always complained of severe headaches after the liberation. The condition got worse, and he lost the feeling in his hands. He was taken to a hospital in Frankfurt where he stayed for about a year and a half, and then he died. According to the doctor, he had died as a result of the injuries caused by the ill treatment. I was then in a children's home in Bad Eibling near Munich.[40]

The claim was rejected.

However, for all the humiliation and pain that the restitution process could bring to adolescent survivors, some who navigated its obstacles gained access to documents that helped to complete the puzzle of their early histories. Some learned their real birth dates, or their parents' true names, or that they had siblings or half-siblings. On some occasions staff at the URO offices chose to conceal information that they had discovered, for fear that it would be too upsetting for young survivors to hear. Jackie Y. recalled that shortly after he got engaged in his late teens, he read something about the restitution process in the newspaper:

Together with my fiancée we went to the United Restitution Office and there we found a very nice lady who listened to what I had to say. She said that as I had been adopted a search must have already been carried out to see whether there were any surviving relatives, but that she would get in touch with the records offices in Vienna to make sure. A few weeks later we were asked to go along to the United Restitution Office as they had some information for me. I was given a small slip of paper. On this paper was the fact that my mother's occupation had been a milliner, her name, date of birth and the dates of our deportations, me to Terezin [Theresienstadt] and her to Minsk, from where she never returned. From these dates we could work out that I had been taken away from my mother when I was five and a half months old and she was deported immediately after this and I was deported three months later. As for any other relations there were no records.[41]

It was not until 1981 that Jackie learned more. During a visit to Israel he made contacts who helped him to secure his long-form birth certificate from the municipal archives in Vienna, which showed that his mother had been unmarried:

This didn't altogether surprise me, but I wondered why nobody had mentioned this fact before. I had asked often enough, and furthermore, why hadn't I been given my mother's birth certificate before now when the United Restitution Office had carried out a search for me? My wife rang up the lady at the Office and on telling her what we had found out she owned up and said she had known all the time, but she didn't want to hurt the poor boy's feelings. She had decided, together with someone else, to with-hold this information. [. . .] We now wondered how many other people there were who were doing the same thing.

The restitution process could thus bring with it valuable information, but at the same time it could deliver a heavy emotional toll. Where claims were rejected, there was anger, humiliation, and a gnawing doubt that the life story, provided as fully as many children could do in the circumstances, was inaccurate at best and untrue at worst. Where claims were honoured, the emotional repercussions were no easier. The psychologist Sarah Moskovitz has called restitution 'the tragic dilemma' for child survivors, who felt that if they accepted the pittance offered by the BEG authorities for the deaths of longed-for parents, they both lessened the guilt of the murderers, and increased their own. Jackie himself recalled this feeling:

> No amount of money could ever compensate for my loss, and I felt that the people who had done this terrible thing to me were brushing me aside with a pittance. When I finally received the money, I felt that I wanted to tear it to shreds and throw it away. This money represented the mother I never knew.

Before the years of their adolescence, many child survivors were aware that there were gaps in their pasts that made little sense and proved stubbornly difficult to fill. However, the question of the past – its shape, its meaning, and its resonance – took on a different urgency as they entered their teens. If before they had simply not known about their early years, now they seemed to encounter deliberate attempts to wall off their access to their own histories, or to suggest that their memories were in fact mere fantasies. We can empathize with the plight of parents and others who strove to protect child survivors from the terrifying truth, but we can equally understand that, to their children, control of the past was a fraught issue in an unequal power relationship. And as this struggle unfolded at a historical moment in which consciousness of the genocide was muted, and knowledge of its processes was still under-developed, there were few avenues open to adolescents hungry to know the facts about their origins. As they entered adulthood, that hunger often grew, and yet most found themselves grappling alone with real and imagined terrors, longings, and ghosts.[42]

# SEVEN

# TRAUMA

Among the 300 child survivors of Theresienstadt who were brought to Britain in the summer of 1945, there were six toddlers under four years old (one of whom was Jackie Y.).[1] Leaders of the Central British Fund, the organization charged with the care of the children, thought that it would be best for the toddlers to be housed in their own dedicated facility. Lady Betty Clarke, the wife of an MP, loaned the agency Bulldogs Bank, her cottage in West Hoathly, Sussex, and the six small children were soon relocated there.[2] There was considerable public interest in the toddlers, and mental health professionals were curious to see how these children, deprived of their mothers during the earliest years of their lives, would develop. Received psychiatric and psychoanalytic wisdom at the time suggested that maternal attention and affection were fundamental to a child's normal psychological development – and thus the six toddlers, separated from their mothers in infancy and housed in the 'Ward for Motherless Children' in Theresienstadt, seemed to present an opportunity to test this theory. Among the experts who saw the Theresienstadt toddlers' potential as experimental subjects was Anna Freud, daughter of Sigmund Freud and one of the founders of the field of child psychoanalysis.[3]

Anna Freud's views on early childhood development had been widely popularized through her writings, and in particular her work with collaborator Dorothy Burlingham at the Hampstead War Nurseries, residential homes for evacuated children that they had run between 1941 and 1945.[4] Freud and Burlingham argued that it was not the violence of war that children found upsetting, but rather the separation from their mothers; indeed, Freud insisted that war fed children's natural appetites for violence, and that the emotional destabilization that came with evacuation was potentially far more damaging to children than the threat of bombs. In this, she was in agreement (at least initially) with other prominent child psychoanalysts of the era, such as John Bowlby, who argued that 'the prolonged separation of small children from their homes is one of the outstanding causes of the development of a criminal character', and that 'maternal deprivation' in early childhood could lead not only to delinquency, but to depression, mental retardation, and loss of affect. If this was the case, then the six Theresienstadt toddlers should have experienced severe emotional and developmental problems.[5]

Anna Freud thus worked to ensure that the six toddlers would be housed in a cosy environment at Bulldogs Bank, but also that they would be carefully observed by staff trained in psychoanalytic methods. She sent two of the care workers who had worked with her at the Hampstead War Nurseries, German émigré sisters Sophie and Gertrud Dann, to run Bulldogs Bank. The Dann sisters took careful notes on the toddlers' day-to-day behaviour. They observed their tantrums, their friendships, and their struggles with a new language. They recorded each time the children comforted themselves by sucking on a thumb or on a feeding bib, each time they wet the bed or played with their genitals. From her offices in London, Anna Freud received these notes, and mulled over their meaning. In 1951 she and Sophie Dann published an article on the children called 'An Experiment in Group Upbringing'. It remains a seminal work in child psychology, referred to in most of the textbooks still used to teach this field to undergraduates today.[6]

Freud and Dann were fascinated by the more unusual elements of the children's behaviour, and in particular the fact that they were wary about forming attachments to any adult, but had strong bonds with each other. The children were 'hypersensitive, restless, aggressive, difficult to handle. They showed a heightened autoerotism and some of them the beginning of neurotic symptoms,' they wrote.[7] For all this, however, Freud and Dann concluded that the children 'were neither deficient, delinquent nor psychotic. They had found an alternative placement for their libido [in the group] and, on the strength of this, had mastered some of their anxieties, and developed social attitudes.' The toddlers thus called into question the fundamental notion that children would invariably be scarred by the loss of a close relationship with their mothers. Despite the fact that they had been separated from their mothers at a very early age, the children appeared to be resilient. Indeed, Freud and Dann concluded the study with the suggestion that John Bowlby and his followers were misguided in their insistence 'that every disturbance of the mother relationship . . . is invariably a pathogenic factor of specific value'.[8] As Freud and Dann saw it, the Bulldogs Bank 'experiment' challenged child psychiatrists and psychoanalysts to reconsider the notion that maternal affection was fundamental to a child's psychological development.

Yet Freud and Dann's work was also a product of its time. We have seen that, following the war, psychoanalytically informed care workers tended to stress that if child survivors had been rendered 'de-normalized' by their war experiences, this was not a permanent state. Care workers often felt that they had to defend their wards against the charge, voiced in the popular press, that Europe's unaccompanied children had been hopelessly tainted by the war. They equally had the issue of funds and fundraising on their minds, for enormous sums were needed for the network of care homes that agencies ran across Europe – and lost causes were unlikely to entice donors to reach for their pocketbooks. Thus there were very real, practical reasons for care workers to insist, in the early years after the war's end, that child survivors had been badly hurt by their experience of persecution – badly hurt enough to require the specialist care of trained experts – but equally that with specialist care, they would be returned to 'normal'. Anna Freud herself did not operate outside of these concerns, despite professing, like other psychoanalysts of the era, that the external world had no place in the Child Guidance Clinic. Part of the funds that had allowed Freud to run the Hampstead War Nurseries, and to sponsor Bulldogs Bank, came from the American Foster Parents' Plan for War Children. The charity's funding of Freud's operations came precisely because Freud and her staff stressed to American donors that, with material and emotional support, the children in their care would go on to live happy, psychologically sound lives.[9]

The conclusions that Anna Freud and Sophie Dann drew in 'An Experiment in Group Upbringing' remained largely unchallenged for more than a decade, and the force that ultimately upended the consensus around their work was the West German restitution process. Here we examine what happened as the restitution process led psychiatrists and psychoanalysts to debate whether child survivors were as resilient as Freud and Dann had suggested in the early 1950s, or whether they had instead suffered lasting psychological damage from their war experiences. We have seen how restitution funds were challenging for child survivors to access, but equally how the process gave some a chance to acquire key pieces of information about their earliest years. Here we examine how the process launched a wide-ranging debate over the concept of psychological 'trauma', a debate in which child survivors played an important role. It was restitution and its discontents, more than any other factor, that led mental health professionals towards a renewed interest in child survivors' psychological development and the question of whether war-torn childhoods could cause long-term psychological harm. It prompted a shift in the relationship between survivors and experts that ultimately left both groups changed. One cannot write the post-war history of child survivors without considering their relationship to the world of mental health experts, and weighing the fears and hopes that they sometimes invested in that world. At the same time, however, one cannot write the post-war history of child psychiatry, psychoanalysis, and developmental psychology without considering child survivors, for experts' work on child survivors fundamentally altered the ways in which these professionals viewed the development of children, the importance of the parent-child relationship, and the very idea of psychological 'trauma'.[10]

What do we mean when we speak of 'trauma'? It is now common in the English language to refer to distressing and emotionally disturbing events as 'traumatic', and to recognize 'trauma' as a conceptual category that explains such events and their short- and long-term consequences. This use of the term, however – and of the set of concepts behind it – evolved only in the latter half of the twentieth century. Indeed, the *Oxford English Dictionary* dates the earliest figurative use of 'trauma' in this sense ('We know the trauma you suffered') to 1977.[11] The way in which 'trauma', as a word and as an idea, entered into general usage to refer to a state of psychological pain is a fascinating development, one that followed profound shifts in how mental health professionals approached the concept during the 1960s and 1970s. These changes had radical effects on clinical psychological practice, on popular understanding, and on academic scholarship (for example, since the 1980s and 1990s, historians have spent a great deal of time exploring the consequences of past 'traumatic' events on present societies). There were many factors that led to this shift in our understanding, but a key factor was the acrimonious debates prompted by the restitution process. It was through the drawn-out cycle of claims, rejections, and appeals to the West German Federal Compensation Law of 1956, the Bundesentschädigungsgesetz (BEG), that psychiatrists and psychoanalysts were forced to question and to debate whether horrific events *could* have lasting effects on an individual, and in so doing they challenged some of the most basic tenets of their professions. As these experts wrangled over the concept of trauma in a hostile, decades-long feud, survivors – and child survivors in particular – found themselves caught between the competing agendas of those who argued that war experiences (no matter how horrific) would have no lasting effects on those who had lived through them at a tender age, and those who argued the opposite: that child survivors had suffered life-long, debilitating, clinical after-effects of persecution.

Before these shifts of the 1960s and 1970s, psychiatrists generally understood psychological trauma as a temporary response to upsetting events. It was assumed that long-term symptoms of psychic distress could not possibly stem from such events; they had to be either genetic or caused (as some psychiatrists argued) by physical injuries in the brain. Indeed, the term 'trauma', which comes from the Greek word for wound, was and remains primarily used in medical contexts to refer to physical wounds. Thus psychiatrists such as Frederick Mott and Charles Myers, some of the first to use the term 'shell shock' to describe emotional disturbances in soldiers during the First World War, thought that the likely cause of such psychic distress was battle-induced lesions in the brain. Around the same time, physicians puzzled over the lasting shock that sometimes afflicted those who had been in railway accidents, but the very fact that this condition was labelled 'railway spine' reveals that professionals saw such psychological complaints as having their roots in physical injury. In an increasingly dangerous, mechanized workplace, it was likewise noticed that those injured in factory accidents sometimes developed ongoing symptoms of shock. However, once governments began to introduce legislation for workers' compensation, the motivations of workers suffering from 'compensation neurosis' were questioned: was this illness or malingering? The issue was divisive, and even those few psychiatrists who began to argue hesitantly that shock may have been brought on by extreme emotions and experiences, and not by physical injury, did not entertain the idea that such psychic states could have *long-term* effects.[12]

Freudian psychoanalysts had a different understanding of 'trauma neurosis', but they similarly did not believe that horrific events could have lasting effects in a healthy individual. Traumas, in the classical Freudian view, either had roots in an individual's inborn constitution or had a sexual etiology and grew out of childhood familial relations. Freudian analysts also resisted admitting the possibility that the symptoms of 'trauma neurosis' could be produced by real-world events; rather, they understood unconscious motivations to be the root cause. Freud himself had argued that it seemed 'highly improbable that a neurosis could come into being because of the objective presence of danger, without any participation of the deeper levers of the mental apparatus'.[13] This conviction that trauma was caused either by innate constitution or by fears and desires that grew out of early family dynamics made for a strained relationship between analysts and the relatively small number of adult Holocaust survivors who sought their help in the late 1940s and 1950s. Psychoanalytically informed mental health experts working for aid agencies in Britain and North America found an alarming range of psychosomatic symptoms in adult survivors: muscle pain, migraines, apathy, anxiety, and disturbances in memory were only some of the frequently reported symptoms. However, these experts proved remarkably resistant to seeing any possible connection between these symptoms and a survivor's experiences during the war. Indeed, they made almost no mention of their patients' wartime pasts in their notes. Even when adult survivors themselves suggested that their emotional troubles might stem from their war experiences, 'the professionals generally paid little heed'.[14] Psychoanalytically informed experts were more open to the idea that horrific war experiences could cause psychic harm in children, but were unsure about whether this harm could endure. A key obstacle in thinking about the potential lasting effects of wartime persecution on children was the then contemporary understanding of how children's capacity to remember develops as they grow.

Classical Freudian psychoanalysts and child developmental psychologists took different perspectives on the issue of memory in children, but experts in both fields insisted that children could not actively remember events that occurred in their early years. Freud had first used the term 'infantile amnesia' to refer to the period before the age of three for which we have no memories at all. According to the Freudian viewpoint, children did indeed have memories of their infancy, but because these memories were overwhelming (particularly the memory of illicit desire for the parent of the opposite sex), the developing ego later repressed them. In their unconscious state these memories continued to motivate behaviour, but could not be actively recalled. Developmental psychologists took a different view of infantile amnesia: such influential thinkers as the Swiss scholar Jean Piaget believed that small children's undeveloped brains could not form lasting memories, and that in children of pre-school age, memory processes were disorganized and fragmentary. Child psychologists thus imagined that terrifying events experienced in early childhood could have no lasting harmful effects on a growing child, because the very memory of these events would simply fade away over time. And while psychoanalysts did credit that a growing brain could retain (repressed) memories of its earliest months and years, they were chiefly concerned with sexual dynamics between parents and children, and tended to disregard external events. Thus Freudian psychoanalysts and classical child psychologists ended up on the same page: both believed that young child survivors could not possibly remember their persecution, and as such could suffer no long-term psychological consequences.[15]

Indeed, it is worth noting here that it was not until the 1980s and 1990s that developmental psychologists' understanding of 'infantile amnesia' changed dramatically, as a new generation of experimental psychologists began to formulate fresh theories regarding why we cannot recall the first three or four years of our lives. Their experiments demonstrated that very young children and even babies can indeed remember events for days, months, and even years – but these early memories are not subsequently retained into adulthood. Researchers such as Robyn Fivush and Katherine Nelson were among the first to argue in the 1980s that the ability to retain early memories was tied to a child's developing communication skills: as children learned to talk about life events, and as parents and other adults helped them to shape their own auto-biographies, children moved out of the phase of 'infantile amnesia'. These researchers further argued that communication skills alone were not enough. Children begin to remember differently at the point where they learn the 'scaffolding' that holds a narrative in place, and start to understand the shape of narrative forms as they are socially constructed.[16] In other words, as you gain the language needed to talk about the past, and as you learn from your parents and others in your social sphere how to tell the story of your life, you retain memories differently. These findings seem particularly poignant for child survivors, who so often had no parent nearby from whom to learn the key skill of how to talk about events in the past, put them in sequence, make sense of them, and incorporate them into the life story. Many child survivors may also have had delayed language acquisition if they were isolated from adult contact (whether in hiding or in a camp or ghetto), or if they had to abandon their mother tongue and quickly begin to learn another language. If memory is fundamentally a social construction, and if child survivors were denied the social environment in which early memory is built, it is reasonable to posit that many may then have experienced a longer period of 'infantile amnesia' than average.[17] At the same time those memories they did possess, however fragmentary and dim, had a significant and lasting impact upon how they related the stories of their early lives.

All this helps us to understand that in the 1950s, when the West German restitution scheme first opened, psychiatrists, psychologists, and psychoanalysts were largely united in the belief that wartime persecutions could not cause a healthy individual lasting psychological harm. Healthy adults were thought to recover quickly from dangerous and frightening events, and children were thought to be unable to remember these at all. Mental health experts had not yet been presented with a compelling reason to question this stance – but the restitution process would change this. It is important to bear in mind here that restitution was indeed a *process*, both for survivors and for the experts who evaluated their claims, and it was one that could drag on for years. Starting from the assumption that there could be no causal link between a claimant's ongoing psychological symptoms and his or her war experiences, the physicians employed by the BEG tended to reject claims for psychological damage, insisting instead that emotionally unstable survivors must already have been unstable before the war. In turn, survivors appealed these rejected claims, and sought out the opinions of more understanding doctors. As this happened, a handful of keen-eyed doctors began to notice that survivors appeared to have a set of symptoms in common. Foremost among these was William Niederland, a German-born, New York-based psychiatrist and psychoanalyst, who found himself in the unique position of clinically observing more than 800 survivors who were applying for compensation via the BEG. He began to notice that the survivors he saw had a number of common symptoms: anxiety, chronic depressive states, sleep disturbances and nightmares, problems of memory and cognition, and physical manifestations such as muscle pains, digestive problems, and headaches. Niederland began to argue that these symptoms were evidence that survivors had endured 'trauma of such magnitude, severity and duration' that they had developed a syndrome that could be seen as a 'recognizable clinical entity', one he dubbed the 'survivor syndrome'.[18] Niederland's work proved to be ground-breaking not only with respect to the treatment of survivors, but in terms of the very conceptualization of psychic trauma.

Niederland's work staked out a territory that was not only different to received psychiatric wisdom, but sat in opposition to the stance of the psychiatrists appointed by the West German restitution authorities, who were by this point employing the traditional psychiatric perspective in order to reject an enormous number of claims. By the end of 1966, the authorities had rejected more than a third of applications from survivors, and this was after a large number of applicants took their rejected claims to a court of appeals: before this, the authorities had rejected more than half of the claims submitted.[19] They argued that symptoms such as chronic anxiety, nightmares, and psychosomatic pains were either congenital or were caused by unresolved incidences from childhood, or were perhaps due to an inability to adjust to post-war life – 'anything', as the historian Dagmar Herzog has written, 'but the persecutions or the camps themselves'.[20] Herzog argues that the authorities did not simply echo medical orthodoxy, but 'self-consciously used every rhetorical strategy at their disposal to refute their critics and justify their decisions'.[21] As a result, clear battle lines began to emerge between orthodox mental health experts (in Germany and elsewhere) and a vanguard of psychiatrists and psychoanalysts who were beginning to accept that surviving horrific events could indeed leave an individual with lasting psychic scars.[22]

These battle lines were political as well as professional. Restitution was tightly bound to the moral question of who was responsible for the lasting damage to bodies and minds caused by Nazi policies and practices. The West German authorities operated in a political and cultural climate in which reparations raised the bitter question of who should pay, literally, for the ongoing suffering of the Nazis' victims. As Herzog argues, they looked to blame applicants' symptoms on genetics, constitution, character, or environment. This was true for a wide swath of potential applicants, and not only for Jewish survivors: the 1956 BEG legislation allowed for compensation claims from all victims who had been persecuted for racial, religious, ideological, or political beliefs (principles that had originally been set out by the US military government during the period of West Germany's occupation), and on the question of compensation for ongoing psychological problems, non-Jewish survivors of concentration camps were as likely to find their claims rejected as were Jewish survivors. The process was influenced by Cold War politics, and by the memory of the war both in West Germany and in a number of other Western European states. It could be a harrowing, soul-crushing experience for claimants suffering from debilitating mental health issues, regardless of their backgrounds or the reasons behind their deportation and internment.[23]

As experts began to stake out territory on either side of the issue of trauma's aftermath, some found themselves fighting to prove, decisively, that horrific events could indeed produce lasting psychological disturbances in an otherwise healthy person. These experts found themselves calling into question Anna Freud and Sophie Dann's work, precisely because some of the psychiatrists employed by the BEG began using Freud and Dann's conclusions to reject the claims of child survivors. The German-born, US-based psychoanalyst Martin Wangh wrote of a mentally ill young woman who had been an infant survivor of Theresienstadt, not unlike Freud and Dann's Theresienstadt toddlers. In denying compensation to this young woman, the authorities' physician used Freud and Dann's work to argue that 'a permanent damage after the persecution is not supported by other findings. We know of Anna Freud's Theresienstadt children who were separated from their parents that their disturbances disappeared after a given time.' If the BEG's psychiatrists were willing to invoke Freud and Dann to deny compensation to child survivors, then it was natural that more sympathetic mental health experts began to question Freud and Dann's very findings. Indeed, Anna Freud herself wrote that she was shocked that her research had been used to support the rejection of child survivors' restitution claims, and remarked she was amazed that any expert could doubt that having been separated from family and interned in a concentration camp could have lasting adverse effects on a child.[24]

By the late 1960s, spurred on by the bitter politics of this debate, those experts of the vanguard changed their approach to the analysis and treatment of child survivors: they began to search for lasting signs of trauma. By this time their numbers were growing, their network was decidedly international, and they were increasingly willing to challenge traditional interpretations in their fields. By the time of the 1967 Congress of the International Psycho-Analytic Association, held in Copenhagen, participants were ready to agree broadly that the classical Freudian view of trauma did little to explain why Holocaust survivors' symptoms seemed so pronounced decades after the persecution.[25] This growing international community of psychiatrists and psychoanalysts were increasingly curious about the long-term, clinical symptoms experienced by some survivors, and the frequent delay in onset of these symptoms (seen by unconvinced psychiatrists as clear evidence that there could be no connection between war experiences and the later emergence of symptoms). They were also concerned about how such 'massive psychic trauma' (in the words of Henry Krystal, a key figure among the vanguard) might affect not only individuals but families.[26]

This led these experts to turn their sights towards both child survivors and children born to survivor parents after the war who themselves had no direct experience of wartime persecution. By the mid-1960s Vivian Rakoff and John Sigal, both researchers in the Psychiatry Department of Montreal's Jewish General Hospital, were puzzling over this issue. Montreal had a sizeable population of Holocaust survivors who had immigrated to Canada after the war, and because the city's hospitals were divided between the (French-language) Catholic and the (English-language) Jewish, the Jewish General Hospital was the first port of call for Jews in the city suffering from psychiatric problems. Rakoff and Sigal had been increasingly struck by how many children of concentration camp survivors had begun to come into the Family Psychiatric Department in need of help, noting that of the nearly 100 Jewish families seen in the unit over the period from 1964 to 1966, a quarter had been 'concentration camp families, a number quite out of proportion to their representation in the Jewish population of Montreal'.[27] The psychiatrists began to wonder whether it was not just survivors who suffered the after-effects of persecution trauma, but whether 'the family itself is a collection of severely disturbed and traumatized individuals'.[28] As psychiatrists working in clinical situations began to speculate that the harm caused by wartime persecution was not only lasting but was even lasting across the generations, psychoanalysts began to reach similar conclusions. More importantly for our purposes, they began to speculate that if children born after the war could be deeply, negatively affected by their parents' war experiences, then it was time to take a closer look at the experiences of children who had themselves lived through the persecutions of the war, even if they were too young to remember. At the Copenhagen congress of psychoanalysts, several experts presented cases of child survivors. The Israeli psychoanalyst H. Z. Winnik spoke of one of his patients, R., a university student born in 1938 in France, who had survived the war in hiding with a Christian family, and who had been returned to her survivor mother at the war's end, only to find that relationship strained and difficult. R.'s psychological problems had begun with the onset of puberty. Before this time, she had been a good student, but as she entered adolescence she became depressed, and developed learning difficulties and severe gastro-intestinal complaints; eventually she had dropped out of school. Winnik observed that three years of psychoanalysis had helped R. to re-enter education and had eased some of her intestinal complaints, but that while she 'managed to adapt herself to normal conditions of work and social demands', she remained afraid of a deeper intimacy in her relationships. Winnik concluded that many of R.'s symptoms corresponded to those found in 'the concentration camp syndrome', even though R. had passed the war years in relative safety and stability with a host family.[29]

Psychiatrists such as Rakoff and Sigal, and psychoanalysts such as Winnik, were interested in the long-term, inter-generational effects of persecution on the young adults who came to their clinics seeking help in the mid-1960s. However, one of their colleagues working in the Netherlands, the psychiatrist and psycho-analyst Hans Keilson, took an even more radical approach: he began to study child survivors in non-clinical settings, and to argue that the debilitating long-term effects of trauma could be found not in some child survivors, but rather in most child survivors, whether they sought treatment for their problems or not. In 1967 Keilson launched what was to become the first major longitudinal psychiatric study of child survivors of the Holocaust. Keilson, a German-born Jew, had qualified as a physician just after the Nazis came to power, and had fled his native Germany for the Netherlands, working as a doctor for the Dutch resistance during the war. Immediately after the war he lent his expertise to L'Esrat Ha-Yeled, a Dutch Jewish organization established to care for the Netherlands' orphaned Jewish child survivors, and he served as their consultant psychiatrist from the end of the war through to 1970. As a researcher he was thus in a unique position to study the long-term psychological issues faced by child survivors, for he had already spent many years working with the 3,500 child survivors who had been helped by L'Esrat Ha-Yeled and other Dutch aid organizations.[30]

In the summer of 1967 Keilson contacted a random sample of 200 of L'Esrat Ha-Yeled's former wards to ask them to participate in his follow-up study. Most agreed, although Keilson noted that even in 'the most positive cases' the grown children resumed contact with their former physician with 'hefty aggressive outbursts'. The children felt that they had been forgotten and ultimately abandoned by their former guardians. One responded to the request to participate by stating, 'You're too late. If only you'd come fifteen years earlier when I needed someone. I feel let down.'[31] As he spoke with the grown children of the Dutch aid organizations, Keilson began to hypothesize that if adult survivors widely suffered from the symptoms associated with 'concentration camp syndrome', then these symptoms would be all the more clearly evident in those who were pre-adolescent children during the war, because they had experienced the humiliation and terror of persecution at their very moment of 'biologically determined ego-weakness'.[32] He drew up a list of symptoms that mirrored that of William Niederland's 'survivors syndrome' (severe anxiety, chronic depression, and somatic symptoms such as headaches and digestive complaints), but also included what he called 'psycho-social' indications, such as divorce and under-performance in school. Then, working on the assumption that there would be no greater injury for a child than separation from the mother, Keilson classified children by the age they were separated from their mothers, and by the number of times that they had subsequently been separated from parental figures such as host parents, and concluded that these 'sequential traumas' of separation had had a particularly insidious effect on the young – and the younger a child had been at the time, the worse the effects. Keilson argued that it did not matter if a child had survived concentration camps or had spent the war in hiding: regardless of the nature of their wartime experiences, child survivors had failed to develop normally (where he defined 'normal development' as having 'no debilitating psycho-social deficiency problems').[33] He concluded that those separated from their mothers between the ages of eighteen months to four years had paid a particularly heavy psychological price, with less than 3 per cent experiencing 'normal development', according to the parameters of his study. Older children had fared somewhat better, he reasoned, but even here Keilson concluded that the vast majority – more than 80 per cent – had been permanently damaged by their war experiences.[34]

Keilson's work marked a clear refutation of the earlier stress on the resilience and adaptability of child survivors. Yet some of the criteria that he used in his assessment of what constituted 'normal' development spoke more to the social dislocations experienced by survivors than to psychological damage. In particular, in looking at indicators such as 'divorce', 'loss of employment', and 'discrepancy between intelligence and education' as indicators of lasting psychic harm, Keilson largely ignored the social contexts that had determined life choices for child survivors. Divorce and separation were becoming increasingly common in the late 1960s and early 1970s, as was job loss after the global economic downturn that followed the 1973 oil crisis – and Keilson did not compare his sample of child survivors to a control group. More troubling was the notion that the failure to pursue or to excel at education indicated a lasting psychic problem, because as we have seen, child survivors were regularly stymied in their quest to pursue better or higher education by their guardians, whether these were surviving parents, relatives, or aid organizations. There was certainly truth in Keilson's assessment that 'severe mental and emotional upsets can lead to an impairment of educational development', but the low expectations and limited educational horizons set out by children's guardians (including the Dutch aid organizations themselves) were never discussed in the study.[35]

Keilson launched his study in 1967, but did not conclude it until 1978, and over this period approaches to both the concept of psychic 'trauma' and the history of the Holocaust changed dramatically. Although the issue of the lasting effects of traumatic experiences was first honed by debates over restitution, the psychiatric literature on this topic only truly blossomed after the Vietnam War, when experts became fascinated by the symptoms of psychological harm that Vietnam veterans experienced months and even years after they had returned to the United States – and, perhaps more importantly, when psychiatrists and anti-war activists launched a large-scale political campaign to win compensation for Vietnam vets struggling with psychiatric complaints.[36] Throughout the 1970s a global network of psychiatrists and psychologists argued for a wholly redesigned conceptualization of 'trauma' and its after-effects, and set about categorizing a new understanding of its symptoms, new diagnostic tools, and new approaches to treatment. This fed into a broader, far-reaching rewriting of the *Diagnostic and Statistical Manual of Mental Disorders* (DSM), the key source used by clinicians to diagnose psychiatric illnesses, which stretched through the 1970s. When DSM-III was published in 1980, one of its most important innovations was the new official designation of Post-Traumatic Stress Disorder (PTSD). Many of the symptoms described by William Niederland in his study of adult Holocaust survivors, and set out again by Keilson in his study of child survivors, were included in the checklist of PTSD symptoms introduced in DSM-III. More importantly, the new designation set out that one of the key indicators of PTSD was the delayed onset of symptoms – an indicator that had caused so many of the BEG's psychiatrists to reject survivors' claims for compensation.[37]

At the same time, public awareness of the history of the Holocaust in many Western countries was changing. It is worth bearing in mind just how far this rising interest in the genocide affected the very experts who were trying to categorize its long-term (and even inter-generational) psychic legacies. When Freud and Dann published their study in 1951, as we have seen, there was little scholarly research on the Holocaust, and public knowledge was also limited. In order to understand what the Theresienstadt toddlers had been through in the camp, Anna Freud had asked her colleagues to introduce her to a few adult Theresienstadt survivors, and her own understanding of life in the camp was based on their stories.[38] By the time that Rakoff and Sigal were treating their young patients in Montreal, and Keilson was beginning his longitudinal study in the Netherlands, this situation had begun to change in earnest. Public understanding of the extent of the wartime persecution of Europe's Jews had grown following the 1961 trial of Adolf Eichmann in Jerusalem. The work of psychiatrists themselves had changed public consciousness of the lasting harm caused by the concentration camp experience, as terms such as 'survivor syndrome' crept into popular usage (at least in the English-language world).[39]

These changes left psychiatrists and psychoanalysts facing what seemed, at the time, like a riddle: if the symptoms of psychological trauma could last for years and even decades after an event, and if, as Keilson suggested, most child survivors exhibited these symptoms, why had mental health experts not noticed this until the 1960s? Experts were keen to see the problem as one of repression, rather than the result of changing historical and cultural contexts. Writing in 1982, the psychologist Martin Bergmann and the psychoanalyst Milton Jucovy argued that the decade after 1945 had been a 'period of latency' for Holocaust survivors, both child and adult, positing that this repression 'appeared to be a moderately healthy and adaptive way of dealing with the Holocaust', but one that was 'achieved only with massive denial and repression of the traumatic period'. They concluded that 'it is not surprising that, eventually, the intolerable memories of the past returned to haunt the survivor'.[40] The presumption that the 'repression' must necessarily lie with the patient, rather than with the expert, was not challenged for a remarkably long time. In the late 1960s the Polish-born, New York-based psychoanalyst Judith Kestenberg undertook a survey of several hundred colleagues, practising in six different countries, regarding their approach to the clinical treatment of child survivors and children of survivors. She was shocked by the response: the survey revealed that it had never occurred to most of her colleagues to draw parallels between a family's wartime persecution and a young person's later mental health problems. It was not that young patients did not want to talk about the Holocaust with their analysts, Kestenberg concluded, but rather the reverse: analysts did not want to discuss it with their patients. 'Child analysts are not immune to the universal idea that children are better off denying and repressing rather than facing fears of a reality that transcends childhood fantasies,' she wrote in 1982. 'The conspiracy of silence may well be shared by the survivor-parents and the psychoanalysts themselves.'[41] Kestenberg's study suggested an uncomfortable truth for experts: that the 'period of latency' had been their own adaptive way of dealing with the horror of the Holocaust, and not that of their patients.

As foundational notions of 'resilience' in the youngest survivors gave way to an insistence on wide-ranging, long-term, and even permanent psychological damage, how did child survivors themselves respond to these shifts? While the psychiatrists and psychoanalysts who called for a reconsideration of the long-term effects of traumatic experiences saw themselves as activists fighting on the side of survivors, survivors themselves did not necessarily welcome this activism. Adult and child survivors alike were often troubled by how far these experts insisted on pathology. They might have felt at times beset by anxieties, they might have struggled to deal with overwhelming memories, but they did not necessarily think of themselves as having debilitating symptoms. Moreover, many felt that they had devoted considerable energy, too much energy in fact, to demonstrating time and again to families, communities, and authorities that they were 'normal' (whether physically, psychologically, or morally). The sympathetic experts' emphasis on long-term damage threatened to destabilize this.

This helps us to understand how child survivors and mental health experts regarded each other in this critical period in the 1960s, 1970s, and early 1980s – and the two-way nature of this gaze is crucial, for experts and survivors deeply influenced each other in this period. As we have seen, experts' encounters with child survivors helped to alter their views on the nature of trauma itself. At the same time, for child survivors, their interactions and confrontations with experts on both sides of the 'trauma' argument began to lead some towards a reckoning with their own identities as survivors. In response to the scepticism of traditional psychiatrists, some child survivors insisted that they did indeed suffer from ongoing anxiety and depression, and that their early experiences had had serious negative effects on their lives. In response to the attentions of sympathetic experts, however, child survivors often felt compelled to stress that while anxieties and attachment issues did mark their adult lives, these problems were not so pronounced that they should be regarded as permanently, irreversibly damaged.

By the late 1970s, as mental health experts and child survivors increasingly sat down together to discuss these issues, such tensions and resentments found their way into the conversation. We can hear this when we listen to oral history interviews conducted at the time. The late 1970s and early 1980s marked a moment in which psychologists began to conduct interview projects with survivors in the hopes of learning more about the psychological legacies of survival, and several of these projects focused specifically on child survivors. The psychologists and psychoanalysts running these projects were convinced of the long-term reach of traumatic events, and as such, they trained the interviewers involved to ask about, and to listen for, signs of trauma disorders in the stories of the child survivors they interviewed. These projects reflected their leaders' preoccupation with the issue of long-term trauma – and at the same time they illustrated just how firmly child survivors themselves could push back against an agenda that seemed, to them, to pathologize their lived experience.

In 1982 Judith Kestenberg launched an interview-gathering project, the International Study of Organized Persecution of Children, which would eventually amass more than 1,500 interviews with adults who had survived the Holocaust as children. Aware from her earlier survey of colleagues that many psychoanalysts were avoiding the issue of a patient's childhood experience of persecution, Kestenberg saw the project as a chance to dig into the difficult issues that others were avoiding, and to do so outside of a clinical setting. She hoped to demonstrate, through these interviews, that child survivors suffered from lasting effects of their traumatic wartime experiences, even when they could not remember them. Kestenberg trained the project interviewers to ask about and to listen for symptoms of trauma disorder in her interviewees, hoping to pinpoint how the then current psychoanalytic scholarship mapped onto child survivors' experience. The survivors interviewed, however, were often wary of this agenda. Many were genuinely grateful that Kestenberg and her team had taken an interest in their lives, and some found themselves revealing elements of their life stories that they had kept hidden from their own parents, spouses, and children. They nonetheless found ways to make the interviewers aware that the litany of questions that probed too insistently for signs of trauma were not only irrelevant, but in some cases ridiculous.

Searching for delicate ways to assert themselves against the 'expert' interviewer, some used humour gently to chastize questioners who were overly keen on hunting for trauma. R.G. was born in Vilna, Poland, in 1937. She was sent with her parents into the Vilna ghetto, where her father died. Her mother then managed to smuggle her out, and she survived the war in hiding with a series of peasant families in the countryside. When Kestenberg interviewed her in August 1984, R.G. tolerated the interview process up to a point, but in the end began to use humour to chide Kestenberg over her questions, a checklist designed to search for symptoms that R.G. did not feel she had:

*Judith Kestenberg:* Do you have any aftermaths of the Holocaust [*sic*]? Do you have any sequelae of this? Do you have any anxieties or hang-ups that are connected with the Holocaust?

*R.G.:* Hang-ups, I don't know. We all have our hang-ups, right?

*J.K.:* How did you feel during your pregnancies? Did you have good pregnancies?

*R.G.:* Yeah, no problems.

*J.K.:* Good deliveries?

*R.G.:* Natural childbirth.

*J.K.:* Were you a very anxious mother?

*R.G.:* Anxious . . . well, I may have been a little bit over-protective with my first one.

*J.K.:* Do you sometimes go hungry without eating?

*R.G.:* No, no. I'm not obsessive about eating at all.

*J.K.:* You are pretty Orthodox, right?

*R.G.:* Well if you ask an Orthodox, I'm not Orthodox.

*J.K.:* But if you ask a conservative, you are, right?

*R.G.:* Well I have a kosher home, and I enjoy my religion. I would get terribly upset if my daughters came home with a non-Jew. As a matter of fact, I think I would be very, very, very upset, and I have told them that from the day they were born, and they tell me: 'Yes, we'll open the oven.' I say: 'That's right, the head goes right in there.'

*J.K.:* Whose head goes in there?

*R.G.:* Mine.

*J.K.:* Your head goes in there.

*R.G.:* That's right.

*J.K.:* When they bring a Gentile home, your head goes in the oven.

*R.G.:* Yes [laughs].[42]

R.G.'s sharp laugh signalled that she saw the irony in a Jewish survivor joking about putting herself into an oven. It took a moment longer, however, for Kestenberg to realize that the joke was on her: R.G. was determined to make it clear that, in searching for trauma symptoms, the psychoanalyst was looking in the wrong places.

The issue of memory frequently provoked interviewees' frustrations. Aware that many young child survivors could not remember their wartime experiences, and convinced that this was because of repression and not due to the natural process of infantile amnesia (just as Edith Ludowyk Gyomroi had assumed in treating 'Elizabeth' – like Gyomroi, Kestenberg was trained in psychoanalysis), Kestenberg and her team devised an interviewing technique that tried to use cues, and invited interviewees to use their imaginations, in an effort to recover 'lost' memories. However, interviewees often chafed at the presumption that their lack of memory was the symptom of a psychological problem. Here is an example from an interview with Gittel H., who had survived Theresienstadt as a toddler and had been less than three years old when liberated from the camp. The interviewer here was Milton Kestenberg, Judith Kestenberg's husband and a noted legal expert on restitution:

*Milton Kestenberg:* Do you remember any Nazis?

*Gittel H.:* No.

*M.K.:* With boots, high boots?

*G.H.:* No. I mean, now I've seen pictures.

*M.K.:* But you don't remember from childhood?

*G.H.:* No.

*M.K.:* Well, when you were in Theresienstadt, didn't you see the guards?

*G.H.:* I don't remember any of that.

*M.K.:* But do you remember boots?

*G.H.:* Boots? No.

*M.K.:* You don't remember any boots? Except from the movies?

*G.H.:* I just know what my grandmother told me.

*M.K.:* I'm trying to help you to recollect.

*G.H.:* I know what you're doing.[43]

Sarah Moskovitz, a psychologist who was one of the interviewers with the Kestenberg project, also conducted her own interview project around this time. Her focus was the children who had spent part of their childhoods in the Weir Courtney care home in Surrey, under the care of Alice Goldberger. Moskovitz carried out two dozen interviews with the former Weir Courtney children over a three-year period from 1977 to 1980, and her interviews capture the complexities of the relationship between psychologists and child survivors in this historical moment. Moskovitz launched her project in the hopes of probing the theory that childhood trauma is the cause of anti-social behaviour in adults. Her erstwhile interviewees were aware of this motive, however, and had reservations about lending their life stories to an effort to test a psychological theory. Some declined to participate, and others used the interview itself to express frustration with psychologists' probings. One of the first survivors that Moskovitz interviewed was Denny M., who had been five years old at the time of his liberation from Theresienstadt. When Moskovitz interviewed him in 1977, he was thirty-seven years old, and happy in his job as a secondary school music teacher. In the interview, he insisted that while he had been a troubled child, he had worked through many of these issues as a teen-ager, and felt normal as an adult:

> I was a very neurotic child, you must have heard. I think I caused distur-bances. I know I slept alone in a room, for several years, I'm not sure why, I had insomnia, it took me a long time to get to sleep; I kept toy guards at the door. I know I had an obsessional fear of death, I remember, when I was eight years old. But compared with so many messed-up adults that I've seen, I think I'm reasonably normal. I don't say I'm free from all anxiety, I certainly can feel things strongly, but it doesn't interfere with my functioning.[44]

In insisting on his own normality, Denny also turned the interview situation around to probe whether the psychologist did not have her own preconceived notions about the 'abnormality' of the Weir Courtney children:

> I sometimes wonder, did you half-expect me and the rest of us to be – somehow, did you, like some other people, feel, well, this person's been through this, he's been through that, he's had an institutional background, no family background – did you intuitively feel you'd meet someone perhaps a bit inarticulate, someone having some mental aberration ... Do [other people] expect us to be not quite right? We've had people from the clinic [Anna Freud's Child Guidance Clinic], for example, hanging around here at parties, and they don't speak to us. They just hang around and look at us, and you wonder what they're there for, what they're looking for.

Most importantly, however, Denny pointedly drew a parallel between the Nazi medical experiments that some of the Weir Courtney children had survived and the readiness of psychologists to continue to see the children as experi-mental test cases after the war. He recalled how disturbed he had been to read Freud and Dann's 1951 study when he was training to be a teacher:

1. Child survivors walk out of a children's barracks in Auschwitz-Birkenau at the liberation. Medical personnel recorded that there were more than 400 young children in the camp in late January 1945, most of them ill and malnourished; 40 per cent had tuberculosis.

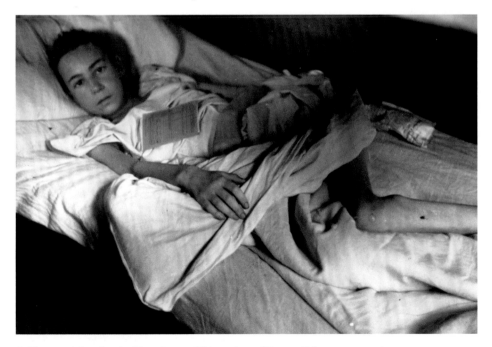

2. Three months after the liberation, a child survivor of Bergen-Belsen concentration camp recuperates in the hospital. When the British Army liberated the camp in April 1945, they found more than 700 children.

3. US troops discovered more than a thousand Jewish children when they liberated Buchenwald concentration camp. Four hundred and thirty of the 'Buchenwald boys' were sent to France for rehabilitation. Their chaperones wrote 'Buchenwald concentration camp orphans' on the side of the train, so that the boys – many of whom were wearing stolen Hitler Youth uniforms – would not be mistaken for captured Germans.

4. Joseph S., a four-year-old survivor of Buchenwald, sits on the footboard of an UNRRA lorry shortly after his liberation from the camp.

5. The 'Buchenwald boys' in their new home in France, a care facility run by the OSE at Taverny. Two of the youngest of the group, Izio R. and Jakob F., are lying at the front.

6. Unlike the 'Buchenwald boys', Joseph S. was reunited with his parents after the war. A year after the liberation, the family returned to Buchenwald for a memorial service, dressing Joseph in his too-small camp uniform.

7. August 1943: Felice Z. poses with Juliette Patoux, the woman who sheltered her during the war on her farm in La Caillaudière, near Vendoeuvres, France. 'I took it for granted that she was my mother,' Felice recalled.

8. June 1946: Judith K. with her foster sister Suzy Enard and another child, in Nay, Pyrénées-Atlantiques, France. Living in hiding with the Enard family 'was the greatest love affair of my life', Judith later recalled.

9. Felice Z. (front row, far left) in the OSE care home at Taverny, where she lived from 1947 to 1951. Beside her is her sister Beate Z., and at the back is her counsellor Hélène Ekhajser. When Felice and Beate were forced to leave Taverny to move to the United States, it was a rupture so painful that 'it was almost as if I broke', Felice remembered.

10. At an OSE reception centre at Les Glycines, France, Judith K. (wearing a hat) awaits onward migration to the United States. She will go on to live with an uncle and aunt she cannot recall, and her new family will ask her to break off all contact with the Enards.

11. Child survivors of Theresienstadt at the Calgarth Estate reception centre in Windermere. The children were part of a cohort of 300 young Theresienstadt survivors, mostly in their teens, who were brought to Britain for rehabilitation in August 1945. Litzi S. is third from left, and beside her is Zdenka H.

12. Alice Goldberger, who cared for the youngest Theresienstadt survivors first at Windermere, and then at a dedicated care home, Weir Courtney, in Lingfield, Surrey. They were later joined by other children who had survived Auschwitz or had spent the war in hiding.

13. Anna Freud, daughter of Sigmund Freud, founded the field of child psychoanalysis, and took a lifelong interest in the children under Alice Goldberger's care.

14. A painting by one of the Weir Courtney children, Hanka T., depicting a cosy domestic scene: a girl with her mother and brother setting a Sukkot table.

15. One of the Weir Courtney boys, Fritz F., painted this scene of soldiers shooting men against a wall, overseen by a Nazi officer. For Fritz, hidden in Budapest during the war, this was a product of imagination rather than memory, although other children at Weir Courtney may have witnessed similar events.

16. Child survivors from Eastern Europe who joined the Bricha after the war in the hopes of immigrating to Palestine. Some ended up interned in British detention centres on Cyprus.

17. A child survivor sits with his suitcases and a wrapper from a bar of Hershey's chocolate at a gathering point for the Bricha. Many children who joined the Bricha did not necessarily want to go to Palestine: they simply wanted to leave the DP camps of Europe as quickly as possible.

18. A campaign poster for the
Canadian Jewish Congress's 'War
Orphans Project', playing on the
widespread fear that child survivors
were being claimed – and baptised – by
Christian families after the war.

19. A fundraising poster used by the Central British Fund to raise money for their war orphans
scheme. The children featured were all under Alice Goldberger's care at Weir Courtney; Zdenka H. is
on the right.

20. Jackie Y. with his adoptive parents at his bar mitzvah.

22. Paulette S. as a young mother in Melbourne in 1967. 'Having two children so little and vulnerable caused my fears and anxieties to come to the surface,' she later wrote.

21. The Weir Courtney children as teenagers, nearly ten years after their arrival in Britain.

23. Ben Lappin, professor of social work at the University of Toronto, at his desk around the time that he wrote his study of the child survivors who had come to Canada with the CJC's war orphans scheme. The book was published in 1963.

24. Psychiatrist Hans Keilson, whose 1979 study of child survivors in the Netherlands was the first to argue that the majority had suffered lasting psychological harm from their wartime experiences.

25. Psychoanalyst Judith Kestenberg launched a ground-breaking interview project with child survivors in 1981, the International Study of Organized Persecution of Children. She was part of a network of mental health professionals who argued that the war had lasting traumatic consequences for these children.

26. Paulette S. on the hunt for her past. Here she poses in front of a monument while attending the International Gathering of Hidden Children in Jerusalem in 1993.

27. Jackie Y., about to have his life story recorded for the Association of Jewish Refugees' 'Refugee Voices' oral history project.

28. Agnes G. in 2018, protesting on-going issues of anti-Semitism in the UK. 'I now feel strongly that it's desperately important that people like me speak out,' she states.

You know, when I was preparing to teach, I came across a reference in a child development textbook to something called 'An experiment in group upbringing', by Anna Freud. It upset me. Did they keep us together as an experiment? Hadn't the Germans experimented on us enough?

Sarah Moskovitz's interviews with Denny and the other Weir Courtney children caused her profoundly to rethink her own assumptions about the long-term psychological impacts of traumatic childhood experiences, arguing in the conclusion of her book that '[life outcomes] are certainly not as bleak as the psychological, particularly the psychoanalytic, literature would have us believe, stressing as it does the absolute centrality of the early mother-child relationship'. If Moskovitz went into her interviews hunting for the long-term effects of trauma, she left them with a better understanding of just how far these grown children battled a stigmatizing everyday reality of constant encounters with people who imagined that they were abnormal. In her conclusions she criticized the 'pathology-seeking' of her fellow therapists:

Has our eagerness for scientific evaluation of functioning restricted our criteria for valuing human beings and led us unwittingly to judgments of superior and inferior, via assorted categories of normal and abnormal? [. . .] It is widely known that survivors overwhelmingly have avoided seeking help from any type of mental health professional. In the literature this has been largely accounted for by lack of trust and pathology on the part of the survivor, rarely to 'professional' attitudes of practitioners which . . . exacerbate fears of being once again stamped, categorized, and made to feel inferior.[45]

Moskovitz's conclusions signalled the extent to which the relationship between mental health experts and child survivors had transformed by the late 1970s and early 1980s. It was not merely that experts had re-envisaged the balance between resilience and trauma for survivors of genocide. Their close contact with child survivors via interview-gathering projects had begun to lay bare just how frustrated these grown children were to find that their life histories were sought, gathered, and analysed not for their human dimension, but to test psychological theories. Mental health experts' ongoing emphasis on psychopathologies, in the words of the journalist Helen Epstein, 'set Holocaust survivors apart from other, "normal" people, including the psychiatrists themselves' – and by the end of the 1970s, then entering middle age, some child survivors found themselves ready to push back against lists of symptoms and clinical terminology that seemed to place them permanently in the realm of 'war-damaged children'.[46]

# EIGHT

# THE LUCKY ONES

In 1966, when she was twenty-six years old, Zilla C. wrote a letter to the OSE staff who had rescued her during the war and cared for her afterwards. She had not been in touch with the agency since leaving their care in 1946, when she was reunited with her Auschwitz-survivor father in Germany. The agency staff asked if Zilla would let them know how things had gone for her since she had been reunited with her father, and she wrote them a letter that set out her story. She detailed the rootlessness of her childhood and adolescent years, explaining how her father had sent her and her brother to live with grandparents in the United States in 1950, and how her grandparents had then placed both children in foster care. She had stayed with her first foster family for a month. She was then placed in a children's home. After some time she went to live with another foster family. Then she was returned to the children's home for another three years. When she was sixteen, the children's home converted into a home for asthmatic children, and she was sent to live with a third foster family. As soon as she reached the legal age of majority, she left foster care as quickly as she could:

> I rented myself a room, and worked as a salesgirl in a ladies' clothing store, a job which I had had since the age of sixteen. Six months later, I married [my husband], who I had met in the children's home at the age of thirteen. I continued to work, as he was attending the graduate school of social work. Two years later, the twins were born, and a year and a half after that, the third boy came along. At present, I am 26 years old, the twins are five, and [the youngest] is four years old. [. . .] Out of a far from ideal childhood

179

comes relative normalcy, and you had a great deal to do with the fact that I am alive. May I, from the bottom of my heart, thank you.[1]

'Relative normalcy'. It was a much sought-after state for many child survivors as they entered adulthood and hoped to put turbulent childhoods and adolescent years behind them – or at least, this is what the rare documents from the time suggest. Child survivors have not, in fact, left much in the archives that can help us to understand how they were feeling in this period, or what meanings their pasts might have had for them as they grappled with starting families, establishing careers, and laying down the pathways that they hoped to follow into later life. We should not, perhaps, be surprised by the firmly positive tone of Zilla's letter, its sense of having succeeded in realizing the prize of a normal life: she clearly wanted to show her former carers that their help had paid off. We can speculate that her emotions might have been more complex under this cheery exterior, but archival documents from the time cannot prove this.

Zilla's later recollections, however, suggest a far more nuanced story of her transition from a turbulent adolescence to young motherhood to middle age. She reappears in the archival record in 1987, when she was forty-seven years old, and was interviewed by Judith Kestenberg for the International Study of Organized Persecution of Children oral history project. By this point, twenty-one years after Zilla had re-established contact with the OSE, we find a person who had firmly set aside the quest for 'relative normalcy' and had instead begun a probing exploration of just how her past marked her out as different from those around her. Her children had grown up, and she had divorced in 1968, only two years after writing her letter to the OSE. She recalled in her interview that she had married at nineteen, and had worked so hard to stake out a 'normal' life for herself that she had never discussed her past with her husband. Ultimately, however, her effort to bury the past could not be sustained. She thought then that she had married her husband primarily because 'he reminded me of my father, and I needed a father, but by the time I was twenty-seven, I no longer needed a father'. What she needed, instead, was to set aside the enormous effort of trying to look and act like everyone around her, although this took a long time:

Until the age of forty, I worked very hard at being normal, and by that I mean pretending that I was not really that different from other people, and at some point I realized that I really never was going to be exactly like other people. There was something there that made me different, or at least feel different.[2]

Zilla tried therapy after her divorce, which she found helpful, but she never discussed her childhood with her therapists. Then one day, in her early forties, she had a dream that moved her to look at her past in a different way:

One night I had this dream. In the middle of my back, between my shoulder blades, was this immense, red, festering wound, and it was in the shape of an official stamp, sort of a little bit long and fancy at the edges. And I knew in the dream that to heal this wound I had to open it. I can feel this in the dream. I take the top skin and slowly begin peeling it back, and inside was maybe an inch deep like a box, and it was filled with millions of little black bugs. What that said to me was that it's time to uncover your past, and that's when I decided that I'm going to do my work on the Holocaust.

She began a masters degree in art of the Holocaust, undaunted by her discovery that 'whenever I brought up the word Holocaust, that would end the conversation very quickly'. At the time of her interview in 1987, she was working towards a PhD in history.[3] Reflecting on her academic work, she observed that it was at once an intellectual undertaking and a journey 'back into my own history. [. . .] I had to [do it]. It was time. My children were grown, they were gone. I was finally alone, and it was time for me to deal with this, and so I did.'

It was not simply a shift in the course of her life, however, that brought Zilla to rethink her past: other changes were taking place around her. In 1982 she was working at the American Jewish Committee as a secretary. When the offices hosted a visit from renowned Nazi hunters Serge and Beate Klarsfeld, Zilla managed to borrow a copy of the not-yet-published English edition of Serge Klarsfeld's *Mémorial de la déportation des Juifs de France*, a painstakingly compiled list of the fates of all the Jews who had been deported from France.[4] Because her family (Zilla, her mother, father, and older brother Eric) had been deported from Germany to the internment camp at Gurs in 1940, she realized that Klarsfeld's work might contain some information on the fate of her mother, about whom she knew little:

> So I go to my desk, and I look at this book, and I start page-by-page. I get to transport number 33 and there . . . it's like discovering a tombstone. I couldn't believe my eyes. There are my parents, both parents together. Deported from Gurs to Auschwitz. When I saw that, I was in a catatonic state. It was as though all the blood drained out of my body. I just sat there, I couldn't believe it. [. . .] It was like everything was converging, it was so bizarre.

Zilla was not alone in sensing, by the late 1970s and early 1980s, that 'everything was converging'. Her trajectory, from a young adult seeking normalcy to a person in mid-life hungry to know more about her past, is a familiar one to many child survivors. This transformation was sparked, in part, by a natural progression in the life cycle: with children growing or grown and career choices established, child survivors had more time and energy to use for a reconsideration of their pasts. At the same time, public interest in the genocide was growing by the 1970s. What was the relationship between child survivors' mounting desire to learn more about their pasts as they entered middle age, and the shifting interests of the world around them?

In asking this question, we are really asking where the points of convergence lie between memory in the individual and that phenomenon generally termed 'collective memory'. At a historical moment in which child survivors were turning the beam of their attention to the history of the Holocaust, the world around them was doing the same. It is tempting to imagine that child survivors were simply mirroring changes that were happening in their societies broadly, but in fact there was no easy or direct causal relationship between shifts in 'collective memory' and child survivors' search for a clearer perspective on the events that had engulfed their families. As the past takes on different roles and representations in politics and culture, individuals respond to these changes, but not in predictable ways. The catalysts that bring an individual into a new relationship with her past are as likely to happen in the intimate world of the family as they are in the wider world of community and society.

Historians who study the 'collective memory' of the Holocaust (by which they generally mean public understanding of and interest in the genocide) have debated for many years what events caused this 'memory' to grow. Some have privileged political, geopolitical, and legal events, linking the growth of interest to the 1961 trial of Adolf Eichmann in Jerusalem to the 1967 Six-Day War and the 1973 Yom Kippur War, to the expansion of Holocaust denial in the 1970s and the collapse of Cold War political structures in the 1990s.[5] In stressing the instrumental role of political events, historians were responding to other scholars – chiefly literary scholars and psychoanalysts – who instead emphasized the centrality of the individual's 'working through' the past, a slow-burn process that these scholars linked to the notions of trauma and repression (and often framed as independent of historical context). From this perspective, the timeline of 'Holocaust memory' looked different: key developments took place far earlier, and individual diarists and memoirists had a greater role to play in shaping a broad collective understanding. The publication of Anne Frank's diary in 1952 (adapted for film in 1959), and the flurry of memoirs published in the mid-to-late 1950s (such as Ka-Tzetnik's *House of Dolls*, which became a best-selling book in the United States in 1955, Elie Wiesel's *La Nuit*, published in France in 1958, or Primo Levi's *Se questo è un uomo*, published for a mass market in Italy in the same year – to mention only a few), were all key events in this rubric.[6] This literature then expanded exponentially from the 1970s onwards. By that time, Holocaust-focused films and television shows, such as the American television miniseries *Holocaust*, which was broadcast in the US in 1978 and in several European countries in 1979, had begun to attract enormous audiences.[7]

If these cultural milestones drove 'memory' for a broad public that had no direct experience of the Holocaust, we might ask how far they shaped remembrance for survivors. How can we understand the relationship between political and cultural episodes, and the intimate world of remembrance in an individual, or a family, or a small circle of friends? For child survivors who had lived through the Holocaust but who could not necessarily remember it, just how important were these trials, these conflicts, these memoirs, these television dramas? If we accept that such events were central both to collective 'memory' and to individual remembrance, we would expect to find that child survivors, often aching to learn more about their pasts, might have responded to them particularly strongly. This does not appear to have been the case, however. When child survivors recalled the moments in their adult lives that brought them into new relationships with their pasts, they rarely mentioned these political incidents and cultural products. The impetus was often far more pedestrian and universal: marriage, the birth of children, divorce, or the death of parents.[8]

This is not to say that child survivors were unaffected by the growth of public interest in the Holocaust. As with Zilla, many returned to thinking about their pasts once the busiest years of child-rearing were over, and it helped that by this time others were beginning to take an interest in their stories. Child survivors did not always welcome the attentions of the psychologists and psychoanalysts who began to ask to study them in the 1970s and 1980s, but welcome or not, this outside interest demanded a response. Those who had spent years quietly changing the subject when asked about their pasts began to find that a willing audience called for a coherent story. Yet many child survivors still did not know very basic details about their own childhoods. How, then, could they tell their life histories to the experts who suddenly wanted to listen?

It was not, moreover, simply a growing Holocaust consciousness that spurred outsiders to want to listen to child survivors' stories. Other aspects of the zeitgeist had shifted by the later decades of the twentieth century. By the 1980s, Western societies were beginning to think about children and childhood experiences in dramatically different ways. Children's voices and stories (as well as their authority as witnesses) entered the legal world in new ways as children began to give courtroom testimony.[9] The concept that children had a specific set of rights was embraced by the United Nations, which adopted the Convention on the Rights of the Child in 1989.[10] Child developmental psychologists began to reconsider the process of memory in very young children in the 1980s, demonstrating that toddlers and even infants were capable of long-term memory, and working to understand why these early memories eventually become inaccessible.[11] All this meant that, by the 1980s, the value of children as witnesses and as agents of memory was taken increasingly seriously, with implications for those who were beginning to think about how they might bear witness to their childhood experience of genocide. Moreover, after the mass social movements of the late 1960s, the very act of speaking out carried a different resonance, as did the idea that those whose voices had traditionally been marginalized in the public sphere deserved to be heard.[12] This new imperative to speak combined with the expanding notion, informed by humanistic psychology, that it was healthy, therapeutic, and positive to voice emotions openly and publicly.[13] These factors could not help but influence child survivors, who found, by this time, that there were not only richer opportunities to explore their pasts in this new context, but different ways to speak about it, and far more ears willing to listen.

The 'memory turn' of the 1970s and 1980s brought child survivors frequent reminders of their past that made thinking about it difficult to avoid. What then of the period before? Historians have worked hard, in recent years, to challenge the supposition that there was a 'silence' on the Holocaust in Western countries before the 1970s. This is a complex issue. In care homes, in families, in humanitarian work, and in communities, we have encountered those who wished to turn away from the genocide in this period, but we have equally encountered those who refused to do so, from agency workers who talked honestly about the past with the children in their care, through to teenaged survivors who challenged silences in their own families. As they moved into adulthood, however, it became harder to maintain this questioning spirit. As we saw in Zilla's letter to the OSE, the moment of young parenthood and of early adult life demanded a different approach to the past. In the 1950s and 1960s many child survivors were eager to present their lives as settled, productive, and calm. To new spouses, new work colleagues, and new neighbours, but also to former carers, child survivors presented their successful integration into 'normal' life as proof not only that they had adapted well, but that the efforts made on their behalf had been good investments – in short, that they had been worth rescuing.

The agencies themselves played a role in this. In the late 1950s, the Canadian Jewish Congress decided to do a follow-up study of the 'war orphans' it had brought to Canada a decade earlier. The CJC was eager to show that its 'children' had embarked upon productive adult lives, which, it felt, would illustrate the ultimate success of its programme. It commissioned Dr Ben Lappin, a long-time CJC member and professor of social work at the University of Toronto, to undertake the study, and Lappin set about trying to track down the more than 1,115 survivors who had come to Canada on the scheme.[14] It quickly became apparent, however, that the young adults who had once been under the agency's care had deliberately removed themselves from its view. Few had remained in the communities where they had been placed under the scheme. Those who had moved had often left no indication of where they were going next. Many had changed their names, adopting anglicized versions of first names, and altering the spelling of family names. When it became clear that the CJC could be of minimal help to Lappin in tracking down its former wards, he placed advertisements in all the Yiddish and Anglo-Jewish newspapers in Canada, hoping to find the children in this way. He received only two replies from former orphans themselves, although he got several responses from spouses of the orphans, who had urged their partners to contact Lappin. However, the former CJC wards 'either kept putting off a reply, or could not work up enough energy to bother responding to the announcement'.[15] They were clearly not keen on the agency tracking them down.

Enlisting the aid of spouses and other relatives, Lappin managed to secure the up-to-date addresses of 237 of the CJC orphans, and he sent them each a questionnaire.[16] The questionnaires, which Lappin designed, asked if the orphans were married and had children, how they would describe their financial circumstances, whether they had been placed in 'free' or 'paid' homes under the scheme, how they would describe their experiences with their foster families and with the agency, whether they were active in their communities, and whether they still participated in Jewish religious life.[17] Given the questionnaire's emphasis on social integration and financial independence, it is perhaps not surprising that only 131 of the 'orphans' felt moved to fill it in. As Lappin himself observed, responses tended to come from a very specific group: those who had most clearly 'succeeded' in terms of economic and social status. These respondents were those who, in Lappin's words, had 'gone on to distinguish themselves': they had gone into the liberal professions, or had founded successful businesses. Lappin also took marriage to be a marker of success, noting with satisfaction that most of the male respondents were married, and all the women were married bar one. The men were all employed, and the women were all housewives (with the exception of the sole single woman, who was a teacher). The children, in their early adult lives, seemed to have fit comfortably into the norms of Canadian society in the 1950s. Lappin concluded that the chief measure of the programme's success was simply that almost all of the children were now living independently, and 'protracted independence in the modern, urban community is not a hit-and-miss affair, but calls forth initiative and brings into sustained play social skills and efficiency of a high order'.[18]

If independence from the agency was the measure of the programme's success, then Ben Lappin's respondents were indeed a highly successful bunch. Yet reading between the lines of their responses, one can detect a discomfort, a tension between the need to set out a picture of a settled, normal life, and a deeper sense that something was amiss. One respondent, when asked to sum up how his life was going, said that he felt he had no right to complain: 'Look at what I started out hoping for twelve years ago and look at what I'm beefing about now. I'm happy alright.'[19] Such assurances suggest that the opposite was in fact true. The CJC was pleased with the results of Lappin's study, and excited by the media buzz that surrounded the publication of his book-length study of the 'war orphans' in 1963, *The Redeemed Children*. Articles appeared in most of Canada's daily papers, and *Maclean's*, the country's pre-eminent weekly news magazine, praised the CJC's work as 'one of the greatest humanitarian acts of the twentieth century'.[20] Yet CJC leaders knew that, beneath the veneer of comfortable success, there was a restlessness. Some of the 'orphans' were desperate to learn more about their pasts, and they wanted to do so quietly. The W. brothers, who were born in Belgium, survived the war in hiding, and had lost their entire family, were desperately searching for information about their pasts by the early 1960s. They recalled that they had had an older sister, but had last seen her when they were younger than five, and could not remember her name. They asked the agency to help them find any remaining relatives, but begged their former carers to keep the search a secret. In particular, they did not want their adoptive parents to find out that they wished to learn more about their lost family, even though the two 'boys' were by then in their mid-twenties.[21] The tension between wanting to know, and wanting to present their lives as happy endings to turbulent beginnings, shaped many child survivors' approach to the past as they moved into adulthood.

In the sweep of time through the 1950s and 1960s, there were moments in which the past interceded sharply in the daily lives of child survivors, but these tended to coalesce around the milestones that marked new life stages, such as engagement and marriage. We have seen how the process of applying to marry in a synagogue proved explosive for Jackie Y., as the need to prove he was Jewish meant he learned, for the first time, that he had been in a concentration camp. He was not alone in this; others shared the infuriating experience of trying to prove, to Jewish communal authorities, that they were indeed Jewish, and found themselves struggling to do so. Esther T., who was aware that she had been in Auschwitz as a child but knew few details, either of how her parents had died or how she herself had survived, encountered a similar scenario when she wanted to marry her Orthodox husband:

> When I was going to get married [the synagogue authorities] asked me all
> this rubbish. 'Where are your parents?' they asked. And that made a problem

to get married properly. You see, you have to have your parents' birth certificate to get married in a shul, and we didn't have it. Don't laugh, you have to prove you're Jewish to get married in a shul, and I couldn't prove it![22]

It is telling that Esther asked her interviewer not to laugh here, for both speaker and listener were aware that the scenario of an Auschwitz survivor struggling to convince some small-minded synagogue authorities that she was Jewish was somewhere between the tragic and the ridiculous. Yet Esther's remarks suggest that marriage could also raise broader questions about identity for child survivors. Sometimes the question was one of religious identity. Survivors who had been raised in care homes, even if these homes had been Jewish, worried that they would not properly understand the running of a religious Jewish household, and that their lack of understanding would expose them as imposters.[23] Sometimes the identity issues were more fundamental. How much could they tell their spouses of who they really were? Would revealing the truth lead to rejection? How far could the past be allowed to enter into the new household? Some reasoned that silence was the best defence against such dangers. Lea R., who spent the war years hidden in the French countryside and who lost her entire family, put this succinctly to an interviewer:

*Interviewer:* Have you ever spoken of your experience?
*Lea R.:* No, not even to my husband.
*Int.:* Why is that?
*L.R.:* Just can't.
*Int.:* Have people asked you about your war experience?
*L.R.:* Yes, and I just say that I lived in France.
*Int.:* Is it because it's so hurtful?
*L.R.:* Yes.[24]

There were perils in speaking about the past to spouses who did not share the experience, and even perils in choosing a spouse. Agnes G., who had survived the war as an infant in Hungary and immigrated with her surviving parents to

England shortly after the war, lost her father to suicide when she was ten years old. This left their household with little money, and locked her into what she called a 'close, claustrophobic' relationship with her mother. She married in 1968, but she felt that the loss of her father had a troubling impact on her choice of partner:

> I was married to a difficult man who had a bad temper and shouted and swore a lot, but because I'd grown up in an environment without a man, with no extended family, although I was well educated, I didn't really know much about men. I assumed that this was how men behaved. By the time I realised that most men didn't behave like that, I had three little boys. [. . .] Because I'd grown up without a father, I felt that the boys in particular needed a father, so I stayed in the marriage longer than I should have.[25]

Decades later, when their marriage was ending, Agnes recalled that one of her husband's parting comments was to accuse her of being 'obsessed with the Holocaust. But he had no idea how it felt for me.'

Jacques F., who had been hidden by the OSE in France during the war and had lived in Taverny before being brought to the US by adoptive parents, similarly found himself in a marriage where he did not feel he could speak of his past. He had married in 1964, and had had a daughter and a son. At the time of his divorce in 1974, he had started to feel a growing need to know more about his past, but 'although I had started to think about it, [my wife and I] really didn't discuss it that much'. The end of a marriage in which his past could not be discussed freed Jacques to give a deeper consideration to his early life. 'That's when I got more into dealing with [the question of] where am I going? By then, I was just about forty years old, and that's a natural time for the mid-life crisis to happen. Forgetting my background, that's going to be true of many people.'[26]

If marriage complicated a child survivor's relationship with her own history, having children could do the same. As they welcomed the birth of daughters and sons, many found themselves consumed with thoughts of the lost mothers and fathers who had once welcomed them. Some were beset by anxieties that,

190

because they had not been cared for by their own parents, they would not know how to parent in turn. Some worries arose not when children were born, but as they grew. How much should they be told, and when? Many found that memories of the past rose up around the time that their children turned the age they themselves had been when they last saw their own murdered parent or parents. Paulette S. recalled that when her daughter turned four:

> That was the age I was when my mother left me. Every time I picked [my daughter] up, I felt how upset my mother must have been when I was her age, and not knowing what was going to happen to me. It reached the point when I couldn't pick her up at all. I couldn't kiss or touch her. It seemed completely beyond my control to fight these feelings. I bought her books, games, anything she needed, but I could not play with her.[27]

After having interviewed a group of child survivors in the late 1970s, the psychologist Sarah Moskovitz wrote that, for her interviewees, the birth of children was redemptive: 'Each birth in the new generation symbolically replaces the lives destroyed and speaks to the dead, as if promising them: neither your seed nor your name nor your line has been destroyed. Naming a child after the dead parent is a symbolic resurrection.'[28] Yet the situation was rarely so emotionally straightforward. The birth of children could awaken latent fears, provoke nightmares, and remind new parents of the lives destroyed as much as it symbolically replicated them. Nor was naming a child after a dead parent a cathartic 'resurrection' alone: it could also be a way for young survivor parents to stake a claim to a part of their own identities, in opposition to the desires of those around them. It was an act that often contested the silence in families as much as it acknowledged the lost mother or father.

We last saw Peter B. as he left his violent and abusive mother and ran away from home at the age of fourteen. When his first child was born, he felt compelled to name the baby boy Eric, after his father. His father, however, had not been killed in the war; instead, he had abandoned his wife and son and fled to Shanghai, while Peter and his mother were deported to Theresienstadt. Peter's decision to name his son after the father who had abandoned him was not a tribute to a parent who had disappeared (Peter had never seen his father again): it was an act of rebellion against his survivor mother. He recalled:

[The name] 'Eric', I realized at the time, would probably alienate my mother. Because she obviously didn't have much love for my father for what he did, or what I perceive he did, which was to abandon us. That's right. So I'm sure that all the hate and all the anger that was in her was directed at him.[29]

In Jackie Y.'s story, we can also see the ways in which the act of naming a child combined a tribute to a dead parent, an act of rebellion against a living parent, and an assertion of identity on the part of the child survivor parent himself. When his first child was born, Jackie wanted to name her after his dead mother Elsa, but his adoptive parents objected, and he acquiesced. When his second daughter was born two years later, however, he was less willing to back down:

This time I told my parents of my intentions; after all, I was a married man with responsibilities. Surely I could do what I wanted. To put it in a nutshell, they objected very strongly, and so I complied with their wishes to a degree. My wife and I chose the name Elisa instead of Elsa, and a second name, Gabi. But when I went to register the birth, I added the name Elsa to the other two names. Now she would be called Elisa Gabi Elsa.[30]

The emotions Jackie was working through at this moment in his life are captured succinctly in this episode, as his need to explore his past rubbed up against his adoptive parents' desire to block it out. That his daughter ended up with two nearly identical names suggests how charged was the tension between Jackie's desire to avoid hurting his adoptive parents and his need to reclaim his past. 'It was my adopted parents' attitude of never understanding me that re-kindled an enormous surge to know more about my background,' he recalled.[31]

The death of a parent (biological or adoptive) could spark a reckoning with the past just as the birth of a child could. It might provoke many sentiments all at once: a dual mourning for the parent who had recently died and for the one (or ones) who had been murdered in the war; a sense that an obstacle to remembering had been removed together with a feeling that remembrance became a burden that then fell largely on the shoulders of the child survivor. This in turn could affect a child survivor's relationship with her or his growing children, and raised the question of just how far the past should enter the family home. Saul A., who survived the Krakow ghetto, life in hiding, and Theresienstadt, recalled that he chose to shield his children from the truth about his childhood, but no longer felt he could continue in silence after his survivor father died:

> I never talked about [my past]. It was too difficult for me to even think about it. From the time I decided to forget about it so that these nightmares would go away, I really pushed it out of the way. What brought it back was, first of all, my father's passing. I guess subconsciously I felt that he was carrying that burden of thinking about it, and telling people about it.[32]

By the time that public interest in the Holocaust began to flourish in the 1970s and 1980s, child survivors had sometimes spent decades caught between the desire to know more about their early years, and the hope of achieving 'relative normalcy'. They had worried about how far to bring their pasts into their marriages and family homes, how much to say to their children as they grew, and how far to assume an additional burden of remembering when parents passed away. As they reached middle age, some began to search for information about their pasts with focused intention. Some undertook an 'internal' soul-searching, hoping to mine their own memories for overlooked details that would help to flesh out the story of their early years. Some conducted an 'external' search, travelling back to the places where they had been born or had spent time during the war. Others took an academic approach, reading the expanding academic literature on the Holocaust to help them understand what had happened to their families. In practical ways, they were better placed to undertake these journeys (metaphorical, intellectual, and literal) than they had been earlier. In middle age, the busyness of their early adult lives was settling. Those who chose to travel in search of information found they had the financial resources to do so (and, by the 1970s and 1980s, international travel had become more affordable). For those originally from Eastern Europe, the slow thawing of the Cold War meant both that previously difficult travel became possible, and also that documents from formerly closed archival collections started to become more easily accessible to private researchers. The search to uncover the past thus became possible in a way that it had not been before.

The idea of the 'internal' search was fed in part by a sea change that was unfolding in the realm of popular psychology in the 1980s, buoyed by a number of best-selling books by authors who claimed to have 'recovered' memories of childhood sexual abuse via therapy that used procedures such as hypnosis and guided imagery. If scholars of psychology looked at this development with both scorn and alarm, this did not stop many practising therapists, members of the legal community, and a broad public from embracing the notion of 'recovered memories', and an expanding number of clinical therapists offered such techniques. We have already seen that some therapists believed that adults who had survived the genocide as young children had repressed their memories, rather than lost them to 'infantile amnesia' – which of course suggested the possibility of their recovery. Some child survivors thus turned to hypnosis to try to fill the holes in their early stories (generally without success).[33] Despite the fact that many experts recognized that these methods led therapists to have undue influence over their patients' memories, 'recovered memory' therapy became both a mainstream practice by the late 1980s and a cultural phenomenon, as the hunger for popular books such as Ellen Bass and Laura Davis's *The Courage to Heal: A Guide for Women Survivors of Child Sexual Abuse* (1988) grew.[34] By the early 1990s, these ideas were being systematically challenged: pressure groups such as the False Memory Syndrome Foundation, created in 1992 by a group of mental health professionals and accused parents, had begun an assertive push-back against the suggestive therapy techniques of the 'recovered memory' movement, and researchers such as the psychologist Elizabeth Loftus were beginning to demonstrate through laboratory work just how easy it was to induce witnesses to misremember events. But for a period in the mid-to-late 1980s the notion of 'recovered memory' held considerable sway in the public imagination, chiefly in the United States, but tangibly in other Western countries as well.[35]

Jacques F. was among those who tried hypnosis in an attempt to piece together elements of his past that danced beyond the reach of his conscious mind. It did not work. When interviewed in 1983, he voiced his frustration that, with the failure of the hypnosis, he had few ideas left about how he could fill in the gaps in his life story, gaps that he found it increasingly difficult to bear:

> I was born in '38, and all I know, from papers that I have, is that my mother was deported in '41 and my father died in '43. I really don't know the mechanics of how I was saved, except through talking to [other child survivors] that most likely the OSE people helped me to find a [wartime host] family. I have forgotten that family's name completely, but I think the name was Bocahut, something like that – it sticks in my mind. I had a sister too, I'm virtually posi-tive that she's my natural sister, but . . . I'm never positive, really, absolutely positive of anything, you know. I don't have anybody to prove it, to show it.[36]

Some preferred to take the notion of a search literally. Around the same time that Jacques was trying hypnosis, Gittel H. decided to travel back to Germany to try to fill in the gaps in her childhood story. She wrote to everyone she could think of who might know anything about her parents, or about her as a child, and made arrangements to meet them. She was unnerved, however, by how unforthcoming some of these contacts were when she showed up in person. She recalled being shocked when one of the families she was supposed to meet refused to see her:

> I was supposed to visit with [a lady who had once clandestinely provided Gittel's mother with milk]. She didn't call. Then I called her, and I had trouble connecting. Finally her daughter answered the mother's phone, and she said that her mother had a cold, and wasn't feeling well. I said, 'I made

some presents for you.' And she said, 'Give them to somebody else, I don't have time,' and she slammed the phone down on me. And there's been no communication with them since, and I don't know why. It bothers me, but there's nothing I can do about it.[37]

The trip left Gittel with much the same feeling that Jacques had described: although she had been given 'a bunch of documents' on the trip to Germany, she still did not know 'what version is true, if any of it is true at all'.[38]

Rather than searching for clues to their own individual pasts, some child survivors took advantage of the growing public interest in the Holocaust to educate themselves about the genocide, in the hopes of placing their family histories within the broader history of the destruction of their native communities. We saw this with Zilla C. Like Zilla, Suzanne N. began to read voraciously about the genocide when she could no longer bear to know so little about the process that had led to her parents' murders:

> As I started learning about the concentration camps through books, movies, newspapers, whatever I could get my hands on, I began to realise that this was where my parents had ended up. That was a very difficult thing for me to absorb, that two of those bodies could have been my mother and father, two of those skeletons, bones. My children certainly learned about that at an early age, about how I felt, because I would sit and cry, and they would crawl up on my lap and ask 'mommy, what's the matter?', and I would tell them what happened to their grandparents.[39]

Whether they took to reading about the Holocaust, or travelled in search of information, or simply explored the spaces within their own minds, as child survivors began to confront the gaps in their life stories, they began to question that well-worn trope that suggested they were 'lucky' to have survived. Psychoanalysts Martin Bergmann and Milton Jucovy, in their 1982 study of child survivors and children of survivors, wrote of a female patient who had been smuggled out of the Warsaw ghetto as a child, and placed with a Catholic host family. Her parents were murdered, but she was later reclaimed by an aunt. The psychoanalysts described how, after extensive therapy and the death of the aunt in question, the patient's sense of herself as lucky began to break down. They quoted her:

> For years I claimed in a big way that I did not suffer from the war, that I was a privileged child in the ghetto (which is true, privileged to have survived, if this is a privilege). I was lucky to have been much loved by my mother and aunt who raised me and still another aunt. Then this whole defensive edifice gave way little by little. The much-loved child really suffered a succession of abandonments. My aunt saved me by taking me out of the ghetto and then when I was ten she abandoned me by leaving for Israel. It was just revenge, for I had survived her daughter and her sister. The privilege is a heavy burden to bear.[40]

It is interesting to note how Bergmann and Jucovy, writing from a moment of profound change for child survivors in the early 1980s, accounted for the waning of this idea that children who survived the Holocaust were among the 'lucky ones'. From their perspective, this concept was a protective structure that child survivors had built around and for themselves, one that 'could only be achieved with massive denial and repression'.[41] It is not surprising, they argued, that these repressed thoughts returned eventually, and the structure crumbled. What the therapists could not see was just how far the world around them was changing, nor how deeply the idea of being 'lucky' was much more than a protective myth that child survivors had built to ward off traumatic thoughts. It was, instead, a narrative that had been created by the social world that surrounded child survivors: the parents, relatives, care workers, and others who had sometimes used that myth to assuage a distressed child, but had equally wielded it to dismiss her fears and her experiences. Now those children were entering middle age, and those adult carers were beginning to pass away. The suggestion that child survivors had been the 'lucky ones' was not a protective talisman that was crumbling under the weight of repressed memories. It was a social construct created in a particular historical context, and that context was coming to an end.

NINE

# BECOMING SURVIVORS

Throughout his childhood and young adult years, and well into adulthood, Harry M. was not sure if he was a survivor. Born in Berlin in 1937, Harry's family – himself, his parents, and two older siblings – left Germany for Antwerp shortly before Kristallnacht, tipped off about the coming destruction by a police officer. In the early years of the war they moved between different Belgian cities, and in 1942 the entire family went into hiding: the parents in a seemingly abandoned flat, and the children with different rescue families and in children's homes. At the age of five, Harry was hidden with the Vanderlindens, a family who sheltered him until the end of the Nazi occupation of Belgium in September 1944. His parents and older siblings also survived, but many members of his extended family were killed.

So were they 'survivors'? Harry felt uncertain, but his older siblings were clear that the answer was no. Harry recalled his sister saying that nothing of import had happened to the family: they had not been caught, and had not starved. 'For a long time,' he remembered, 'that was my view of things: other people were caught, arrested and sent to horrible camps, but we didn't go through any of that.'[1] His family tended not to talk about their war experiences, and Harry felt a particular disconnect with his past, because while his older brother and sister could remember the period in hiding, he could not.

Yet as he grew older, Harry began to feel that his relationship to the past was far more complex, and far more troubled, than his family's narrative conceded. As an undergraduate at the University of Washington in the late 1950s (the family had immigrated to the United States in 1950), Harry began reading what books he could find on the concentration camps, curious to learn more about the genocide that had entangled his childhood. He began to find that he could not talk about his childhood without crying. He tried therapy, but did not have a positive experience; he vividly recalled visiting a psychiatrist in Seattle when he was in his late twenties, who shocked him by suddenly yelling, 'You think you're special, don't you? You think you're special because you think you're lucky.'

Was he lucky – lucky not only to have escaped death, but also to have avoided being a 'survivor'? 'I must say,' he later recalled, 'that all this time I wasn't feeling like a survivor. Those who were in Eastern Europe and were in ghettos and camps, they felt like survivors.' Things were slowly changing, however, not merely around him, but within his family as well. In 1981 Harry's older sister, who had long maintained that nothing of note had happened to the family during the war, attended the first World Gathering of Jewish Holocaust Survivors in Jerusalem. When he asked her why she had attended, his probing 'put her on the defensive', and he began to see that cracks were appearing in the family's story of a relatively benign and fortunate wartime experience. Two years later, Harry learned that a similar event would take place in Washington DC, the first American Gathering of Jewish Holocaust Survivors (hereafter the Gathering), an event that would turn out to be the largest gathering of survivors of the Holocaust that would ever take place. Timed to coincide with the fortieth anniversary of the Warsaw Ghetto Uprising, the event attracted a staggering 16,000 survivors and their families, including roughly 2,400 child survivors.[2] By this point, Harry was married with a child, and living in the Washington DC area. He decided to attend, although he was not sure that he really belonged at a gathering of survivors. He certainly could not have predicted that the event would provide him with a manner of emotional catharsis. He had spent decades trying to convince himself that nothing significant had happened to him during the war. He did not understand why he could not speak about his childhood without crying. Thus he went to the conference uncertain of whether he had any right to be there – but he found that, once there, something remarkable happened. At the time, Ronald Reagan was president of the United States, and he was scheduled to give an address at the Gathering. Harry was not a fan of Reagan's politics. Yet when the president took to the stage at the Gathering to address the tens of thousands of survivors in attendance, Harry 'broke out weeping. It was a recognition of my experience, a validation,' he recalled.

As Harry M. struggled with the issue of whether or not his experiences counted as survival, other child survivors were asking similar questions – and as they did so, they probed the limits of the very notion of who was a 'Holocaust survivor'. It was not a static concept. Its meaning and use had changed radically in the years before the 1980s, and would change even more dramatically from the 1990s onwards. Indeed, although I have used the term 'child survivor' throughout this book, it is important to point out that, in discussing the period before the 1980s, this is anachronistic: no one yet employed this term. Even for adult survivors, the idea of who qualified as a 'survivor', and of what that meant – emotionally, morally, and existentially – was far from clear-cut. In the twenty-first century we have come to take a broad view of who is a Holocaust survivor, and we include all those who were faced with the threat of murder by the Nazis and their collaborators before and during the Second World War, but who lived. This includes not only those who survived concentration camps, but also those who survived in other ways: by hiding, by passing as Aryan, by fleeing to safer zones (such as into the Soviet Union) or leaving continental Europe altogether, or by joining the partisans. The United States Holocaust Memorial Museum (USHMM) defines a Holocaust survivor as 'any persons, Jewish or non-Jewish, who were displaced, persecuted, or discriminated against due to the racial, religious, ethnic, social, and political policies of the Nazis and their collaborators between 1933 and 1945' – thus widening the definition beyond Europe's Jewish population, indisputably the Holocaust's chief target.[3]

Such a wide reading of the term 'survivor', however, is a relatively recent phenomenon. It took more than half a century for the category to coalesce as the standard term for someone who had lived through the genocide.[4] Although 'survivor' was used in English in the early post-war period (usually in combination with the name of a camp, so that a person became a 'Buchenwald survivor' or a 'Belsen survivor'), it was not then a term of choice. In those early years, adult Holocaust survivors were 'displaced persons', and children were 'unaccompanied children' or 'Jewish war orphans', or some other, similar variant. In many European languages, camp survivors called themselves 'deportees', but did so predominantly within the camp associations and *amicales* that flourished in places such as France in the early post-war years. In the world of the DP camps, the survivors were the *Sh'erit Ha-Pletah* – a biblical Hebrew phrase meaning the 'surviving remnant' – but use of this term faded away as the DP camps themselves dissolved into diaspora. With the exception of categories such as 'deportee', these terms emphasized the current state of survivors' lives, and the problems these lives presented – they were displaced, stateless, parentless, scraps that remained of a people. They did not have the backwards-facing focus of 'survivor', which rooted identity in the past, in the act of survival. Rather, they situated survivors in a present beset by difficulties, and were not generally sympathetic; 'DP', in particular, was an epithet that summed up the frustration that aid agencies and governments felt with both the occupants of the DP camps and with the predicament they seemed to represent.[5]

Where the term 'survivor' was used in the post-war period, it had a restricted meaning: it was assumed to refer to a camp survivor. This clearly made it difficult for those who had survived outside of the concentration camps to relate their own experiences to the idea of survival. If they were not survivors, what were they? Were they, as Harry's family maintained for decades, primarily people who had been lucky not to be murdered? This uncertainty about what constituted survival was felt both by child survivors and by adults who had survived outside of the camps, but it was particularly acute for children, as the majority of them had survived in hiding. It complicated child survivors' relationships with their own pasts, for the terms that were used to refer to their experiences made less and less sense as they aged. They were clearly no longer 'unaccompanied children' once they entered adulthood. Were they still 'Jewish war orphans', even once they became parents themselves? What if they had surviving parents? There was no meaningful identity label that encompassed the experiences and emotions that had deeply marked child survivors' formative years.

At the time, the term 'Holocaust survivor' did not have the positive associations that it does now. Survivors now occupy a position of moral authority, one that has developed gradually since the 1990s, but the term once came saddled with implications of culpability and a burden of shame. Annette Wieviorka has argued that the 1961 Eichmann trial created the conditions in which a new social identity developed for survivors, as the trial shifted the spotlight onto their stories and rendered their narratives authoritative, respectable, and worthy of attention.[6] Yet the transformation she pinpoints took several decades to mature. In the early 1980s organizers of the Gathering, in describing the purpose of the conference, expressed hope that it would challenge the public image of survivors as 'shaven, starving people in striped suits'.[7] They were only too aware of the unspoken assumption that survivors 'had done something wrong to live through it', in the words of psychologist Eva Fogelman, that their survival was built around a fundamental moral compromise. From our current vantage point, in which we view survivors as the precious bearers of history, it is difficult to recall that as late as the 1980s concentration camp survivors still engendered as much suspicion as sympathy.[8]

What of the term 'child survivor', which was first used by psychologists such as Sarah Moskovitz in the early 1980s? By that time some child survivors were beginning to approach their histories in new ways, reflecting on the long-term repercussions of their childhoods, and hunting for information that would help them to weave a coherent early-years story out of fragments. As some began to probe their pasts with new energy in mid-life, they sought more and more to plot their individual stories onto a collective one, to frame their experiences within a broader category. The term 'child survivor' suggested the contours of this collective experience. As the sociologist Margaret Somers argues, identities are formed via the narrative patterns of the stories we tell: people construct their identities by locating their own experiences within a repertoire of established narratives. By the 1980s, the story of survival in the

Holocaust was changing, the definition of a 'survivor' becoming more fluid, and this created space for child survivors to place themselves in the frame.[9] It is important to stress here that not all children who survived the Holocaust identified with the term 'child survivor', then or now. The new term made a political argument: it placed individual experiences within a changing public memory, and asserted a new approach to what survival itself meant. Not all those who survived the genocide as children felt aligned with this stance, but for those with whom it resonated the development of the idea of the 'child survivor' fundamentally altered their relationship to their past lives and present identities.

It made a difference that, by the 1980s, another group had begun to dig at the edges of the term 'survivor'. Some children of survivors, born after the war to survivor parents, had begun by the mid-1970s to refer to themselves as 'second-generation survivors', or more broadly as 'the second generation'. This development began with a few small groups in the United States but rapidly took on global dimensions, and was itself firmly rooted in a historical moment informed by the consciousness-raising of the women's movement and the 'rap groups' used by Vietnam War veterans to work through traumatic memories via small-group therapy. The children of survivors at the vanguard of this movement combined the emergent identity politics of the 1970s with practices such as consciousness-raising to explore, via small groups, the impact that their parents' war experiences had had on their own lives, lives which had begun only after the war had ended. They quickly discovered that the homes they had grown up in had many traits in common, and had affected their lives in similar ways. As a collective story emerged, so did the sense of a group identity as a 'second generation' of survivors. The publication of journalist Helen Epstein's 1979 bestseller *Children of the Holocaust* brought the concept of a 'second generation' survivor to a wide English-speaking audience.[10]

The boundaries between the 'second generation' and child survivors were porous. Both groups shared elements of the experience of loss, dislocation, and silences in the household (or non-silences, for many in both groups knew what it was like to live with a survivor parent who could not stop talking about the war). Indeed, a number of child survivors initially tried attending the new 'second generation' groups when these first emerged in the mid-1970s. Yet here, too, child survivors did not feel that they fully belonged; the idea of being in a 'second generation' negated the fact that they had direct, lived experience of the genocide. If they did not 'count' as survivors in the way that adult camp survivors did, but if equally they did not belong with the 'second generation', where did their stories fit? Events such as the Gathering brought these problems into sharp relief, because they afforded these three groups the chance to meet in large numbers, to hear each others' stories – and to argue about whose experiences qualified as 'survival'. At the Gathering, many child survivor participants questioned whether they could call themselves 'survivors' at all; in its wake, however, they began to adopt the term. As well, for the first time, they did this not as individuals but collectively, as attendees worked to establish the first support groups for child survivors in the months and years after the event.

These developments took place in the specific geographic context of the United States, and this was not a coincidence. As the genocide increasingly became the subject of American films, novels, and television programmes, a distinctly American version of its history captured public attention both domestically and beyond, for these cultural products were exported globally.[11] Commentators at the time pondered the strange fact that memory of a European genocide was progressively cultivated in a land far from Europe, and some worried that the slaughter of Europe's Jews was trivialized by this rising cultural fascination. As one observer noted in the *Washington Post* in the lead-up to the Gathering, 'this is another continent, another generation – a new world. The swastika is recycled as a punk button; Auschwitz is a metaphor. And *Holocaust* is a series on TV.'[12] These developments overlapped with new political uses of the genocide in the American context. In 1973, for the first time, the major American Jewish organizations had included the goal of preserving Holocaust memory in their annual agendas. This was then followed by a string of official initiatives geared towards establishing the country's position towards Holocaust remembrance, and fed by political exigencies. A month after the broadcast of the television miniseries *Holocaust* in 1978, President Jimmy Carter announced the creation of a presidential commission on the Holocaust, to be chaired by Elie Wiesel. It was a move that was, as the historian Edward Linenthal writes, 'politics at its best and at its most convenient', a positive gesture that would (it was hoped) help to heal some of the suspicion caused among Jewish leaders by Carter's support for the Palestinian Liberation Organization.[13] In October 1980 the federal government established the United States Holocaust Memorial Council, charged with raising funds for what would become the United States Holocaust Memorial Museum (which opened to the public in 1993). The memory of the Holocaust was becoming a political issue both for Jewish organizations and for the nation in a way that was not yet true in other countries, even arguably in Israel.[14]

Although the United States Holocaust Memorial Museum would not open for another ten years, it was tangible at the Gathering as a future imperative. In March 1983 the federal government had confirmed that two buildings adjacent to the National Mall had been earmarked for the museum, and one of the central events that took place during the Gathering was a symbolic handing over of the keys to these buildings.[15] This meant that certain political pressures linked to the campaign to create the museum had an impact on the Gathering. In particular, planning for the museum had been marked by debates, often heated, concerning how to define 'the Holocaust' and a 'Holocaust survivor'. Although members of the United States Holocaust Memorial Council, Elie Wiesel in particular, argued that the Holocaust was a distinctly Jewish event, state representatives on the council pressed for a view of the Holocaust that went beyond Jewish victims to include all those who were systematically murdered inside the concentration camps. While the Gathering was not directly organized by the Memorial Council, these debates had an impact on the event: organizers pointedly kept their focus on Jewish survivors, but at the same time ensured that the definition of 'survivor' was wide, and that non-survivor family members, particularly children, were encouraged to attend. Indeed, of the 16,000 attendees at the meeting, an estimated 4,000 were children of survivors.[16] By the time of the Gathering, there were hundreds of 'second generation' groups across North America, including a local Washington DC group with nearly 300 members.[17] A second-generation participant in the conference, Jeanette Binstock, speaking to a journalist from the *Washington Post*, recounted that two years previously she had begun to reconsider her own identity as the child of a survivor, and this had prompted her to listen deeply, for the first time, to her survivor father's story. 'Before,' she said, 'I wondered how and if I should tell my children about the war. Now that I really know what happened, it's a matter of necessity: I have to tell them.'[18]

The organizers of the Gathering thus tried to keep their definition of 'survivor' broad enough to encourage all those with family links to the Holocaust to attend, yet their efforts still fell short of embracing the particular experience of child survivors. Child survivors who attended faced frequent reminders that they did not quite fit into the organizers' vision of a typical participant. For example, organizers invited participants to write their stories down on a form that had been prepared for the purpose, and the form asked them to specify which of four experiences they had had during the war: camp, ghetto, hideout, or forest. This suggested a broad understanding of pathways to survival, yet did not quite encompass the experiences of child survivors, the majority of whom had survived not in hideouts, but in hiding. Even in the event's open approach towards the concept of 'survival', a degree of exclusion reinforced child survivors' sense of non-belonging.[19]

It was nonetheless a catalytic moment for child survivors, and we can document this in real time, because the event's organizers came up with the novel idea of having roving volunteers record spontaneous interviews with participants. These volunteers, armed with cassette tape recorders, roamed the halls of the convention centre, and recorded more than 300 interviews with attendees. Because participants did not know about this interview project in advance, the interviews were raw and unrehearsed, and they captured the mood of child survivors at a moment in which many were questioning their identities even as the tape recorders rolled.[20] In these interviews we hear child survivors struggling with the fundamental question of what to call themselves, and how to assert their right to tell their stories at all. If child survivors were unsure about how to define their stories, the volunteer interviewers seemed equally unsure of how to categorize their interviewees, opting in the end to gather them under the heading of 'orphans': an awkward categorization given that most of those questioned were then in their forties, and not all had lost their parents. The recourse to the term 'orphan' suggests that for all the good intentions of the event's organizers to cast as broad a net around the term 'survivor' as possible, those collecting the interviews bowed to an unspoken hierarchy that privileged the experiences of older survivors. As 'orphans', child survivors' losses were real, but their own experience of surviving the genocide was incidental – the use of 'orphans' implied that their parents were the real victims.

In response, many of the child survivors interviewed at the Gathering framed their own stories first and foremost with reference to their parents, or to others in their family who had died in or survived the concentration camps. Felicia N., born in Berlin in 1935, described herself in the opening of her interview as a 'child of non-survivors', clearly to contrast her experience with that of the 'second generation', who referred to themselves as children of survivors. So unsure was Felicia of the value of her own experience that she began her interview with the story of her aunt, an Auschwitz survivor who had never given an interview of her own. Felicia's story of survival, however, was harrowing in its own right. On the eve of Kristallnacht, at the age of four, her mother had sent her alone to go and live with her father, who had moved to Paris in 1937 in search of work. Her father's situation, however, was so precarious that he had to resort to 'hustling for food', and the child spent her days alone in their small flat. One afternoon in 1942 she learned from her playmates that her father had been arrested, leaving her utterly alone in Paris, without even a key to get back into her flat. She was helped first by the concierge of her building, then by staff at an Orthodox Jewish care home, and finally by a host family who hid her when the care home closed. Telling her story to a stranger for the first time, and hesitant about where to place her emphasis, Felicia spent much of her interview praising the bravery of her rescuers, recalling that 'survival was a matter of luck, occasionally of planning, and in my case of the good . . . no, good will will never translate it enough . . . of the giving, sharing of other people's lives, and I mean their lives at stake, their heads on the chopping block'. The interview seemed to leave her baffled, however, by the problem of how to tell the story of her own feelings and memories, which burst through in unguarded moments. The small details in her story revealed a cavernous world of fear and pain below the gratitude towards her rescuers, such as when she recalled being so lonely and frightened after her father's arrest that she took the only possession she had from her parents – a scarf that her mother had given her – and ripped it up and ate it piece by piece, 'as if to hold on to this mother that I had not seen since I was four years old'.[21]

If the testimonies gathered at the conference reflected a moment in which child survivors were beginning to consider just how far their narratives 'counted' as stories of survival, interviews carried out in the years following reflected a shift towards a collective understanding of a distinct 'child survivor' identity – and many of those who had attended the Gathering later pinpointed it as the moment where this shift had begun. Jacques F. gave an interview in 1991 in which he recalled that the Gathering had marked a pivotal moment for him in two ways. First, it was the moment in which he found out the truth about what had happened to his parents. There was a copy of Serge Klarsfeld's *Memorial* volume at the conference, and Jacques recalled the shock of consulting it and finding his parents' names:

> I met someone who asked about my parents, and I didn't know anything, so this person took me to see the Klarsfeld book *Memorial to the Jews Deported from France*. The person said 'Do you know when they were sent?', but I didn't know anything except their last name. I went through every convoy until I eventually found the name K. [Jacques's birth name]. I found my father on page 38. [. . .] That was one of the emotional moments of my life, just seeing them on paper.[22]

Second, the Gathering brought Jacques the chance to form what would become lasting relationships with other child survivors. Attendees were able to take away lists of names and telephone numbers of others with similar backgrounds, which gave child survivors the practical information they needed to begin to form networks. In a more expansive sense the conference was a moment during which many child survivors recognized, in meeting each other, the collective aspects of their life histories. In 1985 Jacques was one of the founders of a group for child survivors in the Washington–Baltimore area. He recalled in his interview that 'the '83 conference was the catalyst [for the group], because we got a bunch of names. But clearly, it was going to happen, because there were other people feeling the same way, people in their mid-40s starting to have their mid-life crises.'

Like Jacques F., Felice Z. reflected, in two later interviews, on how the Gathering had cemented a sense of belonging to a wider group.[23] We earlier saw Felice as she left the care home at Taverny and immigrated to the United States; one of the highlights of the Gathering for Felice was meeting Jacques, because while they did not remember each other, they were amazed to discover that they had been at Taverny together. Felice did not join a child survivors' group until some years later, after attending the first International Gathering of Hidden Children in New York in May 1991, but her anger over how she was treated by older survivors at the 1983 Gathering motivated her to begin to seek out others who shared her background:

There was this Holocaust conference. I questioned whether I should go because I'd never been in a camp, I have nothing to show for it, I wasn't in this camp or that camp and I used to want to have a number [tattooed on my arm] so I could show people the pain. [. . .] They used to say 'You were a child, what do you know? You don't remember.' This is one of the things they used to tell me at the conference, 'Oh, you don't remember.' This is why the [1991] Hidden Child conference was good: there was a pain there, but a different kind of pain. The pain of loss.[24]

Jacqueline R., born in 1938 in Paris, had been smuggled into neutral Switzerland by the OSE in 1943, and had spent the remainder of the war with a Swiss family. Her parents survived, but she was not returned to them until 1948. Attending the Gathering spurred her to seek out others like her:

[Being at the Gathering] was like a great burden was lifted from my shoulders. I felt such pride in being a Jew and [here she starts to cry] found such strength from the people I met there. [. . .] [Following this] I felt the need to meet with my own generation, I felt so alone, and you really feel the lack of people in your own age group, because so many were killed.[25]

In 1985 Jacqueline began working with others to set up a group for child survivors in New York. Like Felice, she attended and was deeply moved by the first Hidden Child conference in 1991. Interviewed in 1992, Jacqueline recalled that the Gathering had marked the beginning, for her, of a journey to better understand her past:

It kind of brought everything together, because I've been working on this since 1983, and I feel I now have an understanding of how and in what way it formed me and influenced my behaviour, my beliefs, my values, and it also gave me a greater understanding of my parents: what they went through, their losses, their experiences, their relationship to me.

As Jacqueline suggested, the growth of a collective identity as 'child survivors' took work: psychic, emotional, and intellectual, personal and shared. The Gathering provided a context and a moment in which child survivors began to fit their own life stories into a broader, changing story of who a Holocaust survivor could be, and what dimensions survival could assume. This was not just about claiming the mantle of 'survivors' for themselves: it was about exploring what it meant to survive in a fundamentally different way. Through this process they contributed to a transformation in public understanding, for we are all now familiar with the term 'child Holocaust survivor'.

In 1982 Jacques F. attended one of the regular meetings of a group of concentration camp survivors in his area. He later recalled just how deeply he felt out of place in this group. 'It was really difficult to relate to them,' he remembered, 'and for them to relate to us. Because from our point of view, we didn't have any of that, and from their point of view, we didn't really suffer.'[26] A few years later, shortly after his emotional experience at the Gathering, Harry M. attended the same group, and came away with the same impressions. He, Jacques, and a handful of others decided to organize a separate group for younger survivors. 'There were seven of us at our first meeting,' Harry recalled, 'but we kept expanding from there.'[27]

This was the moment of the formation of the Association of Child Survivors in the Washington–Baltimore Area, a child survivors' group that continues to meet to this day. It was clear to members from that first meeting that the group filled a gap, but they did not initially agree on its fundamental purpose. What precisely was to be gained from coming together? Some wanted to invite a therapist to lead the group, as was being done elsewhere; others firmly rejected the notion of making therapy the group's key function.[28] Paul Z., one of the group's early members, recalled:

Initially we spent a great deal of time on the question of whether we should get professionals to conduct our group. And I and many others were very strongly against it. I am not in principle against therapists, but I didn't think that I wanted a therapy group in that context. I often resisted the [impulse in the] child survivor group to explain things in terms of psychology. You can be happy or unhappy regardless. You can have a good marriage or a bad marriage regardless. It's not a good idea to blame everything on that.[29]

Having rejected the idea that they needed guidance from a therapist, early members recalled that they focused instead on the strength that came out of knowing they had a shared background. 'In a way,' Paul considered, 'these are the people who . . . well, I considered them the classmates that I don't have.' Jacques went further: 'All I can tell you is that people in their mid-40s and early 50s who have lived with this . . . the best medicine is to get together and talk about it and somehow start to open up. To meet people who have had the same experience. You don't have to explain to our group.' Harry recalled that the group also rejected the idea of collaborating with the older survivor group early on. They made a few attempts to bring the 'older' and 'younger' groups together for discussions, but 'the older ones said "What do you know? You were just children"', which further reinforced for the child survivors their need for separateness.[30]

In the wake of the Gathering, hundreds of similar groups for child survivors formed across the United States and Canada, continental Europe, the United Kingdom, Australia, and elsewhere, highlighting the transnational impact of these changes.[31] For many of those involved in these groups, the experience deeply altered their relationship with their past. As Harry and Jacques suggested, there was a rebellious aspect to the decision, an assertion both of difference and of validity. On the other side of the Atlantic, Henri O., who joined the Child Survivors' Association of Great Britain shortly after its formation in the early 1990s, similarly recalled the satisfaction in discovering that child survivors felt independent enough, and saw the value of their experiences clearly enough, that they rejected the criticisms of older survivors and forged their own networks. 'We don't need you,' he recalled members of his group thinking about the older survivors' groups. 'We're young enough, we're in our fifties, we can do our own thing – and so we broke away.' When asked what members did in those early meetings, he remembered that 'we talked: you don't need to explain yourself.'[32]

As they established these new networks, the term 'child survivor' became an essential element of their group identity, a cipher for a host of particular experiences. Daisy M., one of the founding members of the first of these groups (the Child Holocaust Survivors' Group of Los Angeles, formed with the help of psychologist Sarah Moskovitz in 1982 – the only child survivor group to pre-date the Gathering), later remembered the thrill that accompanied the discovery of this new term:

> What struck me and others present that first day was the term 'child survivor'. Many of us had never realized that we were a unique, and valid, group. Survivors who had never before been acknowledged and recognized specifically for what defined us as a special group. At the end of that

memorable meeting, some of us decided to meet again and to explore this 'new' subject further. That is how we began.[33]

Held within the term was not only a recognition of a shared war experience, but equally an acknowledgement that child survivors had in common a set of painful post-war experiences. They had constantly been told that they were too young to remember, or that they had not really suffered, or that they were lucky above all else. In the term was an appreciation of the pain caused by decades of having heard that their childhood experiences did not really matter, and a rejection of the assumptions behind such thinking. As Paulette S., who joined the child survivors' group in Melbourne, Australia, shortly after its creation, later remembered:

> I have been told so often that I was too young to remember or to be affected by what happened in my early childhood. Nothing could be further from the truth. I remember so much, but in an incoherent and fragmentary way. It has taken a lifetime for me to piece these fragments together with the help of family members, official documents and history books. It is taking me just as long to understand how deeply affected I have been by my experiences. The turning point came when I joined the Child Survivors Group in Melbourne in 1992 and for the first time heard other people tell their stories. I could relate to those stories. Just as importantly, I was overwhelmed by the support offered by the group and no longer felt alone. [. . .] There had been times that I thought I was crazy, but now I had the context to understand how deeply confused I had been, through no fault of my own.[34]

In 1987 representatives of a number of child survivor groups on the US East Coast met to discuss forming an umbrella organization that could represent this growing network. They held their first conference in 1988, and continue to hold conferences to this day. The umbrella organization was officially constituted in 1997, calling itself the World Federation of Jewish Child Survivors of the Holocaust. By the time it published its first newsletter in 1999, it represented thirty-eight groups in twelve different countries; within a decade this had grown to fifty-three groups in fifteen countries on four continents.[35] The network of groups had become global, and as it expanded it brought with it more and more child survivors, who often felt an aching relief to have their experiences not only understood, but represented and respected. Stefanie Seltzer, the president of the World Federation, wrote at the time that she fielded a daily barrage of telephone calls from child survivors, who 'often speak of the more than half-century of their silence. Some, whose adult children know nothing of their history, sob as they speak.'[36] The very existence of representational organizations allowed the collective story of the 'child survivor' to take shape in the public sphere, and this in turn encouraged individuals to see their own experiences as part of something bigger, something of value, a story that needed to be told. In asserting a sense of generational belonging, in mapping out the shape of a narrative that was deliberately neither that of adult survivors nor that of the 'second generation', these former 'orphans' moved their own subjective experience to the centre of their stories. Once this had been accomplished, it was possible to talk about the past in very different ways.

# TEN

# STORIES

In 1997, when he was fifty-seven years old and living in London, Denny M. volunteered to tell his life story to an interviewer from the Survivors of the Shoah Visual History Foundation project (now known as the Visual History Archive, or VHA). Initially, this probably seemed like a good deed. The project had the ambitious goal of collecting 50,000 interviews with Holocaust survivors. At the time, relatively few survivors living in Britain had participated, and project staff were approaching survivor networks in the hope of increasing these numbers. Denny and a few of the other child survivors from his circle offered their participation.

Denny had given an interview about his life before, although twenty years had passed since he had told his story to psychologist Sarah Moskovitz. We have seen how clear-eyed Denny had been in flipping that interview around to ask whether the psychologist might have had preconceived notions about the 'normality' of child survivors. If he had been disturbed by certain questions that Moskovitz had asked him all those years before, he had nonetheless been able to assert his version of events over her authority – after all, the subject they had been discussing was his own psychological development. But the questions posed by the interviewer from the Survivors of the Shoah project rattled Denny profoundly. They probed too far and too relentlessly at something about which he felt far less sure: the factual details of his own early life.

The interviewer began by asking Denny where and when he had been born, which thankfully were questions he could answer. But then she asked about his mother, and Denny felt compelled to make it clear that he had very little information about his birth parents:

I don't actually remember her, I don't remember what she looked like, I know that she was born in Berlin . . . I have very little information about my mother. I don't know what her profession was, and I know virtually nothing about her at all . . . I have no record, no information either first-hand or through records, of any of those things.[1]

His attempt to signal to the interviewer that he was uncomfortable with a conversation about the facts of his early life failed. She continued to press. She asked about his father: 'I have no information. I don't know his profession, schooling, or what he was like as a person.' She asked if he had been aware that he was Jewish: no, not until later. She asked about his recollection of smells and of tastes; he had none. Then she asked if he could describe his daily routine in Theresienstadt, and Denny's composure broke. He struggled to find the words to explain to this interviewer, insisting as she did on a coherent story, that his memories of the camp were nothing but fragments that he struggled to fit together:

I couldn't do that, that would be too . . . I couldn't cope with . . . because I don't have enough . . . because my memories of those years were completely incohesive. I think a lot of the time I might have slept, so I probably . . . I can't actually think of a special routine, except possibly having meals of one sort or another. That time is a kind of jumble of memories, of things which now don't make very much sense, and probably didn't even make sense at the time.

Denny's interview is nearly unbearable to watch, or at least I found it so. Again and again the interviewer asked questions about factual details that Denny could not answer, and he began to retreat viscerally from the camera. His answers became monosyllabic. His face took on a hardened quality. Finally, his voice crackling with suppressed anger, his brow furrowed with the effort to find the right words, he made one last attempt to show his interviewer the harm that her questions were causing:

216

My memories are very scattered. I can't build a story out of any of this, really, at all. Because it was too . . . it was too . . . I was too young to remember very much. [. . .] I don't think it's a kind of amnesia. It isn't because I want to forget it.

In examining child survivors' post-war lives and memories, we have thus far been looking at an intimate world: the conversations (and silences) about the past that child survivors had within their families and communities, and inside of their own heads. By the 1980s and 1990s, however, the situation was changing. Some of those who had been children during the Holocaust were beginning to think of themselves as 'child survivors', and at the same time audiences for their stories were expanding. Psychologists and historians were actively seeking their accounts. These changes brought with them both sizeable opportunities and considerable pressures: survivors like Denny were often grateful for external interest in the stories of their lives, but equally frustrated by the fact that interviewers expected these stories to take on a certain shape, one that was an uncomfortable fit for memories that were fragmentary and difficult to plumb for meaning.

Despite these limitations, however, interviews conducted in this period are fascinating historical sources. Indeed, they are among the key sources used in this book, and as such they have been our window onto child survivors' life experience as a whole. If we have been able to explore and reflect upon how child survivors experienced family reunification, or how they felt as they left care homes, how they negotiated their adolescent years or what it meant for them to become parents, this is only because they discussed these issues in the wave of interviews conducted in this period. Without these interviews, we would struggle to reconstruct the events and emotions that shaped their lives. They are valuable sources for other reasons as well. Because the process of giving an interview was new for child survivors in this period, neither interviewers nor participants had yet figured out how best to do it. These early interviews were paradoxically both more and less free, more and less circumscribed by internal and external notions of what a child survivor's interview *should* be, than were interviews conducted later. In some cases, such as Denny's, this meant that child survivors struggled to get their stories to conform to the expectations of an interview format designed for adult survivors. In other cases, this meant that child survivors felt free to discuss sensitive issues and emotions in a way that they would not later, once social expectations around what was an appropriate 'child survivor's story' began to crystallize.

We talk about our histories all the time, with our families, with our friends and colleagues, and in our communities – but it is a very different experience to give your life history in an interview. If you have never done so, it is worth taking a moment to imagine how you would approach it, for this manner of narrating requires not simply that you tell the story of who you are, but that you make sense of your pathways and justify your choices, in front of a person who is likely a stranger, and with recording equipment on display. All the large-scale Holocaust oral history projects of the 1980s and 1990s included child survivors in their collections, thus signalling that the founders of these projects understood children's experiences as *survivors'* experiences. Child survivors thus found themselves facing a new set of audiences keen to insert their stories into the broader frame of Holocaust history. The very existence of these new listeners fundamentally changed the way in which many child survivors spoke about their pasts. The goals of these oral history projects, and the motivations of their creators, had a powerful effect on the shape of child survivors' stories as they emerged into the public sphere.[2]

Here we examine how different factors shaped the ways in which child survivors told their stories: the concept of 'testimony'; the approaches used by different interview projects; the gradual creation of an established narrative for the stories of child survivors, which made it easier for interviewees to say certain things when recounting their experiences, and more difficult to say others; and the importance of changes in collective Holocaust consciousness through the 1980s and 1990s (particularly in the United States), which affected the understanding both of those telling their stories, and of those listening. Changing historical contexts naturally affected every aspect of these stories, from the language used to the political and ideological concerns that motivated – consciously or otherwise – what child survivors said to their new audiences, and what these audiences heard.[3]

Readers will note that I use the word 'stories' here, although I am aware that it is a term that makes some survivors uncomfortable, bringing with it as it does suggestions of fabrications, inventions, and even falsehoods. This is not the sense in which I use it. Every interview is a story: a performance of the self and its past for a particular audience, shaped by certain expectations and historical contingencies, which seeks to fit certain recognizable patterns. We always tell the story of our pasts through the lens of the present, in a way that makes sense to and for our current lives and audiences. As the oral historian Alessandro Portelli argues, there is a complex relationship between the 'time of the telling' in an interview and the 'time of the event': we speak about remembered past events in an interview, but we do so via a self that offers this narrative in a specific historical moment.[4] We should not be surprised to find that the way in which we tell the stories of our lives changes over time; this is true for child survivors as it is for everyone else.

When we tell our stories, we shape them onto a scaffolding constructed of many intangible factors, such as our understanding of the expectations of the listener, or the extent to which there exists an established pattern for the narrative that speakers can draw on (consciously or unconsciously). In the 1980s and 1990s there was not yet a precedent for telling a 'child survivor's' story in the semi-public format of the interview. Child survivors had not yet acquired the sense that their stories should follow a certain pattern, or stay within certain agreed (if unspoken) limits. Because of this, there was room, in these early interactions, to speak of things that later became uncomfortable or impolitic.[5]

Child survivors, like all people, shape their stories to fit the expectations of their listeners, and this involves drawing on certain tropes. In Western cultures, where we discuss children and childhood, one of the most powerful and predictable contemporary tropes is that of innocence. But in the early years of collecting child survivors' interviews, before 'child survivor' had firmly rooted itself as an identity in the minds of speakers and listeners, the notion that stories of wartime childhoods should hinge on the idea of innocence did not yet exert a strong influence. This meant both that interviewers felt free to ask questions that would later become indelicate, and narrators felt free (or at least freer) to answer candidly. There are many examples of this from early interviewing projects, where we can find liberal discussions of emotions such as anger, guilt, and shame, and issues such as revenge. Here we will hone in on the topic of revenge, because the notion that children might have dreamed of, sought, and carried out violent acts of revenge so deeply vitiates the 'childhood innocence' narrative that it has all but disappeared from the narratives of child survivors today. Yet it chimes powerfully with one of the central themes of this book: that thinking of children primarily as passive victims reflects neither the historical record nor the realities of children's potential as agents. While an 'innocent' child caught in war is most frequently portrayed as the object of violence, the child who carries out an act of revenge is demonstrably a histor-ical actor, however uncomfortable we might be with the idea of children as distributors of rough justice.

If we are reluctant today to see children in this way, this was certainly not the attitude of the adults who worked with child survivors in the immediate aftermath of the war. If anything, many of these adults saw children who had survived the genocide as bent on both symbolic and actual retribution against the Germans and their local collaborators. This was in many ways a moral panic. Dorothy Macardle sparked fears when she wrote that child concentra-tion camp survivors had 'maniacal cravings for revenge' after having lived for so long 'in an atmosphere of active and purposeful evil'; the violence of the camps, she argued, would not be easily erased from children's psyches or prac-tices. Bernard Gillis of the World Jewish Congress voiced similar concerns that children who had survived camps contained 'a restless cruelty. They seemed to feel the need to discharge their pent-up fury by inflicting upon others some of the torment and humiliation they had themselves suffered.' Greta Fischer, a social worker who worked with UNRRA to establish a children's centre at

Kloster Indersdorf (and later assisted with the CJC's war orphans programme), recorded that 'nearly all' of the children at the centre shared an attitude of intense and burning hatred of the Germans and of all things German, and that they dreamt and spoke of revenge compulsively. Fischer and her team worried that the ferocity of these emotions would slow children's rehabilitation, but other humanitarian aid workers argued that they were in fact a healthy response to months and years of degradation and humiliation. Social worker Margot Hicklin recalled that, at the Windermere reception centre in the summer of 1945, some of the boys who had survived Theresienstadt broke the chairs that were arranged on the porches of their houses. When one of the educators asked why the chairs kept being broken, one of the boys replied that it was 'because we did not have a chance of breaking the heads of the Nazis in our camp'. Hicklin wrote that 'this degree of insight and wisdom, calmly brought forth, silenced further inquiry. It was a sign of the returning confidence and honesty in this group, and was well worth a dozen admittedly very slightly-built chairs.'[6]

If adults in the early post-war period were so preoccupied with the idea that children wanted revenge, we might ask why the topic disappeared from later narratives. The answer is complex. There was, of course, a gulf between adult fears and the reality of children's lives: children might have fantasized about revenge without ever taking concrete action. But what of those who did? How did they later tell their stories? The historian Atina Grossman has observed that revenge was one of a host of emotions that punctuated the relationships between Jewish survivors and Germans in the immediate post-war period, emotions that later were 'shelved and forgotten, deemed insignificant and discomforting, by both Jews and Germans'.[7] The question is when this erasure from collective memory took place, and the answer is that it was likely a gradual process that unfolded over decades, and took different forms for different audiences. Historian Naomi Seidman recognized this when she pointed out, in an article that provoked heated polemics among scholars, that there were fundamental differences between the French version of Nobel Peace Prize winner Elie Wiesel's autobiographical *Night* and the original Yiddish version (*Un di velt hot geshvign*, published in Argentina in 1956). Wiesel, who was sixteen at the time of his liberation from Buchenwald, wrote in the French version of his book that following the liberation, 'some of the young men went to Weimar to get some potatoes and clothes – and to sleep with girls. But of revenge, not a sign.' As Seidman found, however, in the original Yiddish version the German girls were not slept with, they were raped – and even this was insufficient to fulfil the 'historical commandment of revenge' that Wiesel called for in his original Yiddish text. As Seidman argued, the Yiddish version describes for its Jewish readers a 'scene of lawless retribution' in which 'rape is a frivolous dereliction of the obligation to fulfil the "historical commandment of revenge"'; the French version, on the other hand, presented its largely Catholic readership with a 'far more innocent picture of the aftermath of war'. It is this innocent picture that ultimately came to take precedence, the violence of the original version largely forgotten until Seidman published her article in 1996.[8]

Yet this discomfort with the idea of revenge may have become entrenched more recently than it first appears. In 1981 the psychoanalyst Judith Kestenberg founded the International Study of Organized Persecution of Children interviewing project (later referred to as the Kestenberg Archive of Testimonies of Child Holocaust Survivors). Most of the interviews for the project were conducted in the mid-1980s. Kestenberg and the interviewers who worked with her regularly asked their interviewees if they had thought about or engaged in acts of revenge after the war – and, indeed, if they continued to think about such acts. When interviewees denied having had (or continuing to have) desires for revenge, Kestenberg's team did not hesitate to press the point:

*Judith Kestenberg:* And tell me, when you were in the ghetto, when you were in hiding, did you feel that you want to get revenge?
*R.G. (born in Vilna in 1937):* No, I don't think so.
*J.K.:* Did you ever have thoughts of revenge later like you will get back at them? Now if you saw a German or Lithuanian . . .
*R.G.:* Listen, I mean, I grew up in Germany. I was the only Jewish girl in an all-German school.

*J.K.:* I know you didn't do anything to the Germans, but if you saw a Nazi who was in the Vilna Ghetto and you could do something to him, what would you do?

*R.G.:* You mean violently?

*J.K.:* I don't know which, I'm asking.

*R.G.:* No, I don't think I could do anything. I might verbally say something.

*J.K.:* What would you say?

*R.G.:* I don't know. Maybe . . . I might not even say anything, I might just ignore them. I don't know.[9]

While in her writings Kestenberg denied that child survivors had wanted retribution against Germans, her team's insistence on questioning interviewees about it turned up a considerable number who both remembered longing for revenge in the early post-war period and professed that they still desired it:

*Milton Kestenberg:* If you would see a Nazi on the street and there is no one else around, and you know that it's one of the guys who shot . . . who is responsible for the deaths of many Jews and you have a gun . . .

*L.A. (born in 1939 in Warsaw):* I would shoot him.

*M.K.:* You have no problem shooting him?

*L.A.:* No. No feeling at all. I would shoot him on the spot. If I had a gun, I would shoot him right away.

*M.K.:* You wouldn't talk to him or anything?

*L.A.:* I would just call him: 'You dirty Nazi', and that's about it. As a matter of fact, I would shoot him very slowly to let him suffer. I would shoot a Polack too.[10]

Kestenberg's psychoanalytically informed project was perhaps unique in asking pointedly about the question of revenge, but the issue cropped up nevertheless in other interviewing projects during this period, sometimes around the margins of the 'official' interview. Janek E., born in Poland in 1936, was interviewed for the Survivors of the Shoah VHA project in 1994, the year of the project's creation. Like Denny and many other child survivors interviewed for the project, he felt frustrated that he could not answer many of the questions the interviewer asked, pleading at points to end the interview early, and insisting towards the end that 'I did a terrible job [with this interview], but I did the best I could.' The interview seemed to conclude; the tape shut off. But then suddenly the taping resumed, with the interviewer clearly having put her list of questions aside. When the recording began again, she was in the midst of telling Janek a story about someone she knew who was a child in the Warsaw ghetto and who shot a German soldier. Not realizing, perhaps, that the recording had recommenced, Janek recalled that he had done something similar shortly after the war (when he would have been around ten years old): 'That was nothing, it was nothing. I mean, I shot somebody that I recognized, it was a German guard who used to beat us. He says "No, it wasn't me, it wasn't me!" And I just, I had a gun after the war, and I shot him.' Janek added this detail almost as a casual aside. However, his revelation of this memory of retributive violence clearly piqued the interviewer's interest, and she began to probe for further details. At the same time Janek seemed to realize that the camera was rolling, and one can see in his face the fear that he has revealed too much, that the information was too incriminating. Nonetheless, he answered the interviewer's questions:

*Janek E.:* When I was young, life didn't mean anything. You lived for the day. I carried a gun when I was young.

*Interviewer:* How did you get it?

*J.E.:* I don't know if I bought it, or if somebody gave me the gun; I really don't remember.

[He then describes seeing a guard from the Flossenbürg concentration camp, where he had been imprisoned with his father.]

*J.E.:* I shot him. I mean, it didn't mean anything to shoot somebody after the war. We used to do that.

*Int.:* Did you see others?

*J.E.:* Yes, yes, definitely. In [the DP camp at] Salzheim we used to do that. The Jewish guards that we used to catch, we would severely punish them or turn them over to prosecute them, because there were quite a few Jewish inmates that used to turn on the Jews, but now I look back on it, I don't hold it against them, because they had to survive.[11]

Here the interview came to an abrupt end, with the suggestion that Janek has ultimately forgiven the Jewish inmates who collaborated with the Germans in the camp – but had no regrets about shooting the German guard. What is telling, however, is that although he went on to give other interviews, Janek's story of revenge later disappeared from his narrative. As if he had imbibed his first interviewer's surprise at hearing his story and realized that the idea of a ten-year-old shooting an adult lay too far outside the bounds of what was expected from a child survivor's story, Janek recrafted his story to conform to what his listeners expected to hear. He shifted towards a narrative that scrubbed out complex emotions that seemed to clash with the idea of innocence. And he was not alone. Issues such as revenge faded from later oral history with child survivors, as interviewers stopped asking, and participants stopped volunteering details that did not fit easily with the emerging sense of what a child survivor's story *should* look like.

Why do we interview people about the past, and how do we classify stories that we have collected in this way? I am an oral historian by training, which means that I study the past through interviews with people who lived through historic events, and so I think of these exercises in telling the life story as *oral history interviews*. Yet this has not traditionally been the term of choice to describe interviews with Holocaust survivors (or survivors of other genocides): for decades, scholars have here instead preferred the term 'testimony'. This question of classification might seem pedantic on the surface: we might ask whether it really makes a difference how we label these interviews. Yet such classifications in fact have had enormous implications for how survivors of genocide have presented their stories, and the term 'testimony' has an exclusionary dimension that is rarely acknowledged. 'Testimony', and the related term 'bearing witness', have clear roots in a juridical context, where witnesses to events set their memories out publicly and (it is hoped) authentically, credibly, logically, and truthfully. For a witness in such a context to be seen as credible, his or her version of events should also be consistent – it should not change over time. However, the notion of 'Holocaust testimony', while it has its roots in such juridical contexts (particularly the post-war trials for war crimes, and later trials for crimes against humanity such as that of Adolf Eichmann in 1961), evolved out of circumstances that were more academic than legal. As public interest in the Holocaust expanded through the 1970s and 1980s, the writings of 'Holocaust revisionists' (a term that was, and remains, generally a code for 'Holocaust deniers') simultaneously proliferated.[12] The growth of this so-called revisionism from the 1970s onwards had an enormous influence on credible research into the Holocaust, persuading leading researchers to avoid using subjective accounts in their work. Professional historians of the first generation to work on Holocaust history feared that any slide towards subjective experience in their research would only provide fodder for revisionists. Foundational texts such as Raul Hilberg's *The Destruction of the European Jews* firmly rejected the use of survivor accounts, relying instead on the cold officialdom of perpetrator-authored documents to tell the story of the genocide. Dori Laub, a psychoanalyst who founded one of the early video interview projects and himself a child survivor, recalled how adamantly some historians in this era rejected the use of first-hand accounts, asserting that 'it was utterly important to remain accurate, lest the revisionists in history discredit everything'.[13]

At the same time, scholars in other fields interested in the Holocaust – particularly literary scholars and psychologists – began to repudiate the historians' insistence on discounting individual memory. They set about collecting the first-hand accounts of Holocaust survivors, borrowing terms such as 'witness' and 'testimony' from the legal context to assert the value of individual memory, its ability to speak to and about an aspect of the genocide that historians had chosen to ignore. As the literary scholar Sara Horowitz notes, 'the word "testimony" and its expansion to include a burgeoning set of survivor narratives performed a kind of ethical work. It was a corrective in a conversation about the Holocaust that resisted incorporating survivors' memories.'[14] As projects aiming to collect audio or video 'testimony' with Holocaust survivors expanded over a period from the late 1970s to the mid–1990s, the very act of 'giving Holocaust testimony' became routinized and institutionalized. 'Testimony' became the accepted modality for gathering and for classifying oral history with survivors of the Holocaust.

The problem, however, is that a 'witness' providing 'testimony' understands the function of an interview in a particularly strict way. The emphasis must necessarily be on objectivity, on facts, and on events set out in a logical order. Both speakers and listeners understand 'testimonies' to be consistent and accurate narratives of past events. Child survivors, unsure of the veracity of their memories and often unable to put remembered events into a logical order, struggled to get their stories to conform to the 'testimonial' frame. They sometimes lacked the very basic facts needed to tell a coherent story of their early years, but perhaps more importantly, they were often aware that the pieces of information available to them, the scraps they had been able to gather from surviving relatives or from official documents, might not in fact be true. Recalling Jacques F., who was not even certain that his sister was indeed his sister, child survivors sometimes questioned the authenticity of their own received histories. If 'testimony' is, as the historian and psychoanalyst Henry Greenspan argues, simply one genre of survivors' retelling, it was one that was fundamentally ill-suited to the stories of child survivors.[15]

If the founders of these interviewing projects were asking child survivors to provide 'testimony', to what end did they want them to testify? The expectations at the core of these early projects dramatically shaped what interviewees felt they could and should say to interviewers. Through the nature of the questions asked and responses sought, some projects favoured redemptive or cathartic narratives, stories that stressed how survivors had overcome their traumatic pasts to live full lives in the present. Others favoured what Henry Greenspan has called 'psychiatric discourses': narratives that reflected on the lasting consequences of trauma on a survivor's life. Interviewees, reading the social cues from their interviewers and taking on board the goals of the projects, shaped their stories accordingly, stressing either the celebratory or the traumatic, and testifying either to continuing dislocation or ultimate redemption.

Most of the projects that favoured 'psychiatric discourses' were, unsurprisingly, founded and run by psychotherapists and psychoanalysts. Several such projects were launched in the late 1970s and 1980s, of which the most influential was the project known since 1987 as the Fortunoff Video Archive for Holocaust Testimonies, housed at Yale University since 1982.[16] Most important for our purposes, however, is Judith Kestenberg's International Study of Organized Persecution of Children project, because it was and remains the only major interview project to focus exclusively on child survivors.[17] Kestenberg's primary goal was to understand how children experience and remember persecution, and how this affects their psychological health. She believed that having been hunted by the Nazis had left what she called an 'indelible influence' on children, no matter how young they had been at the time, and with her team of interviewers she developed 'kinesthetic techniques' that prompted interviewees to tell their stories without relying on concrete memories, but rather by drawing on their senses and their imaginations. Those conducting the interviews would ask, for example, not how a toddler survivor remembered the train that took her to Theresienstadt, but rather who she imagined might have held her during the journey. They would ask if she could recall particular textures or smells.

In choosing this approach, Kestenberg and her team were influenced by wider debates about the nature of how children remember, and specifically how they remember traumatic events, that entered public discourse in the United States in the 1980s. We have seen previously that this was a period in which scholars working in experimental psychology first began to demonstrate, via laboratory experiments, that very young children (even infants) could remember events across months and even years, although these memories faded as children grew. At the same time as this experimental research was redefining how academic psychologists approached children's memories, fashions in popular psychology embraced the idea of 'recovered memories', which seemed to offer the promise that forgotten childhood experiences (and upsetting experiences in particular) could be retrieved from the depths of the unconscious adult mind via techniques such as hypnosis and guided imagery. The methods used by Kestenberg and her team bore striking similarities to those used by 'recovered memory' therapists. They employed guided imagery techniques, privileged emotions and sensations, and discouraged their interviewees from doubting the validity of the memories that they 'recovered'.

We have previously looked at how some child survivors interviewed by Kestenberg and her team were uncomfortable with her project's focus on trauma and its long-term effects. Some interviewees were equally wary of the project's focus on 'remembering' via imagery, emotions, and senses. Aniko S., born in 1942 in Szeged, Hungary, was too young to remember being deported from the Szeged ghetto to Theresienstadt with her mother and brother, so her interviewer for the Kestenberg project took her through a series of guided imagery exercises. Her interview highlights just how far some Kestenberg interviewers went in asserting that imaginings and sensations should be taken seriously as memories – and just how uncomfortable that made some interviewees, who felt that their 'testimony' had a duty to reflect the truth. When the interviewer asked Aniko to imagine the person who cut her hair when the toddler arrived at Theresienstadt, Aniko hesitated, but then ventured that it might have been a 'middle-aged woman', that she might have worn a khaki uniform, and that she 'seems to be blond':

*Aniko S.:* But I truly believe that I don't have any memories, you know.
*Interviewer:* But listen, you are telling me so many memories. I never heard anyone tell me so many memories, so how can you tell me you have no memories?
*A.S.:* I just thought that I don't have any.
*Int.:* Well, look, you even remembered what this woman looked like, right? And in such detail.
*A.S.:* I never saw, I mean I never thought that I could see her.

*Int.:* You are trying to talk yourself into not having any memories, but you see the reason for it probably is because you want memories like an adult, and that can't be. You can only have memories from the time when you were a child, and the kind of things you experienced – that she had dirty blond hair, that, how old she was – you are telling me things that children observe.

When the interviewer asked again what colour something was, however, Aniko baulked, and attempted to stake out some territory between what was imagined and what was known:

*A.S.:* I don't know. I can try to remember, but I want to be truthful, you know.
*Int.:* You are very truthful. I can't talk you into anything, and I shouldn't.[18]

It does not take a great leap of the imagination to recognize that the interviewer was in fact trying quite hard to talk Aniko into believing that her responses to leading questions about colours and sensations were in fact memories. As a child of two, Aniko had been unambiguously in the period of 'infantile amnesia' when she arrived at Theresienstadt: she could not possibly recall her admission to the camp.

The Kestenberg project collected stories that were collaborative fantasies, in some cases, and participants were aware of this, and at times upset by it. Their upset betrayed a confusion over the project's basic goals. Were the interviews meant to be therapy? If so, the fantasy element seemed less harmful. But interviewees were likely aware that the project's primary goal was to analyse children's lived experience of persecution, and participants familiar with the genre of 'testimony' understood that, in this sense, they were being asked for an objective account of the impact of persecution on their lives.[19] Here, guided imagery techniques and an insistence that vaguely felt sensations must constitute memories was less acceptable to participants, who already doubted their role as witnesses. Whatever might have been the attitude of

Kestenberg and her team to the 'recovered memory' craze of the era, the techniques they used were very much marked by their historical moment, and few would use such techniques now – which might explain why so few subsequent researchers have used Kestenberg's collection.[20]

If Kestenberg's collection was typical of those taking a psychological approach to oral history with child survivors, then the interviews collected for the Survivors of the Shoah VHA project typified the 'redemptive' or 'cathartic' approach to building an interview narrative. Established in 1994 by the film director Steven Spielberg, the project was shaped fundamentally by its founder's cinematic vision. Spielberg's film *Schindler's List*, with its redemptive story line, had been released the year before to great box-office success, and Spielberg had been moved by the stories of the Polish survivors who had worked as advisers on the film. The VHA owed a greater debt to the film than simply honouring the survivors who had participated in its making, however: the celebratory tone that marks the film's finale served as a 'source narrative' for the collection, as the historian Noah Shenker has argued, 'linking the archival project with its own narrative stakes in fostering hope and tolerance'.[21] The VHA's interviewers coaxed survivors towards redemptive narratives – which they referred to as 'testimony' – in a number of ways. They asked set questions that encouraged interviewees to give a linear account of their experiences, and broke the interview into a tripartite division that was, as Shenker points out, 'reminiscent of the traditional Classical Hollywood Cinema paradigm', with 20 per cent of the interview focusing on the period leading up to the war, 60 per cent exploring the war itself, and an additional 20 per cent looking at the years since. Most importantly, however, at the end of the interview each survivor was asked to give a message concerning 'what he or she would hope to leave as a legacy for future generations', and following this, the survivor's family were invited to come before the video cameras.[22] This aspect of the interview format owed much to the closing scenes of *Schindler's List*, when the film changed from black and white to colour and subtitle text informed viewers that while 'there are fewer than four thousand Jews left alive in Poland today, there are more than six thousand descendants of the Schindler Jews'.[23] In both cases, the camera focused on children and grandchildren to impart an optimistic message: that the Nazis failed to destroy Europe's Jews, and that survivors had re-established the chain of generations.

The VHA interviews were also shaped by the project's ambitions of scale. The founders hoped that the collection would become the largest in the world, setting out an initial goal of gathering 50,000 interviews – a goal they reached by 1999 (and there are now more than 54,000 interviews in the archive).[24] They emphasized quantity over quality. Interviewers, who sometimes had only minimal training, worked through a questionnaire-style list of biographical questions, and sought (at least in the initial years of the project) to fix the length of the interview at two hours. They were discouraged from establishing a dialogue with survivors, and were trained instead to focus on their set list of questions. The result was an assembly-line approach to interviewing that tended to condense the panoply of potential Holocaust narratives into a recognizable shape, and to flatten out the dynamic between interviewer and interviewee.[25]

The VHA's approach posed difficulties for all survivors interviewed, but it created particular problems for child survivors, because they were often unable to answer the census-like questions of the interviewers, as we have seen in the case of Denny M. This could lead to a breakdown of trust between interviewer and interviewee, as child survivors became increasingly resentful at being asked questions they could not answer. The interviewers' insistence on following the set questions seemed to expose the gaps in child survivors' knowledge of their own pasts, and rather than fill these gaps with imaginings or sensory explorations as the Kestenberg interviews did, they punctured the narrative, sometimes accompanied by the distraught emotional cues of increasingly flustered interviewees. Zdenka H., born in Prague in 1939 and deported to Theresienstadt as a toddler, was interviewed for the VHA project in 1997. The interviewer began by asking her about her parents:

*Interviewer:* What was your mother's name?
*Zdenka H.:* I can give you her name, but I can't tell you anything about her, because I don't remember. I haven't got any recollections of her.

Yet despite the fact that Zdenka clarified from the outset she had no memories of her mother, the interviewer – following the list of questions – asked again:

*Int.:* Do you remember anything about your mother?
*Z.H.:* As I've already said, no.

When she was questioned about her mother a third time, Zdenka finally lost patience: 'When [the matron of my care home] asked me [about my mother], I couldn't say anything to her then! I have no memories! My earliest memories are in the camp.'[26]

If interviews conducted for projects such as the Fortunoff collection aimed to have a therapeutic role for survivors, it would be difficult to say the same for the VHA interviews. Many child survivors found the experience unnerving. Zdenka recalled her frustration at the experience in a 2007 interview:

[The interviewer] asked me what toys there were in Terezin, and what smells can you remember, and what Jewish holidays. But how could there be Jewish holidays in a camp, and toys? [. . .] We were told that anyone interviewing grown-ups who were children had had special training, but how can you ask those sorts of questions? I mean, I was three and a half when I went to the camp. How can I remember that? I only have three or four definite memories of the camp. Having my hair shaved, sleeping on a bunk, and somewhere running around naked in the snow . . . but these are very vivid memories.[27]

Just as was the case with Kestenberg's project, the trust between VHA interviewers and participants fractured over the question of memory. If Kestenberg's interviewees felt uncomfortable referring to imaginings as memories, however, VHA interviewees baulked at questions that seemed superfluous, misguided, and demanding of more detail than could be provided. They were aware, like Zdenka, that no small child could remember in this way. Indeed, one of the strengths of Kestenberg's approach was that she and her team understood that children's memories are inherently fragmented, that they often hinge on sensory experiences, and generally do not adhere to sequential narrative structures.

The literary theorist Geoffrey Hartman has used the term 'frame conditions' to explain how interviews with Holocaust survivors are shaped by factors such as displacement in time, the use of non-native languages, and the spirit in which the interview is conducted. Interviewees reveal or conceal information in response to these frame conditions, holding back when they sense that they will not be given the chance to tell the story they want to tell, or constructing narratives that fit the shape they assume the listener wants to hear.[28] We have seen here how the frame conditions of many early interviewing projects circumscribed the stories that child survivors felt they could tell. In 'psychological' interviews such as Kestenberg's, interviewers' willingness not only to explore fantasy images and sensations but to employ them as memories sat uncomfortably with interviewees' desire to tell their stories as they felt they knew them – complete with their absences and uncertainties. In projects such as the VHA, by contrast, the focus on detailed, linear narratives upset many child survivors who recognized that their particular way of remembering could not possibly fit the constrictions of the interviewer's questionnaire. Nor did child survivors embrace the VHA's imposition of a cathartic narrative pattern, particularly where the interview techniques tended to lay bare the gaps in their stories. There is little catharsis to be had in revealing a broken life narrative. And over all of these frame conditions lay the additional stricture of the idea of 'testimony', used by all of these early interview projects: a concept that seemed to demand a coherence and a logicality to which child survivors' memories refused to bend.

As audiences for child survivors' stories expanded beyond the intimate worlds of their families to include psychologists and scholars who sought to gather their 'testimony' for a range of reasons, this began to lend their stories an aspect that was built of more than personal meanings. The shape of a collective 'child survivor' story began to emerge. As we have seen, this process made it easier for child survivors to relate certain elements of their stories, and more challenging to relate others. It lent those who were reticent about speaking a template around which they could construct a narrative. But we should not fall into the trap of assuming that this made it easier to speak. Some struggle to tell their stories to this day.

The term 'composure', as it is used by oral historians, was first coined by the historian Graham Dawson to describe how individuals tell the stories of their lives while drawing on the tropes, patterns, and symbols that are embedded in their culture. Oral historians use the term both to describe how a speaker composes a story, and how that speaker presents the story as a coherent whole, as recognizable and even comfortable. 'Discomposure', on the other hand, is what happens when a speaker cannot align his or her subjective experience with collective discourse; the result is a sense of unease that can seem to make a story fall apart. This sense of a fragmented self is often what stands out when we listen to interviews conducted with child survivors in the 1980s and 1990s. It is what we encounter when Denny insists on the piecemeal nature of his memories, or when Aniko ventures that she really had no memories at all, and could not honestly tell the story of her life in the camp.[29]

When we reflect on stories about the Holocaust, the issue of composure becomes even more complex, because many interview-gathering projects have employed a rhetoric of 'legacies' and 'transmission', a presumption that the moral imperative at the heart of the project is a future-oriented one. Survivors' stories are, in this rubric, an inheritance that speaker-donors pass on to an imagined future audience.[30] Stories told as legacies for the future, however, make certain demands on both speakers and listeners. Both parties may assume that such stories must be intelligible – for what use is a story for future generations if it cannot be understood? Both parties might equally assume that such stories must present a well-composed self, for a broken and fragmented one may seem to be a toxic gift to pass forwards. The rhetoric of 'legacies' thus calls on speakers to present a successful journey of self-discovery, in which the most fundamental elements of the child survivor's life story – the uncertainties, the absences of memory – become muted. The often shocking moments when a child survivor discovers important details about his or her past (think of Jackie Y. learning first that he was adopted, next that he had been born abroad, and finally that he was liberated from a concentration camp) become, in such well-composed narratives, steps towards the construction of an integrated self, rather than how they were likely experienced at the time: moments of personal crisis where the very sense of self was pulled apart.

Sometimes it simply takes some rehearsal to weave a coherent story out of rupture. In interviewing child survivors for this project, most of those with whom I spoke had given interviews multiple times. Like any skill, making sense of your life for an interviewer is one that is honed with practice. Occasionally, however, one of my informants had never before told her life story, and this revealed just how far composure is a state achieved through hard graft, both for speakers and for listeners. I will never forget an interview I conducted early in my research with the only participant in this project who wished to remain anonymous. I will call her Leora. Our interview began as most do, with the exchange of a few pleasantries and small exercises in getting comfortable with one another, but Leora quickly began to look tense. 'I don't know what to tell you,' she whispered. I ventured that she should start by telling me her name and her date and place of birth (a technique for starting an interview that I have long used, for the practical reason that it prevents mix-ups with recordings). But she could not do this, because she did not know where she was born, or when – nor did she know her own birth name. She wrung her hands, looking helpless. I tried to assure her that I had come to hear about her life since the war, and that I was most interested in the person she was now, not the one she had been at birth – but the huge fact of the loss of her most basic identity, her very name, sat heavily in the space between us.[31]

Leora told me about how she had been sheltered during the war by a peasant woman in the French countryside. The woman had been very poor; they often went hungry together, and in the winter they shivered together. A kind of love grew up between them, but like other hidden children in France, the child was removed from the woman's care at the war's end. Leora did her best to tell me this story that she had never told anyone (not her own husband, not her own children); it was halting, it was hesitant, but it was her story, and we could both recognize it as such. But we were proceeding together towards a rupture so profound that the story could not cut through it. During her years in hiding, it had not mattered to Leora or to her carer that no one seemed to know her real name. At the war's end, however, the girl was suddenly forced to realize just how vast was the hole in the centre of her life. Without knowing her name, there was no hope of searching for Leora's parents, who might still be alive, or of looking for surviving siblings or other family members. There was no way to reconnect the child to any part of her origins. She was a blank slate, a child who had come from nowhere.

The emptiness of this realization was too much. There was no way for Leora to tell the story of being no one, of the grinding work it had been to slowly, slowly go forwards from that desolation. Nor was I really equipped to hear this, for at that point I had not yet learned how to be attuned to a narrative that seemed on the surface to have no content, its absences so loud that they were deafening. Bereft of words, the shape of the story collapsing around us, we simply sobbed.

## ELEVEN

# SILENCES

Let us go back, for a moment, to the late 1940s, to the countryside manor house of Weir Courtney in the village of Lingfield, Surrey. In December 1945 it was partially converted into a care home for child survivors, all of whom were under the age of twelve at the time. By mid-1946 two dozen children lived there. Anna Freud played a key role in assembling the home's female staff: most were German and Austrian Jewish pre-war refugees, and almost all had worked for Freud at the Hampstead War Nurseries, where they received training in her 'double approach' of direct observation of children combined with psychoanalytic reconstruction.[1]

Under the guidance of matron Alice Goldberger, staff worked to create a warm, welcoming, and open environment for the children of Weir Courtney, and an essential part of this environment was talking about the past. Goldberger recorded, in her monthly reports, how keen the children were to discuss what they had witnessed during the war, and how staff encouraged them to talk. Once they had settled into life in Weir Courtney, Goldberger recorded, 'they slowly started talking about the lost mother and the real "home"'. These discussions were not easy. Some of the children, particularly those who had been in Auschwitz, 'tell horror stories about the camp very often'. 'They still dream of horrors in the camps or of reunions with relations who were killed,' Goldberger wrote in June 1946. 'It is a great relief, though, that they can talk freely about their experiences and fears.'[2]

Goldberger's policy of encouraging children to talk about the war was both a key aspect of daily life at Weir Courtney, and a vital element of how staff portrayed their work to the outside world. The care home was frequently covered by the British press in the mid- to late 1940s, and reporters wrote effusively about the staff's insistence on the psychological benefits for the children of talking about the war. The journalist Howard Byrne wrote in 1948 that, three years after the war's end, the Weir Courtney children's psychological recuperation was due in large part to this practice of speaking about the past:

> Miss Goldberger knew that rapid physical improvement was no proof that [the children] had mended equally well underneath. Unless their neurotic troubles could be detected and treated in childhood, they might suffer untold miseries in later life. So, no matter how tragic their memories, the children were encouraged to face their past and put their feelings about it into words. One little girl said suddenly during a trip to the village: 'I can't forgive my mother. She came into the room, gave me a piece of bread, and said she would come back soon, but she never came.' . . . When the child was told why her mother had been unable to keep her promise, she lost the sense of rejection from which she had suffered, and no longer hated her mother.[3]

As an institution that operated under the patronage of Anna Freud, psychoanalytic principles were a fundamental part of Weir Courtney's everyday functioning. Goldberger herself was training as a lay psychoanalyst. As was the case in other homes, hostels, and children's colonies where staff followed contemporary psychoanalytic theories and practices, Goldberger and her team believed that encouraging children to speak about what they had witnessed during the war had a therapeutic effect. Recalling the past and speaking about it, they reasoned, would help children to process their painful memories and move forward with their lives.

The idea that it is healthy and healing to discuss painful past events, to 'let things out' via a public or semi-public airing, is a keystone of contemporary therapeutic culture, and one that historians generally trace to the rise of humanist psychology in the 1960s, and its many and varied intersections with popular culture.[4] However, with the expanding influence of psychoanalysis in the early post-war period, it was an idea that caught on in certain environments and communities well before the 1960s. The policy of speaking about the past that Goldberger and her staff advocated was thus not all that unusual. Indeed, as we have seen, similar approaches were used elsewhere where child survivors lived in group environments, and 'mental hygiene' experts such as Paul Friedman encouraged the practice. There were of course also many adult carers who felt that talking about the war would reopen wounds that seemed to be healing, or would prevent children from focusing on the present and the future. They hoped that young children would naturally forget the war years, and did not want to distract them from this gradual amnesia by inviting them to revisit the past. However, the advocates of speaking were not a tiny minority, and they argued widely and publicly that talking about the war was a vital part of a broader programme meant to guide survivor children towards a certain normative state, psychologically, emotionally, and morally. Many care workers argued that it was a necessary therapeutic step in the process of mental rehabilitation for children who had survived the genocide.

The archives offer us ample evidence that Weir Courtney was an environment in which such 'therapeutic' speaking about the past was greatly encouraged. However, if we turn away from the archives and focus instead on later oral history and memoir material created by the Weir Courtney children themselves, we face an intriguing conundrum: not one of the children remembers Weir Courtney in these terms. They remember Goldberger and her staff with love and with respect, they remember the home as a warm environment, but they do not remember it as a place where they could speak about what they had been through during the war. Indeed, many recall not only that they did not speak about their pasts there, but that they *were not allowed to do so*: they remember a silence that was imposed from above. Bela R., a toddler survivor of Theresienstadt who spent a year at the Bulldogs Bank care home before arriving at Weir Courtney, recalled that:

> Throughout my childhood, nobody bothered to explain very much about anything. We were told to go here, do that – and it made life much more

difficult, because we had to work things out for ourselves. So we did a lot of inner soul searching, but very quietly, because we were always told not to talk about it. We were forbidden to speak German, so we had to learn English very quickly, and nobody spoke about the past; certainly nobody encouraged us. It was almost a non-written rule that nobody discussed the camps or anything that had happened to us. We were always looking forward to what we were doing next week, tomorrow. So there was never any going back at all to the past, it was like a complete disconnection from my past. That was quite hard for a five-year-old to deal with. [. . .] I suppose the idea was, presumably, that the experiences were so awful that they tried to close the door on it and say forget about it, and let's replace all those bad memories with good memories.[5]

Bela R. was the very first child survivor that I interviewed for this project, and what I remember most about the afternoon I spent in her company was her fervent commitment to seeking out the truth. Thus I do not want to imply here that her account is in any way false: on the contrary, I think it speaks to a very deep truth. It suggests that it matters not only that we tell our stories: it matters *why* we do so. If the archival record gives us clear evidence that Weir Courtney was an environment in which conversations about the wartime past were encouraged, but the children involved remember the opposite, we should question what purposes such acts of speaking served. What made these conversations so deeply forgettable that all that remains in memory is silence? In asking such questions, we probe the very function of speaking about the past, and the connection between acts of speaking and later memories.

Throughout this book, we have looked at memory and its place in a person's life over time, through changing historical contexts and crests and eddies in the life cycle. We have seen how speaking and silence about the wartime past have been themes that marked child survivors' lives through every decade of the post-war era. The Weir Courtney example reveals much about the nature of remembering the Holocaust in the early years after the war's end, but also about the memory of that memory in later years. The meaning-laden disconnect between environments of speaking and memories of silence suggests that when children and adults talked about the past in the wake of the war, they approached such discussions from very different vantage points. What adults hoped to achieve by talking at times diverged radically from children's own needs and desires – and this tension between adult intentions and children's reactions left an imprint on how such 'therapeutic' acts of speaking were later remembered.

What do we mean when we talk about silence? Throughout this book we have encountered many examples both of silence and of attempts to rupture it. We have seen how a widespread belief that young children would not remember the war encouraged some parents and carers not to speak about it, and we have seen how some children challenged this reticence as they grew older. We have likewise seen the very different type of silence that permeated environments such as the Taverny care home, where children did not necessarily talk with each other about their personal wartime experiences, but drew comfort from the knowledge that they had a shared history. We have looked at the tension between memory in the individual and 'silence' at the societal level, and how this began to shift as popular interest in the Holocaust grew from the 1970s onwards. When historians discuss 'silence' surrounding the Holocaust, it is generally this latter phenomenon that they have in mind. For decades, both historians and survivors alike argued that the early years after the war's end were distinguished not merely by a lack of public interest in the Holocaust, but by a more fundamental rejection of the voices of survivors, who wanted to speak but found deaf ears everywhere they turned. This notion was widely accepted up until the dawn of the twenty-first century. It was a 'comfortable consensus', as the historian David Cesarani has argued, one that hinged on the assumption that the years between 1945 and 1970 were so barren a stretch that they were 'not even worth exploring'.[6]

Survivors contributed to this notion of an impenetrable post-war silence, because so many maintained that they could find no one willing to listen to their stories in the early post-war decades. However, as Henry Greenspan has argued, this vision was very much coloured by survivors' later experiences. When survivors began to give testimony en masse in the 1980s and 1990s, they did so in a climate where the Holocaust had become a culturally and politically salient topic, where the very term 'Holocaust survivor' had begun to draw respect, recognition, and enhanced status. In the receptive climate of the 1990s, earlier decades must indeed have seemed marked by a powerful quiescence.[7] We might therefore interpret the mystery of the Weir Courtney children's memories of not speaking about the past through this lens. As we have seen, by the time that child survivors began giving interviews in large numbers in the 1980s and 1990s, they had long lived with a variety of types of silence, both their own and that of others: in adoptive and foster families, with marriage partners and with their own children, in their places of work and in their communities, and inside themselves. From this vantage point, it may well have appeared that the years before they first gave interviews were indeed a desert in which no one allowed them to tell their stories, no one listened, and no one cared.

However, over the past decade historians – myself included – have chipped away slowly but firmly at the 'myth of silence'. They have documented the wide range of early Holocaust commemorations and memorials, the myriad grassroots gestures to keep alive the memory of Europe's murdered Jews, the fervour with which survivors collected early testimony and formed historical commissions to document the genocide, the importance of early academic studies, and the simple fact that in families, communities, and with a wider public, (some) Jews were indeed doing a great deal to remember and to mourn the murdered. Moreover, historians have demonstrated that survivors themselves had considerable agency in this process. So great has been this sea change in our understanding of the early post-war period that some have argued that we are now discussing the 'silence that never was'.[8]

From this perspective, we might interpret the Weir Courtney story as one where the idea of not having been able to talk about the wartime past was so persuasive that it became, in time, the only possible interpretation. It seemed to be a truism that needed no challenge, even though it was in fact a construction – a social expectation of an earlier period of silence – that had emerged over time. Oral historians have long explored the ways in which dominant, collective memories of the past can obscure the complexity of an individual's own story. Indeed, because in an interview situation both the speaker and the listener are generally familiar with these dominant narratives, they can be present almost as a 'third person in the room': the person speaking may map her own story onto the agreed collective one, because she believes that this is precisely what the person listening expects to hear. Conversely, where an individual's story resists attempts to conform to the dominant model, that person will often insist that her story is not worth telling or hearing, because it is not what she assumes the interviewer wants to hear. In this scenario, evidence of the fact that a great deal of speaking about the past happened in care homes like Weir Courtney was discarded from grown children's later stories because it made no sense. It was so far beyond the notion of a dominant silence that there was no room for it to enter into individual stories. It became unfathomable.[9]

This is a reasonable explanation for the speaking–silence disjuncture that we find in the Weir Courtney example, but it only tells us part of the story. We can begin to explore other factors by probing the nature of the speaking that took place in environments such as Weir Courtney after the war. We might ask what adults hoped to achieve when they invited children to discuss the past, and explore where adult goals and beliefs mapped onto children's own needs and desires, and where they diverged. Many adults fervently believed that encouraging children to free themselves of their psychological burdens through speaking served children's best interests, but the situation was more complex. Children brought their own agendas to these post-war memory projects, and they often had good reasons to guard aspects of their pasts carefully for themselves.

The adults who encouraged these conversations about the past were not a united group. They saw children's testimony as serving a variety of different purposes, and we can divide them into three broad camps: the interviewers, the testimony gatherers, and the believers in child psychology. The interviewers were those adults who asked children to tell their stories for a very specific reason: either to help them to trace their relatives, or to determine if they qualified for immigration schemes. The adults involved in this case were principally those who worked for aid agencies; they were responsible for compiling a child's personal case file, and their chief motivation was to gather information about a child's background. A child might in fact encounter several such interviewers as they passed between different care agencies, en route to new care homes, new regions, and new countries. One of the key organizations conducting these interviews was UNRRA's Child Search Branch, which was tasked among other things with reconnecting unaccompanied children with their surviving relatives. The Child Search Branch conducted extensive interviews with unaccompanied children throughout the DP camps of Europe, and aimed to interview all children old enough to talk about their experiences. While the organization's staff were not psychologists, they had exposure to new psychoanalytic models of childcare, and generally believed that the process of interviewing children was an important component of their rehabilitation. The interviews often lasted for hours, and the staff used a variety of tricks and tools, such as having the children sing songs in their native languages, to encourage them to open up.[10]

There is no doubt that many of the staff working for bodies like the Child Search Branch believed they had the best interests of children at heart when they asked them to speak about the war, but this does not mean that children were always willing participants in the interview process. Child Search Branch officers had certain goals, and the children did not necessarily share these. The officers were tasked with reuniting children with their relatives, but not all children wanted this, and even young children could conceal information in order to avoid a forced return to their families, communities, or nations of origin. They gave false names, false birthdates, different nationalities and home towns, and some simply stopped talking when they realized that interested adults were in fact 'interviewing' them. For example, a Child Search Branch officer wrote in 1949 of a boy who 'is very difficult to handle. As soon as he is aware of being interviewed he does not answer.' Officers had tried to interview the child several times; he had given them two different names, two different nationalities, birthdates in 1932, 1936, and 1937, and several birth towns. The more that Child Search Branch officers pressed, the more that the boy's true identity seemed to recede. They finally closed his case in 1951, after he disappeared from the care home where he was living.[11]

Some child survivors, of course, had ample practice in concealing aspects of their life histories, having survived the war with false identities. Relatively young children might have lived the majority of their lives with false identities; indeed, at the war's end, some had forgotten their true identities entirely, as we saw with the case of Leora. For others, the original and fictional components of their identities had merged so seamlessly that neither child nor enquiring adult could later untangle them. These children, moreover, had often developed a deep mistrust of adults with authority. Adults working for aid agencies may have been willing listeners and great believers in talking as a therapeutic intervention, but they were nonetheless asking children to recount their stories in order to establish whether or not those children qualified for further support or for immigration schemes. Even very young children could be aware that such interviews required them to draw on those skills of concealment, creative imagining of the recent past, and outright fabrication that they had cultivated during the war. From this perspective, we can see that such acts of speaking did not necessarily serve a therapeutic purpose, whatever agency caseworkers might have believed.

Indeed, as we have seen, some children readily altered their stories to fit the needs of immigration schemes. Here we might ask, what became of these imagined stories over time? What place did they hold in later memory? Aaron B.*, born in Białystok in July 1935, was interviewed by officers from the Canadian Jewish Congress in 1947, in the hopes of joining the Canadian war orphans scheme. His case file gave a succinct overview of his life story, recording that he had lived with his parents in Vilna until 1941, at which point his notes recorded that his 'parents took him to friends in the country. Parents were deported to labour camp. Aunt found him and took him to Lodz, after she heard that both parents were in this camp.' His notes listed his mother as Halina B. and his father as Chaim B., both deported to Estonia and 'killed in concentration camp 1943'.

---

* pseudonym

It also listed as a 'maternal relative' his aunt Ruth B., who was in the nearby DP camp at Hallein, and was training with the Organization for Rehabilitation and Training (ORT) to be a seamstress.[12]

Despite the fact that CJC officers were carefully checking that the orphans they found in the DP camp children's homes and colonies were indeed full orphans, no one seems to have questioned why the woman given as Aaron's maternal aunt had his father's last name. Aaron was accepted onto the CJC programme, and arrived in Canada from Austria in February 1948. Ruth B. arrived two months later, her ORT training meaning she could join a scheme intended to bring skilled DPs into the country. The CJC remained oblivious to the fact that something was not right with Aaron's story, although by the time his file closed in 1950 they seemed to have grown suspicious. The last document in his file, dated 2 February 1950, mentions that 'Mrs. B. is the "aunt" who came here as a D.P. tailor.'[13]

Aaron's account of his own past as told to CJC officers was a fabrication born of necessity. The two people he named as his father and mother were in fact his maternal aunt and her husband, who were indeed murdered in a concentration camp. He told CJC officers that his parents took him to the countryside to hide; what he did not report was that his mother, Ruth, went into hiding with him, and was with him in hiding throughout the war years. It was his mother, not his aunt, who took him to Łódź after the war, and then on to a DP camp in Strobl, Austria. Aaron's story reminds us that the accounts children gave to interviewers from the aid agencies after the war were often blatantly untrue – but for good reason. It was a cruel policy that allowed children to emigrate but not their surviving parents, and children were more than capable of bending their stories so that they could fit the requirements of an unjust system. Aaron's account of his wartime experience reveals the child as a subject in his own right, using the means at his disposal to subvert imposed rules, and to get himself and his mother out of the DP camp and onwards to a new life.

But if this was a necessary deception in 1947, what place did it hold in Aaron's life story after the need for the deception had passed? In an interview he gave to the Shoah Foundation VHA project in 1998, Aaron did not mention the fact that he hid the truth about his mother's survival for years. He recalled in the interview that the care home where he lived in the DP camp in Strobl 'was for children who were orphans . . . I recall most of the other children who were there were missing both parents', thus suggesting that he was already adept at pretending that he was a full orphan when CJC officers arrived in the camp in 1947. But this long-term, dedicated act of concealment, which demanded his energies from 1945 to at least 1950 (and possibly longer), was absent from his later story. Instead, Aaron suggested in the interview that there had never been any need to lie to CJC staff about his mother's survival, mentioning that 'in Canada and the United States they had a debate, and the governments said they would take orphans. By the time they decided this, there was a shortage of orphans, because most of them had gone to Israel. So they said if we can't have orphans, we'll take half orphans.' However, the CJC never made any such policy change. Fifty years on, the original deception in Aaron's account had taken on some complex permutations, revealing the impetus that moves us all to smooth out ragged elements of our narratives, to offer a tidy explanation for a messy trajectory.

The habit of concealment was also, perhaps, a tricky one to break, for Aaron and for many other child survivors. As sympathetic listeners in the present, we can understand exactly why Aaron and his mother felt they had to hide the truth of their relationship for so long. We can imagine that to get out of a desperate situation in a refugee camp, any one of us might have similarly bent the truth. But for grown child survivors who had out of necessity devoted years to crafting and re-crafting their life stories in order to conceal as much as to reveal, layers of false identities and imagined histories sometimes ended up woven so deeply into the life story that they could not be untangled. It is impossible to know how far, in cases such as Aaron's, the silence was a conscious choice.[14]

Who has the right to a child's story? In Aaron B.'s case, CJC staff required the boy's history as a prerequisite for immigration; Aaron's own contribution to this exchange was a doctored version of the past. What about cases where there was no such plum dangling in return for the story? In the months and years after the end of the war, throughout the DP camps of Europe and beyond, volunteers worked to collect eyewitness reports of survivors of the genocide, and children were included in these schemes. In fourteen different European countries, Jewish survivors founded historical commissions, documentation centres, and small-scale projects to record the recent destruction of European Jewry. At its apex, there were nearly fifty such projects in the British and American occupation zones of Germany alone.[15] These initiatives, largely run by volunteers who were survivors themselves, were rooted in a number of impulses. Aware of Nazi efforts to destroy all evidence of crimes against the Jews, and wanting to protect the cultural heritage of lost communities, the historical commissions aimed to record every vestige of the Jewish past, collecting not only documents and photographs left by the Nazis in their hasty retreat, but also the diaries and letters of victims, the stories of survivors, and the songs, poems, and tales from a Jewish world that had disappeared.[16] This work was intended to provide evidence of the extent of Nazi crimes in both a legal and a pedagogical sense. The Nuremberg court had established that Nazi Germany had murdered 5.7 million Jews, two-thirds of the Jewish population of Europe, but states in Western Europe and the Soviet zone of influence alike were keen to downplay or ignore the specific nature of the persecution of the Jews. This only increased as the Cold War began to develop, and West Germany moved from being a defeated opponent to a key ally.[17] Thus the activists who set out after the war to interview survivors did so with a specific intent: they saw themselves as gathering evidence that could be used in the trials of Nazi criminals, as well as wielded to educate states, institutions, and a non-Jewish populace about the nature and breadth of Nazi crimes.[18]

These interview projects were grassroots ones, but they were not small: the largest of them, the Central Jewish Historical Commission in Poland, collected roughly 7,300 eyewitness reports, of which 400 were with children. Across the many such projects run in the early years after the war, volunteers collected thousands of accounts from children.[19] The 'testimony gatherers' were not of one mind when it came to children's stories. Some felt that children's accounts had an authenticity and emotional relevance that adult accounts did not, imagining them to be apolitical and genuine. Others questioned whether children's accounts had much value as historical documents, but agreed to gather them nonetheless because they imagined that they had a psychological value, both for the children speaking, and for experts trying to understand how children had coped with persecution.[20] But even where those gathering children's stories agreed that speaking about the past had a therapeutic effect for children, the accounts themselves were circumscribed less by the demands of therapy, and more by the gatherers' desire to document Nazi crimes. They contained little or nothing on life before the war, not because children did not want to speak about this, but because the gatherers asked children to focus on the persecution they had suffered. The accounts generally closed with the liberation. The goal of these projects was not to relate a child's whole life story, with its continuities and contingencies between past and present. The goal, in the eyes of adult gatherers, was to record evidence of persecution for legal and educational purposes. Knowing this, it is not difficult to see how the aims of adults listening and the needs of children speaking often differed.

It is tricky to unpick, in these early post-war children's accounts, just where we encounter the child's voice, and where we encounter the interviewer's. With the exception of the twenty children's interviews recorded by the Latvian-born, US-based psychologist David Boder on a wire tape recorder in 1946, the accounts were written down.[21] Some older children wrote their stories in their own hand, but for younger children the adult listener was both the recorder and the editor of the story. The accounts were heavily edited and highly selective: in order to fit the purposes that adults had in mind, children were asked to speak and write to a certain script, following the guidelines set out by the various historical commissions. Indeed, given that the adults writing down the stories wanted to focus the reader's attention on the facts of persecution, they may well have weeded out anything they considered to be superfluous or distracting, including the children's very emotions.[22] Where the accounts were published (such as with Maria Hochberg-Mariańska's 1947 collection *The Children Accuse*, which included fifty-five children's stories from the Central Jewish Historical Commission's collection), it is clear that adult editors were looking for particular types of stories. Hochberg-Mariańska had fought in Żegota, the Polish underground organization that provided assistance to Jews, and she wrote in the introduction to the collection that 'all my own experiences in the resistance, all the years of working and fighting, seemed insignificant and feeble, something unworthy of being mentioned in comparison with [the children's] terror and their quiet suffering and heroism'. In her eyes the book was to serve as 'an indictment not just of Nazi policies and actions against Jewish children, but also of the post-war world that so easily forgot the murder of the Jews', and she selected the stories in the book accordingly.[23] One wonders about the extent to which the accounts of children who did not suffer quite so quietly and heroically were deliberately set aside.

Yet many of the adults involved in these projects seemed blithely unaware of just how far their own motivations, the restrictions of the environment, the children's ongoing suspicion of authority figures, their practice in maintaining dual identities, and their own perception of the need to conceal certain elements of their histories, all worked to ensure that children were not really free to speak as they might have wanted. The adults involved continued to believe, in many cases, that speaking would have a positive and therapeutic effect on children. For some children this may have been the case. But it is difficult to regard as healing any account of the past in which children themselves had so little freedom to shape the parameters. Any remnants of the tensions that existed between the children speaking and the adults recording were largely edited out of the accounts that made their way into the archives of the historical commissions, but in a few cases there remain compelling glimpses. This is particularly true for smaller testimony projects, where the adults involved were less likely to be strict in their adherence to a script set out by the historical commissions.

One such example is the collection of forty-two children's testimonies gathered by Shlomo Tsam, the head teacher of a Hebrew school in Polish Bytom (Silesia), who left Poland for a DP camp in Germany in the autumn of 1945.[24] Tsam compiled the accounts into a manuscript, and deposited it with the Central Jewish Historical Commission in Poland. What is noteworthy about Tsam's work is that, although he edited out the questions and comments that he posed to the children, elements of a dialogue remained in some of the final edited accounts – as did evidence that the dialogue was fraught. The extent to which the children may not have been willing or enthusiastic participants in the process is revealed by one girl's brief account:

> A lot of things I cannot repeat. A lot of things I must not tell. A lot of things I am ashamed to tell. You will not believe me anyway. [. . .] Why did I run away from the Horyn? And which village did I run to? And how was I rescued? It is none of your business![25]

The girl's response suggests not only that she resented Tsam's insistence on focusing on the practicalities and facts of her persecution, but also that she felt he would not be able to understand her story, even though Tsam was a survivor himself. We see this in Tsam's other interviews as well. Another girl, Buzha W., who was then nine years old, began to tell Tsam about her wartime experience of hiding in fields and orchards with her three-year-old sister, Shulamit, but she abruptly ended the account shortly after beginning:

> The Germans fired on the forest. I lost my parents – and until now, [Shulamit and I] have been wandering through the villages of Aleksandrovka, Netreba, etc. Nobody begrudged us bread, but nobody let us stay overnight, so we learned to spend the night in a field or in an orchard, and sometimes we used to steal into a cowshed.
>
> Shulamit used to say then, 'Buzha, do you see what a faithful mother the calf has? Look how she licks its ears. I wish I had been a little calf!' And when she saw the cat on a bed of boards over a stove, she used to say, 'I wish I had been a cat!' Then she would start looking at her little finger and smiling at it. But I don't want to tell anyone about that.[26]

These brief interviews reveal the tension between Tsam's insistence on focusing on facts and the children's own insistence that facts were an irritating distraction: it was emotions that mattered. Buzha W. realized that the memory of witnessing her little sister's agonizing longing for their mother, so central to the girl's war experience but so peripheral to a factual narrative, was of little value to Tsam as an interviewer. Seeing this, the child did what young children often do when they want to assert their own wills against adult authority: she stopped speaking. There was too little room, in the testimony-gathering process, for children's own emotions, questions, and ways of speaking, and thus they some-times chose to sabotage the experiment by removing their voices.

Like so many of his peers, Tsam believed that inviting children to tell their stories would serve a therapeutic purpose, but the accounts he collected attest to something more complex. His primary goal was to establish the facts of the children's persecution, and some of the children clearly resisted participating in this fact-finding mission. It is telling, moreover, to note that just as was the case for the children of Weir Courtney, Tsam's young interviewees later recalled nothing of these interactions. When scholars Boaz Cohen and Beate Müller traced Tsam's former interviewees in 2011, not one could remember ever having recounted their stories in this way, although they recognized the stories as their own. The act of speaking, seen by adults as so valuable and potentially healing for children in the post-war moment, could clearly be of so little importance to the children involved that it left no trace in their memories whatsoever. One wonders if Tsam's grown interviewees recalled, instead, an enforced silence.[27]

We have seen that adult interviewers and 'testimony gatherers' tended to subscribe to the belief that talking about the persecution was healthy for chil-dren: it may not have been their primary motivation, but nonetheless it played a role. There were also, of course, adults for whom the assumed therapeutic benefits of inviting children to speak were in and of themselves the key goal. These were the childcare experts and care workers who, informed by psycho-analytic thinking on the benefits of talking therapy, believed that encouraging children to talk about the past was a basic and integral part of their psycholog-ical rehabilitation. Thanks to historians' efforts to challenge and unpick the 'myth of silence', we now have a firm understanding of just how extensive early testimony projects like the ones discussed above were, but less attention has been paid to those who encouraged speaking not to collect, record, commemorate or memorialize, but rather to rehabilitate psyches.

It is a subject that turns on its head the idea that Holocaust survivors wanted to speak, but no one wanted to listen to their stories. Psychoanalytically informed experts in the early post-war period argued that the opposite was true: they believed that survivors, including child survivors, were inclined *not* to speak about the war, and that it was the task of care workers to ensure that they did not stay silent, even when they seemed to want to do so. The psychiatrist Paul Friedman, after meeting with children in Europe's DP camps, wrote of the need to press child and adult survivors alike to confront their wartime experiences. 'To one degree or another, [the survivors] have all stifled their true feelings, they have all denied the dictates of conscience and social feeling in the hope of survival, and they have all been warped and distorted as a result,' he wrote in 1948. The solution, he argued, was to make them talk about their experiences during the war:

> Such a feat of remembering is, in truth, both impossible and cruel except in an atmosphere of love and understanding that will bolster the patient's weakened confidence and carry her through the first stages of the inevitable shock. The task is to bring her back into human society after her experience on its outermost edges.[28]

We have seen that in the immediate post-war period experts such as Friedman sought the psychological and emotional rehabilitation of survivor children. What role did they imagine that remembering might play in this process? Care staff trained in then modern approaches to child psychology were overwhelmingly in agreement that encouraging children to talk about their pasts would, in the words of one care worker, 'free them from their terrible psychological burden. The most important task is, naturally, to induce them to talk.'[29] This approach was both new, and largely untested. Prominent child psychoanalysts were not in agreement as to whether talking therapy should be used with children in analysis. There was not a great deal of evidence to demonstrate that having children speak did indeed serve a therapeutic role, although there were numerous anecdotal reports from care staff in the field suggesting that children's emotions and behaviour seemed to improve after speaking about the war with adults. It is worthwhile, however, to question what outcomes adult care workers hoped to see when they encouraged (and even forced) children to talk about the wartime past. It is clear that, for some care workers, speaking about the past was seen as an essential component of a wider programme of psychological reconstruction for children. The goal was, ultimately, to settle children into a normative emotional and behavioural state, the better to prepare them for subsequent steps such as adoption. Like Paul Friedman, Margot Hicklin, who worked with children at the Windermere reception centre, imagined that the children 'will have done their best to forget or distort in their own minds' their war experiences, but that urging them to talk was a necessary step in preparing young survivors for eventual adoption. 'Children who seem to have "forgotten" their own past,' she wrote, 'are the ones who are least likely to adapt themselves to new family ties.' She argued that these children 'could not endure the family atmosphere because it broke through years of defence and "forgetting" to the pain of the original loss', and were at risk of later developing neuroses and difficult behaviour such as 'stealing, withdrawal of affection and trust, running away, or illness'.[30]

Thus for all their certainty that encouraging children to speak was therapeutic, adults who advocated such speaking had a rather instrumentalist approach to its purpose: they hoped to steer the children towards feelings and behaviours that would satisfy (or at least not frighten off) potential adopters or foster families. In this rubric, care workers imagined that the children's memories carried a destructive impulse that needed to be tamed and managed through speaking. The goal was not to help children integrate their war experiences into the narrative of their lives as a whole, but rather to release them from the burden of these memories, so that they could move forwards into a world of new families (where new parents and siblings were unlikely to want to know, or to hear, about the horrors of the war). Thus for all the talk of speaking about the past as a therapeutic intervention, we might equally see it as an attempt to sanitize survivor children's behaviour, feelings, psyches, and even memories. It was, at least in some instances, intended to help children lay aside the aspects of their identities that were connected to these memories, rather than to embrace them.

We have seen where this could lead. Post-war carers did indeed attempt to spruce up survivor children for adoption, and in adoptive homes many children would find the door to the past utterly blocked. We saw this in the story of Jackie Y., and we can see it if we return to the story of Bela R., who like Jackie was adopted at a young age from Weir Courtney. Bela's adoptive parents set out to scrub the five-year-old of her own memories, forcing her to re-invent herself:

> I was told to forget about the past, to try to put the past behind as best I could. I had no choice. You can't imagine the massive change in my life that took place. A new name, a new identity. Not exactly a new manufactured past, but almost. Like the past just didn't happen. It was almost like somebody had wiped the tape clear, but there was some residual memory.[31]

Like Jackie Y., Bela's desire to learn more about her past led to clashes with her adoptive parents as she grew into an adolescent and then an adult. The many barricades to the past that her adoptive family set in place took decades to disassemble; some could only be removed after her adoptive parents' deaths. In memory, those obstacles might well be described as 'silence', although Bela herself made lifelong efforts to chip away at this deliberate forgetting.[32]

Seen in this light, the fact that none of the Weir Courtney children could later recall speaking about the past in the care home becomes far less surprising. The act of speaking may have served care workers' desires and fears, but it is more difficult to see it as serving children's needs. If one of the goals of such speaking projects was to steady children's psyches so they would be more desirable as adoptees, children had their own reasons to resist these attempts. After all, as we have seen, many were not keen to leave the safe, known world of the care home for the unknown world of a new family. Equally, where children could see that there was some reward to be had for relating their memories – even if the reward was simply the approval of their care workers – then they may have obliged adults by providing stories about the recent past, but doctored the stories to fit the context. We can see this if we return to the story of Mina R., whom we met at the book's very beginning. Mina decided one day to tell matron Alice Goldberger that she had seen her mother shot through the head right in front of her. Goldberger wrote in her August 1946 report that Mina seemed to be 'much quieter and clearer since, has spoken logically and has lost her silly expression and the frozen grin on her face. She gets treatment every week at [Anna Freud's] Child Guidance Clinic and the doctor has seen the change in her as well.'[33] Yet Goldberger went on to record that this sudden improvement in Mina's mental condition was short-lived. Six years later, in October 1952, Goldberger was shocked to learn 'that Mina's mother is alive in Germany, and is enquiring about her daughter'.[34]

How are we to interpret Mina's act of speaking about the past? We can see that it took place within an important framework, one in which she knew she was expected to speak, and would please her carers by doing so. And this is precisely what happened: even her doctor was happy to see what appeared to be an improvement in her condition. But while Mina spoke of witnessing her mother's murder, her mother was in fact alive. The value of her story lies not in its faith to the facts, but in its very departure from them: children such as Mina did not hesitate to present creatively re-imagined pasts for adult consumption when the need arose. Her story appears, on the surface, to be a horrifying tale of a child seeing her mother killed, but it might equally be read as a small act of defiance, a small assertion of will, a brief window onto the child herself as a subject.

Such a reading subverts the hierarchy between adults and children, and helps us to think about acts of speaking, and indeed silences, in a new light. Returning to the case of Weir Courtney, we can see that talking about the past did happen there after the war, and it was encouraged, but what adults hoped to get out of the experience was rather different from what children expected. So complex, tangled, and potentially oppositional was the conversation about the past between adults and children, so laden with conflicting hopes and divergent fears, that it disappeared from children's later memories altogether. Care workers may have used talking as a tool to mitigate the burdens of memory, to lighten them, even to erase them – but they did not, perhaps, want to explain them.

In response, wary children fabricated suitable pasts. They concealed. They were aware that they were not free to speak as they wanted and needed, and they guarded their memories as a precious, private inheritance where they could. It is no wonder, then, that we find these early post-war conversations shot through with children's efforts to refute, to conceal, and to adapt memories to fit the requirements imposed by their carers and other adults. Where records of these conversations exist in case files and in children's post-war 'testimony', we should view them as complicated sources: they reveal attempts to shape early post-war memory of the Holocaust, but they equally allude to the failure of such attempts.

They also tell us a great deal about the present, and about what memory means to us as we age. In that early post-war moment many advocates of therapeutic speaking worked from the assumption that having children talk about the past would quieten it. It would box the past in, tame it, and then a child could move on. This is not how memory works. This book has charted the ways that childhood memories provided an insistent percussion over the span of a life: chiming away in the background, sometimes barely heard, sometimes deafening, insisting that they not be silenced, nor set aside, nor even dealt with, but incorporated into the whole. We have looked at the decades-long battle that many child survivors had to fight for access to their own pasts. We have seen how they attempted to make sense of their memories over time. With this in mind, we can better understand why 'silence' is so prominent a theme in later life stories, and why earlier acts of speaking left so little imprint: if the purpose of speaking is ultimately to shut off the past, then silence reigns.

# CONCLUSION
## THE LAST WITNESSES

Trauma. Testimony. Survival. Silence.

Through decades of research into the Holocaust, these have been among the core concepts that have guided scholars in their studies. They have become fundamental to our understanding of the genocide. Yet when looked at through the prism of child survivors' lives, each one appears newly foreign; the fit is no longer adequate. Child survivors themselves have challenged the concepts behind these terms, if not the terms themselves. When experts came looking for 'trauma' in their stories, child survivors questioned this external quest to seek pathologies in their experiences. When scholars solicited their 'testimony', child survivors spoke from an uncomfortable space caught between the desire to give a logical and truthful account of their past, and the impossibility of doing so. When others expressed doubt that their experiences counted as 'survival', child survivors doubted themselves – but then insisted that the very idea of survival had to change to accommodate their lives. When they contemplated the decades of 'silence', they acknowledged that what conversations had taken place about the past had failed to fulfil their needs, longing, or curiosity.

We have followed the paths of child survivors from the moment the war ended, as they left hiding places, camps, and ghettos. They entered into new relationships with the adults around them: surviving parents and relatives, foster and adoptive parents, aid agency workers and others who regarded them as psychologically and emotionally 'de-normalized', and worried about how best to return them to normative behaviours and feelings. They were claimed (or left aside) by many different parties, and these competing claims moved them, physically and existentially, across regional, national, and global boundaries. Whether they returned to live with their families of origin, spent the remainder of their childhoods in care homes, or were taken in by foster or adoptive families, as they grew they began to be troubled by the divide between their fragmentary memories and the versions of the past that the adults around them offered or allowed. They began to probe. They challenged their carers over access to the past. As they entered adulthood and the world around them began to take a sustained interest in the Holocaust, those who wanted were able to learn more about the fate of their families and communities of origin. Some came to adopt the new term 'child survivor' to reference their own lives and experiences. Some found new audiences for their stories, and this demanded a new way of telling the story. Some aspects of the past came to the foreground; others became more and more difficult to articulate. Throughout this journey, many were driven by the insistent question: Who am I? Over the seven decades of their post-war lives, child survivors have had to approach this question from an ever-shifting variety of angles. Seventy-five years after the war's end, some might ask: Who am I now? What does knowing about the past give a person? What does not knowing?

Child survivors' stories have now made their way into the canon of 'Holocaust survival' narratives. The weight of acceptance and authority has brought with it a different way of speaking about the past, and child survivors have in some ways repackaged their experiences accordingly. Some have profoundly re-crafted their identities. In an interview she conducted with me in 2014, Agnes G. spoke of the depths of this transformation, as her marriage ended, she moved to Sheffield to take up a Master's degree in Holocaust history, and the core of her life shifted from being a housewife and mother to taking on the social role of the survivor:

> My identity has changed. I've gone from being a middle-class . . . well, you
> know, living in a village in Worcestershire for sixteen years, and then moving
> to Sheffield. I am now a Holocaust survivor. And then in the last five years,
> I've become a Holocaust survivor who writes about the Holocaust. [. . .] I
> suppose the thing is that you always think that your life and your family and
> what's happened to you is somehow normal, even if you know it isn't. So

when people sit there with their jaw dropped, and say 'What an amazing story, you're such an inspiration!', and so on, I look around, because I don't feel that that's me. It has changed how I perceive myself. I now feel strongly that it's desperately important that people like me speak out. You know, I sometimes say to people, when I stand and speak to them, 'You have to think about the six million who are standing behind me and can't speak for themselves.'[1]

Those who choose to speak publicly about their pasts now generally do so from the vantage point of lives successfully lived. The anxieties and uncertainties that once dominated their horizons have faded. In interviews conducted in recent years, they often want to stress that their stories have happy endings. They are further encouraged to do so, as we have seen, by the format of many contemporary interviewing projects, which emphasize the inspirational, the redemptive, and the legacy-building aspects of survivors' stories. What has been lost in this way of telling the story is just how far child survivors' narratives speak to the multiple ruptures of the self over time, and indeed how deeply these ruptures are part of the essential fabric of the story. To discover herself as a survivor, Agnes had to relinquish the self that rooted its identity in being a wife and a mother of a certain social standing; this was not a slow shift, but rather a deliberate and monumental break. The break transformed her as an individual, and it transformed her place in her community.

Agnes largely welcomed these changes, but for some, the new status of 'survivor' reinforced an old feeling of loneliness and difference. Erwin B. felt this most keenly when, some years before his death in 2017, he got involved with an organization that invites survivors to tell their stories to local children, and the children then create a piece of theatre out of the survivor's story. Erwin, who had never had children of his own, relished the chance to work with children, but felt his isolation sharpen when the project came to an end:

When I saw the children act out my story, I felt relief – as if I was suddenly appreciated, as if I was at the centre of things. After the show, I received all sorts of compliments from my friends in the kibbutz. It was a wonderful feeling after all the years of stress. I wasn't used to people asking about me, or being interested in me. I have lived in [the Ein Harod kibbutz] for sixty years. Yet they never asked me what I went through in the Holocaust, and it seems to me that I never told them. And now I am 76 years old.

I have lived alone for ten years, and the warmth and love I received through [the work with the children] had a powerful influence on me. After years of loneliness, I had someone to share experiences with. It was like a stone came out of my heart. But now that it's all over, I feel empty. I no longer have contact with the children. It's hard for me.[2]

As identities have changed, and as child survivors' places in their communities have changed, so too have their stories. As we have seen, having a receptive audience, particularly an audience that hopes to see a story as redemptive, demands that the speaker builds a coherent and logical story – and over time, and with practice, many child survivors have done precisely this. For such a narrative to function, however, aspects of the past that damage this sense of composure must necessarily fade into the background. Chad McDonald writes of the case of Bernard G., who came to Britain as a child on the Kindertransport, leaving behind parents and a sister who were then deported to Riga and murdered. In a 2009 memoir he described how his parents had written him brief letters until their deportation, letters which meant that 'I knew they were still alive.' He had given a similar account in 2004, mentioning that he had received short letters from his parents. An earlier interview, however, added a piercing detail that was absent from later accounts: as an adult, he had found these letters so painful, their presence in his house so overwhelming, that he had eventually burned them. What later became unbearable to explore, as his story became more practised, was the raft of emotions linked both to the letters themselves and to the decision to destroy them: the guilt, the pain, and the need to take steps to bring aspects of the past under some semblance of control. The act of destroying the letters spoke to a moment in Bernard's own life when the past had reared up and overwhelmed him. As greater composure entered his narrative, it was this moment that no longer sat easily with the rest of his story.[3]

The need for composure in a story does not always sit comfortably alongside other pressures, such as the desire for authenticity. We have seen just how hard many child survivors had to fight to find out the truth about their pasts, from their parents' fates to the trajectories of their own early lives. Just as is the case with the issue of composure, where a survivors' need to smooth over the fractured elements of their story interacts with an audience's desire to hear a tale of how the broken self can be mended, so the desire for an authentic story comes both from within and without. After decades of working to root out the facts of their early lives, many child survivors quite rightly now relish the chance to savour the fruits of that long labour: if their stories remain incomplete, if essential facts still evade their grasp, many can now tell a more complete story than they could have at earlier points in their lives. Accompanying that hard-won victory has been the gradual dampening of any lingering elements of uncertainty. At the same time, audiences for these stories have perhaps become less comfortable with uncertainty. The concept of 'testimony' requires the known. Thus the unknown – the deep and fundamental unknown that has been such an intrinsic element of so many child survivors' stories through so much of their lives – has increasingly moved to the margins, partly because what really happened is now better understood, and partly because an expectation of 'what really happened' is built into the 'testimony' format. This too dictates what child survivors feel they can and cannot say.

In 1995 a book that purported to be the memoir of a child Holocaust survivor was published first in German, and then soon after in multiple other languages. The English translation was titled *Fragments: Memories of a Childhood, 1939–1948*. The book told the story of how the author, whose name appeared on the title page as Binjamin Wilkomirski, was separated from his parents during the massacre of the Jews of Riga. He escaped by boat to

Poland, and was taken to Majdanek concentration camp, and then to another camp that was possibly Auschwitz. At the end of the war he was brought to a Jewish orphanage in Kraków. Finally, when he was about seven years old, the author was sent to Switzerland, where he was adopted.

Many elements of this story would have been recognizable and resonant to child survivors. The author wrote eloquently of his own doubts about the nature and validity of his memories, and also of the long period of work required to make sense out of them, writing that 'years of research, many journeys back to the places where I remember things happened, and countless conversations with specialists and historians have helped me to clarify many previously inexplicable shreds of memory'.[4] Some of the book's more tentative and cautious descriptions seemed to harden as time went by. The author describes having seen, as a small child, a man who might have been his father crushed against a wall by a moving vehicle, but in some translations the book's jacket stated unambiguously that the author had seen his father killed. In the book, the second camp to which the author was sent was unidentified, but in promotional material – and by the author himself in interviews – it was named as Auschwitz.

Three years after its publication a young Swiss writer named Daniel Ganzfried published two pieces in the Swiss weekly *Weltwoche* that argued that *Fragments* was in fact a work of fiction. The author's name was not Binjamin Wilkomirski, but Bruno Dössekker; he had been born in Switzerland in 1941 to an unmarried mother, spent time in an orphanage as a child, and had then been adopted by the Dössekker family. As *Fragments* came under greater scrutiny, every aspect of the story began to unravel, and as it did so, it raised some difficult questions. Why would a person *make up* such a terrible past? What happens when we question a survivor's story: do we not risk subjecting them to a second attempt at annihilation? Because the author told a child survivor's story with such eloquence, he himself became something of an exemplar. As the writer Blake Eskin has noted of the case, however, once a person becomes an ideal, questioning his or her story challenges more than that person's individual integrity: it can seem to damage the credibility of related accounts.

Fabricated Holocaust memoirs render legitimate ones suspect; questioning one seems to raise questions about them all.

Wilkomirski/Dössekker's book is not the only fictionalized account professing to be a child survivor's true story that has been published since the early 1990s – it is simply the best-known case. It won literary awards, and was widely praised as a potential new classic of Holocaust literature until it was exposed as a fabrication. I asked many of the people I interviewed for this project if they had read *Fragments* or knew of the controversy surrounding it. Most had not read it, and many had not even heard of it, but they were aware nonetheless of a genre of pseudo-memoirs, and in response many underscored the need to allow only absolutely verifiable facts into their stories. Thus faux memoirs such as *Fragments* have changed the way that child survivors regard and tell their own stories, making them worry, sometimes very deeply, about the potential charge that aspects of their story might be altered or embellished. Over the course of their lives, they had sometimes put a great deal on the line to gain access to even the most basic facts about their backgrounds. Some had paid a high price for that effort to learn the truth in terms of their relationship with their families and their parents (whether biological or adoptive). Most of us take our knowledge of such facts for granted, but for many child survivors these were hard-won certainties – and they grasped them tightly as individuals and with a communal spirit, for if one false account impinges on the veracity of all accounts, then a collective decision to privilege the known acts as a bulwark that protects all.

Over time, these knowns have been woven into their stories, but also into the expectations of their audiences. When we tell our stories, we always do so for the consumption of a broader audience. This book has looked at how child survivors have told their stories over time, and thus memory and narrative lie here at the intersection of the private and the public, the personal and the shared. We have seen how individual memory has never been isolated from outside expectations concerning what child survivors should remember and how they should remember it, and growing children's responses to these pressures were complex and subversive, stubborn and human. The people whose stories form the core of this book were almost universally told, as children, that they would and should forget the war years. Instead, their memories – and their struggle to access them and make sense of them – have been a continuous backdrop to their life stories. It is true, of course, that most of us revisit our childhood memories continually as we age, but we have likely not found ourselves facing quite so many internal and external obstacles as we assess the space between our current selves and our understanding of our pasts.

Yet now, as we enter the third decade of the twenty-first century, and even the very youngest child survivors enter their mid-seventies, those obstacles have changed. For some, internal obstacles remain and will likely always remain. A few of those I contacted when I was conducting interviews for this project politely but firmly declined. They did not wish to talk about their past: not to a researcher, not to their partners, not to their children, not to anyone. It was and remains too unbearable to gaze at directly. For those who are willing to talk, who wish to talk, and who feel a duty to do so, however, there is a world of potential audiences. Many of the child survivors in this book speak regularly at schools, in museums and at memorial events, in addition to giving recorded oral history interviews. A key impetus driving this activity is the passage of time. Time has, ultimately, made them the last generation of Holocaust survivors, the last witnesses to the destruction. That status has brought with it a not inconsiderable pressure. As the bearers of these final stories, child survivors sometimes feel a deep sense of duty to relate them – even, perhaps, as audiences have lost sight of the very specific historical context which was the backdrop to the Holocaust, and have looked more readily to these stories as symbols of a transition from ultimate horror to 'inspirational' rebuilding.

One of the women I interviewed for this project, Cywia P., has gone on since I interviewed her in 2015 to tell her story regularly at public events such as the United States Holocaust Memorial Museum's 'First Person' speaker series (under her anglicized and married name, Sylvia R.). She is a wonderful speaker, and her story is utterly compelling. One can find several videos of her telling her story on the Internet; one website describes it as 'heartwarming and inspiring, [demonstrating] the courage of a young child who in the face of constant fear and loneliness found hope, love, and kindness that sustained her during her early years and throughout her life'. In the multiple recordings online, Cywia never greatly varies her way of telling it. The story goes like this.

She was born in January 1935, in Łódź, Poland. German forces occupied Łódź in September 1939, and not long after Cywia found herself trapped in the ghetto with her father, mother, and older sister. When deportations from the ghetto began, the girl's resourceful father began to search for places to hide her, a pursuit that he kept up for years, and to which she owes her life. These moments in hiding while raids were conducted and others were taken away to their deaths were terrifying for the child, and one episode in particular she recalls as 'the worst part' of her entire five years in the ghetto. There was a cemetery on the other side of the wall that circled the courtyard where the family lived. During one raid, Cywia's father helped her to climb the wall, and he dug a shallow hole in the cemetery. He told her to lie in it, to be still and quiet and to wait, and he covered her with grass and straw. She lay in the hole all night, and all through the next day. The terror of that stay in the cemetery was difficult to expunge. 'After coming out of the hole,' she recalled, 'I became really scared of everything. And it lasted for a long time, even when I was an adult. For forty years I dreamed that I was in the hole, and the Germans were coming to kill me.'[5]

This is not, however, the version of her story that Cywia told me in 2015 – or not quite. The difference arose out of my intentions as much as hers. When she has spoken in recent years about her early life, she has done so to audiences who wanted primarily to hear about the Holocaust. The rest of her life, the many years that have followed, was reduced to a specific role in these accounts focused on the genocide: it was included largely to demonstrate the success of her later reconstruction of herself (or, if readers will tolerate a decidedly non-Jewish image, her metaphorical resurrection after having been buried in the cemetery). When I interviewed her, however, I was a different audience with a very different intention: I wanted to hear about her life after the war, to reverse the dynamic that allowed the Holocaust to take up so much space in her life story while compressing everything else down to an 'inspirational' or 'heart-warming' message. She told me about her family's entrapment in the ghetto, and her father's many efforts to hide her. She told me the story of 'the worst part', the burial in the cemetery, and the decades of fear and nightmares that followed. But then almost as an aside, she remarked that the night in the cemetery, and those years in the ghetto, had not been the hardest part of her life. No. The hardest part of her life was the grief that followed the death of her husband, many, many years after the end of the war.[6]

This struck me as a radical narrative, because it challenged the reductionism that forms much of our current approach to survivors' stories, an approach that assumes that what happened during the war was necessarily the worst thing that could ever happen to a person – and that life afterwards has in turn been a slow, steady march away from horror towards successful rebuilding. In an instant, Cywia subverted the dynamic that made me the reverential listener, and her the bearer of a precious witness account. The key moment of rupture in her life had been a pedestrian one: the death of her spouse. The war and its horrors retreated; the regular moments of mourning and loss that punctuate all human lives entered the foreground. It made me think of the closing words of another of my interviewees, Jackie Y., who I had interviewed at the end of 2014. His words captured so well an impulse that, I felt, tugged at the core of all these stories. 'I think, in the end,' he said with a sigh, 'that I and my past are like two trains. It's gone that way, and I've gone this way.'[7]

# NOTES

## INTRODUCTION

1. Interview with Litzi H. (born S.), 27 March 1995, interviewer Vanessa Ring, USC (University of Southern California) Shoah Foundation Visual History Archive.
2. 'Lingfield Colony' report, August 1946, Alice Goldberger collection, 2007.423, USHMMA.
3. There have been a number of recent edited volumes on children in and after the Holocaust. See in particular Simone Gigliotti and Monica Tempian (eds), *The Young Victims of the Nazi Regime: Migration, the Holocaust, and Postwar Displacement* (London: Bloomsbury, 2016); Henning Borggräfe, Akim Jah, Nina Ritz, and Steffen Jost, with Elisabeth Schwabauer (eds), *Freilegungen: Rebuilding Lives – Child Survivors and DP Children in the Aftermath of the Holocaust and Forced Labour* (Göttingen: Wallstein Verlag, 2017); and Sharon Kangisser Cohen, Eva Fogelman, and Dalia Ofer (eds), *Children in the Holocaust and its Aftermath: Historical and Psychological Studies of the Kestenberg Archive* (Oxford: Berghahn Books, 2017).
4. Joseph Schwartz, 'Jewish Children in Europe Today', *New York Times*, 1 October 1948.
5. JDC figures can be found in Zorach Warhaftig and Jacob Freid, *Uprooted: Jewish Refugees and Displaced Persons after Liberation* (New York: American Jewish Congress, 1946), p. 119; and in the *Jewish Chronicle*, 13 July 1945, p. 1. For later historians' use of these figures, see Debórah Dwork, *Children with a Star: Jewish Youth in Nazi Europe* (New Haven: Yale University Press, 1991), p. xii. Many historians subsequently adopted this figure from Dwork.
6. The JDC estimated that there were 60,000 such children in Europe in 1947, in addition to the 35,000 cared for in JDC-funded homes, and the 85,000 living with parents or relatives who were supported by JDC funds. See *New York Times*, 11 February 1947.
7. Susanne Urban, ' "More Children are to be Interviewed": Child Survivors' Narratives in the Child Search Branch Files', in Borggräfe et al., *Freilegungen*, p. 73. For the JDC's revised figures, see Jacques Bloch, 'The Jewish Child in Europe: Rehabilitation Work of the OSE', *Jewish Chronicle*, 6 November 1948. On refugees in the Soviet Union, see in particular the essays in Mark Edele, Sheila Fitzpatrick, and Atina Grossmann (eds), *Shelter from the Holocaust: Rethinking Jewish Survival in the Soviet Union* (Detroit, MI: Wayne State University Press, 2017). It is worth noting that the JDC figures also did not include children who fled as refugees immediately before the war on Kindertransport schemes, although their numbers were considerable: 10,000 went to Britain alone.
8. Adolescents were, of course, mature enough to understand danger in a systematic way, able to care for themselves, and far more likely to be admitted to a concentration camp or used as slave labour than younger children, all of which helps to account for their higher survival rate. As well, although circumcision posed a unique danger to Jewish boys during the Holocaust, older girls may have found themselves with greater responsibility for the care of younger siblings, which increased their own vulnerability. On parallels with child refugees today, see Rebecca Clifford, 'Britain's Response to WWII Child Refugees Puts Modern Society to Shame', *The Conversation*, 8 February 2017.

9. See in particular Tara Zahra, *The Lost Children: Reconstructing Europe's Families after World War II* (Cambridge, MA: Harvard University Press, 2011), Daniella Doron, *Jewish Youth and Identity in Postwar France: Rebuilding Family and Nation* (Bloomington, IN: Indiana University Press, 2015); Ruth Balint, 'Children Left Behind: Family, Refugees and Immigration in Postwar Europe', *History Workshop Journal*, 82 (2016), pp. 151–72, and the articles in Gigliotti and Tempian (eds), *The Young Victims of the Nazi Regime*.

10. Later the Oeuvre de Secours aux Enfants (OSE) would assume responsibility for removing children from Gurs, but Felice and her sister were taken out of the camp slightly before this date. On this see Laura Hobson Faure, 'Orphelines ou soeurs? Penser la famille juive pendant et après la Shoah', 20 & 21. *Revue d'histoire*, 145 (2020), pp. 91–104. See also Katy Hazan, *Les Orphelins de la Shoah: Les Maisons de l'espoir, 1944–1960* (Paris: Belles Lettres, 2000).

11. Interview with Felice Z. S. (born Z.), 23 April 1983, interviewer unstated, 'American Gathering of Jewish Holocaust Survivors' collection, RG-50.477*1361, USHMMA.

12. Interview with Denny M., 31 July 1997, interviewer Miriam Feldman-Rosman, USC Shoah Foundation VHA.

13. Interview with Nicole D., 10 May 1995, catalogue no. 15431, interviewer Lyn Smith, Imperial War Museum Archive.

14. As I wanted every child in this book to have had the lived experience of the war (even if they could not recall it), I have not included the stories of children who escaped continental Europe before the war on Kindertransport schemes.

15. 'Lingfield Colony' report, August 1946, Alice Goldberger collection, 2007.423, USHMMA.

16. Nicholas Stargardt, 'Children's Art of the Holocaust', *Past and Present*, 161 (1998), pp. 191–235. On agency in children's history, see the articles in the first issue of the *Journal of the History of Childhood and Youth* (2008), and especially Mary Jo Maynes, 'Age as a Category of Historical Analysis: History, Agency, and Narratives of Childhood', *Journal of the History of Childhood and Youth*, 1 (2008), pp. 114–24.

17. Christine Wells, Catriona Morrison, and Martin Conway, 'Adult Recollections of Childhood Memories: What Details can be Recalled?', *The Quarterly Journal of Experimental Psychology*, 67:7 (2013), pp. 1,249–61.

## CHAPTER 1: ANOTHER WAR BEGINS

1. On the history of the OSE, see Sabine Zeitoun, *Histoire de l'OSE: de la Russie tsariste à l'occupation en France* (Paris: L'Harmattan, 2010). See also Debórah Dwork, *Children with a Star: Jewish Youth in Nazi Europe* (New Haven, CT: Yale University Press, 1991), pp. 55–65.

2. Between 8,000 and 10,000 Jewish children in France were hidden with host families during the war. See Daniella Doron, *Jewish Youth and Identity in Postwar France: Rebuilding Family and Nation* (Bloomington, IN: Indiana University Press, 2015), p. 12.

3. Zilla's story is reconstructed here both from archival records and from her later oral history. See 'Zilla C.', RG-43.113M, USHMMA. For her later oral history, see interview with Zilla C., 14 November 1987, interviewer Judith Kestenberg, Kestenberg Archive of Testimonies of Child Holocaust Survivors, Hebrew University of Jerusalem Archives. Details of Zilla's rescue by the young French Catholic woman Jacqueline Prandi can be found on the website of Yad Vashem: http://db.yadvashem.org/righteous/family.html?language=en&itemId=6956109 (accessed 3 June 2020). Zilla C. died in 2007.

4. Interview with Zilla C., Kestenberg Archive.

5. Dwork, *Children with a Star*, p. 257.

6. The Gurs camp was originally built to house refugees fleeing the Spanish Civil War in 1939, but in the autumn of 1940, some months after the fall of France to the Nazis, 6,500 Jews from the Baden and Palatinate regions of Germany were deported there as part of Operation Wagner-Bürckel.

7. Before Felice and Beate were removed from the camp, their parents wrote beseechingly to the children's uncle in the United States, asking for help (which did not come): 'Things are really bad for the children. Beate has lost a lot of weight, and all of us are too thin and unrecognisable. Please do something before it is too late.' Letter from David, Hugo, and Leopold Z. to Julius Z., 15 December 1940, Felice Z. S. collection, USHMMA.

8. Interview with Felice Z. S. (born Z.), 2 February 1998, interviewer Rosalie Franks, USC Shoah Foundation VHA.

9. Ibid.

10. Interview with Felice Z. S. (born Z.), 30 December 1992, interviewer Joni Sue Blinderman, Fortunoff Video Archive for Holocaust Testimony, Yale University Library.

11. It was obviously easier to hide a sole child than siblings or a family group. A single child could more easily be passed off as a relative or an evacuee from a bombed-out area, and if they were young enough in many countries children did not require identity papers. See Dwork, *Children with a Star*, p. 34.

12. I have deliberately used the term 'host family' rather than 'rescue family' in this book, although I found this a difficult decision, because the actions of some of these families were jaw-droppingly brave, and the word 'rescue' is only too fitting in these cases. The term 'host family', however, is broad enough to encompass the wider range of experiences that reflect the reality of hidden children's lives: some host families risked their own lives to shelter Jewish children, and others did not; some were paid for their troubles; some used hidden children as free labour; some did not understand the dangers involved and grew to regret their choice as the situation became more perilous; and some cared for the children hidden with them as if they were their own children, regardless of the dangers. This last option was the experience of both Zilla C. with Jacqueline Prandi, and Felice Z. with Juliette Patoux, and both Zilla and Felice later worked to have their rescuers (and here the word is apt) recognized by Yad Vashem as Righteous among the Nations. Juliette and her husband Gaston were recognized in 1971 (after Gaston's death), and Jacqueline Prandi was recognized in 2013 (six years after Zilla's own death).

13. On children's experiences in hiding, see Susanne Vromen, *Hidden Children of the Holocaust: Belgian Nuns and their Daring Rescue of Young Jews from the Nazis* (Oxford: Oxford University Press, 2010); Diane Wolf, *Beyond Anne Frank: Hidden Children and Postwar Families in Holland* (Berkeley, CA: University of California Press, 2007); Nahum Bogner, *At the Mercy of Strangers: The Rescue of Jewish Children with Assumed Identities in Poland* (Jerusalem: Yad Vashem, 2009); Emunah Gafny, *Dividing Hearts: The Removal of Jewish Children from Gentile Families in Poland in the Immediate Post-Holocaust Years* (Jerusalem: Yad Vashem, 2009); and Mary Fraser Kirsh, 'Remembering the "Pain of Belonging": Jewish Children Hidden as Catholics in Second World War France', in Simone Gigliotti and Monica Tempian (eds), *The Young Victims of the Nazi Regime: Migration, the Holocaust, and Postwar Displacement* (London: Bloomsbury, 2016). In addition to aid organizations such as the OSE, networks of political parties, youth groups such as the Jewish Scouts and university student clubs, and Protestant and Catholic organizations all worked to hide children during the war; see Dwork, *Children with a Star*, p. 35.

14. The Netherlands was a unique case in this regard, as the organization charged with caring for orphaned Jewish children after the war did not demand that they be systematically removed from their rescuers. See chapter 3, endnote 21, for further details.

15. Interview with Maurits C., 9 June 1986, interviewer Debórah Dwork, quoted in Dwork, *Children with a Star*, p. 263.

16. Independent Commission of Experts Switzerland – Second World War (ICE), *Switzerland and Refugees in the Nazi Era* (Bern: BBL, 1999), p. 174.

17. See Michal Ostrovsky, ' "We are standing by": Rescue Operations of the United States Committee for the Care of European Children', *Holocaust and Genocide Studies*, 29:2 (2015), pp. 230–50.

18. ICE, *Switzerland and Refugees*, p. 167.

19. On the flight to and return from the Soviet Union, see especially Mark Edele, Sheila Fitzpatrick, and Atina Grossmann (eds), *Shelter from the Holocaust: Rethinking Jewish Survival in the Soviet Union* (Detroit, MI: Wayne State University Press, 2017).

20. ICE, *Switzerland, National Socialism, and the Second World War* (final report) (Zurich: Pendo Verlag, 2002). An unknown number of these children were Jewish.
21. Robert Gildea, *Fighters in the Shadows: A New History of the French Resistance* (London: Faber & Faber, 2015), pp. 199–200. See also Zeitoun, *Histoire de l'OSE*, pp. 35–60, and Renée Posnanski, *Les Juifs en France pendant la Seconde Guerre Mondiale* (Paris: Hachette, 1997), pp. 409–26.
22. This policy was in place until the end of 1943, but many families did not in fact see each other again until the war's end.
23. SHEK was a pre-war organization founded in 1933, but during the war it was commissioned by the national police to find families for the children who were with their parents in the Swiss internment camps. By the close of the war, there were more than 2,500 children in SHEK's care, and over half of these were placed in foster homes. See Salome Lienert, *Das Schweizer Hilfswerk für Emigrantenkinder, 1933–1947* (Zurich: Chronos Verlag, 2013); and Sara Kadosh, 'Jewish Refugee Children in Switzerland, 1939–1950', in J. K. Roth and Elisabeth Maxwell (eds), *Remembering for the Future* (London: Palgrave Macmillan, 2001), pp. 1,207–23.
24. Interview with Cecile S. (born H.), 25 October 1988, interviewers Bernard Weinstein and Selma Dubnick (Kean College Oral History Project), Fortunoff Video Archive for Holocaust Testimonies, Yale University Library.
25. ICE, *Switzerland and Refugees*, p. 122.
26. This and subsequent quotations from interview with Cecile S. (née H.), FVA.
27. Doc. 239, 'Jewish Refugee Records', RG-58.001 M.0384, USHMMA.
28. Ibid.
29. Ibid. and 'Cecile and Esther R.', 'Case files from the Schweizer Hilfswerk für Emigrantenkinder', J.255, RG-58.003M, USHMMA.
30. Interview with Cecile S. (born H.), FVA.
31. Interview with Litzi H. (born S.), USC Shoah Foundation VHA.
32. Interview with Litzi H. (born S.), USC Shoah Foundation VHA; interview with Denny M., 31 July 1997, interviewer Miriam Feldman-Rosman, USC Shoah Foundation VHA.
33. On Theresienstadt, see Tara Zahra, *The Lost Children: Reconstructing Europe's Families after World War II* (Cambridge, MA: Harvard University Press, 2011), pp. 78–87, and Nicholas Stargardt, *Witnesses of War: Children's Lives under the Nazis* (London: Pimlico, 2006).
34. Interview with Denny M., USC Shoah Foundation VHA.
35. Stargardt, *Witnesses of War*, pp. 197–228.
36. Sarah Moskovitz, *Love Despite Hate: Child Survivors of the Holocaust and their Adult Lives* (New York: Schocken Books, 1983), p. 11.
37. Martin Gilbert, *The Boys: The Story of 732 Young Concentration Camp Survivors* (London: Weidenfeld & Nicolson, 1996), p. 236.
38. Zahra, *The Lost Children*, p. 86; and H. G. Adler, *Theresienstadt, 1941–1945: The Face of a Coerced Community* (Cambridge: Cambridge University Press, 2017), p. 315.
39. Interview with Peter D. (born B.), 27 May 1984, interviewer Sarah Moskovitz, Kestenberg Archive of Testimonies of Child Holocaust Survivors, Hebrew University of Jerusalem Archives.
40. Ibid.
41. Ibid.
42. Dwork, *Children with a Star*, p. 157.
43. Mark Mazower, *Hitler's Empire: Nazi Rule in Occupied Europe* (London: Allen Lane, 2008).
44. Stargardt, *Witnesses to War*, p. 183.
45. Nechama Tec, *Jewish Children Between Protectors and Murderers* (Washington, DC: USHMM, 2005), p. 8.
46. Interview with Sybil H., 2 August 1985, interviewer Judith Kestenberg, Kestenberg Archive of Testimonies of Child Holocaust Survivors, Hebrew University of Jerusalem Archives; 'Alfus CM-1 file', digital documents 78873070_1 to 78873071_4, ITS Digital Archives, USHMMA; 'Esther H. T/D file', digital documents 93106671_1 to 93106689_2, and

'Sybil H. T/D file', digital documents 9351167_1 to 93511695_2, ITS Digital Archives, USHMMA.

47. Danuta Czech, *Auschwitz Chronicle, 1939–1945* (New York: Holt, 1997), p. 674.
48. Nikolaus Wachsmann, *KL: A History of the Nazi Concentration Camps* (London: Abacus, 2016), p. 356.
49. Helena Kubica, 'Children', in Yisrael Gutman and Michael Berenbaum, *Anatomy of the Auschwitz Death Camp* (Bloomington, IN: University of Indiana Press, 1994), p. 413.
50. Ibid, p. 413.
51. Ibid, p. 414. Also see Nili Keren,'The Family Camp', in Gutman and Berenbaum, *Anatomy of the Auschwitz Death Camp*, pp. 428–40.
52. Wachsmann, *KL,* p. 359.
53. Stargardt, *Witnesses to War*, p. 222. A few were twins (or were siblings who appeared to be twins), singled out and sent to the block where Josef Mengele and his staff performed medical experiments. Some ended up, through unknown means, in the children's blocks, together with non-Jewish children from every part of Europe, including large numbers who had arrived with civilian transports from the occupied territories of the Soviet Union after September 1943. On this see also Kubica, 'Children', p. 422.
54. Stargardt, *Witnesses to War*, p. 227. Sybil's mother, aunt, and uncle all survived.
55. Kubica, 'Children', p. 424. A Russian medical commission examined 180 of these children, aged six months to fourteen years, immediately after the liberation of the camp. They reported that the majority of the children were suffering from diseases, 60 per cent showed vitamin deficiency, and 40 per cent had tuberculosis. All were underweight by 5 to 17 kilograms, despite the fact that the majority of them had been transported to Auschwitz in the second half of 1944, and had spent only a few months there.
56. Interview with Sybil H., Kestenberg Archive.
57. It is interesting that this detail about the bread stood out both in Sybil's mind, and in Wala's, although the two had not seen each other since 1945: when psychoanalyst Judith Kestenberg tracked Wala down in Warsaw in 1985, Wala recalled seeing Sybil, at the moment of liberation, with a whole loaf of bread. Asking where she got the bread, Wala recalled that Sybil said 'I "organised" it', using the camp slang for looting. Interview with Wala D., 27 July 1985, interviewer Judith Kestenberg, Kestenberg Archive of Testimonies of Child Holocaust Survivors, Hebrew University of Jerusalem Archives. On the slang use of the term 'organising', see Stargardt, *Witnesses to War,* p. 365.
58. Wala recalled that Sybil, at nearly four years old, was not the youngest child in the children's blocks.
59. Interview with Sybil H., Kestenberg Archive.

## CHAPTER 2: THE ADULT GAZE

1. Judith Hemmendinger and Robert Krell, *The Children of Buchenwald* (Jerusalem: Gefen Publishers, 2000).
2. Naomi Seidman, 'Elie Wiesel and the Scandal of Jewish Rage', *Jewish Social Studies*, 3:1 (1996), pp. 1–19, here p. 8.
3. Judith Hemmendinger, *Revenus du néant* (Paris: L'Harmattan, 2002), pp. 7–10.
4. Judith Hemmendinger, 'Readjustment of Young Concentration Camp Survivors through a Surrogate Family Experience' (paper from Third International Conference on Family Therapy, Jerusalem, 1979), no pp. See also Eugène Minkowski, *Les Enfants de Buchenwald* (Geneva: Union OSE, 1946).
5. Hemmendinger, 'Readjustment of Young Concentration Camp Survivors'. On the story of the Buchenwald boys and Hemmendinger's involvement, see also Alex Grobman, *Rekindling the Flame: American Jewish Chaplains and the Survivors of European Jewry, 1944–1948* (Detroit, MI: Wayne State University Press, 1993); Daniella Doron, *Jewish Youth and*

*Identity in Postwar France: Rebuilding Family and Nation* (Bloomington, IN: Indiana University Press, 2015), ch. 4; Katy Hazan and Eric Ghozian (eds), *A la Vie! Les enfants de Buchenwald, du shtetl à l'OSE* (Paris: Fondation pour la mémoire de la Shoah, 2005); Judith Hemmendinger, *Survivors: Children of the Holocaust* (Bethesda, MD: National Press, 1986), and Tara Zahra, *The Lost Children: Reconstructing Europe's Families after World War II* (Cambridge, MA: Harvard University Press, 2011), pp. 114–16.

6. Ibid, p. 4.

7. Ibid, pp. 4–7.

8. Phyllis Bottome, 'The Jewish Child', *The Jewish Chronicle*, 31 October 1947.

9. Michal Shapira, *The War Inside: Psychoanalysis, Total War, and the Making of the Democratic Self in Postwar Britain* (Cambridge: Cambridge University Press, 2013).

10. On the history of social work, see John Ehrenreich, *The Altruistic Imagination: A History of Social Work and Social Policy in the United States* (Ithaca, NY: Cornell University Press, 1985); and Roy Lubove, *The Professional Altruist: The Emergence of Social Work as a Career, 1870–1930* (Cambridge, MA: Harvard University Press, 1965).

11. 'They Learn to Be Children Again', *John Bull*, 9 October 1948.

12. Anna Freud and Sophie Dann, 'An Experiment in Group Upbringing', *The Psychoanalytic Study of the Child*, vol. VI (New York: International Universities Press, 1951), pp. 127–68.

13. Alice Bailey, *The Problems of the Children in the World Today* (New York: Lucis, 1946), quoted in Zahra, *The Lost Children*, p. 10.

14. On the print press coverage, newsreels, and radio reports from liberated Bergen-Belsen and Buchenwald concentration camps, see Joanne Reilly, *Belsen: The Liberation of a Concentration Camp* (London: Routledge, 1998), ch. 3.

15. On the British 'war orphan scheme', see Martin Gilbert, *The Boys: The Story of 732 Young Concentration Camp Survivors* (London: Weidenfeld & Nicolson, 1996); and Mary Fraser Kirsh, 'The Lost Children of Europe: Narrating the Rehabilitation of Child Holocaust Survivors in Great Britain and Israel', unpublished PhD thesis, University of Wisconsin-Madison, 2012.

16. Reilly, *Belsen*, ch. 3.

17. Margot Hicklin, *War-Damaged Children: Some Aspects of Recovery* (London: Association of Psychiatric Social Workers, 1946).

18. Ibid.

19. It is interesting to note that Hicklin, who knew perfectly well that her young charges had survived Theresienstadt, referred to them as 'children from Belsen, Buchenwald, and Auschwitz', because these were the names that her readers were familiar with, as they were 'daily pronounced in the Nuremberg trials'. Hicklin, *War-Damaged Children*, p. 10.

20. Maxwell Luchs to AJDC Paris, 7 June 1946, digital document NY AR 45-54 00205 0920, JDC Archives.

21. Paul Friedman, 'Psychiatric Report', 18 September 1947, folder CYP.98, 'Cyprus Operation, 1945–1949', JDC Archives. Friedman also reviewed the report's main findings for an article in the magazine *Commentary*: see Paul Friedman, 'The Road Back for the DPs: Healing the Psychological Scars of Nazism', *Commentary*, 1 December 1948.

22. Friedman, 'The Road Back for the DPs'.

23. Ibid.

24. Shapira, *The War Inside*, p. 1.

25. On the shift from bodies to minds in childcare advice, see also Cathy Urwin and Elaine Sharland, 'From Bodies to Minds in Childcare Literature: Advice to Parents in Inter-War Britain', in Roger Cooter (ed.), *In the Name of the Child: Health and Welfare in England, 1880–1940* (New York: Routledge, 1992), pp. 174–99. The JDC consulted with Anna Freud over the choice of Paul Friedman to lead the study of children in the DP camps: see William Schmidt to Paul Friedman, 8 June 1946, digital document NY AR 45-54 00205 0915, JDC Archives.

26. Urwin and Sharland, 'From Bodies to Minds', p. 191. It was not that there were no experts promoting an 'emotional' approach earlier: psychoanalyst Susan Isaacs, for example, took a psychodynamic approach through the 1920s and 1930s that drew on children's emotions.

However, the hygienist approach remained by far the most influential, in Britain and else-where in the Anglo-American sphere. It was the event of the war itself that allowed this to change.

27. On Paul Friedman's support for the 'mental hygiene' movement, see William Schmidt to Paul Friedman, 14 June 1946, digital document NY AR 45-54 00024 0847, JDC Archives.

28. Summary of volunteers' discussions, HA 2-5/10/11, MFDoc 052, Rose Henriques Archive, Wiener Library.

29. Indeed, it is worth noting that Paul Friedman hardly mentioned the issue of play in his reports on child survivors, but the wide press coverage that accompanied the release of his 1947 report focused on how he 'told of seeing children liberated from concentration camps who did not know how to play. He saw toys given to children who did not know what to do with them' (see for example *New York Times*, 11 February 1947). Adults were equally disturbed by children's play during the war: see Nicholas Stargardt, *Witnesses of War: Children's Lives under the Nazis* (London: Pimlico, 2006), pp. 174–8; and Patricia Heberer, *Children during the Holocaust* (Lanham, MD: AltaMira Press, 2011), pp. 284–90.

30. Toby Shafter, 'How DP Children Play', *Congress Weekly*, 26 March 1948.

31. Melanie Klein, Anna Freud, and others had argued for more than a decade that play revealed the inner emotional and psychic state of a child. Klein believed that children's play could be used in psychoanalytic sessions in the same way as free association could be used for adults – an idea that other analysts initially greatly criticized, but which is still effectively used in child psychoanalysis today. See Shapira, *The War Inside*, p. 90.

32. Of course, the issue of 'juvenile delinquency' had broad repercussions in the Cold War period; see the classic work of sociologist Stanley Cohen, *Folk Devils and Moral Panics* (London: MacGibbon and Kee, 1972).

33. 'Rescuing 150,000 Children from Delinquency' (report on a speech by Bernard B. Gillis, vice-chair of British branch of the World Jewish Congress), *Jewish Telegraph Agency*, 16 September 1955.

34. Shafter, 'How DP Children Play'.

35. *Jewish Chronicle*, 17 October 1947.

36. Urwin and Sharland, 'From Bodies to Minds', p. 191; Zahra, *The Lost Children*, p. 19.

37. Paul Friedman, 'Cyprus: Psychiatric Report', folder CYP.98, 'Cyprus Operation, 1945–1949', JDC Archives. See also 'Cyprus Camp for Jewish Kids Seen as a Psychological Limbo', *New York Times*, 5 November 1947.

38. Friedman, 'Cyprus: Psychiatric Report', section 2, p. 7.

39. Zvi Friedmann, unpublished memoir, p. 29, USHMMA.

40. Elie Wiesel quoted in Katy Hazan, *Les Orphelins de la Shoah: Les Maisons d'espoir, 1944–1960* (Paris: Belles Lettres, 2000), p. 249.

## CHAPTER 3: CLAIMING CHILDREN

1. On the Hungarian labour battalions (a forced labour system into which Jewish men were conscripted), see in particular the work of Randolph Braham: *The Hungarian Labor Service System, 1939–1945* (New York: Columbia University Press, 1977); *The Politics of Genocide: The Holocaust in Hungary* (New York: Columbia University Press, 1981); and *The Wartime System of Labor Service in Hungary: Varieties of Experience* (Boulder, CO: Rosenthal Institute for Holocaust Studies, 1995).

2. On the occupation of Hungary, see the work of Randolph Braham cited above, and also David Cesarani (ed.), *Genocide and Rescue: The Holocaust in Hungary, 1944* (Oxford: Berg, 1997). A number of safe houses, under the protection of the embassies of neutral countries and agencies, were set up in Budapest in 1944. This included a number of dedi-cated safe houses for children (some under the auspices of the International Red Cross, and others run by religious and Zionist organizations). See Robert Rozett, 'International

Intervention: The Role of Diplomats in Attempts to Rescue Jews in Hungary', in Randolph Braham (ed.), *The Nazis' Last Victims: The Holocaust in Hungary* (Detroit, MI: Wayne State University Press, 1998), pp. 137–52.

3. This and subsequent quotations from an interview with Robert Z. (born Robert B.), 14 December 1995, interviewer Cheryl Wetstein, USC Shoah Foundation Visual History Archive.

4. Like other children in this study, Robert awaited onward transport at an OSE-run children's home in France, in this case the home at Les Glycines, Seine-et-Oise.

5. 'Report on Robert B.', 14 July 1950, Cb 03 (Robert B.), UJRA records, CJCA.

6. On the link between enuresis and psychological trauma in children as it was understood at the time, see Amanda Jane Jones, *Bringing Up War Babies: The Wartime Child in Women's Writing and Psychoanalysis at Mid-Century* (London: Routledge, 2018), pp. 130–2. For a more recent perspective, see for example William Lane M. Robson and Alexander K. C. Leung, 'Secondary Nocturnal Enuresis', *Clinical Pediatrics*, 39:7 (2000), pp. 379–85; and Tal Eidlitz-Markus, Avinoam Shuper, and Jacob Amir, 'Secondary Enuresis: Post-Traumatic Stress Disorder in Children after Car Accidents', *Israeli Medical Association Journal* (*IMAJ*), 2 (2000), pp. 135–7.

7. 'Report on Robert B.', 14 July 1950, Cb 03 (Robert B.), UJRA records, CJCA.

8. Joseph Schwartz, 'Jewish Children in Europe To-day', *New York Times*, 1 October 1948.

9. Tara Zahra, *The Lost Children: Reconstructing Europe's Families after World War II* (Cambridge, MA: Harvard University Press, 2011), p. 13.

10. While some 'unaccompanied children' immigrated via designated schemes managed by these overseas aid agencies, many others immigrated to the same countries in family groups outside of these schemes. Since the countries involved did not record whether incoming migrants were Jewish, it is impossible to assess the total numbers of survivor children who immigrated to a given destination after the war.

11. Although definitive numbers are impossible to establish, it is likely that more children were hidden in France than in any other country: an estimated 10,000 children were hidden with Christian (chiefly Catholic) host families and institutions during the war, the majority of whom survived. Hidden children thus accounted for roughly a third of the total of 30,000 children who survived the Holocaust in France. See Daniella Doron, *Jewish Youth and Identity in Post-war France: Rebuilding Family and Nation* (Bloomington, IN: Indiana University Press, 2015), p. 12.

12. Quoted in ibid, p. 85.

13. Ibid, p. 53.

14. *Jewish Chronicle*, 21 November 1947.

15. Michael Marrus, 'The Vatican and the Custody of Jewish Child Survivors', *Holocaust and Genocide Studies*, 21:3 (2007), pp. 378–403; Annette Wieviorka, *Déportation et génocide* (Paris: Plon, 1992), p. 390.

16. Franck Caestecker, 'The Reintegration of Jewish Survivors into Belgian Society, 1943–47', in David Bankier (ed.), *The Jews Are Coming Back: The Return of the Jews to their Countries of Origin after World War II* (Oxford: Berghahn Books, 2005), pp. 72–107.

17. Doron, *Jewish Youth*, p. 57; Wieviorka, *Déportation*, p. 388; Katy Hazan, 'Récuperer les enfants cachés: Un impératif pour les oeuvres juives dans l'après-guerre', *Archives Juives*, 37:2 (2004), pp. 16–31.

18. For further readings on efforts to recuperate 'lost children' in different countries, see Diane Wolf, *Beyond Anne Frank: Hidden Children and Postwar Families in Holland* (Berkeley, CA: University of California Press, 2007); and Joel S. Fishman, 'The War Orphan Controversy in the Netherlands: Majority-Minority Relations', in J. Michman and T. Levie (eds), *Dutch Jewish History: Proceedings of the [Second] Symposium on the History of Jews in the Netherlands, 28 November–3 December 1982, Tel-Aviv/Jerusalem*, pp. 421–32 (on the Netherlands); Luc Dequeker, 'Baptism and Conversion of Jews in Belgium, 1939–1945', in Dan Michman (ed.), *Belgium and the Holocaust: Jews, Belgians, Germans* (Oxford: Berghahn Books, 1998), pp. 235–71 (on Belgium); Nahum Bogner, *At the Mercy of Strangers: The Rescue of Jewish Children with Assumed Identities in Poland* (Jerusalem: Yad Vashem, 2009) (on Poland).

19. The case received global attention when French courts ordered in 1952 that Brun return the children to their Israeli aunt, and in response Brun hid the children, in collaboration with church officials. In June 1953 monks revealed that the children were hidden in the Basque region. See Catherine Poujol, *L'Affaire Finaly: Les Enfants cachés* (Paris: Berg International, 2006). Doron also gives a useful summary of the case and its implications in *Jewish Youth*, pp. 68–73.

20. *Jewish Chronicle*, 5 September 1947. Unlike in other Western European countries, authorities in the Netherlands did not privilege returning an orphaned Jewish child to his or her relatives after the war, and claimed Jewish orphans as wards of the state. This meant, in practice, that host families had a better chance of winning official support where they hoped to keep a child in the Netherlands than elsewhere. See Joel S. Fishman, 'Jewish War Orphans in the Netherlands: The Guardianship Issue, 1945–1950', *Wiener Library Bulletin*, 27 (1973–4), pp. 31–6. Cases such as that of Ruth Heller were by no means unique. One of the children interviewed for this study, Robert T., was still in the home of his wartime host family in 1947 when his grandfather came to claim him. The grandfather ended up trying to flee the country with the six-year-old Robert, but the pair were caught, and Robert was returned to the Netherlands to live in an orphanage. The case was widely reported in the Dutch national and local press: see *Het Vrije Volk*, 18 July 1947; *Nieuwe Leidsche Courant*, 18 July 1947; and *Leidsche Courant*, 18 July 1947. I thank Robert and his daughter Miriam for sharing copies of these articles with me.

21. *Jewish Chronicle*, 8 April 1951.

22. *New York Times*, 18 November 1949.

23. In private, agency workers often acknowledged that statistics on 'lost children' were inflated, but were hesitant to make such admissions public, as the issue rallied public attention, and helped major aid organizations such as the JDC – supported entirely by donations to the United Jewish Appeal – continue to raise sufficient operational funds. In effect, the issue of 'lost children' loosened donors' purse strings, and as such it became more and more difficult for the agencies to admit that the scale of the problem was in fact minimal. See Doron, *Jewish Youth*, p. 65; and Poujol, *Les enfants cachés*, p. 29.

24. Paulette Szabason Goldberg, *Just Think It Never Happened* (Victoria, Australia: Makor Jewish Community Library, 2002).

25. Ibid, pp. 34–5. Although it is tempting to see such dramatic tales of kidnapping as a trick of memory – these removals might have felt so sudden and unexplained to young children that they remembered them as kidnapping – there is ample evidence in the archives that Jewish agencies did in fact abduct children from non-Jewish rescuers in this manner. See Doron, *Jewish Youth*, p. 77.

26. Paul Friedman, 'The Road Back for the DPs: Healing the Psychological Scars of Nazism', *Commentary*, 1 December 1948.

27. Ivan Jablonka has pointed out that the post-war history of child survivors was fundamentally transnational. See Ivan Jablonka, 'Introduction', in idem (ed.), *L'Enfant-Shoah* (Paris: Presses Universitaires de France, 2014), pp. 11–30.

28. Between 1945 and the mid-1950s, the International Tracing Service received nearly 350,000 requests for help in finding missing children. See Keith Lowe, *Savage Continent: Europe in the Aftermath of World War II* (London: Viking, 2012), p. 27.

29. Avinoam J. Patt, 'Introduction', in Avinoam J. Patt and Michael Berkowitz (eds), *We Are Here: New Approaches to Jewish Displaced Persons in Postwar Germany* (Detroit, MI: Wayne State University Press, 2010), p. 3.

30. Lynn Taylor, *In the Children's Best Interests: Unaccompanied Children in American-Occupied Germany, 1945–1952* (Toronto: University of Toronto Press, 2017), pp. 30–40.

31. By 1946 the JDC was responsible for 70 per cent of the budget of French Jewish organizations, and was helping more than 40,000 people. See Laura Hobson Faure, *Un 'Plan Marshall juif': La présence juive américaine en France après la Shoah, 1944–1954* (Paris: Armand Colin, 2013).

32. Antoine Burgard, '"Une Nouvelle Vie dans un nouveau pays": Trajectoires d'orphelins de la Shoah vers le Canada (1947–1952)', unpublished PhD thesis (Université Lumière Lyon 2, 2017), p. 60; Zahra, *The Lost Children*, p. 12.

33. Zahra, *The Lost Children*, p. 12. On the 'infiltrees' see especially Zeev Mankowitz, *Life Between Memory and Hope* (Cambridge: Cambridge University Press, 2009); on the Bricha, see Yehuda Bauer, *Flight and Rescue: Brichah* (Jerusalem: Magnes Press, 1970).

34. Susanne Urban, 'Unaccompanied Children and the Allied Child Search', in Simone Gigliotti and Monica Tempian (eds), *The Young Victims of the Nazi Regime: Migration, the Holocaust, and Postwar Displacement* (London: Bloomsbury, 2016), p. 280.

35. Burgard, ' "Une Nouvelle Vie dans un nouveau pays" ', p. 54.

36. In response to this and to the Harrison report of August 1945, UNRRA constructed Jewish-only DP camps in the US zone of occupied Germany, particularly around Munich. The first of these camps was Feldafing, built in a former Hitler Youth camp; the largest was Föhrenwald.

37. We have seen that psychiatrist Paul Friedman was particularly interested in the plight of child survivors trapped on Cyprus. His report on children in the Cyprus camp can be found at Paul Friedman, 'Cyprus: Psychiatric Report', folder CYP.98, 'Cyprus Operation, 1945–1949', JDC Archives.

38. 'Report on Jewish Infiltree Children', 1946, folder 7.27, Rachel Greene Rottersman papers, USHMMA. See also Taylor, *In the Children's Best Interests*, ch. 5.

39. Urban, 'Unaccompanied Children', p. 290.

40. On UNRRA age limits, see Susanne Urban, ' "More Children Are to Be Interviewed": Child Survivors' Narratives in the Child Search Brach Files', in Henning Borggräfe, Akim Jah, Nina Ritz, and Steffen Jost, with Elisabeth Schwabauer (eds), *Freilegungen: Rebuilding Lives – Child Survivors and DP Children in the Aftermath of the Holocaust and Forced Labour* (Göttingen: Wallstein Verlag, 2017), p. 71. Children were disqualified from these schemes if they appeared to have poor physical or mental health. On disabilities and disqualifications see Ruth Balint, 'Children Left Behind: Family, Refugees and Immigration in Postwar Europe', *History Workshop Journal*, 82 (August 2016), pp. 151–72. On the South African scheme, which never achieved its quota of 400 children, see Suzanne D. Rutland, 'A Distant Sanctuary: Australia and Child Holocaust Survivors', in Gigliotti and Tempian (eds), *The Young Victims*, p. 78.

41. Doron, *Jewish Youth*, p. 84.

42. Jacques Bloch, 'The Jewish Child in Europe: Rehabilitation work of the OSE', *Jewish Chronicle*, 6 November 1948.

43. Ben Lappin, *The Redeemed Children: The Story of the Rescue of War Orphans by the Jewish Community of Canada* (Toronto: University of Toronto Press, 1963), p. 15.

44. Ibid, p. 16; Margarete Myers Feinstein, 'Jewish Observance in Amalek's Shadow: Mourning, Marriage and Birth Rituals among Displaced Persons in Germany', in Patt and Berkowitz, *We Are Here*, p. 276.

45. Central British Fund committee meeting notes, 12 November 1945, CBF collection, reel 37, Wiener Library.

46. Quoted in Rutland, 'A Distant Sanctuary', p. 75.

47. There were a number of violent pogroms in post-war Poland, the most significant of which was the Kielce pogrom of July 1946, in which forty-two Holocaust survivors were killed and many others wounded. There were also deliberate attacks by Polish nationalists on orphanages housing Jewish child survivors. On this see Karolina Panz, ' "They did not want any more Jews there": The Fate of Jewish Orphans in Podhale, 1945–1946', in Borggräfe et al., *Freilegungen*, pp. 93–104. Lena Kuchler, director of the Jewish orphanage at Zakopane, was so concerned about these attacks that she smuggled the children under her care out of Poland illegally, and relocated the entire orphanage to Paris. See Lena Kuchler-Silbermann, *My Hundred Children* (London: Souvenir, 1961). In Paris, a number of the older children from this orphanage were interviewed by David Boder, the Lithuanian-American academic who recorded the only known early reel-to-reel recordings of interviews with child and adult Holocaust survivors. On the work of David Boder, see Alan Rosen, *The Wonder of their Voices: The 1946 Holocaust Interviews of David Boder* (Oxford: Oxford University Press, 2010); Alan Rosen, ' "We Know Very Little in America": David Boder and Un-Belated

278

Testimony', in David Cesarani and Eric Sundquist (eds), *After the Holocaust: Challenging the Myth of Silence* (London: Routledge, 2012), pp. 102–14; Rachel Deblinger, 'David P. Boder: Holocaust Memory in Displaced Persons Camps', in Cesarani and Sundquist (eds), *After the Holocaust*, pp. 115–26; and Donald L. Niewyk (ed.), *Fresh Wounds: Early Narratives of Holocaust Survival* (Chapel Hill, NC: University of North Carolina Press, 1998). The Boder interviews can be found online and in translation at https://iit.aviaryplatform.com/collections/231 (accessed 3 June 2020).

48. Although the state of Israel was created in May 1948, according to Morris Laub the British continued to hold Jewish immigrants 'of fighting age' on Cyprus until 1949. See Morris Laub, *Last Barrier to Freedom: Internment of Jewish Holocaust Survivors on Cyprus, 1946–1949* (Jerusalem: Magnes Press, 1985).

49. After the war, between 72,000 and 100,000 Jewish DPs immigrated to the United States, and between 100,000 and 120,000 immigrated to Israel. Adara Goldberg estimates that 35,000 Holocaust survivors eventually immigrated to Canada. See Adara Goldberg, *Holocaust Survivors in Canada: Exclusion, Inclusion, Transformation, 1947–1955* (Winnipeg: University of Manitoba Press, 2015). For Australia, Suzanne Rutland states that by 1961 the small Jewish population had tripled in size to 61,000, largely thanks to post-war immigration. See Rutland, 'A Distant Sanctuary', p. 72.

50. The IRO became an official body in 1948, although it had in fact been created by a preparatory commission in April 1946. It ceased activities in 1952, and was replaced by the United Nations High Commissioner for Refugees, which exists to this day.

51. On the effects of the JDC's budget cuts on the OSE, see Katy Hazan, *Les Enfants de l'après-guerre dans les Maisons de l'OSE* (Paris: Somogy Editions d'Art, 2012), p. 17.

52. Mary Fraser Kirsh, 'The Lost Children of Europe: Narrating the Rehabilitation of Child Holocaust Survivors in Great Britain and Israel', unpublished PhD thesis (University of Wisconsin-Madison, 2012), p. 134. On the British scheme, see also Martin Gilbert, *The Boys: The Story of 732 Young Concentration Camp Survivors* (London: Weidenfeld & Nicolson, 1996).

53. CBF committee meeting minutes, 15 November 1945, reel 37, file 198/6; CBF committee meeting minutes, undated but after 4 December 1945, reel 37, file 198/11, Wiener Library.

54. The Australians partly fulfilled their quota by raising the age limit first to sixteen, and then to twenty-one by 1950. Although the AJWS was searching for children in the camps from 1945 onwards, the first group of children only arrived in Australia in January 1948, by which time the JDC budget cuts had encouraged the OSE to participate in selecting children for the Australian scheme. Regarding the Canadian scheme, there is no agreement, either in the CJC files or among later historians, on the total number of children brought to Canada. During the tenure of the scheme from 1947 to 1952, the CJC gave the official number of 'orphans' as 1,116, but later agency statistics cite 'over 1,200 Jewish orphans'. Later historians have given the total variously as 1,121 (Burgard, ' "Une Nouvelle Vie dans un nouveau pays" ', p. 39), or 1,123 (Fraidie Martz, *Open Your Hearts: The Story of the Jewish War Orphans in Canada* [Montreal: Véhicule Press, 1996]; and Goldberg, *Holocaust Survivors in Canada*). Figures compiled by the regional CJC offices in 1959 put the total at 1,275; see Lappin to Saalheimer, 20 July 1959, CA box 71, folder 659, 'Study on war orphans', UJRA collection, CJCA.

55. See the December 1947 issue of the USCOM quarterly bulletin *Orphans of the Storm*. The majority of the youngest children were non-Jewish 'Lebensborn' children taken by the ITS's Child Search Branch from Nazi Germanization centres. On USCOM, see Michal Ostrovsky, ' "We Are Standing By": Rescue Operations of the United States Committee for the Care of European Children', *Holocaust and Genocide Studies*, 29:2 (2015), pp. 230–50. On the impacts of the 1948 DP Act, see Leonard Dinnerstein, *America and the Survivors of the Holocaust* (New York: Columbia University Press, 1982), p. 288. See also Mark Wyman, *DPs: Europe's Displaced Persons* (New York: Cornell University Press, 1998); Haim Genizi, *America's Fair Share: The Admission and Resettlement of Displaced Persons, 1945–1952*

(Detroit, MI: Wayne State University Press, 1993); and Beth B. Cohen, 'American Jews and Holocaust Survivors, 1946–54', in Patt and Berkowitz, *We Are Here*.

56. On the Canadian case, particularly useful are Irving Abella and Harold Troper, *None Is Too Many: Canada and the Jews of Europe, 1933–1948* (Toronto: University of Toronto Press, 2012); Franklin Bialystok, *Delayed Impact: The Holocaust and the Canadian Jewish Community* (Montreal: McGill-Queen's University Press, 2000); Burgard, ' "Une Nouvelle Vie dans un nouveau pays" '; Martz, *Open Your Hearts*; and Goldberg, *Holocaust Survivors in Canada*.

57. The 1947 order-in-council is reprinted in Lappin, *The Redeemed Children*, p. 12. The federal government stipulated that the children had to be cared for by accredited casework agencies, which meant in practice that the CJC had to hire social workers trained in the casework model to administer the care of the orphans. It is interesting to note that this insistence on professional casework standards was in the 1947 Privy Council order, but not in the original 1942 one, illustrating just how greatly standards of childcare had shifted in the period after the war.

58. Manfred Saalheimer to Ruth and William Hirsch, Ca Subject Files (FOR-MED), box 26, 'Homes, Prospective 1947–1949', UJRA, CJCA.

59. Ca Subject Files (FOR-MED), box 26, 'Homes, Prospective 1947–1949', UJRA, CJCA. The fact that some of the families that inquired about adoption from the programme stated their preference for infants three years after the war's end demonstrates a rather nebulous understanding of the situation in Europe. See also Manfred Saalheimer, 'Bringing Jewish Orphan Children to Canada', *Canadian Jewish Review*, 5 December 1947, pp. 7 and 82.

60. *Peterborough Evening Examiner*, 14 November 1947.

61. On the problems associated with foster families for children on the British Kindertransport scheme, see Judith Tydor Baumel, *Never Look Back: The Jewish Refugee Children in Great Britain, 1938–1945* (West Lafayette, IN: Purdue University Press, 2012). The CJC chiefly used the children's centres at Prien and Wartenberg, and the Aglasterhausen International Children's Center near Heidelberg, for this purpose. The CJC had only three officers on the ground in Europe (Ethel Ostry, Manfred Saalheimer, and Lottie Levinson), and thus relied heavily on other agencies to interview children and prepare their case files, chiefly the JDC, the IRO, and OSE. On this see Burgard, ' "Une Nouvelle Vie dans un nouveau pays" ', pp. 145–74. On UNRRA children's centres, see Verena Buser, 'Displaced Children: 1945 and the Child Tracing Division of the United Nations Relief and Rehabilitation Administration', *The Holocaust in History and Memory*, 7 (2014), pp. 109–23; and Taylor, *In the Children's Best Interests*, pp. 60–9.

62. 'Rejections, Prien and Wartenberg', 1948, box Cb 01, UJRA, CJCA.

63. Quoted in Lappin, *The Redeemed Children*, p. 49.

64. Ibid, p. 37. In the CJC archives, I was only able to find sixty-seven files for children born in the period from 1935 to 1944. The first contingent of CJC children sailed to Halifax on 13 September 1947, and the final child arrived on the scheme on 10 March 1952.

65. Lappin, *The Redeemed Children*, p. 53.

66. Ibid, p. 60.

67. Ibid, p. 56.

68. Ibid, p. 85; 'Outline for Homefinding Committee', 1948, file 'Home Finding Committee, emergency 1948', box 26, Ca Subject Files (FOR-MED), UJRA collection, CJCA.

69. Greta Fischer, 'The Refugee Youth Program in Montreal, 1947–1952', unpublished Masters thesis in social work (McGill University, 1955).

70. Lappin, *The Redeemed Children*, p. 745.

71. 'Z., Freda, 1948–9', Cb 03, UJRA collection, CJCA.

72. 'R., Tomas, 1949–1952', Cb 03, UJRA collection, CJCA.

73. 'J., Marcel' (pseudonym), Cb 03, UJRA collection, CJCA. Marcel's status as an 'unaccompanied child' had been verified by Rachel Rottersman. Rottersman was the head of Aglasterhausen children's centre, and also played an important role in tracing relatives

of unaccompanied children for UNRRA. Her fascinating papers can be found in the United States Holocaust Memorial Museum Archives (Rachel Greene Rottersman papers).

74. 'J., Marcel', 1948–1950, Cb 03, UJRA collection, CJCA.

75. Esther Gorosh to H. Frank, September 1949, 'J., Marcel', 1948–1950, Cb 03, UJRA collection, CJCA.

76. Estelle Mindess to Manfred Saalheimer, 26 July 1950, 'J., Marcel', 1948–1950, Cb 03, UJRA collection, CJCA. This is the last document in Marcel's case file.

77. On the designated scheme for tailors, see Bialystok, *Delayed Impact*, pp. 50–6. Dorota was not eligible, however, to emigrate on the same scheme as her aunt.

78. 'J., Dorota (pseudonym), 1948–1958', Cb 03, box 35, UJRA collection, CJCA.

79. Ibid.

80. Clare Greenwald to Manfred Saalheimer, 24 November 1949, 'J., Dorota, 1948–1958', Cb 03, box 35, UJRA collection, CJCA.

81. Quoted in Sophie S. to CJC Vancouver office, 20 September 1949, 'J., Dorota, 1948–1958', Cb 03, box 35, UJRA collection, CJCA.

82. It is clear that, at some point, documents were removed from Dorota's file: her case file closed in 1958, but the last document currently in the file is dated 1949. This frequently happened with CJC files; in some instances nearly the entire contents of the case file folders have been removed. I was unable to trace Dorota herself, so cannot be sure how her story ended, nor how she came to understand it over time as she grew up.

## CHAPTER 4: FAMILY REUNIONS

1. 'Form to be used for referring unaccompanied children for immigration to Canada', 1948, B., Isak [pseudonym], 1948–1949, Cb 03, box 32, UJRA collection, CJCA.

2. 'Report for period from 3 October 1948 to 3 April 1949', B., Isak, 1948–1949, Cb 03, box 32, UJRA collection, CJCA.

3. Isak B. case file, digital document numbers 78956203 through 78956208 and 109400522 through 109400548, ITS Digital Archive, USHMMA.

4. Thelma Tessler to Manfred Saalheimer, 11 February 1949, B., Isak, 1948–1949, Cb 03, box 32, UJRA collection, CJCA.

5. Director of area no. 7, IRO Headquarters, to APO 407 U.S. Army, 5 April 1949, digital document 84173576, ITS Digital Archive, USHMMA.

6. Rebecca Jinks, *Representing Genocide: The Holocaust as Paradigm?* (London: Bloomsbury, 2016), p. 139.

7. Of the 100 children in this study, a handful were never separated from their parents during the war; these children sometimes found the post-war transition smoother.

8. Daniella Doron, *Jewish Youth and Identity in Postwar France: Rebuilding Family and Nation* (Bloomington, IN: Indiana University Press, 2015), pp. 5–15; Maud Mandel, *In the Aftermath of Genocide: Armenians and Jews in Twentieth-Century France* (Durham, NC: Duke University Press, 2003).

9. Mary Fraser Kirsh, 'The Lost Children of Europe: Narrating the Rehabilitation of Child Holocaust Survivors in Great Britain and Israel', unpublished PhD thesis (University of Wisconsin-Madison, 2012), p. 2.

10. Tara Zahra, *The Lost Children: Reconstructing Europe's Families after World War II* (Cambridge, MA: Harvard University Press, 2011), pp. ix–x.

11. On UNRRA and its work with children, see Ben Shephard, *The Long Road Home: The Aftermath of the Second World War* (London: Bodley Head, 2010), pp. 300–44.

12. Quoted in Kirsh, 'The Lost Children of Europe', p. 145.

13. USCOM quarterly report no. 1, 1 December 1947, p. 2, press clippings collection, Wiener Library.

14. Ben Lappin, *The Redeemed Children: The Story of the Rescue of War Orphans by the Jewish Community of Canada* (Toronto: University of Toronto Press, 1963), p. 68.
15. Anna Freud and Dorothy Burlingham, *War and Children* (London, 1943), p. 45. Many of the experts associated with child welfare in this period followed Freud and Burlingham; for example, Thérèse Brosse, a French cardiologist who by the post-war period had become an expert in child 'mental hygiene', wrote in 1946 that the 'trauma' of war for children was principally the separation from their mothers. See Thérèse Brosse, *War-Handicapped Children: Report on the European Situation* (Paris: UNESCO, 1950).
16. Laura Lee Downs's work demonstrates that the equivalent notion made few inroads in the French context, where it continued to be considered healthy to send children to the countryside without their parents, even after the war ended. See Laura Lee Downs, 'Milieu Social or Milieu Familial? Theories and Practices of Childrearing among the Popular Classes in 20th-Century France and Britain: The Case of Evacuation (1939–45)', *Family and Community History*, 8:1 (May 2005), pp. 49–66.
17. Bowlby quoted in Zahra, *The Lost Children*, p. 65.
18. Joanne Reilly, *Belsen: The Liberation of a Concentration Camp* (London: Routledge, 1998), pp. 50–77; Michael Berkowitz and Suzanne Brown-Fleming, 'Perceptions of Jewish Displaced Persons as Criminals in Early Postwar Germany: Lingering Stereotypes and Self-Fulfilling Prophecies', in Avinoam J. Patt and Michael Berkowitz (eds), *We Are Here: New Approaches to Jewish Displaced Persons in Postwar Germany* (Detroit, MI: Wayne State University Press, 2010), pp. 167–93.
19. IRO child care officer Yvonne de Jong in a June 1948 report, quoted in Zahra, *The Lost Children*, p. 110. While many care workers fretted over female survivors' maternal instincts, they tended to consider widowed men unfit to resume the care of their children. See Zahra, *The Lost Children*, p. 103.
20. Dorothy Hardisty, executive director of the Movement for the Care of Children from the Camps, quoted in Kirsh, 'The Lost Children of Europe', p. 143. Agencies such as the Central British Fund tried to maintain some control over the process by guarding the right to remove a child survivor from their parents' or relatives' home at any point, although they rarely did so in practice.
21. Zahra, *The Lost Children*, p. 102. By 1953 the OSE noted that more and more 'social cases' were coming into their care homes: children who had one or both parents but who could no longer live in the family home due to their parents' poor physical or mental health. Some children had been removed from their families by the courts. See 'OSE maisons d'enfants 1953', file 50 (1949–1953), Erich A. Hausmann papers, RG-58.026, USHMMA.
22. Interview with Erwin Shmuel B., July 1979, interviewed by Sarah Moskovitz, quoted in Sarah Moskovitz, *Love Despite Hate: Child Survivors of the Holocaust and their Adult Lives* (New York: Schocken Books, 1983), p. 195.
23. Memorial book for Erwin B., Kibbutz Ein Harod Meuhad Archives. I thank Anat Zisling, the kibbutz archivist, for sharing this with me.
24. Interview with Erwin Shmuel B., in Moskovitz, *Love Despite Hate*, pp. 196–7.
25. Ibid.
26. Interview with Erwin B., 26 June 2001, interviewer Renée Messi, Kibbutz Ein Harod Meuhad Archives.
27. Memorial book for Erwin B., Kibbutz Ein Harod Meuhad Archives.
28. Diane Wolf, *Beyond Anne Frank: Hidden Children and Postwar Families in Holland* (Berkeley, CA: University of California Press, 2007), p. 163.
29. Diane Wolf found that children's relationships with their surviving parents were often 'distant, cold, and detached'. See ibid, pp. 163–4, 200.
30. Shoshana Felman, 'Education and Crisis', in Shoshana Felman and Dori Laub, *Testimony: Crises of Witnessing in Literature, Psychoanalysis, and History* (New York: Routledge, 1992), pp. 44–6.
31. These were the findings of a study by Dutch psychologist Bloeme Evers-Emden, quoted in Wolf, *Beyond Anne Frank*, p. 181.

32. Interview with Henri O., 15 December 2014, interviewer Rebecca Clifford. See also Henri O., 'A Bridge Too Far', in The Child Survivors' Association of Great Britain, *We Remember: Child Survivors of the Holocaust Speak* (Leicester: Matador, 2011), pp. 113–24.
33. On the issue of jealousy, see Eva Fogelman, 'The Psychology behind Being a Hidden Child', in Jane Marks, *The Hidden Children: The Secret Survivors of the Holocaust* (New York: Ballantine Books, 1993), pp. 292–307.
34. This was equally true for many children of survivors. Here, see in particular Helen Epstein, *Children of the Holocaust: Conversations with Sons and Daughters of Survivors* (New York: G. P. Putnam & Sons, 1979).
35. Interview with Saul A., 13 January 1985, interviewer D.A., Kestenberg Archive of Testimonies of Child Holocaust Survivors, Hebrew University of Jerusalem Archives. Helen Epstein also describes several similar cases in her *Children of the Holocaust.*
36. Bernard Trossman, 'Adolescent Children of Concentration Camp Survivors', *Canadian Psychiatric Association Journal*, 13:2 (April 1968), pp. 121–3.
37. Interview with Eric C., 23 October 1995, interviewer Gary Lubell, USC Shoah Foundation Visual History Archive.
38. Interview with Judith S. (born K.), 20 January 1993, interviewer Joni-Sue Blinderman, Fortunoff Video Archive for Holocaust Testimonies, Yale University Library.
39. AJDC Paris to AJDC Berlin, 19 August 1946, digital document 85308968, ITS Digital Archive, USHMMA.
40. Wolf, *Beyond Anne Frank,* p. 271.
41. Interview with Daisy G. (born L.), 29 July 1987, interviewer Judith Kestenberg, Kestenberg Archive of Testimonies of Child Holocaust Survivors, Hebrew University of Jerusalem Archives.
42. Maurice Halbwachs, *Les Cadres sociaux de la mémoire* (Paris: Presses Universitaires de France, 1925).

## CHAPTER 5: CHILDREN OF THE CHÂTEAU

1. Erich Hausmann, *J'Aurais Pu Choisir les Accents circonflexes!* (Paris: FSJU-Hamoré, 2007), p. 45. Interview with Felice Z. S. (born Z.), 2 February 1998, interviewer Rosalie Franks, USC Shoah Foundation VHA. The OSE care home in the Château de Vaucelles at Taverny still exists: it is still managed by the OSE, and is now called the Maison d'enfants Elie Wiesel. Hausmann later married and had six children of his own. He remained director at Taverny until 1957.
2. Interview with Felice Z. S. (born Z.), USC Shoah Foundation VHA.
3. Ibid.
4. Interview with Hélène Weksler (born Ekhajser), March 1994, quoted in Katy Hazan, *Les Orphelins de la Shoah: Les Maisons de l'espoir, 1944–1960* (Paris: Les Belles Lettres, 2000), pp. 307–8. She also recalled discussing practical, future-oriented topics such as jobs and careers, sexual education, and how to find a marriage partner.
5. Interview with Felice Z. S. (born Z.), 30 December 1992, interviewer Joni Sue Blinderman, Fortunoff Video Archive for Holocaust Testimonies, Yale University Library.
6. Daniella Doron, *Jewish Youth and Identity in Postwar France: Rebuilding Family and Nation* (Bloomington, IN: Indiana University Press, 2015), p. 119.
7. 'Evaluation of Bad-Schallerbach Children's Home in U.S. Zone Austria', 5 June 1951, p. 2, Syma Crane papers, series 1, USHMMA.
8. Klok's biography is taken here from the finding aid for her personal papers collection, located at the United States Holocaust Memorial Museum Archive: https://collections. ushmm.org/findingaids/1997.A.0373_01_fnd_en.pdf (accessed 3 June 2020).
9. 'Evaluation of Bad-Schallerbach Children's Home in U.S. Zone Austria', 5 June 1951, pp. 6, 13, 21, USHMMA.

10. Quoted in Boaz Cohen, 'Survivor Caregivers and Child Survivors: Rebuilding Lives and the Home in the Postwar Period', *Holocaust and Genocide Studies*, 32:1 (2018), pp. 49–65; here 62 f 15.

11. Lena Kuchler tells her story beautifully in her autobiographical *My Hundred Children* (London: Souvenir Press, 1961), originally published in Yiddish as *Meine Kinder* in Paris in 1948. On the anti-Semitic attacks on the Zakopane orphanage, see Karolina Panz, ' "They did not want any more Jews there": The Fate of Jewish Orphans in Podhale, 1945–1946', in Henning Borggräfe, Akim Jah, Nina Ritz, and Steffen Jost (eds), *Freilegungen: Rebuilding Lives – Child Survivors and DP Children in the Aftermath of the Holocaust and Forced Labour* (Göttingen: Wallstein Verlag, 2017), pp. 93–104.

12. Interview with Lena Kuchler, 8 September 1946, interviewer David P. Boder. A copy of the transcript of this interview is available via the Voices of the Holocaust project, at https://iit. aviaryplatform.com/collections/231 (accessed 3 June 2020).

13. On children's courts, see Christian Höschler, 'International Families? Community Living in the IRO Children's Village Bad Aibling, 1948–1951', in Borggräfe et al. (eds), *Freilegungen*, pp. 105–24, here p. 113.

14. Ernst Papanek, *Out of the Fire* (New York: William Morrow, 1975), pp. 86–7.

15. On Papanek, see his fascinating autobiographical work *Out of the Fire*. See also Tara Zahra, *The Lost Children: Reconstructing Europe's Families after World War II* (Cambridge, MA: Harvard University Press, 2011), pp. 99–100. On Corti, see Christian Höschler, 'International Families? Community Living in the IRO Children's Village Bad Aibling, 1948–1951', in Borggräfe et al. (eds), *Freilegungen*. See also the work of Corti's co-worker Elisabeth Rotten: *Children's Communities: A Way of Life for War's Victims* (Paris: UNESCO, 1949). The Pestalozzi Children's Village in the Swiss town of Trogen was founded in accordance with Corti's suggestions, which were also widely taken up in homes for child survivors across Europe.

16. Doron, *Jewish Youth*, p. 136; Zahra, *The Lost Children*, pp. 105–6.

17. Doron, *Jewish Youth*, p. 137.

18. Zahra, *The Lost Children*, p. 19.

19. Post-war debates concerning families versus communal living have been well covered by other scholars, and thus I have not gone into great detail here. See especially Zahra, *The Lost Children*, pp. 59–87, and Doron, *Jewish Youth*, pp. 118–61.

20. Of the roughly thirty children who spent time at Weir Courtney, only eight were placed with foster families, and most of these were the very youngest. There were attempts to have some of the older children fostered, but these children – only slightly older than their adopted peers, but able to articulate their wishes clearly – refused, and matron Alice Goldberger respected their wishes. The situation may have been further complicated by the fact that foreign-born children could not legally be adopted in Britain until the mid-1950s. 'Reports to foster parents in America', Alice Goldberger papers, series 4, USHMMA.

21. Olga Gurvic is quoted in Doron, *Jewish Youth*, p. 124.

22. Ibid, pp. 126–7.

23. Quoted in ibid. p. 130. On Vivette Samuel, born Vivette Hermann in Paris in 1919, see Katy Hazan, *Les Enfants de l'après-guerre dans les Maisons de l'OSE* (Paris: Somogy Editions d'Art, 2012), p. 17.

24. Doron, *Jewish Youth*, p. 131. The OSE did place approximately 1,500 children with foster families, but this was not the privileged route that it was in the Canadian case, for example. On the difficulties French Jews faced in getting their property back after the war, see Maud Mandel, *In the Aftermath of Genocide: Armenians and Jews in Twentieth-Century France* (Durham, NC: Duke University Press, 2003).

25. 'OSE maisons d'enfants 1953', p. 4, file 50, Erich A. Hausmann papers, RG-58.026, USHMMA.

26. Doron, *Jewish Youth*, p. 158.

27. In particular, Hausmann was friends with OSE leaders Bô Cohn and Andrée Salomon, whom he had met via pre-war Jewish youth movements.

28. Hausmann's autobiographical information is taken here from his personal papers, held at the ETH Zürich, a digital copy of which can be found at the United States Holocaust Memorial Museum Archive. See also his autobiographical *J'Aurais Pu Choisir les Accents circonflexes!* (Paris: FSJU-Hamoré, 2007). Many of the children at Fontenay-aux-Roses accompanied Hausmann to Taverny. Hausmann remained at Taverny as director until 1957. He died in 2008.

29. Ekhajser passed through several concentration camps as an adolescent, including Auschwitz and Ravensbrück. See Hazan, *Les Enfants de l'après-guerre*, p. 69, and Hazan, *Les Orphelins de la Shoah*, pp. 307–8.

30. Hausmann, *J'Aurais Pu Choisir*, pp. 30, 40–2. On Irène Opolon, see Susan Gross Solomon's fascinating paper 'Patient Dossiers and Clinical Practice in 1950s French Child Psychiatry', *Revue d'histoire de l'enfance 'irrégulière'*, 18 (2016), pp. 275–96.

31. Hausmann, *J'Aurais Pu Choisir*, pp. 47–52.

32. Ibid, p. 47.

33. Paulette Szabason Goldberg, *Just Think It Never Happened* (Victoria, Australia: Makor Jewish Community Library, 2002), p. 47.

34. Ibid, pp. 43–4.

35. Ibid, p. 44.

36. Interview with Jacques F. (born K.), 24 November 1991, interviewers Myra Katz and Froma Willen, Fortunoff Video Archive for Holocaust Testimonies, Yale University Library.

37. Interview with Beate Z. M. (born Z.), 20 January 1998, interviewer Rosalie Franks, USC Shoah Foundation VHA.

38. Hazan, *Les Enfants*, p. 12.

39. Hausmann notes in his memoir that over time the 'victims of the Shoah moved out, and the victims of decolonization moved in' to Taverny, as Jewish refugees from North Africa began to arrive in mainland France, sometimes so impoverished and overwhelmed that they no longer felt they could care for their children.

40. Hausmann, *J'Aurais Pu Choisir*, p. 57.

41. Eugénie (Jenny) Masour, who was responsible for overseas placements for OSE wards, quoted here in Laura Hobson Faure, 'Orphelines ou soeurs? Penser la famille juive pendant et après la Shoah', *Revue d'histoire*, 145 (2020), pp. 91–104. I am grateful to Laura for sharing an early copy of this paper with me.

42. Hobson Faure, 'Orphelines ou soeurs?'.

43. Szabason Goldberg, *Just Think It Never Happened*, pp. 51–3.

44. Interview with Felice Z. S. (born Z.), USC Shoah Foundation VHA.

45. Felice Z. to J. Patoux, 18 January 1951, 'Felice Z. S. collection', USHMMA.

46. Regine C. to Erich Hausmann, 12 July 1981, file 52, Erich A. Hausmann papers, RG-58.026, USHMMA.

## CHAPTER 6: METAMORPHOSIS

1. Jackie Y., 'Lost and Waiting to Be Found' (unpublished memoir), 2005. I am grateful to Jackie for sharing a copy of his memoir with me.

2. Interview with Jackie Y., 16 December 2014, interviewer Rebecca Clifford, author's collection.

3. Jackie Y., 'Lost and Waiting to Be Found'.

4. Interview with Jackie Y., author's collection.

5. Jackie Y., 'Lost and Waiting to Be Found'.

6. Examples include Gerald Reitlinger's *The Final Solution: An Attempt to Exterminate the Jews of Europe* (New York: Vallentine Mitchell), which was first published in 1953 but had only a limited circulation, and Léon Poliakov's *Bréviaire de la haine* (Paris: Calmann-Levy), which was published as a small run in French in 1951, and then in a scarcely larger English edition (as *Harvest of Hate*) in 1954. On early Holocaust historiography, see Michael Marrus, *The Holocaust in History* (Hanover, NH: University Press of New England, 1987).

7. There is much helpful information on the yizkor books via the Yizkor Books Project: www. jewishgen.org/Yizkor (accessed 3 June 2020).

8. Hasia Diner, *We Remember with Reverence and Love: American Jews and the Myth of Silence after the Holocaust, 1945–1962* (New York: New York University Press, 2009); Laura Jockusch, *Collect and Record! Jewish Holocaust Documentation in Early Postwar Europe* (Oxford: Oxford University Press, 2012).

9. On the DP Act, see Beth Cohen, *Case Closed: Holocaust Survivors in Postwar America* (New Brunswick, NJ: Rutgers University Press, 2007).

10. Gill Rossini, *A Social History of Adoption in England and Wales* (Barnsley: Pen and Sword, 2014), pp. 99–111. By the 1950s this was changing: the work of child psychoanalysts such as John Bowlby suggested that it was not psychologically healthy to ban all discussion of the birth family, and better to tell a child the truth early on than to risk the tremendous shock that could follow a later discovery. We thus see the beginnings, in this period, of 'natural' adoption societies that advocated honesty about adoption between children and parents. This approach, however, remained a minority one until the 1970s.

11. In England and Wales, it remained illegal to adopt a foreign-born child until the mid-1950s, and even then it was a bureaucratic challenge for families to do so. Even the 1950 Adoption Act, which sought to modernize the legal process of adoption in the wake of the growth in illegitimate births that took place during the war, had not established a pathway for the adoption of foreign-born children, despite the fact that many of the families who had taken in the 10,000 children of the Kindertransport hoped to adopt their wards formally.

12. Interview with Gittel H., 9 February 1985, interviewer Milton Kestenberg, Kestenberg Archive of Testimonies of Child Holocaust Survivors, Hebrew University of Jerusalem Archives.

13. Interview with Peter D. (born B.), 27 May 1984, interviewer Sarah Moskovitz, Kestenberg Archive of Testimonies of Child Holocaust Survivors, Hebrew University of Jerusalem Archives.

14. Interview with Denny M., 31 July 1997, interviewer Miriam Feldman-Rosman, USC Shoah Foundation VHA.

15. Ibid.

16. Sarah Moskovitz, *Love Despite Hate: Child Survivors of the Holocaust and their Adult Lives* (New York: Schocken Books, 1983), p. 228.

17. Katy Hazan, *Les Enfants de l'après-guerre dans les Maisons de l'OSE* (Paris: Somogy Editions d'Art, 2012), p. 12.

18. Ibid, p. 42; Daniella Doron, *Jewish Youth and Identity in Postwar France: Rebuilding Family and Nation* (Bloomington, IN: Indiana University Press, 2015), p. 152.

19. Interview with Jackie Y., author's collection.

20. Interview with Peter D. (born B.), Kestenberg archive.

21. Interview with Felice Z. S. (born Z.), USC Shoah Foundation VHA.

22. Interview with Suzanne A. (born N.), 22 January 1990, interviewer Lisa Newman, Toronto Jewish Congress Archives of the Holocaust Project, USC Shoah Foundation VHA.

23. 'Report, June to November 1949', 'N., Suzanne 1947–1950', box 37, Cb 03, UJRA collection, CJCA.

24. This and subsequent quotations from interview with Suzanne A. (born N.), USC Shoah Foundation VHA.

25. Edith Ludowyk Gyomroi, 'The Analysis of a Young Concentration Camp Victim', *The Psychoanalytic Study of the Child*, XVIII (1963), pp. 484–510, here p. 488.

26. See chapter 7, notes 21 and 22.

27. Gyomroi, 'The Analysis of a Young Concentration Camp Victim', pp. 496–7.

28. 'Anfragekarte', 24.11.1987, in Central Names Index, International Tracing Service collection, 0.1, document 47004551, WLA.

29. From 1949 to 1953 individual states in West Germany issued their own indemnification regulations based on those published by the occupying forces; when the Federal Republic was formed, these various laws were replaced by the BEG. See Milton Kestenberg, 'Discriminatory

Aspects of the German Indemnification Policy: A Continuation of Persecution', in Martin S. Bergmann and Milton E. Jucovy (eds), *Generations of the Holocaust* (New York: Columbia University Press, 1982), pp. 62–79, here p. 63.

30. Anne Rothfeld, 'A Source for Holocaust Research: The United Restitution Organization Files', *Perspectives on History: The Newsmagazine of the American Historical Association*, April 2000.

31. On child survivors and children of survivors in the indemnification process, see Kestenberg, 'Discriminatory Aspects'. On the process in general, see Michael Bazyler, *Holocaust Justice: The Battle for Restitution in America's Courts* (New York: New York University Press, 2003); Stuart E. Eizenstat, *Imperfect Justice: Looted Assets, Slave Labor, and the Unfinished Business of World War II* (New York: Perseus Books, 2003); Marilyn Henry, *Confronting the Perpetrators: A History of the Claims Conference* (New York: Vallentine Mitchell, 2007); Christian Pross, *Paying for the Past: The Struggle over Reparations for Surviving Victims of the Nazi Terror* (Baltimore, MD: Johns Hopkins University Press, 1998); Ronald W. Zweig, *German Reparations and the Jewish World: A History of the Claims Conference* (Boulder, CO: Westview, 1987); and Elazar Barkan, *The Guilt of Nations: Restitution and Negotiating Historical Injustices* (New York: W. W. Norton, 2000).

32. URO Köln to L. Montefiore, 30 September 1959, A2049/198/13, West London Synagogue Archives, Hartley Library, University of Southampton.

33. Subsequent amendments to the legislation, and a decades-long process of appeals against rejections, meant that compensation was extended well beyond the initial 1958 deadline, and for some groups (including some child survivors) it continues to this day.

34. Interview with Mirjam S., September 1978, interviewer Sarah Moskovitz, in Moskovitz, *Love Despite Hate*, pp. 184–5. Mirjam S. passed away in 2017.

35. Ibid.

36. URO Köln to Germany Embassy, London, 18 February 1959, A2049/198/13, West London Synagogue Archives, Hartley Library, University of Southampton.

37. Kestenberg, 'Discriminatory Aspects', p. 66.

38. Interview with Janek E. (pseudonym), 30 September 1994, interviewer Klara Firestone, USC Shoah Foundation VHA. Because I use Janek's URO records here, and researchers using these records must sign a waiver ensuring an applicant's full anonymity, I have had to use a pseudonym (throughout the book) for Janek – even though he gave his VHA interview in his own name.

39. Oscar Myer to Janek E., Janek E. file (pseudonym), box 1, MS1U-13-4, URO Los Angeles records, RG-28.004, USHMMA; grammatical errors in the original. The information provided by the URO adviser was only partially correct: Budzyn was a forced labour camp in District Lublin, and became a sub-camp of Majdanek in the early autumn of 1943. Janek, however, could not have known that it was a forced labour camp rather than a closed ghetto – a somewhat arbitrary distinction, in any case, for a child who was trapped there and knew that his siblings had been murdered there.

40. Statement dated 16 April 1957, Janek E. file (pseudonym), box 1, MS1U-13-4, URO Los Angeles records, RG-28.004, USHMMA. The file does not preserve Janek's original English statement, only the German translation, so I have here translated from the German back into English.

41. Jackie Y., 'Lost and Waiting to Be Found'.

42. Moskovitz, *Love Despite Hate*, p. 228.

## CHAPTER 7: TRAUMA

1. See Martin Gilbert, *The Boys: The Story of 732 Young Concentration Camp Survivors* (London: Weidenfeld & Nicolson, 1996), pp. 254–86, and Elisabeth Young-Bruehl, *Anna Freud: A Biography* (New York: Summit Books, 1989), pp. 320–2.

2. The 300 children who arrived from Theresienstadt in August 1945 were the first children to come to Britain under the 'thousand orphans' scheme managed by the Central British Fund. The youngest of these children were sent to Weir Courtney, with the exception of the six toddlers: they joined the Weir Courtney group after their initial year under observation at Bulldogs Bank. Jackie Y. was the oldest of the six toddlers, and was three and a half when he was brought to Britain.

3. No one at the time noted the disturbing irony of using child concentration camp survivors as subjects for ongoing experiments. As psychologist John Sigal would write many years later of child survivors, 'anyone interested in testing theories of human development dreams of being able to conduct a study that would permit one to determine the long-term consequences of deviations from normative rearing at various earlier development stages'. The question of whether or not this was ethical was never broached, neither at the time of Freud's work, nor at the time of Sigal's later writing. Sigal in foreword to Hans Keilson, *Sequential Traumatization in Children: A Clinical and Statistical Follow-Up Study on the Fate of the Jewish War Orphans in the Netherlands* (Jerusalem: Magnes Press, 1979), p. xi.

4. On the history of the Hampstead War Nurseries, see Michal Shapira, *The War Inside: Psychoanalysis, Total War, and the Making of the Democratic Self in Postwar Britain* (Cambridge: Cambridge University Press, 2013), pp. 66–77.

5. Anna Freud and Sophie Dann, 'An Experiment in Group Upbringing', *The Psychoanalytic Study of the Child*, vol. VI (1951), pp. 127–68. On the work of John Bowlby, see Shapira, *The War Inside*, pp. 198–214; Tara Zahra, *The Lost Children: Reconstructing Europe's Families after World War II* (Cambridge, MA: Harvard University Press, 2011), pp. 65–6; and Young-Bruehl, *Anna Freud*, pp. 322–3.

6. Freud and Dann, 'An Experiment in Group Upbringing'. For current clinical perspectives, see for example Salman Akhtar, *The Mother and her Child: Clinical Aspects of Attachment, Separation, and Loss* (New York: Jason Aronson, 2012).

7. Freud and Dann, 'An Experiment in Group Upbringing'.

8. Ibid. Further details concerning where Freud and Bowlby's arguments diverged can be found in Anna Freud, 'Discussion of Dr. John Bowlby's Paper', *The Psychoanalytic Study of the Child*, XV (1960), pp. 53–62.

9. Dagmar Herzog, *Cold War Freud: Psychoanalysis in an Age of Catastrophes* (Cambridge: Cambridge University Press, 2017), p. 92. On Anna Freud's connection to the American Foster Parents' Plan for War Children, see Amanda Jones, *Bringing up War Babies: The Wartime Child in Women's Writing and Psychoanalysis at Mid-Century* (New York: Routledge, 2018), pp. 78–80.

10. Useful texts concerning post-war developments in psychology and psychoanalysis and the concept of 'trauma' include: Mari Jo Buhle, *Feminism and its Discontents: A Century of Struggle with Psychoanalysis* (Cambridge, MA: Harvard University Press, 1998); Eli Zaretsky, *Secrets of the Soul: A Social and Cultural History of Psychoanalysis* (New York: Vintage, 2005); George Makari, *Revolution in Mind: The Creation of Psychoanalysis* (New York: HarperCollins, 2008); and John Burnham (ed.), *After Freud Left: A Century of Psychoanalysis in America* (Chicago, IL: University of Chicago Press, 2012). Useful sources on the history of post-traumatic stress disorder as a diagnosis include: Yael Danieli (ed.), *International Handbook of Multigenerational Legacies of Trauma* (New York: Springer, 1998); Leo Eitinger and Robert Krell, *The Psychological and Medical Effects of Concentration Camps and Related Persecutions on Survivors of the Holocaust* (Vancouver: University of British Columbia Press, 1985); Charles R. Figley, *Trauma and its Wake: The Study and Treatment of Post-Traumatic Stress Disorder*, vol. 1 (Hove: Psychology Press, 1985); Mardi Jon Horowitz (ed.), *Essential Papers on Post-Traumatic Stress Disorder* (New York: New York University Press, 1999); and Andreas Maercker, Zahava Salomon, and Matthias Schutzwohl (eds), *Post-Traumatic Stress Disorder: A Lifespan Developmental Perspective* (New York: Bertrams, 1999).

11. *Oxford English Dictionary* digital edition.

12. Michael R. Trimble, 'Post-Traumatic Stress Disorder: History of a Concept', in Figley, *Trauma and its Wake*, pp. 5–14; Adrian C. Brock (ed.), *Internationalizing the History of Psychology* (New York: New York University Press, 2006), p. 236; Tracey Loughran, 'Shell Shock, Trauma, and the First World War: The Making of a Diagnosis and its Histories, *Journal of the History of Medicine and Allied Sciences*, 67:1 (January 2012), pp. 94–119.

13. Freud quoted in Martin S. Bergmann and Milton E. Jucovy (eds), *Generations of the Holocaust* (New York: Columbia University Press, 1982), p. 9.
14. Beth B. Cohen, 'American Jews and Holocaust Survivors, 1946–54', in Avinoam J. Patt and Michael Berkowitz (eds), *We Are Here: New Approaches to Jewish Displaced Persons in Postwar Germany* (Detroit, MI: Wayne State University Press, 2010).
15. On the Freudian viewpoint, see Wolfgang Schneider and Michael Pressley (eds), *Memory Development between Two and Twenty*, 2nd edn (Mahwah, NJ: Lawrence Erlbaum Associates, 1997), p. 3. On Piaget and his influence, see Patricia J. Bauer, 'Development of Memory in Early Childhood', in Nelson Cowan (ed.), *The Development of Memory in Childhood* (Hove: Psychology Press, 1997), p. 84, and Robyn Fivush, 'Event Memory in Early Childhood', ibid, p. 140. Psychologists today do not necessarily agree on what causes 'infantile amnesia', but they do concur that, with slight variations across different cultures, we cannot directly remember events from the earliest years of our lives. In a 2000 meta-analysis, D. C. Rubin found that the mean age of earliest memories was three and a half, but for some individuals the period of 'infantile amnesia' can stretch as late as six or seven years old. See D. C. Rubin, 'The Distribution of Early Childhood Memories', *Memory*, 8:4 (2000), pp. 265–9. Psychologists have also demonstrated that although many adults firmly *believe* that they retain memories from before the age of three, this is in fact an illusion. See in particular Christine Wells, Catriona Morrison, and Martin Conway, 'Adult Recollections of Childhood Memories: What Details Can Be Recalled?', *The Quarterly Journal of Experimental Psychology*, 67:7 (2013), pp. 1249–61.
16. See for example Robyn Fivush, 'The Functions of Event Memory: Some Comments on Nelson and Barsalou' (1988), pp. 277–82; Robyn Fivush, Catherine Haden, and Salimah Adam, 'Structure and Coherence of Preschoolers' Personal Narratives over Time: Implications for Childhood Amnesia', *Journal of Experimental Child Psychology*, 60 (1995), pp. 32–50; and Katherine Nelson, 'The Psychological and Social Origins of Autobiographical Memory', *Psychological Science*, 4:1 (1993), pp. 1–8.
17. Fivush, Haden, and Adam, 'Structure and Coherence of Preschoolers' Personal Narratives over Time', pp. 32–56; Nelson, 'The Psychological and Social Origins of Autobiographical Memory', pp. 1–8; David B. Pillemer and Sheldon H. White, 'Childhood Events Recalled by Children and Adults', in Hayne W. Reese (ed.), *Advances in Child Development and Behaviour* (San Diego, CA: Academic Press, 1989), pp. 297–340; Fivush, 'The Functions of Event Memory', pp. 277–82.
18. William G. Niederland, 'Clinical Observations on the "Survivor Syndrome"', *International Journal of Psycho-Analysis*, 49 (1968), pp. 313–15.
19. Ibid, p. 98.
20. Herzog, *Cold War Freud*, p. 90.
21. Ibid, p. 90.
22. Scholars have tended to suggest that West German psychiatrists were uniquely intransigent in refusing to credit that traumatic events could have long-term consequences, but the truth is that there were psychiatrists throughout Western Europe, and in North America as well, who were equally guarded in their approach. This remained true well into the 1970s. Here see Svenja Goltermann, *The War in their Minds: German Soldiers and their Violent Pasts in West Germany* (Ann Arbor, MI: University of Michigan Press, 2017).
23. Most academic work on the restitution process has focused on the claims of Jewish survivors, but non-Jewish survivors faced equally daunting prospects in attempting to secure compensation. Recent work is shedding light on how restitution for non-Jewish victims of the Nazis was negotiated, secured, and distributed. The research of Susanna Schrafstetter is notable here; see her 'The Diplomacy of *Wiedergutmachung*: Memory, the Cold War, and the Western European Victims of Nazism, 1956–1964', *Holocaust and Genocide Studies*, 7:3 (2003), pp. 459–79.
24. Milton Kestenberg, 'Discriminatory Aspects of the German Indemnification Policy: A Continuation of Persecution', in Bergmann and Jucovy, *Generations of the Holocaust*, pp. 62–79. Indeed, by 1960, Freud was arguing that her earlier work on the Theresienstadt

toddlers had been overly optimistic about their long-term mental health: 'These children who had undergone repeated traumatic separations from birth or infancy onward achieved comparatively stable relationships during their latency period; but from preadolescence onward they displayed almost without exception withdrawn, depressive, self-accusatory or hostile mood swings.' See Anna Freud, 'Discussion of Dr. John Bowlby's Paper,' pp. 53–62, here p. 59.

25. Bergmann and Jucovy, *Generations of the Holocaust*, pp. 10–11.
26. Two books consolidated this early scholarship: Henry Krystal (ed.), *Massive Psychic Trauma* (New York: International Universities Press, 1968), and Henry Krystal and William G. Niederland, *Psychic Traumatization: After Effects in Individuals and Communities* (Boston: Little, Brown, 1971).
27. Vivian Rakoff, J. J. Sigal, and N. B. Epstein, 'Children and Families of Concentration Camp Survivors', *Canada's Mental Health*, 14:4 (July–August 1966), pp. 24–6, here p. 24. See also Vivian Rakoff's earlier article in the general-circulation Jewish periodical *Viewpoints*, the earliest article published on the issue of mental health problems in children of survivors: Vivian Rakoff, 'Long-Term Effects of the Concentration Camp Experience', *Viewpoints* (March 1966), pp. 17–21. In addition, at roughly the same time, Rakoff and Sigal's colleague at McGill University in Montreal, Bernard Trossman, began to see increasing numbers of children of survivors visiting the university's medical clinic regarding mental health issues; see Bernard Trossman, 'Adolescent Children of Concentration Camp Survivors', *Canadian Psychiatric Association Journal*, 13:2 (April 1968), pp. 121–3.
28. Rakoff, Sigal, and Epstein, 'Children and Families', p. 25.
29. H. Z. Winnik, 'Contribution to Symposium on Psychic Traumatization through Social Catastrophe', *International Journal of Psycho-Analysis*, 49 (1968), pp. 298–301. Winnik's paper was presented at the 1967 Copenhagen conference. Others at the conference spoke of child and adolescent survivors as well, including US-based psychoanalyst Hans Fink, who described his treatment of the adolescent survivor Joseph, and concluded that 'his illness cannot be explained primarily as the result of unresolved, unconscious, infantile conflicts'. See Hans Fink, 'Development Arrest as a Result of Nazi Persecution during Adolescence', *International Journal of Psycho-Analysis*, 49 (1968), pp. 327–9.
30. There is a useful guide to the history of the Dutch aid organizations in Keilson's book, *Sequential Traumatization in Children*. See also Diane Wolf, *Beyond Anne Frank: Hidden Children and Postwar Families in Holland* (Berkeley, CA: University of California Press, 2007), and Joel S. Fishman, 'Jewish War Orphans in the Netherlands: The Guardianship Issue, 1945–1950', *Wiener Library Bulletin*, 27 (1973–4), pp. 31–6.
31. Keilson, *Sequential Traumatization*, pp. 12–18.
32. Ibid, p. 48.
33. Ibid, p. 80.
34. Ibid, p. 82. Keilson completed his study in 1978, and it was first published in German in 1979.
35. Wolf, *Beyond Anne Frank*, pp. 95–125.
36. Ian Hacking, 'Memory Sciences, Memory Politics', in Paul Antze and Michael Lambek (eds), *Tense Past: Cultural Essays in Trauma and Memory* (New York: Routledge, 1996), pp. 67–87; Ruth Leys, *Trauma: A Geneaology* (Chicago, IL: University of Chicago Press, 2000), pp. 5–17.
37. American Psychiatric Association, 'Post-Traumatic Stress Disorder', *Diagnostic and Statistical Manual of Mental Disorders*, 3rd edn (Washington, DC: American Psychiatric Association, 1980).
38. Freud and Dann, 'An Experiment in Group Upbringing'. See also Mary Fraser Kirsh, 'The Lost Children of Europe: Narrating the Rehabilitation of Child Holocaust Survivors in Great Britain and Israel', unpublished PhD thesis (University of Wisconsin-Madison, 2012), p. 137.
39. By the late 1970s the term 'survivor syndrome' had made its way decisively into the North American English-language press, where it was used in reference not only to Holocaust survivors, but also to survivors of other, far more common events, such as natural disasters.

40. Bergmann and Jucovy, *Generations of the Holocaust*, pp. 4–6.
41. Judith Kestenberg, 'Psychoanalytic Contributions to the Problem of Children of Survivors from Nazi Persecution', *Israel Annals of Psychiatry and Related Disciplines*, 10:4 (1972); Judith and Milton Kestenberg, 'Background of the Study', in Bergmann and Jucovy, *Generations of the Holocaust*, pp. 33–43, here pp. 37–8. See also Helen Epstein, *Children of the Holocaust: Conversations with Sons and Daughters of Survivors* (New York: G. P. Putnam & Sons, 1979), pp. 217–18.
42. Interview with R.G., 17 August 1984, interviewer Judith Kestenberg, Kestenberg Archive of Testimonies of Child Holocaust Survivors, Hebrew University of Jerusalem Archives.
43. Interview with Gittel H., 9 February 1985, interviewer Milton Kestenberg, Kestenberg Archive of Testimonies of Child Holocaust Survivors, Hebrew University of Jerusalem Archives. When the journalist Helen Epstein conducted interviews with children of Holocaust survivors in the late 1970s, she noted that many of the sons and daughters of survivors profiled in her book had had similarly frustrating encounters with psychiatrists and psychoanalysts, although in their case the frustration concerned the expert's checklist of symptoms regarding their parents. Epstein cites, for example, the case of Ruth Alexander, who went to visit a university psychiatrist when she was an undergraduate, and describes how he asked questions about her survivor parents' social life and digestive upsets that made her feel 'very uncomfortable. I felt that he didn't know about me and he thought he did. I didn't like the way he started pulling out all those questions. I thought: Who the hell does he think he is?' Quoted in Epstein, *Children of the Holocaust*, p. 200.
44. Interview with Denny M., July 1977, interviewer Sarah Moskovitz, *Love Despite Hate: Child Survivors of the Holocaust and their Adult Lives* (New York: Schocken Books, 1983), pp. 92–100.
45. Moskovitz, *Love Despite Hate*, p. 226.
46. Epstein, *Children of the Holocaust*, pp. 202–3.

## CHAPTER 8: THE LUCKY ONES

1. 'Cecilia W. to A. Eisenstadt, OSE Paris', 1966, doc. 12, file 6, RG-43.113M, USHMMA.
2. This and all subsequent quotes from interview with Zilla C.,14 November 1987, interviewer Judith Kestenberg, Kestenberg Archive of Testimonies of Child Holocaust Survivors, Hebrew University of Jerusalem Archives.
3. Zilla's doctoral study was later published as *Suicide in French Thought from Montesquieu to Cioran* (New York: Peter Lang, 1999). At the time of her death in 2007 she was writing a second book on the role of intellectuals in post-war France that explored how some worked to conceal their wartime actions in the post-war period.
4. Serge Klarsfeld, *Le Mémorial de la déportation des Juifs de France* (Paris: Association des Fils et Filles des Déportés Juifs de France, 1978). The English edition was published in 1983 as *Memorial to the Jews Deported from France, 1942–1944* (New York: B. Klarsfeld Foundation, 1983). Klarsfeld's book was enormously important to survivors whose loved ones had been deported from France. As the historian Annette Wieviorka writes, on the book's publication 'families whose dead had no graves at last knew the fate of their relatives'. See Annette Wieviorka, *The Era of the Witness*, trans. Jared Stark (Ithaca, NY: Cornell University Press, 2006), p. 29. See also my *Commemorating the Holocaust: The Dilemmas of Remembrance in France and Italy* (Oxford: Oxford University Press, 2013), p. 58.
5. Among the canonical works by historians in this area are Wieviorka, *The Era of the Witness*; Peter Novick, *The Holocaust and Collective Memory* (London: Bloomsbury, 2001); Henry Rousso, *The Vichy Syndrome: History and Memory in France since 1944*, trans. Arthur Goldhammer (Cambridge, MA: Harvard University Press, 1991); and Tony Judt's epilogue to his excellent *Postwar: A History of Europe since 1945* (London: Pimlico, 2007).

6. The English edition of Elie Wiesel's *Night* appeared in 1960, trans. Stella Rodway (London: Panther Books), and the English edition of Primo Levi's *If This Is a Man* was first published in 1959 (New York: Orion Press). These works are well known to English-language readers, yet are not necessarily the most important memoirs of the late 1950s and early 1960s for readers of other European languages (including Yiddish), or of Hebrew.
7. Wieviorka, *The Era of the Witness*, pp. 98, 107. In the US the miniseries drew 120 million viewers.
8. Of the survivors whose stories are explored in this study, a handful recalled in interviews the emotional impact of the television miniseries *Holocaust*, and one mentioned the impact of the Eichmann trial. None of the others mentioned *any* of the events that scholars have privileged in their discussions of memory. This does not mean that these events had no import for child survivors at the time they occurred (as interviews may have been conducted years or even decades later), but it does suggest we should look beyond the standard canon of 'vectors of memory' as we weigh the factors that influenced child survivors' own remembering over time.
9. On the first use of child witnesses in American courtrooms, and the implications of this shift, see Michael Sherwin, 'The Law in Relation to the Wishes and Feelings of the Child', in Ronald Davie, Graham Upton, and Ved Varma (eds), *The Voice of the Child: A Handbook for Professionals* (London: Falmer Press, 1996).
10. The concept of children's rights, however, pre-dated the Convention by several decades: the first Declaration of the Rights of the Child was drafted by Save the Children founder Eglantyne Jebb, and endorsed by the League of Nations General Assembly in 1924.
11. For a useful overview of these developments, see Robyn Fivush, 'Event Memory in Early Childhood', in Nelson Cowan (ed.), *The Development of Memory in Childhood* (Hove: Psychology Press, 1997), pp. 139–57.
12. Wieviorka, *The Era of the Witness*, pp. 96–7.
13. Eva Illouz, *Saving the Modern Soul: Therapy, Emotions, and the Culture of Self-Help* (Berkeley, CA: University of California Press, 2008).
14. See chapter 3, n. 55, for a discussion of the number of children who immigrated to Canada on the CJC scheme.
15. Ben Lappin, *The Redeemed Children: The Story of the Rescue of War Orphans by the Jewish Community of Canada* (Toronto: University of Toronto Press, 1963), p. 156.
16. Ibid, p. 156. Those who lived in Toronto were also asked if they would be willing to be interviewed by a volunteer from the Council of Jewish Women. Sadly, no record of these precious interviews survives, although a list of the questions that interviewers asked can be found in 'Note to interviewers, 4 September 1959', 'Study on war orphans', folder 659, CA box 71, UJRA collection, CJCA.
17. Copies of the blank questionnaire can be found in 'Questionnaire – European Youth Group Study', folder 659, CA box 71, UJRA collection, CJCA. Although the CJC archivists and I searched through the entire collection, and made enquiries at other archives across Canada, no trace could be found of the completed questionnaires. We concluded that, after finishing his study, Ben Lappin likely destroyed them.
18. Lappin, *The Redeemed Children*, p. 156. Lappin's entire report on the questionnaires can be found on pp. 146–56. His conclusions are clear from the very title of his book: the CJC's programme had 'redeemed' the children from their wartime experiences, transforming them into solid Jewish Canadian citizens.
19. Ibid.
20. Sidney Katz, 'The Redeemed Children: The Story of One of the Great Humanitarian Acts of the Twentieth Century', *Maclean's*, 10 February 1962, pp. 11–13, 42–4. For the CJC's reaction to the *Maclean's* article, see IOI no. 2598, January 1962, CJCA.
21. Mintz to Heinz Frank, 7 August 1962, W. file, Cb 03, UJRA collection, CJCA.
22. Interview with 'Esther Traubova Mandel' (pseudonym), November 1978, interviewer Sarah Moskovitz, in *Love Despite Hate: Child Survivors of the Holocaust and their Adult Lives* (New York: Schocken Books, 1983), p. 134.

23. This was particularly true for women who, on marriage, were expected to run a kosher kitchen: even if they had been raised in a kosher care home, few had direct experience of managing a kosher kitchen in a private household.

24. Interview with Lea R., 24 November 2010, catalogue no. 33131, interviewer Lyn Smith, Imperial War Museum Archive.

25. Interview with Agnes G.-S. (born G.), 22 October 2014, interviewer Rebecca Clifford, author's collection.

26. Interview with Jacques F. (born K.), 24 November 1991, interviewers Myra Katz and Froma Willen, Fortunoff Video Archive for Holocaust Testimonies, Yale University Library.

27. Paulette Szabason Goldberg, *Just Think It Never Happened* (Victoria, Australia: Makor Jewish Community Library, 2002), p. 94.

28. Moskovitz, *Love Despite Hate*, p. 234.

29. Interview with Peter. D. (born B.), 27 May 1984, interviewer Sarah Moskovitz, Kestenberg Archive of Testimonies of Child Holocaust Survivors, Hebrew University of Jerusalem Archives.

30. Jackie Y., 'Lost and Waiting to Be Found', unpublished memoir, 2005, p. 6.

31. Ibid, p. 6.

32. Interview with Saul A., 13 January 1985, interviewer D.A., Kestenberg Archive of Testimonies of Child Holocaust Survivors, Hebrew University of Jerusalem Archives.

33. The use of hypnosis and guided imagery to 'recover' memories of childhood sexual abuse grew alongside psychologists' expanding interest in the notion of trauma, as explored in the last chapter. Yet even at the time most psychologists and psychoanalysts rejected the claims of the 'memory recovery' advocates, recognizing that their methods were too greatly influenced by the therapist's own input. See B. J. Cohler, 'Memory Recovery and the Use of the Past: A Commentary on Lindsay and Read from Psychoanalytic Perspectives', *Applied Cognitive Psychology*, 8 (1994), pp. 365–78.

34. For an overview that situates the 'recovered memory' craze in its historical context, see the introduction to Wolfgang Schneider and Michael Pressley (eds), *Memory Development between Two and Twenty*, 2nd edn (Mahwah, NJ: Lawrence Erlbaum, 1997), pp. 24–5. On the influence of Bass and Davis's book, see Blake Eskin, *A Life in Pieces* (London: Aurum Press, 2002), pp. 66–8.

35. Elizabeth Loftus, 'Creating False Memories', *Scientific American*, 277:3 (September 1997), pp. 70–5. See also idem, 'Tricked by Memory', in Jeffrey Jaclyn, Glenace Edwall, and Donald A. Ritchie (eds), *Memory and History: Essays on Recalling and Interpreting Experience* (Lanham, MD: University Press of America, 1994), pp. 17–32; Eugene Winograd, 'The Authenticity and Utility of Memories', in Robyn Fivush and Ulrich Neisser (eds), *The Remembering Self: Construction and Accuracy in the Self-Narrative* (Cambridge: Cambridge University Press, 1994), pp. 243–51; and S. J. Dallam, 'Crisis or Creation: A Systematic Examination of False Memory Claims', *Journal of Child Sexual Abuse*, 9:3 (2002), pp. 9–36.

36. Interview with Paul K., Jacques F. (born K.), and Felice Z. S. (born Z.), April 1983, interviewer unknown, American Gathering of Jewish Holocaust Survivors Oral History Collection, RG-50.477.1361, USHMMA. A couple of years after he gave this interview, Jacques received a copy of his personal dossier from the OSE, and was able to confirm that his host family's name had indeed been Bocahut.

37. Interview with Gittel H., 9 February 1985, interviewer Milton Kestenberg, Kestenberg Archive of Testimonies of Child Holocaust Survivors, Hebrew University of Jerusalem Archives.

38. Interview with Gittel H. (second interview), interviewer I.B., Kestenberg Archive of Testimonies of Child Holocaust Survivors, Hebrew University of Jerusalem Archives.

39. Interview with Suzanne A. (born N.), 22 January 1990, interviewer Lisa Newman, Toronto Jewish Congress Archives of the Holocaust Project, USC Shoah Foundation VHA.

40. Martin S. Bergmann and Milton E. Jucovy, prelude, in *Generations of the Holocaust* (New York: Columbia University Press, 1982), p. 6.

41. Ibid.

## CHAPTER 9: BECOMING SURVIVORS

1. Interview with Harry M., 23 April 2015, interviewer Rebecca Clifford, author's collection.
2. 16,000 participants were estimated to have attended the Gathering although up to 30,000 people attended the public events in the evenings. See Mike Feinsilber, '16,000 Survivors with 16,000 Stories', *Associated Press*, 12 April 1983. The estimate of 2,400 child survivors is my own, based on a careful reading of the thirty-two folders (comprising thousands of pages) of written personal testimony collected at the Gathering ('American Gathering of Jewish Holocaust Survivors collection', RG-02.002, USHMMA), as well as the oral testimony collected at the Gathering ('American Gathering of Jewish Holocaust Survivors oral history collection', RG-50.119, USHMMA, and 'Oral history interviews of the Bay Area Oral History Project', RG-50.477, USHMMA). Child survivors produced roughly 15 per cent of this written testimony, and 13 per cent of the oral testimony, giving an estimate of 2,000–2,400 child survivor attendees. However, because many child survivors in attendance felt uncertain about whether they could in fact call themselves survivors, some may well have held back from providing testimony. If this was the case, we can assume the actual numbers to be higher.
3. See the USHMM website for the definition: www.ushmm.org/remember/the-holocaust-survivors-and-victims-resource-center/survivors-and-victims (accessed 3 June 2020). The inclusivity of the USHMM's definition was the result of debates, sometimes bitter and always political, that preceded its opening in 1993. On the issue of non-Jewish survivors and the history of the museum, see Edward T. Linenthal, *Preserving Memory: The Struggle to Create America's Holocaust Museum* (New York: Viking, 1995), pp. 114–23.
4. Laura Jockusch and Avinoam J. Patt, 'Holocaust Survivors Diasporas', in Hasia Diner (ed.), *Oxford Handbook of Jewish Diasporas* (New York: Oxford University Press, forthcoming).
5. See Jockusch and Patt, 'Holocaust Survivors Diasporas'. For examples of the early use of the term survivor, see Joseph W. Schwarz, *The Redeemers: A Saga of the Years 1945–1952* (New York: Farrar, Straus and Young, 1953); and Robert Muhlen, *The Survivors: A Report on the Jews in Germany Today* (New York: T. Y. Crowell, 1962). The first critical analysis of a large number of survivor testimonies was Terrence Des Pres, *The Survivor: An Anatomy of Life in the Death Camps* (New York: Oxford University Press, 1976). The book found a wide readership and contributed significantly to establishing the term 'survivor' as a cipher for a distinct set of Holocaust experiences.
6. Annette Wieviorka, *The Era of the Witness*, trans. Jared Stark (Ithaca, NY: Cornell University Press, 2006), pp. 88 and 102.
7. Site organizer Lawrence Goldberg, quoted in the *Washington Post*, 9 April 1983.
8. *Washington Post* staff, *The Obligation to Remember* (Washington, DC: The Washington Post, 1983), p. 34. Fogelman's work on the psychological issues faced by children of survivors was ground-breaking. She was among the first psychologists to organize therapy groups for children of survivors, establishing the first such group in Boston in 1976. Her work became widely known when it was discussed by journalist Helen Epstein. See Helen Epstein, 'Heirs of the Holocaust', *New York Times Magazine*, 19 June 1977, p. 175.
9. Margaret R. Somers, 'The Narrative Constitution of Identity: A Relational and Network Approach,' *Theory and Society*, 23 (1994), p. 614.
10. See Helen Epstein, *Children of the Holocaust: Conversations with Sons and Daughters of Survivors* (New York: G. P. Putnam & Sons, 1979). For excellent academic work on this issue by scholars who are also children of survivors, see in particular Arlene Stein, *Reluctant Witnesses: Survivors, Their Children, and the Rise of Holocaust Consciousness* (Oxford: Oxford University Press, 2014), and Marianne Hirsch, *The Generation of Postmemory: Writing and Visual Culture After the Holocaust* (New York: Columbia University Press, 2012).
11. Wieviorka, *Era of the Witness*, p. 119.
12. Charles Fenyvesi, '"The trick is to remember and to forget": Surviving the Holocaust', reprinted in *The Obligation to Remember* (Washington, DC: The Washington Post, 1983), p. 38. The writer refers here to the miniseries *Holocaust*, aired on US television in 1978.

13. Linenthal, *Preserving Memory*, pp. 17–23.
14. On the creation of the Memorial Council, see Linenthal, *Preserving Memory*, pp. 38–56. On the development of Holocaust memory in Israel, see Tom Segev, *The Seventh Million: The Israelis and the Holocaust* (New York: Henry Holt, 2000).
15. Then vice president George Bush Sr officially handed the keys over to Elie Wiesel, chair of the United States Holocaust Memorial Council, during the Gathering. See *Washington Post* staff, *The Obligation to Remember*, p. 46.
16. A special programme of events was organized for children of survivors, spearheaded by Menachem Rosensaft, head of the International Network of Children of Jewish Holocaust Survivors and himself the child of survivors, who was born in Bergen-Belsen DP camp immediately after the war. Rosensaft organized a similar programme of events at the 1981 conference in Jerusalem, and the International Network of Children of Jewish Holocaust Survivors was formed out of relationships established in Jerusalem. In this sense, the Jerusalem Gathering was likely a more significant moment for children of survivors than it was for child survivors.
17. Epstein, *Children of the Holocaust*. See also *Washington Post* staff, *The Obligation to Remember*, p. 34. It is interesting to note that, in the United States (and possibly elsewhere), groups for children of survivors pre-dated groups for child survivors by nearly a decade.
18. Neil Henry, 'The Children: Inheritors of a Painful Legacy', reprinted in *The Obligation to Remember*, p. 34.
19. 'American Gathering of Jewish Holocaust Survivors collection', RG-02.002, USHMMA.
20. There are 320 interviews in the collection, of which roughly forty are with child survivors (they are catalogued in two separate record groups, but are all from the Gathering: RG-50.119 and RG-50.477, USHMMA).
21. Interview with Felicia N., interviewer unspecified, 11 April 1983, American Gathering of Jewish Holocaust Survivors Oral History collection, RG-50.119*0099, USHMMA. Felicia died in 2011. Her rescuer, Mme Renée Vérité, was a cook at the care home where Felicia was placed, run by the Jewish underground organization Rue Amelot. When the care home was closed, the children went into hiding, and Mme Vérité took a number of children from the orphanage to her home in Bienfay (Somme), where she hid them for the duration of the war. In 1995 she was recognized by Yad Vashem as a Righteous among the Nations. See Yad Vashem's website for further details: http://db.yadvashem.org/righteous/family.html?language=en&itemId=4018052 (accessed 3 June 2020).
22. Interview with Jacques F. (born K.), interviewed by Myra Katz and Froma Willen, 24 November 1991, Fortunoff Video Archive for Holocaust Testimonies, Yale University Library. All subsequent quotations in this section are from this interview.
23. Interview with Felice Z. S. (born Z.), interviewed by Joni Sue Blinderman, 30 December 1992, Fortunoff Visual Archive for Holocaust Testimonies, Yale University Library; interview with Felice Z. S. (born Z.), interviewed by Rosalie Franks, 2 February 1998, Shoah Foundation Visual History Archive.
24. Interview with Felice Z. S. (born Z.), FVA. Felice also attended the second International Gathering of Hidden Children in Jerusalem in 1993.
25. Interview with Jacqueline R., interviewed by Dana Kline and Lucille B. Ritro, 13 June 1992, Fortunoff Visual Archive for Holocaust Testimonies, Yale University Library.
26. Interview with Harry M., author's collection; interview with Jacques F. (born K.), FVA.
27. Interview with Harry M., author's collection.
28. The earliest of the therapy-oriented groups were the one affiliated with psychologist Sarah Moskovitz in Los Angeles and the one affiliated with psychoanalyst Judith Kestenberg in New York.
29. Interview with Paul Z., 24 April 2015, interviewer Rebecca Clifford, author's collection.
30. Interview with Paul Z., author's collection; interview with Jacques F. (born K.), FVA; interview with Harry M., author's collection.
31. See, for example, the Shoah Visual History Foundation interview with Litzi H. for an account of the establishment of the first of these groups in Australia in 1987, or the

interview with Joanna M. for an account of the formation of the first parallel organization in Great Britain in the early 1990s. Interview with Felizitas (Litzi) H. (born S.), 27 March 1995, interviewer Vanessa Ring, Shoah Foundation VHA; interview with Joanna M. (born Bela R.), 15 February 1998, interviewer Shirley Murgraff, Shoah Foundation VHA.

32. Interview with Henri O., 15 December 2014, interviewer Rebecca Clifford, author's collection.
33. Daisy Miller, 'A Bit of Child Survivor History', *Mishpocha* (autumn 1999), p. 8.
34. Paulette Szabason Goldberg, *Just Think It Never Happened* (Victoria, Australia: Makor Jewish Community Library, 2002), p. 3.
35. *Mishpocha* (spring 1999); *Mishpocha* (spring 2007).
36. 'Letter from the Chair', *Mishpocha* (spring 1999), p. 2.

## CHAPTER 10: STORIES

1. Interview with Denny M., 31 July 1997, interviewer Miriam Feldman-Rosman, USC Shoah Foundation VHA.
2. There were earlier testimony-gathering projects, most notably that of the Israeli Holocaust authority Yad Vashem, which has had an oral history department since the 1950s. However, the late 1970s saw a flourishing of such interview-gathering projects in the United States, projects that have gone on to become the most significant and best-used collections of Holocaust survivors' stories. See Lynn Abrams, *Oral History Theory* (London: Routledge, 2010), p. 154.
3. As Lynn Abrams notes, these projects were part of a broader trend in the United States 'to encourage "victims" to see themselves as "survivors"', whether they had lived through sexual assault or the Holocaust'. See Abrams, *Oral History Theory*, p. 154.
4. Alessandro Portelli, *The Battle of Valle Giulia: Oral History and the Art of Dialogue* (Madison, WI: University of Wisconsin Press, 1997), p. 185.
5. Rachel Deblinger makes a similar point when she observes that David Boder, interviewing adult and child survivors in 1946, did not hesitate to ask questions that would later seem insensitive, in part because what survivors told him was so unprecedented that he literally could not understand it. His interviews captured details of sexual abuse, prisoners' violence against each other, and retributive violence – details that would disappear from later interviews. See Rachel Deblinger, 'David P. Boder: Holocaust Memory in Displaced Persons Camps', in David Cesarani and Eric Sundquist (eds), *After the Holocaust: Challenging the Myth of Silence* (London: Routledge, 2012), pp. 115–26. Conversely, Christopher Browning has argued the opposite: that certain taboo subjects have only in recent years made their way into survivors' interviews. See Browning, *Remembering Survival: Inside a Nazi Slave-Labor Camp* (New York: W. W. Norton, 2011).
6. Dorothy Macardle, *Children of Europe* (London: Victor Gollancz, 1949), p. 245; Margot Hicklin, *War-Damaged Children: Some Aspects of Recovery* (London: Association of Psychiatric Social Workers, 1946); Bernard Gillis quoted in 'Rescuing 150,000 Children from Delinquency', *Jewish Telegraphic Agency* (16 September 1955); 'Greta Fischer Papers', p. 26, RG-19.034*01, USHMMA. See also Michael Berkowitz and Suzanne Brown-Fleming, 'Perceptions of Jewish Displaced Persons as Criminals in Early Postwar Germany: Lingering Stereotypes and Self-fulfilling Prophecies', in Avinoam J. Patt and Michael Berkowitz (eds), *We Are Here: New Approaches to Jewish Displaced Persons in Postwar Germany* (Detroit, MI: Wayne State University Press, 2010), pp. 167–93. On moral panics, see Stanley Cohen, *Folk Devils and Moral Panics* (London: MacGibbon and Kee, 1972).
7. Atina Grossman, 'Entangled Histories and Lost Memories: Jewish Survivors in Occupied Germany, 1945–49', in Patt and Berkowitz (eds), *We Are Here*, pp. 14–30, here p. 17.
8. Naomi Seidman, 'Elie Wiesel and the Scandal of Jewish Rage', *Jewish Social Studies*, 3:1 (1996), pp. 1–19; here p. 5.

9. Interview with R.G., 17 August 1984, interviewer Judith Kestenberg, Kestenberg Archive of Testimonies of Child Holocaust Survivors, Hebrew University of Jerusalem Archives.

10. Interview with L.A., 25 November 1989, interviewer Milton Kestenberg, Kestenberg Archive of Testimonies of Child Holocaust Survivors, Hebrew University of Jerusalem Archives.

11. Interview with Janek E. (pseudonym), 30 September 1994, interviewer Klara Firestone, USC Shoah Foundation VHA. Because I refer to Janek's URO records in chapter 6, I have had to employ a pseudonym throughout the book – even though Janek gave his VHA interview in his own name.

12. Some Holocaust 'revisionists', such as David Irving in Britain and Robert Faurisson in France, received enormous media coverage in this period, which served to amplify their theories.

13. Raul Hilberg, *The Destruction of the European Jews*, 3rd edn (New Haven, CT: Yale University Press, 2003); Shoshana Felman and Dori Laub, *Testimony: Crises of Witnessing in Literature, Psychoanalysis, and History* (New York: Routledge, 1992), p. 59.

14. Sara Horowitz in Henry Greenspan, Sara R. Horowitz, Éva Kovács, et al., 'Engaging Survivors: Assessing "Testimony" and "Trauma" as Foundational Concepts', *Dapim: Studies on the Holocaust*, 28:3 (2014), pp. 190–226, here p. 194.

15. Henry Greenspan, in Greenspan et al., 'Engaging Survivors', p. 193.

16. The Fortunoff project currently has roughly 4,400 videotaped interviews in its holdings, including 220 interviews with child survivors born in or after 1935.

17. There were smaller projects launched in the late 1970s, such as the interviews Sarah Moskovitz collected for her book *Love Despite Hate*, or the interviews collected by historian Yaffa Eliach that are now housed in the Museum of Jewish Heritage in New York, but these were limited in scope. Moskovitz also worked as an interviewer for Kestenberg's project, and for the Fortunoff collection.

18. Interview with Aniko S., 21 April 1985, interviewer J.S.K., Kestenberg Archive of Testimonies of Child Holocaust Survivors, Hebrew University of Jerusalem Archives.

19. I say 'likely' here because I was not able to discover how far Kestenberg's team provided participants with information about the project as a whole (for example, in the form of a project information sheet or consent form).

20. For examples of how the Kestenberg interviews have recently been used by scholars, see Sharon Kangisser Cohen, Eva Fogelman, and Dalia Ofer (eds), *Children in the Holocaust and its Aftermath: Historical and Psychological Studies of the Kestenberg Archive* (Oxford: Berghahn Books, 2017). I myself think the Kestenberg interviews are fantastic sources, but not necessarily for the purpose that Kestenberg originally intended. What these interviews illustrate so compellingly is how grown child survivors were making sense of their pasts in mid-life, in the specific historical context of the 1980s; how the interaction between interviewers and interviewees shaped child survivors' stories in this period; and how we might understand what motivated researchers in this period to take an interest in child survivors.

21. Noah Shenker, *Reframing Holocaust Testimony* (Bloomington, IN: Indiana University Press, 2015), pp. 112–13.

22. VHA guidance literature is quoted in Annette Wieviorka, *The Era of the Witness*, trans. Jared Stark (Ithaca, NY: Cornell University Press, 2006), p. 114; and Shenker, *Reframing Holocaust Testimony*, p. 119.

23. *Schindler's List*, dir. Steven Spielberg, 1993.

24. The collection now includes interviews with survivors of the Armenian, Cambodian, and Rwandan genocides, the 1937 Nanjing Massacre in China, and of ongoing conflicts in the Central African Republic, south Sudan, and Myanmar.

25. Wieviorka, *The Era of the Witness*, pp. 114–15.

26. Interview with Zdenka H., 29 July 1997, interviewer Miriam Feldman-Rosman, USC Shoah Foundation VHA.

27. Interview with Zdenka H., 2007 (exact date not given), interviewer Sheila Melzack, 'The Girls' collection, WLA. When I interviewed Zdenka myself in 2017, I asked her about her

VHA interview, and she recalled that the experience was 'horrible', and she had never again glanced at the videotaped copy that the Shoah Foundation had given her.

28. Geoffrey Hartman, 'The Humanities of Testimony: An Introduction', *Poetics Today*, 27:2 (2006), pp. 249–60.
29. On composure and discomposure, see Graham Dawson, *Making Peace with the Past? Memory, Trauma and the Irish Troubles* (Manchester: Manchester University Press, 2007); and Abrams, *Oral History Theory*, pp. 66–70.
30. Henry Greenspan, 'On Testimony, Legacy and the Problem of Helplessness in History', *Holocaust Studies*, 13:1 (2007); pp. 44–56.
31. Interview with 'Leora' (pseudonym), 15 December 2014, interviewer Rebecca Clifford, author's collection.

## CHAPTER 11: SILENCES

1. On Anna Freud's 'double approach', see Nick Midgley, 'Anna Freud: The Hampstead War Nurseries and the Role of the Direct Observation of Children for Psychoanalysis', *International Journal of Psychoanalysis*, 88:4 (2007), pp. 939–59.
2. 'Lingfield Colony reports' (April, October, June 1946 respectively), Alice Goldberger collection, 2007.423, USHMMA.
3. Howard Byrne, 'They Learn to be Children Again', *John Bull*, October 1948.
4. See especially the sociologist Eva Illouz, *Saving the Modern Soul: Therapy, Emotions, and the Culture of Self-Help* (Berkeley, CA: University of California Press, 2008). Illouz argues that new beliefs about the emotional benefits of talking therapy emerged in the period between the First and Second World Wars, but that these only became 'widely available' after the 1960s.
5. Interview with Bela R., 2007, interviewer Sheila Melzack, 'The Girls' project, WLA.
6. David Cesarani, introduction, in David Cesarani and Eric Sundquist (eds), *After the Holocaust: Challenging the Myth of Silence* (London: Routledge, 2012), p. 1.
7. Henry Greenspan, *The Awakening of Memory: Survivor Testimony in the First Years after the Holocaust* (Washington, DC: USHMM, 2000); Hasia Diner, *We Remember with Reverence and Love: American Jews and the Myth of Silence after the Holocaust, 1945–1962* (New York: New York University Press, 2009), p. 369. Diner refers specifically to survivors' memories of a 'deafening silence' in American Jewish communities in the 1950s and 1960s.
8. Boaz Cohen, 'The Children's Voice: Postwar Collection of Testimonies from Child Survivors of the Holocaust', *Holocaust and Genocide Studies*, 21:1 (2007), pp. 73–95.
9. Rebecca Clifford, 'Emotions and Gender in Oral History: Narrating Italy's 1968', *Modern Italy*, 17:2 (2012), pp. 209–22.
10. Susanne Urban, ' "More Children are to be Interviewed": Child Survivors' Narratives in the Child Search Brach Files', in Henning Borggräfe, Akim Jah, Nina Ritz, and Steffen Jost, with Elisabeth Schwabauer, *Freilegungen: Rebuilding Lives – Child Survivors and DP Children in the Aftermath of the Holocaust and Forced Labour* (Göttingen: Wallstein Verlag, 2017), p. 78. See also Verena Buser, 'Displaced Children: 1945 and The Child Tracing Division of the United Nations Relief and Rehabilitation Administration', in *The Holocaust in History and Memory*, 7 (2014), pp. 109–23.
11. Julia Reus, ' "Everywhere Where Human Beings Are, We Can Find Our Children": On the Organization of the ITS Child Search Branch', in Borggräfe et al., *Freilegungen*, p. 51.
12. We should be alert to the possibility that while the CJC as a whole sought to ensure that all the children on their scheme were full orphans, individual CJC officers may have been complicit in bending these rules.
13. Pearl Leibovitch of the Jewish Child Welfare Bureau to the CJC, 2 February 1950, 'Aaron B.' file, 1947–50, Cb 03, UJRA collection, CJCA.
14. Interview with Aaron B., 17 May 1998, interviewer Yana Katzap, USC Shoah Foundation VHA.

15. David Cesarani, introduction, in *After the Holocaust*, p. 16.
16. Laura Jockusch, *Collect and Record! Jewish Holocaust Documentation in Early Postwar Europe* (Oxford: Oxford University Press, 2012), p. 4.
17. Here see in particular Jeffrey Herf, *Divided Memory: The Nazi Past in the Two Germanys* (Cambridge, MA: Harvard University Press, 1997), and Pieter Lagrou, *The Legacy of Nazi Occupation: Patriotic Memory and National Recovery in Western Europe, 1945–1965* (New York: Cambridge University Press, 2000).
18. On the historical commissions, see in particular Jockusch, *Collect and Record!* See also Ada Schein, '"Everyone Can Hold a Pen": The Documentation Project in the DP Camps in Germany', in David Bankier and Dan Michman (eds), *Holocaust Historiography in Context: Emergence, Challenges, Polemics and Achievements* (New York, 2008), pp. 103–34.
19. Boaz Cohen and Beate Müller, 'A Teacher and his Students: Child Holocaust Testimonies from Early Postwar Polish Bytom', *East European Jewish Affairs*, 46:1 (2016), pp. 68–115, here p. 71. See also Cohen, 'The Children's Voice', pp. 111–12. Of the Central Jewish Historical Commission's interviews with children, fifty-five were edited and published in a 1947 volume in Polish (Maria Hochberg-Mariańska and Noe Grüss, *Dzieci Oskarżają*; translated into English as *The Children Accuse*), and a shorter Yiddish edition published in Buenos Aires in 1947 as *Kinder-Martyrologie*.
20. Laura Jockusch, *Collect and Record!*, p. 264, footnote 152; Cohen, 'The Children's Voice', pp. 87–9.
21. Of the twenty children Boder interviewed, almost all were adolescents: unlike many other testimony gatherers, Boder worried that asking young children to speak about the persecution could be psychologically harmful.
22. Cohen and Müller note that many of the children's accounts seem strangely devoid of emotion, and speculate that emotional content may have been deliberately removed. See Cohen and Müller, 'A Teacher and His Students', pp. 68–115, here p. 70.
23. Quoted in Cohen, 'The Children's Voice', pp. 80, 84.
24. Boaz Cohen and Beate Müller, 'The 1945 Bytom Notebook: Searching for the Lost Voices of Child Holocaust Survivors', in *Freilegungen: Überlebende – Erinnerungen – Transformationen* (Göttingen: Wallstein Verlag, 2013). Tsam appears to have written down the children's accounts while in the DP camp. He immigrated to the US in 1949.
25. Interview with A.F., interviewer Shlomo Tsam, in Cohen and Müller, 'A Teacher and his Students', p. 82. Four of the forty-two children interviewed by Tsam wanted to remain anonymous, and A.F. was one of these.
26. Interview with Buzha (Busia) W., interviewer Shlomo Tsam, in Cohen and Müller, 'A Teacher and his Students', pp. 89–90. Weiner left Poland for a German DP camp, was briefly housed at the children's centre in Prien, and then immigrated to the US in April 1947.
27. On children's post-war accounts more broadly, see in particular the work of Boaz Cohen. See also Joanna Beata Michlic; see in particular her 'Jewish Children in Nazi-Occupied Poland: Survival and Polish-Jewish Relations during the Holocaust as Reflected in Early Postwar Recollections', *Search and Research – Lectures and Papers*, XIV (Jerusalem: Yad Vashem, 2008), p. xiv.
28. Paul Friedman, 'The Road Back for the DPs: Healing the Psychological Scars of Nazism', *Commentary* (1 December 1948).
29. Miriam Warburg, 'Children Without Parents', *Jewish Chronicle*, 15 April 1949.
30. Margot Hicklin, *War-Damaged Children: Some Aspects of Recovery* (London: Association of Psychiatric Social Workers, 1946), pp. 8, 12.
31. Interview with Bela R., 'The Girls' project.
32. Interview with Joanna M. (born Bela R.), 21 October 2014, interviewer Rebecca Clifford, author's collection.
33. 'Lingfield Colony report', August 1946, p. 2, Alice Goldberger collection, 2007.423, USHMMA.
34. 'Lingfield Colony report', October 1952, Alice Goldberger collection, 2007.423, USHMMA.

## CONCLUSION: THE LAST WITNESSES

1. Interview with Agnes G.-S. (born G.), 22 October 2014, interviewer Rebecca Clifford, author's collection. Agnes is a historian and author who has published three books on Holocaust history.
2. Memorial book for Erwin B., Kibbutz Ein Harod Meuhad.
3. Chad McDonald, '"We Became British Aliens": Kindertransport Refugees Narrating the Discovery of their Parents' Fates', *Holocaust Studies*, 24:4 (2018), pp. 395–417. On the notion that changes in a survivor's narrative reflect the need to bring an unmasterable past under control, see in particular Mark Roseman, *A Past in Hiding: Memory and Survival in Nazi Germany* (New York: Metropolitan Books, 2000).
4. Quoted in Elena Lappin, 'The Man with Two Heads', *Granta*, 66 (1999), p. 13.
5. www.kentlandstowncrier.com/2018/05/presentation-by-child-holocaust-survivor-sylvia-rozines/ (accessed 3 June 2020). For an example of Cywia's 'First Person' interviews (under her anglicized married name, Sylvia R.), see www.youtube.com/watch?v=o_dIkuC8668 (accessed 3 June 2020).
6. Interview with Sylvia R. (born Cywia P.), 22 May 2015, interviewer Rebecca Clifford, author's collection.
7. Interview with Jackie Y., 16 December 2014, interviewer Rebecca Clifford, author's collection.

# BIBLIOGRAPHY

All translations from other languages are my own, unless otherwise stated.

## ARCHIVAL SOURCES

American Jewish Joint Distribution Committee, New York City
    1945–54 records
    Cyprus Operation records, 1945–9

Canadian Jewish Congress Archives (CJCA)
    IOI collection
    United Jewish Relief Agencies of Canada collection (UJRA)

Hartley Library, University of Southampton
    West London Synagogue archives

Hebrew University of Jerusalem Archives
    Kestenberg Archive of Testimonies of Child Holocaust Survivors

Illinois Institute of Technology
    Voices of the Holocaust Project, online at https://iit.aviaryplatform.com/collections/231

Imperial War Museum, London
    Oral History collection

United States Holocaust Memorial Museum Archives, Washington DC (USHMMA)
    Alice Goldberger papers
    American Friends Service Committee records
    American Gathering of Jewish Holocaust Survivors collection
    Bay Area Oral History Project collection
    Case files from the Schweizer Hilfswerk für Emigrantenkinder (SHEK)
    Erich A. Hausmann papers
    Felice Z.S. papers
    Greta Fischer papers
    International Tracing Service collection
    Jewish Refugee records, Switzerland
    Oeuvre de Secours aux Enfants records (OSE)
    Oral History collection
    Rachel Greene Rottersman papers

# BIBLIOGRAPHY

Syma Crane papers
United Restitution Office Los Angeles and Toronto collections

USC Shoah Foundation Institute
Visual History Archive (VHA)

Wiener Library Archives, London (WLA)
Central British Fund for German Jewry collection
Dann Family papers
International Tracing Service collection
Press clippings collection
Rose Henriques archive
The Girls oral history collection

Yad Vashem, Jerusalem
The Righteous Among the Nations Database, online at https://righteous.yadvashem.org

Yale University Library
Fortunoff Video Archive for Holocaust Testimonies (FVA)

## PRINTED PRIMARY AND SECONDARY SOURCES

Abella, Irving, and Troper, Harold, *None Is Too Many: Canada and the Jews of Europe, 1933–1948* (Toronto: University of Toronto Press, 2012)

Abrams, Lynn, *Oral History Theory* (London: Routledge, 2010)

Adler, H. G., *Theresienstadt, 1941–1945: The Face of a Coerced Community* (Cambridge: Cambridge University Press, 2017)

Akhtar, Salman, *The Mother and her Child: Clinical Aspects of Attachment, Separation, and Loss* (New York: Jason Aronson, 2012)

Althoff, Becky, 'Observations on the Psychology of Children in a D.P. Camp', *Journal of Social Casework*, XXIX:1 (1948), pp. 17–22

American Psychiatric Association, 'Post-Traumatic Stress Disorder', in *Diagnostic and Statistical Manual of Mental Disorders*, 3rd edn (Washington, DC: American Psychiatric Association, 1980)

Anderson, Mark, 'Child Victim as Witness to the Holocaust: An American Story?', *Jewish Social Studies*, 14:1 (2007), pp. 1–22

Andlauer, Anna, *The Rage to Live: The International D.P. Children's Center Kloster Indersdorf, 1945–46* (self-published, 2012)

Auslander, Leora, 'Coming Home? Jews in Postwar Paris', *Journal of Contemporary History*, 40:2 (2005), pp. 237–59

Azouvi, François, *Le Mythe du grand silence: Auschwitz, les Français, la mémoire* (Paris: Fayard, 2012)

Bailey, Alice, *The Problems of the Children in the World Today* (New York: Lucis, 1946)

Bailly, Danielle (ed.), *Traqués, Cachés, Vivants: Des Enfants juifs en France (1940–1945)* (Paris: L'Harmattan, 2004)

Balint, Ruth, 'Children Left Behind: Family, Refugees and Immigration in Postwar Europe', *History Workshop Journal*, 82 (2016), pp. 151–72

Bankier, David (ed.), *The Jews Are Coming Back: The Return of the Jews to Their Countries of Origins after World War II* (Oxford: Berghahn Books, 2005)

Bardgett, Susanne, 'Belsen and the BBC: What Wireless Listeners Learned', *History Today*, 56:8 (2006), pp. 30–7

Bardgett, Susanne, Cesarani, David, Reinisch, Jessica, and Steinert, Johannes-Dieter (eds), *Survivors of Nazi Persecution in Europe after the Second World War. Vol. I: Landscapes after Battle* (London: Vallentine Mitchell, 2010)

Barkan, Elazar, *The Guilt of Nations: Restitution and Negotiating Historical Injustices* (New York: W. W. Norton, 2000)

Bauer, Patricia J., 'Development of Memory in Early Childhood', in Nelson Cowan (ed.), *The Development of Memory in Childhood* (Hove: Psychology Press, 1997)

Bauer, Yehuda, *American Jewry and the Holocaust: The American Jewish Joint Distribution Committee, 1939–1945* (Detroit, MI: Wayne State University Press, 1981)

——*Flight and Rescue: Brichah* (Jerusalem: Magnes Press, 1970)

——*My Brother's Keeper: A History of the American Jewish Joint Distribution Committee, 1929–1939* (Philadelphia, PA: Jewish Publication Society of America, 1974)

——*Out of the Ashes: The Impact of American Jews on Post-Holocaust European Jewry* (New York: Pergamon Press, 1989)

Baumel-Schwartz, Judith Tydor, 'Jewish Refugee Children in the USA (1934–45): Flight, Resettlement, Absorption', in Simone Gigliotti and Monica Tempian (eds), *The Young Victims of the Nazi Regime: Migration, the Holocaust and Postwar Displacement* (London: Bloomsbury, 2016), pp. 11–30

——*Never Look Back: The Jewish Refugee Children in Great Britain 1938–1945* (West Lafayette, IN: Purdue University Press, 2012)

——*Unfulfilled Promise: Rescue and Resettlement of Jewish Refugee Children in the United States 1934–1945* (Juneau: Denali, 1990)

Bazyler, Michael, *Holocaust Justice: The Battle for Restitution in America's Courts* (New York: New York University Press, 2003)

Beaglehole, Ann, ' "The Children Are a Triumph": New Zealand's Response to Europe's Children and Youth, 1933–49', in Simone Gigliotti and Monica Tempian (eds), *The Young Victims of the Nazi Regime: Migration, the Holocaust and Postwar Displacement* (London: Bloomsbury, 2016), pp. 91–112

Bergmann, Martin S., and Jucovy, Milton E. (eds), *Generations of the Holocaust* (New York: Columbia University Press, 1982)

Berkowitz, Michael, and Brown-Fleming, Suzanne, 'Perceptions of Jewish Displaced Persons as Criminals in Early Postwar Germany: Lingering Stereotypes and Self-Fulfilling Prophecies', in Avinoam J. Patt and Michael Berkowitz (eds), *We Are Here: New Approaches to Jewish Displaced Persons in Postwar Germany* (Detroit, MI: Wayne State University Press, 2010), pp. 167–93

Bessel, Richard, and Schumann, Dirk (eds), *Life After Death: Approaches to a Cultural and Social History of Europe during the 1940s and 1950s* (Cambridge: Cambridge University Press, 2003)

Bialystok, Franklin, *Delayed Impact: The Holocaust and the Canadian Jewish Community* (Montreal: McGill-Queen's University Press, 2000)

Blackstock, Charity, *Wednesday's Children* (London: Hutchinson, 1966)

Bluglass, Kerry, *Hidden from the Holocaust: Stories of Resilient Children who Survived and Thrived* (London: Praeger, 2003)

Boder, David P., *I Did Not Interview the Dead* (Urbana, IL: University of Illinois Press, 1949)

Bogner, Nahum, *At the Mercy of Strangers: The Rescue of Jewish Children with Assumed Identities in Poland* (Jerusalem: Yad Vashem, 2009)

Borggräfe, Henning, Jah, Akim, Ritz, Nina, and Jost, Steffen, with Schwabauer, Elisabeth (eds), *Freilegungen: Rebuilding Lives – Child Survivors and DP Children in the Aftermath of the Holocaust and Forced Labour* (Göttingen: Wallstein Verlag, 2017)

Braham, Randolph, *The Hungarian Labor Service System, 1939–1945* (New York: Columbia University Press, 1977)

——*The Nazis' Last Victims: The Holocaust in Hungary* (Detroit, MI: Wayne State University Press, 1998)

——*The Politics of Genocide: The Holocaust in Hungary* (New York: Columbia University Press, 1981)

——*The Wartime System of Labor Service in Hungary: Varieties of Experience* (Boulder, CO: Rosenthal Institute for Holocaust Studies, 1995)

Brauner, Alfred, and Brauner, Françoise, *L'Accueil des enfants survivants* (Paris: Cahier du groupement de recherches practiques pour l'enfance, 1994)

Brock, Adrian C. (ed.), *Internationalizing the History of Psychology* (New York: New York University Press, 2006)

Brosse, Thérèse, *War-Handicapped Children: Report on the European Situation* (Paris: UNESCO, 1950)

Brown-Fleming, Suzanne, *Nazi Persecution and Postwar Repercussions: The International Tracing Service Archive and Holocaust Research* (Lanham, MD: Rowman & Littlefield, 2016)

Browning, Christopher, *Remembering Survival: Inside a Nazi Slave-Labor Camp* (New York: W. W. Norton, 2011)

Bruttmann, Tal, Ermakoff, Ivan, Mariot, Nicolas, and Zalc, Claire (eds), *Pour Une Micro-Histoire de la Shoah* (Paris: Seuil, 2012)

Buhle, Mari Jo, *Feminism and its Discontents: A Century of Struggle with Psychoanalysis* (Cambridge, MA: Harvard University Press, 1998)

Burgard, Antoine, ' "Une Nouvelle Vie dans un nouveau pays": Trajectoires d'orphelins de la Shoah vers le Canada (1947–1952)', unpublished PhD thesis (Université Lumière Lyon 2, 2017)

Burnham, John (ed.), *After Freud Left: A Century of Psychoanalysis in America* (Chicago, IL: University of Chicago Press, 2012)

Buser, Verena, 'Displaced Children: 1945 and The Child Tracing Division of the United Nations Relief and Rehabilitation Administration', *The Holocaust in History and Memory*, 7 (2014), pp. 109–23

Caestecker, Franck, 'The Reintegration of Jewish Survivors into Belgian Society, 1943–47', in David Bankier (ed.), *The Jews Are Coming Back: The Return of the Jews to their Countries of Origin after World War II* (Oxford: Berghahn Books, 2005), pp. 72–107

Cahn, Eric, *Maybe Tomorrow: A Hidden Child of the Holocaust* (Arvada, CO: Casan Publishing, 1995)

Cahn, Zilla, *Suicide in French Thought from Montesquieu to Cioran* (New York: Peter Lang, 1999)

Celinscak, Mark, *Distance from the Belsen Heap: Allied Forces and the Liberation of a Nazi Concentration Camp* (Toronto: University of Toronto Press, 2015)

Cesarani, David, 'Camps de la mort, camps de concentration et camps d'internement dans la mémoire collective britannique', *Vingtième Siècle. Revue d'histoire*, 54 (1997), pp. 13–23

——(ed.), *Genocide and Rescue: The Holocaust in Hungary, 1944* (Oxford: Berg, 1997)

Cesarani, David, and Sundquist, Eric (eds), *After the Holocaust: Challenging the Myth of Silence* (London: Routledge, 2012)

Clifford, Rebecca, 'Britain's Response to WWII Child Refugees Puts Modern Society to Shame', *The Conversation* (8 February 2017)

——*Commemorating the Holocaust: The Dilemmas of Remembrance in France and Italy* (Oxford: Oxford University Press, 2013)

——'Emotions and Gender in Oral History: Narrating Italy's 1968', *Modern Italy*, 17:2 (2012), pp. 209–22

——'Families after the Holocaust: Between the Archives and Oral History', *Oral History*, 46:1 (2018), pp. 42–54

——'Who Is a Survivor? Child Holocaust Survivors and the Development of a Generational Identity', *Oral History Forum d'histoire orale*, 37 (2017)

Close, Kathryn, *Transplanted Children: A History* (New York: USCOM, 1953)

Cohen, Beth B., 'American Jews and Holocaust Survivors, 1946–54', in Avinoam J. Patt and Michael Berkowitz (eds), *We Are Here: New Approaches to Jewish Displaced Persons in Postwar Germany* (Detroit, MI: Wayne State University Press, 2010)

——*Case Closed: Holocaust Survivors in Postwar America* (New Brunswick, NJ: Rutgers University Press, 2007)

——*Child Survivors of the Holocaust: The Youngest Remnant and the American Experience* (New Brunswick, NJ: Rutgers University Press, 2018)

Cohen, Boaz, 'The 1945 Bytom Notebook: Searching for the Lost Voices of Child Holocaust Survivors', in Rebecca Boehling, Susanne Urban, and René Bienet (eds), *Freilegungen: Überlebende – Erinnerungen – Transformationen* (Göttingen: Wallstein Verlag, 2013), pp. 122–37

——' "And I Was Only a Child": Children's Testimonies, Bergen-Belsen 1945', in Suzanne Bardgett and David Cesarani (eds), *Belsen 1945: New Historical Perspectives* (London: Vallentine Mitchell, 2006), pp. 153–69

——'The Children's Voice: Postwar Collection of Testimonies from Child Survivors of the Holocaust', *Holocaust and Genocide Studies*, 21:1 (2007), pp. 73–95

——'Survivor Caregivers and Child Survivors: Rebuilding Lives and the Home in the Postwar Period', *Holocaust and Genocide Studies*, 32:1 (2018), pp. 49–65

Cohen, Boaz, and Horvath, Rita, 'Young Witnesses in the DP Camps: Children's Holocaust Testimony in Context', *Journal of Modern Jewish Studies*, 11:1 (2012), pp. 103–25

Cohen, Boaz, and Müller, Beate, 'A Teacher and his Students: Child Holocaust Testimonies from Early Postwar Polish Bytom', *East European Jewish Affairs*, 46:1 (2016), pp. 68–115

Cohen, Daniel G., *In War's Wake: European Refugees in the Postwar Order* (Oxford: Oxford University Press, 2011)

Cohen, Stanley, *Folk Devils and Moral Panics* (London: MacGibbon and Kee, 1972)

Cohler, B. J., 'Memory Recovery and the Use of the Past: A Commentary on Lindsay and Read from Psychoanalytic Perspectives', *Applied Cognitive Psychology*, 8 (1994), pp. 365–78

Cole, Tim, *Holocaust City: The Making of a Jewish Ghetto* (London: Routledge, 2003)

Cole, Tim, Giordano, Alberto, and Knowles, Anne Kelly (eds), *Geographies of the Holocaust* (Bloomington, IN: Indiana University Press, 2014)

Cowan, Nelson (ed.), *The Development of Memory in Childhood* (Hove: Psychology Press, 1997)

Czech, Danuta, *Auschwitz Chronicle, 1939–1945* (New York: Holt, 1997)

Dallam, S. J., 'Crisis or Creation: A Systematic Examination of False Memory Claims', *Journal of Child Sexual Abuse*, 9:3 (2002), pp. 9–36

Danieli, Yael (ed.), *International Handbook of Multigenerational Legacies of Trauma* (New York: Springer, 1998)

Davie, Maurice, *Refugees in America: Report of the Committee for the Study of Recent Immigration from Europe* (New York: Harper & Brothers, 1947)

Davie, Ronald, Upton, Graham, and Varma, Ved (eds), *The Voice of the Child: A Handbook for Professionals* (London: Falmer Press, 1996)

Dawson, Graham, *Making Peace with the Past? Memory, Trauma and the Irish Troubles* (Manchester: Manchester University Press, 2007)

De Young, Alexandra, Kenardy, Justin, and Cobham, Vanessa, 'Trauma in Early Childhood: A Neglected Population', *Clinical Child and Family Psychology Review*, 14:3 (2011), pp. 231–50

Deblinger, Rachel, 'David P. Boder: Holocaust Memory in Displaced Persons Camps', in David Cesarani and Eric Sundquist (eds), *After the Holocaust: Challenging the Myth of Silence* (London: Routledge, 2012), pp. 115–26

Dequeker, Luc, 'Baptism and Conversion of Jews in Belgium, 1939–1945', in Dan Michman (ed.), *Belgium and the Holocaust: Jews, Belgians, Germans* (Oxford: Berghahn Books, 1998), pp. 235–71

Des Pres, Terrence, *The Survivor: An Anatomy of Life in the Death Camps* (New York: Oxford University Press, 1976)

Diner, Hasia R., *We Remember with Reverence and Love: American Jews and the Myth of Silence after the Holocaust, 1945–1962* (New York: New York University Press, 2009)

Dinnerstein, Leonard, *America and the Survivors of the Holocaust* (New York: Columbia University Press, 1982)

Dodd, Lindsey, *French Children under the Allied Bombs, 1940–45: An Oral History* (Manchester: Manchester University Press, 2016)

Doron, Daniella, *Jewish Youth and Identity in Postwar France: Rebuilding Family and Nation* (Bloomington, IN: Indiana University Press, 2015)

——'Lost Children and Lost Childhoods: Memory in Post-Holocaust France', in Seán Hand and Steven T. Katz (eds), *Post-Holocaust France and the Jews, 1945–1955* (New York: New York University Press, 2015), pp. 85–117

Downs, Laura Lee, *Childhood in the Promised Land: Working-Class Movements and the Colonies de Vacances in France, 1880–1960* (Durham, NC: Duke University Press, 2002)

——'Milieu Social or Milieu Familial? Theories and Practices of Childrearing among the Popular Classes in 20th-Century France and Britain: The Case of Evacuation (1939–45)', *Family and Community History*, 8:1 (2005), pp. 49–66

Draper, Paula, 'Canadian Holocaust Survivors from Liberation to Rebirth', *Canadian Jewish Studies*, 4 (1997), pp. 39–42

Draper, Paula, and Troper, Harold (eds), *Archives of the Holocaust, Vol. 15: National Archives of Canada, Ottawa, and Canadian Jewish Congress Archives, Montreal* (New York: Garland Publishing, 1991)

Dwork, Debórah, *Children with a Star: Jewish Youth in Nazi Europe* (New Haven, CT: Yale University Press, 1991)

Eckl, Marlen, ' "This Tear Remains Forever . . .": German-Jewish Refugee Children and Youth in Brazil (1933–45): Resettlement Acculturation, Integration', in Simone Gigliotti and Monica Tempian (eds), *The Young Victims of the Nazi Regime: Migration, the Holocaust, and Postwar Displacement* (London: Bloomsbury, 2016), pp. 51–70

Edele, Mark, Fitzpatrick, Sheila, and Grossmann, Atina (eds), *Shelter from the Holocaust: Rethinking Jewish Survival in the Soviet Union* (Detroit, MI: Wayne State University Press, 2017)

Ehrenreich, John, *The Altruistic Imagination: A History of Social Work and Social Policy in the United States* (Ithaca, NY: Cornell University Press, 1985)

Eidlitz-Markus, Tal, Shuper, Avinoam, and Amir, Jacob, 'Secondary Enuresis: Post-Traumatic Stress Disorder in Children after Car Accidents', *IMAJ*, 2 (2000), pp. 135–7

Eitinger, Leo, and Krell, Robert, *The Psychological and Medical Effects of Concentration Camps and Related Persecutions on Survivors of the Holocaust* (Vancouver: University of British Columbia Press, 1985)

Eizenstat, Stuart E., *Imperfect Justice: Looted Assets, Slave Labor, and the Unfinished Business of World War II* (New York: Perseus Books, 2003)

Engel, David, 'Patterns of Anti-Jewish Violence in Poland, 1944–1946', *Yad Vashem Studies*, 26 (1998), pp. 43–85

Epstein, Helen, *Children of the Holocaust: Conversations with Sons and Daughters of Survivors* (New York: G. P. Putnam & Sons, 1979)

——'Heirs of the Holocaust', *New York Times Magazine* (19 June 1977)

Eskin, Blake, *A Life in Pieces* (London: Aurum Press, 2002)

Feldman, David, Mazower, Mark, and Reinisch, Jessica (eds), *Postwar Reconstruction in Europe: International Perspectives, 1945–1949* (Oxford: Oxford University Press, 2011)

Felman, Shoshana, and Laub, Dori, *Testimony: Crises of Witnessing in Literature, Psychoanalysis, and History* (New York: Routledge, 1992)

Figley, Charles R., *Trauma and its Wake: The Study and Treatment of Post-Traumatic Stress Disorder*, vol. I (Hove: Psychology Press, 1985)

Finder, Gabriel, 'Yizkor! Commemoration of the Dead by Jewish Displaced Persons in Postwar Germany', in Alon Confino, Paul Betts, and D. Schumann (eds), *Between Mass Death and Individual Loss: The Place of the Dead in Twentieth-Century Germany* (New York: Berghahn Books, 2008)

Fink, Hans, 'Development Arrest as a Result of Nazi Persecution during Adolescence', *International Journal of Psycho-Analysis*, 49 (1968), pp. 327–9

Fischer, Greta, 'The Refugee Youth Program in Montreal, 1947–1952', unpublished Masters thesis in social work (McGill University, 1955)

Fishman, Joel S., 'Jewish War Orphans in the Netherlands: The Guardianship Issue, 1945–1950', *Wiener Library Bulletin*, 27 (1973–4), pp. 31–6

——'The War Orphan Controversy in the Netherlands: Majority-Minority Relations', in J. Michman and T. Levie (eds), *Dutch Jewish History: Proceedings of the [Second] Symposium on the History of Jews in the Netherlands*, 28 November–3 December 1982, Tel-Aviv/Jerusalem, pp. 421–32

Fivush, Robyn, 'Event Memory in Early Childhood', in Nelson Cowan (ed.), *The Development of Memory in Childhood* (Hove: Psychology Press, 1997), pp. 139–57

——'The Function of Event Memory: Some Comments on Nelson and Barsalou', in Ulric Neisser and Eugene Winograd (eds), *Remembering Reconsidered: Ecological and Traditional Approaches to the Study of Memory* (New York: Cambridge University Press, 1988), pp. 277–82

Fivush, Robyn, Haden, Catherine, and Adam, Salimah, 'Structure and Coherence of Preschoolers' Personal Narratives over Time: Implications for Childhood Amnesia', *Journal of Experimental Child Psychology*, 60:1 (1995), pp. 32–56

Fogelman, Eva, 'Intergenerational Group Therapy: Child Survivors of the Holocaust and Offspring of Survivors', *Psychoanalytic Review*, 75:4 (1988), pp. 619–40

——'The Psychology behind Being a Hidden Child', in Jane Marks, *The Hidden Children: The Secret Survivors of the Holocaust* (New York: Ballantine Books, 1993), pp. 292–307

Fogg, Shannon, *The Politics of Everyday Life in Vichy France: Foreigners, Undesirables, and Strangers* (Cambridge: Cambridge University Press, 2009)

Freud, Anna, 'Discussion of Dr. John Bowlby's Paper', *The Psychoanalytic Study of the Child*, XV (1960), pp. 53–62

Freud, Anna, and Burlingham, Dorothy, *War and Children* (London, 1943)

Freud, Anna, and Dann, Sophie, 'An Experiment in Group Upbringing', *The Psychoanalytic Study of the Child*, vol. VI (1951), pp. 127–68

Friedländer, Saul, *When Memory Comes* (Madison, WI: University of Wisconsin Press, 1979)

Friedman, Paul, 'The Road Back for the DPs: Healing the Psychological Scars of Nazism', *Commentary* (1 December 1948)

Gafny, Emunah Nachmany, *Dividing Hearts: The Removal of Jewish Children from Gentile Families in Poland in the Immediate Post-Holocaust Years* (Jerusalem: Yad Vashem, 2009)

Gallant, Mary, *Coming of Age in the Holocaust: The Last Survivors Remember* (Lanham, MD: University Press of America, 2002)

Gatrell, Peter, *The Making of the Modern Refugee* (Oxford: Oxford University Press, 2013)

Gay, Ruth, *Safe Among the Germans: Liberated Jews after World War Two* (New Haven, CT: Yale University Press, 2002)

Genizi, Haim, *America's Fair Share: The Admission and Resettlement of Displaced Persons, 1945–1952* (Detroit, MI: Wayne State University Press, 1993)

Gershon, Karen (ed.), *We Came as Children* (London: Victor Gollancz, 1966)

Gigliotti, Simone, and Monica Tempian (eds), *The Young Victims of the Nazi Regime: Migration, the Holocaust, and Postwar Displacement* (London: Bloomsbury, 2016)

Gilbert, Martin, *The Boys: The Story of 732 Young Concentration Camp Survivors* (London: Weidenfeld & Nicolson, 1996)

Gildea, Robert, *Fighters in the Shadows: A New History of the French Resistance* (London: Faber & Faber, 2015)

Goldberg, Adara, *Holocaust Survivors in Canada: Exclusion, Inclusion, Transformation, 1947–1955* (Winnipeg: University of Manitoba Press, 2015)

Goldberg, Paulette Szabason, *Just Think It Never Happened* (Victoria, Australia: Makor Jewish Community Library, 2002)

Goltermann, Svenja, *The War in their Minds: German Soldiers and their Violent Pasts in West Germany* (Ann Arbor, MI: University of Michigan Press, 2017)

Greenspan, Henry, *The Awakening of Memory: Survivor Testimony in the First Years after the Holocaust* (Washington, DC: USHMM, 2000)

——'The Humanities of Contingency: Interviewing and Teaching Beyond "Testimony" with Holocaust Survivors', *The Oral History Review*, 8 (2019), pp. 360–79

——'On Testimony, Legacy and the Problem of Helplessness in History', *Holocaust Studies*, 13:1 (2007), pp. 44–56

Greenspan, Henry, Horowitz, Sara R., Kovács, Éva, et al., 'Engaging Survivors: Assessing "Testimony" and "Trauma" as Foundational Concepts', *Dapim: Studies on the Holocaust*, 28:3 (2014), pp. 190–226

Grobman, Alex, *Rekindling the Flame: American Jewish Chaplains and the Survivors of European Jewry, 1944–1948* (Detroit, MI: Wayne State University Press, 1993)

Grossmann, Atina, *Jews, Germans, and Allies: Close Encounters in Occupied Germany* (Princeton, NJ: Princeton University Press, 2007)

Gurvic, Olga, *Quelques Problèmes de l'enfance abandonée* (Geneva: OSE, 1946)

Gutman, Yisrael, and Saf, Avital (eds), *She'erit Hapletah, 1944–1948: Rehabilitation and Political Struggle* (Jerusalem: Yad Vashem, 1990)

Gyomroi, Edith Ludowyk, 'The Analysis of a Young Concentration Camp Victim', *The Psychoanalytic Study of the Child*, XVIII (1963), pp. 484–510

Hacking, Ian, 'Memory Sciences, Memory Politics', in Paul Antze and Michael Lambek (eds), *Tense Past: Cultural Essays in Trauma and Memory* (New York: Routledge, 1996)

Halbwachs, Maurice, *Les Cadres sociaux de la mémoire* (Paris: Presses Universitaires de France, 1925)

Harris, Mark Jonathan, and Oppenheimer, Deborah, *Into the Arms of Strangers: Stories of the Kindertransport* (London: Bloomsbury, 2000)

Hartman, Geoffrey, 'The Humanities of Testimony: An Introduction', *Poetics Today*, 27:2 (2006), pp. 249–60

Hausmann, Erich, *J'Aurais Pu Choisir les Accents circonflexes!* (Paris: FSJU-Hamoré, 2007)

Hazan, Katy, *Les Enfants de l'après-guerre dans les Maisons de l'OSE* (Paris: Somogy Editions d'Art, 2012)

——*Les Orphelins de la Shoah: Les Maisons de l'espoir, 1944–1960* (Paris: Belles Lettres, 2000)

——'Récuperer les Enfants cachés: Un impératif pour les oeuvres juives dans l'après-guerre', *Archives Juives*, 37:2 (2004), pp. 16–31

Hazan, Katy, and Ghozian, Eric (eds), *A La Vie! Les Enfants de Buchenwald, du shtetl à l'OSE* (Paris: Fondation pour la mémoire de la Shoah, 2005)

Heberer, Patricia, *Children during the Holocaust* (Lanham, MD: AltaMira Press, 2011)

Hemmendinger, Judith, 'The Children of Buchenwald: After Liberation and Now', in Shalom Robinson (ed.), *Echoes of the Holocaust* (Jerusalem: Jerusalem Center for Research into the Late Effects of the Holocaust, 1994)

——'Readjustment of Young Concentration Camp Survivors through a Surrogate Family Experience' (paper presented at the Third International Conference on Family Therapy, Jerusalem, 1979)

——*Revenus du néant* (Paris: L'Harmattan, 2002)

——*Survivors: Children of the Holocaust* (Bethesda, MD: National Press, 1986)

Hemmendinger, Judith, and Krell, Robert, *The Children of Buchenwald* (Jerusalem: Gefen Publishers, 2000)

Henry, Marilyn, *Confronting the Perpetrators: A History of the Claims Conference* (New York: Vallentine Mitchell, 2007)

Herf, Jeffrey, *Divided Memory: The Nazi Past in the Two Germanys* (Cambridge, MA: Harvard University Press, 1997)

Herzog, Dagmar, *Cold War Freud: Psychoanalysis in an Age of Catastrophes* (Cambridge: Cambridge University Press, 2017)

Heuman, Johannes, *The Holocaust and French Historical Culture, 1945–65* (Basingstoke: Palgrave Macmillan, 2015)

Hicklin, Margot, *War-Damaged Children: Some Aspects of Recovery* (London: Association of Psychiatric Social Workers, 1946)

Hilberg, Raul, *The Destruction of the European Jews*, 3rd edn (New Haven, CT: Yale University Press, 2003)

Hirsch, Marianne, *Family Frames: Photography, Narrative and Postmemory* (Cambridge, MA: Harvard University Press, 1997)

——*The Generation of Postmemory: Writing and Visual Culture after the Holocaust* (New York: Columbia University Press, 2012)

Hitchcock, William I., *The Bitter Road to Freedom: A New History of the Liberation of Europe* (London: Faber & Faber, 2009)

Hobson Faure, Laura, 'Orphelines ou soeurs? Penser la famille juive pendant et après la Shoah', *20 & 21. Revue d'histoire*, 145 (2020), pp. 91–104

——'Penser L'Accueil des immigrés juifs: l'American Jewish Joint Distribution Committee et les oeuvres sociales juives françaises après la Shoah', in Colette Zytnicki (ed.), *Terre d'exil, terre d'asile. Migrations juives en France aux XIXe et XXe siècles* (Paris: L'Eclat, 2010)

——*Un 'Plan Marshall juif': La présence juive américaine en France après la Shoah, 1944–1954* (Paris: Armand Colin, 2013)

Hobson Faure, Laura, and Vanden Daelen, Veerle, 'Imported from the United States? The American Jewish Welfare System in Post-WWII Europe: The Cases of Belgium and France, 1944–1960', in Avinoam Patt, Atina Grossmann, Linda G. Levi, and Maud S. Mandel (eds), *The Joint Distribution Committee: 100 Years of Jewish History* (Detroit, MI: Wayne State University Press, 2017)

Hobson Faure, Laura et al. (eds), *L'Oeuvre de Secours aux Enfants et les populations juives au XXe siècle* (Paris: Armand Colin, 2014)

Hochberg-Mariańska, Maria, and Grüss, Noë (eds), *The Children Accuse*, trans. Bill Johnston (London: Vallentine Mitchell, 1996)

Hoffman, Eva, *After Such Knowledge: A Meditation on the Aftermath of the Holocaust* (London: Vintage, 2004)

Holborn, Louise, *The International Refugee Organization. A Specialized Agency of the United Nations: Its History and Work, 1946–1952* (Oxford: Oxford University Press, 1956)

Holian, Anna, *Between National Socialism and Soviet Communism: Displaced Persons in Postwar Germany* (Ann Arbor, MI: University of Michigan Press, 2011)

Horowitz, Mardi Jon (ed.), *Essential Papers on Post-Traumatic Stress Disorder* (New York: New York University Press, 1999)

Höschler, Christian, 'International Families? Community Living in the IRO Children's Village Bad Aibling, 1948–1951', in Henning Borggräfe, Akim Jah, Nina Ritz, and Steffen Jost, with Elisabeth Schwabauer (eds), *Freilegungen: Rebuilding Lives – Child Survivors and DP Children in the Aftermath of the Holocaust and Forced Labour* (Göttingen: Wallstein Verlag, 2017), pp. 105–24

Humbert, Laure, ' "When Most Relief Workers Had Never Heard of Freud": UNRRA in the French Occupation Zone, 1945–1947', in Sandra Barkhof and Angela Smith (eds), *War and Displacement in the Twentieth Century: Global Conflicts* (London: Routledge, 2014), pp. 199–223

Illouz, Eva, *Saving the Modern Soul: Therapy, Emotions, and the Culture of Self-Help* (Berkeley, CA: University of California Press, 2008)

Independent Commission of Experts Switzerland – Second World War (ICE), *Switzerland and Refugees in the Nazi Era (Interim Report)* (Bern: BBL, 1999)

——*Switzerland, National Socialism, and the Second World War (Final Report)* (Zurich: Pendo Verlag, 2002)

Jablonka, Ivan, *Histoire des grands-parents que je n'ai pas eus* (Paris: Seuil, 2012)

Jablonka, Ivan (ed.), *L'Enfant Shoah* (Paris: Presses Universitaires de France, 2014)

Jinks, Rebecca, *Representing Genocide: The Holocaust as Paradigm?* (London: Bloomsbury, 2016)

Jockusch, Laura, *Collect and Record! Jewish Holocaust Documentation in Early Postwar Europe* (Oxford: Oxford University Press, 2012)

Jockusch, Laura, and Patt, Avinoam J., 'Holocaust Survivors Diasporas', in Hasia R. Diner (ed.), *Oxford Handbook of Jewish Diasporas* (New York: Oxford University Press, forthcoming)

Jones, Amanda, *Bringing Up War Babies: The Wartime Child in Women's Writing and Psychoanalysis at Mid-Century* (New York: Routledge, 2018)

Judt, Tony, *Postwar: A History of Europe since 1945* (London: Pimlico, 2007)

Kadosh, Sara, 'Jewish Refugee Children in Switzerland, 1939–1950', in J. K. Roth and Elisabeth Maxwell (eds), *Remembering for the Future* (London: Palgrave Macmillan, 2001)

Kangisser Cohen, Sharon, *Child Survivors of the Holocaust in Israel: Social Dynamics and Post-War Experiences* (Brighton: Sussex Academic Press, 2005)

Kangisser Cohen, Sharon, Fogelman, Eva, and Ofer, Dalia (eds), *Children in the Holocaust and its Aftermath: Historical and Psychological Studies of the Kestenberg Archive* (Oxford: Berghahn Books, 2017)

Kaplan, Jacob, *L'Affaire Finaly* (Paris: Cerf, 1993)

Kaplan, Marion, *Between Dignity and Despair: Jewish Life in Nazi Germany* (Oxford: Oxford University Press, 1998)

Karpf, Anne, *The War After: Living with the Holocaust* (London: Minerva, 1997)

Kavanaugh, Sarah, *ORT, the Second World War and the Rehabilitation of Holocaust Survivors* (London: Vallentine Mitchell, 2008)

Keilson, Hans, *Sequential Traumatization in Children: A Clinical and Statistical Follow-Up Study on the Fate of the Jewish War Orphans in the Netherlands* (Jerusalem: Magnes Press, 1992)

Keren, Nili, 'The Family Camp', in Yisrael Gutman and Michael Berenbaum (eds), *Anatomy of the Auschwitz Death Camp* (Bloomington, IN: Indiana University Press, 1994)

Kestenberg, Judith, 'Memories from Early Childhood', *Psychoanalytic Review*, 75:4 (1988), pp. 561–71

——'Psychoanalytic Contributions to the Problem of Children of Survivors from Nazi Persecution', *Israel Annals of Psychiatry and Related Disciplines*, 10:4 (1972)

Kestenberg, Judith, and Brenner, Ira (eds), *The Last Witness: The Child Survivor of the Holocaust* (Washington, DC: American Psychiatric Press, 1996)

Kestenberg, Judith, and Fogelman, Eva (eds), *Children During the Nazi Reign: Psychological Perspective on the Interview Process* (London: Praeger, 1994)

Kestenberg, Judith, and Kestenberg, Milton, 'Background of the Study', in Martin S. Bergmann and Milton E. Jucovy (eds), *Generations of the Holocaust* (New York: Columbia University Press, 1982), pp. 33–43

Kestenberg, Milton, 'Discriminatory Aspects of the German Indemnification Policy: A Continuation of Persecution', in Martin S. Bergmann and Milton E. Jucovy (eds), *Generations of the Holocaust* (New York: Columbia University Press, 1982), pp. 62–79

Kieval, Hillel J., 'Legality and Resistance in Vichy France: The Rescue of Jewish Children', *Proceedings of the American Philosophical Society*, 124:5 (1980), pp. 339–66

Kirsh, Mary Fraser, 'The Lost Children of Europe: Narrating the Rehabilitation of Child Holocaust Survivors in Great Britain and Israel', unpublished PhD thesis (University of Wisconsin-Madison, 2012)

——'Remembering the "Pain of Belonging": Jewish Children Hidden as Catholics in Second World War France', in Simone Gigliotti and Monica Tempian (eds), *The Young Victims of the Nazi Regime: Migration, the Holocaust, and Postwar Displacement* (London: Bloomsbury, 2016)

Klarsfeld, Serge, *French Children of the Holocaust: A Memorial* (New York: New York University Press, 1996)

——*Le Mémorial de la déportation des Juifs de France* (Paris: Association des Fils et Filles des Déportés Juifs de France, 1978)

——*Memorial to the Jews Deported from France, 1942–1944* (New York: B. Klarsfeld Foundation, 1983)

Knox, Katherine, and Kushner, Tony, *Refugees in an Age of Genocide: Global, National and Local Perspectives during the Twentieth Century* (London: Frank Cass, 1999)

Kolinski, Eva, *After the Holocaust: Jewish Survivors in Germany after 1945* (London: Pimlico, 2004)

Königseder, Angelika, and Wetzel, Juliane, *Waiting for Hope: Jewish Displaced Persons in Post-World War II Germany*, trans. John A. Broadwin (Evanston, IL: Northwestern University Press)

Kovarsky, Marcel, 'Casework with Refugee Children', *Jewish Social Service Quarterly*, 24 (June 1948), pp. 402–7

Krell, Robert Suedfeld, Peter, and Soriano, Erin, 'Child Holocaust Survivors as Parents: A Transgenerational Perspective', *American Journal of Orthopsychiatry*, 74:4 (2004), pp. 502–8

Krell, Robert, and Glassner, Martin Ira (eds), *And Life Is Changed Forever: Holocaust Childhoods Remembered* (Detroit, MI: Wayne State University Press, 2006)

Krell, Robert, and Sherman, Marc I. (eds), *Medical and Psychological Effects of Concentration Camps on Holocaust Survivors* (New Brunswick, NJ: Transaction Publishers, 1997)

Krystal, Henry (ed.), *Massive Psychic Trauma* (New York: International Universities Press, 1968)

Krystal, Henry, and Niederland, William G. (eds), *Psychic Traumatization: After Effects in Individuals and Communities* (Boston, MA: Little, Brown, 1971)

Kubica, Helena, 'Children', in Yisrael Gutman and Michael Berenbaum, *Anatomy of the Auschwitz Death Camp* (Bloomington, IN: Indiana University Press, 1994)

Kuchler-Silbermann, Lena, *My Hundred Children* (London: Souvenir, 1961)

Lagrou, Pieter, *The Legacy of Nazi Occupation: Patriotic Memory and National Recovery in Western Europe, 1945–1965* (New York: Cambridge University Press, 2000)

Langer, Lawrence L., 'The Dilemma of Choice in the Death Camps', in Alan Rosenberg and Gerald Myers (eds), *Echoes from the Holocaust: Philosophical Reflections on a Dark Time* (Philadelphia, PA: Temple University Press, 1988), pp. 118–27

——*Holocaust Testimonies: The Ruins of Memory* (New Haven, CT: Yale University Press, 1993)

Lappin, Ben, *The Redeemed Children: The Story of the Rescue of War Orphans by the Jewish Community of Canada* (Toronto: University of Toronto Press, 1963)

Lappin, Elena, 'The Man with Two Heads', *Granta*, 66 (1999), pp. 7–66

Laqueur, Walter (ed.), *The Holocaust Encyclopedia* (New Haven, CT: Yale University Press, 2001)

Laub, Morris, *Last Barrier to Freedom: Internment of Jewish Holocaust Survivors in Cyprus, 1946–1949* (Jerusalem: Magnes Press, 1985)

Lavsky, Hagit, *New Beginnings: Holocaust Survivors in Bergen-Belsen and the British Zone in Germany* (Detroit, MI: Wayne State University Press, 2002)

Lazare, Lucien (ed.), *The Encyclopedia of the Righteous Among the Nations: France* (Jerusalem: Yad Vashem, 2003)

Lenroot, Katherine, 'The United States Program for the Care of Refugee Children', *Proceedings of the National Conference of Social Work* (1941)

Levi, Primo, *If This Is a Man* (New York: Orion Press, 1959)

Levy, Daniel, and Sznaider, Natan, *The Holocaust and Memory in the Global Age* (Philadelphia, PA: Temple University Press, 2005)

Leys, Ruth, *Trauma: A Geneaology* (Chicago, IL: University of Chicago Press, 2000)

Lienert, Salome, *Das Schweizer Hilfswerk für Emigrantenkinder, 1933–1947* (Zurich: Chronos Verlag, 2013)

Linenthal, Edward T., *Preserving Memory: The Struggle to Create America's Holocaust Museum* (New York: Viking, 1995)

Loftus, Elizabeth, 'Creating False Memories', *Scientific American*, 277:3 (1997), pp. 70–5

——'Tricked by Memory', in Jeffrey Jaclyn, Glenace Edwall, and Donald A. Ritchie (eds), *Memory and History: Essays on Recalling and Interpreting Experience* (Lanham, MD: University Press of America, 1994), pp. 17–32

London, Louise, *Whitehall and the Jews, 1933–1948: British Immigration Policy, Jewish Refugees and the Holocaust* (Cambridge: Cambridge University Press, 2001)

Loughran, Tracey, 'Shell Shock, Trauma, and the First World War: The Making of a Diagnosis and its Histories', *Journal of the History of Medicine and Allied Sciences*, 67:1 (January 2012), pp. 94–119

Lowe, Keith, *Savage Continent: Europe in the Aftermath of World War II* (London: Viking, 2012)

Lubove, Roy, *The Professional Altruist: The Emergence of Social Work as a Career, 1870–1930* (Cambridge, MA: Harvard University Press, 1965)

Macardle, Dorothy, *Children of Europe* (London: Victor Gollancz, 1949)

Maercker, Andreas, Salomon, Zahava, and Schutzwohl, Matthias (eds), *Post-Traumatic Stress Disorder: A Lifespan Developmental Perspective* (New York: Bertrams, 1999)

Makari, George, *Revolution in Mind: The Creation of Psychoanalysis* (New York: HarperCollins, 2008)

Mandel, Maud, *In the Aftermath of Genocide: Armenians and Jews in Twentieth-Century France* (Durham, NC: Duke University Press, 2003)

Mankowitz, Zeev, *Life Between Memory and Hope* (Cambridge: Cambridge University Press, 2009)

Marks, Jane, *The Hidden Children: The Secret Survivors of the Holocaust* (New York: Ballantine Books, 1993)

Marrus, Michael, *The Holocaust in History* (Hanover, NH: University Press of New England, 1987)

——*The Unwanted: European Refugees in the Twentieth Century* (New York: Oxford University Press, 1985)

——'The Vatican and the Custody of Jewish Child Survivors', *Holocaust and Genocide Studies*, 21:3 (2007), pp. 378–403

Martz, Fraidie, *Open Your Hearts: The Story of the Jewish War Orphans in Canada* (Montreal: Véhicule Press, 1996)

Masour-Ratner, Jenny, and Hazan, Katy, *Mes Vingt Ans à l'OSE* (Paris: Le Manuscrit, 2006)

Maynes, Mary Jo, 'Age as a Category of Historical Analysis: History, Agency, and Narratives of Childhood', *Journal of the History of Childhood and Youth*, 1 (2008), pp. 114–24

Mazower, Mark, *Dark Continent: Europe's Twentieth Century* (London: Penguin, 1998)

——*Hitler's Empire: Nazi Rule in Occupied Europe* (London: Allen Lane, 2008)

McDonald, Chad, ' "We Became British Aliens": Kindertransport Refugees Narrating the Discovery of their Parents' Fates', *Holocaust Studies*, 24:4 (2018), pp. 395–417

McLaughlin, Jeff, and Schiff, Vera, *Bound for Theresienstadt: Love, Loss and Resistance in a Nazi Concentration Camp* (London: McFarland and Company, 2017)

Michlic, Joanna B., 'Jewish Children in Nazi-Occupied Poland: Survival and Polish-Jewish Relations during the Holocaust as Reflected in Early Postwar Recollections', *Search and Research – Lectures and Papers* (Jerusalem: Yad Vashem, 2008), p. xiv

——' "The War Began for Me after the War": Jewish Children in Poland, 1945–1949', in Jonathan Friedman (ed.), *The Routledge History of the Holocaust* (London: Routledge, 2011), pp. 482–97

——'Who Am I? Jewish Children Search for Identity in Postwar Poland', *Polin: Studies in Polish Jewry*, 20 (2007), pp. 98–121

Michman, Dan, *The Emergence of Jewish Ghettos during the Holocaust* (Cambridge: Cambridge University Press, 2011)

Midgley, Nick, 'Anna Freud: The Hampstead War Nurseries and the Role of the Direct Observation of Children for Psychoanalysis', *International Journal of Psycho-Analysis*, 88:4 (2007), pp. 939–59

Minkowski, Eugène, *Les Enfants de Buchenwald* (Geneva: Union OSE, 1946)

Moskovitz, Sarah, *Love Despite Hate: Child Survivors of the Holocaust and their Adult Lives* (New York: Schocken Books, 1983)

Moskovitz, Sarah, and Krell, Robert, 'The Struggle for Justice: A Survey of Child Holocaust Survivors' Experiences with Restitution', in John K. Roth and Elisabeth Maxwell (eds), *Remembering for the Future: The Holocaust in an Age of Genocide. Vol. 2: Ethics and Religion* (New York: Palgrave, 2001), pp. 923–37

Muhlen, Robert, *The Survivors: A Report on the Jews in Germany Today* (New York: T. Y. Crowell, 1962)

Müller, Beate, 'Trauma, Historiography and Polyphony: Adult Voices in the CJHC's Early Postwar Child Holocaust Testimonies', *History & Memory*, 24:2 (2012), pp. 157–95

Myers Feinstein, Margarete, *Holocaust Survivors in Postwar Germany, 1945–1957* (Cambridge: Cambridge University Press, 2010)

——'Jewish Observance in Amalek's Shadow: Mourning, Marriage and Birth Rituals among Displaced Persons in Germany', in Avinoam J. Patt and Michael Berkowitz (eds), *We Are Here: New Approaches to Jewish Displaced Persons in Postwar Germany* (Detroit, MI: Wayne State University Press, 2010)

Nelson, Katherine, 'The Psychological and Social Origins of Autobiographical Memory', *Psychological Science*, 4:1 (1993), pp. 1–8

Nicholas, Lynn H., *Cruel World: The Children of Europe in the Nazi Web* (New York: Vintage, 2006)

Niederland, William G., 'Clinical Observations on the "Survivor Syndrome"', *International Journal of Psycho-Analysis*, 49 (1968), pp. 313–15

Niewyk, Donald L. (ed.), *Fresh Wounds: Early Narratives of Holocaust Survival* (Chapel Hill, NC, and London: University of North Carolina Press, 2011)

Norton, Jennifer Craig, *The Kindertransport: Contesting Memory* (Bloomington, IN: Indiana University Press, 2019)

Novick, Peter, *The Holocaust and Collective Memory* (London: Bloomsbury, 2001)

Ofer, Dalia, Ouzan, Françoise, and Baumel-Schwartz, Judith Tydor (eds), *Holocaust Survivors: Resettlement, Memories, Identities* (Oxford: Berghahn Books, 2011)

Ogilvie, Sarah, and Miller, Scott, *Refuge Denied: The St. Louis Passengers and the Holocaust* (Madison, WI: University of Wisconsin Press, 2006)

Ostrovsky, Michal, '"We Are Standing By": Rescue Operations of the United States Committee for the Care of European Children', *Holocaust and Genocide Studies*, 29:2 (2015), pp. 230–50

Panz, Karolina, '"They Did Not Want Any More Jews There": The Fate of Jewish Orphans in Podhale, 1945–1946', in Henning Borggräfe, Akim Jah, Nina Ritz, and Steffen Jost, with Elisabeth Schwabauer (eds), *Freilegungen: Rebuilding Lives – Child Survivors and DP Children in the Aftermath of the Holocaust and Forced Labour* (Göttingen: Wallstein Verlag, 2017), pp. 93–104

Papanek, Ernst, *Out of the Fire* (New York: William Morrow, 1975)

Passerini, Luisa, 'Work Ideology and Consensus under Italian Fascism', *History Workshop Journal*, 8:1 (1979), pp. 82–108

Patt, Avinoam J., *Finding Home and Homeland: Jewish Youth and Zionism in the Aftermath of the Holocaust* (Detroit, MI: Wayne State University Press, 2009)

Patt, Avinoam J., and Berkowitz, Michael (eds), *We Are Here: New Approaches to Jewish Displaced Persons in Postwar Germany* (Detroit, MI: Wayne State University Press, 2010)

Perra, Emiliano, 'Narratives of Innocence and Victimhood: The Reception of the Miniseries Holocaust in Italy', *Holocaust and Genocide Studies*, 22:3 (2008), pp. 411–40

Pillemer, David B., and White, Sheldon H., 'Childhood Events Recalled by Children and Adults', in Hayne W. Reese (ed.), *Advances in Child Development and Behaviour* (San Diego, CA: Academic Press, 1989), pp. 297–340

Poliakov, Léon, *Bréviaire de la haine* (Paris: Calmann-Levy, 1951)

Portelli, Alessandro, *The Battle of Valle Giulia: Oral History and the Art of Dialogue* (Madison, WI: University of Wisconsin Press, 1997)

——*The Death of Luigi Trastulli and Other Stories: Form and Meaning in Oral History* (Albany, NY: State University of New York Press, 1991)

——*The Order Has Been Carried Out: History, Memory, and Meaning of a Nazi Massacre in Rome* (New York: Palgrave Macmillan, 2003)

——'What Makes Oral History Different?', in Robert Perks and Alistair Thomson (eds), *The Oral History Reader*, 2nd edn (New York: Routledge, 2006), pp. 32–42

Posnanski, Renée, *Les Juifs en France pendant la Seconde Guerre Mondiale* (Paris: Hachette, 1997)

Poujol, Catherine, '1945–1953: Petite Chronique de l'affaire des enfants Finaly', *Archives Juives*, 37:2 (2004), pp. 7–15

——*L'Affaire Finaly: Les Enfants cachés* (Paris: Berg International, 2006)

Pross, Christian, *Paying for the Past: The Struggle over Reparations for Surviving Victims of the Nazi Terror* (Baltimore, MD: Johns Hopkins University Press, 1998)

Proudfoot, Malcolm, *European Refugees, 1939–1952: A Study in Forced Population Movement* (London: Faber & Faber, 1957)

Rakoff, Vivian, 'Long-Term Effects of the Concentration Camp Experience', *Viewpoints* (March 1966), pp. 17–21

Rakoff, Vivian, Sigal, J. J., and Epstein, N. B., 'Children and Families of Concentration Camp Survivors', *Canada's Mental Health*, 14:4 (July–August 1966), pp. 24–6

Reilly, Joanne, *Belsen: The Liberation of a Concentration Camp* (London: Routledge, 1998)

Reinisch, Jessica, 'Internationalism in Relief: The Birth (and Death) of UNRRA', *Past and Present* (2011), pp. 258–89

Reinisch, Jessica, and White, Elizabeth (eds), *The Disentaglement of Populations: Migration, Expulsion and Displacement in Post-War Europe, 1944–9* (Basingstoke: Palgrave Macmillan, 2011)

Reitlinger, Gerald, *The Final Solution: An Attempt to Exterminate the Jews of Europe* (New York: Vallentine Mitchell, 1953)

Reus, Julia, '"Everywhere Where Human Beings Are, We Can Find Our Children": On the Organization of the ITS Child Search Branch', in Henning Borggräfe, Akim Jah, Nina Ritz, and Steffen Jost, with Elisabeth Schwabauer (eds), *Freilegungen: Rebuilding Lives – Child Survivors and DP Children in the Aftermath of the Holocaust and Forced Labour* (Göttingen: Wallstein Verlag, 2017), pp. 41–69

Robson, William Lane M., and Leung, Alexander K. C., 'Secondary Nocturnal Enuresis', *Clinical Pediatrics*, 39:7 (2000), pp. 379–85

Roseman, Mark, *A Past in Hiding: Memory and Survival in Nazi Germany* (New York: Metropolitan Books, 2000)

Rosen, Alan, '"We Know Very Little in America": David Boder and Un-Belated Testimony', in David Cesarani and Eric Sundquist (eds), *After the Holocaust: Challenging the Myth of Silence* (London: Routledge, 2012), pp. 102–14

——*The Wonder of Their Voices: The 1946 Holocaust Interviews of David Boder* (Oxford: Oxford University Press, 2010)

Rossini, Gill, *A Social History of Adoption in England and Wales* (Barnsley: Pen and Sword, 2014)

Rossler, Peter, *The Words to Remember It: Memoirs of Child Holocaust Survivors* (Melbourne: Scribe, 2009)

Roth, John K., and Maxwell, Elisabeth (eds), *Remembering for the Future: The Holocaust in an Age of Genocide. Vol. 3: Memory* (New York: Palgrave, 2001)

Rothberg, Michael, *Multidirectional Memory: Remembering the Holocaust in the Age of Decolonization* (Stanford, CA: Stanford University Press, 2009)

Rothfeld, Anne, 'A Source for Holocaust Research: The United Restitution Organization Files', *Perspectives on History: The Newsmagazine of the American Historical Association* (April 2000)

Rotten, Elisabeth, *Children's Communities: A Way of Life for War's Victims* (Paris: UNESCO, 1949)

Rousso, Henry, *The Vichy Syndrome: History and Memory in France since 1944*, trans. Arthur Goldhammer (Cambridge, MA: Harvard University Press, 1991)

Rozett, Robert, 'International Intervention: The Role of Diplomats in Attempts to Rescue Jews in Hungary', in Randolph Braham (ed.), *The Nazis' Last Victims: The Holocaust in Hungary* (Detroit, MI: Wayne State University Press, 1998), pp. 137–52

Rubin, D. C., 'The Distribution of Early Childhood Memories', *Memory*, 8:4 (2000), pp. 265–9

Rutland, Suzanne D., 'A Distant Sanctuary: Australia and Child Holocaust Survivors', in Simone Gigliotti and Monica Tempian (eds), *The Young Victims of the Nazi Regime: Migration, the Holocaust, and Postwar Displacement* (London: Bloomsbury, 2016)

——'Postwar Anti-Jewish Refugee Hysteria: A Case of Racial or Religious Bigotry?', *Journal of Australian Studies*, 77 (2003), pp. 69–79

Saalheimer, Manfred, 'Bringing Jewish Orphan Children to Canada', *Canadian Jewish Review* (5 December 1947), pp. 7 and 82

Salvatici, Silvia, '"Help the People to Help Themselves": UNRRA Relief Workers and European Displaced Persons', *Journal of Refugee Studies*, 25:3 (2012), pp. 428–51

Samuel, Vivette, *Rescuing the Children: A Holocaust Memoir* (Madison, WI: University of Wisconsin Press, 2002)

Schein, Ada, '"Everyone Can Hold a Pen": The Documentation Project in the DP Camps in Germany', in David Bankier and Dan Michman (eds), *Holocaust Historiography in Context: Emergence, Challenges, Polemics and Achievements* (New York, 2008), pp. 103–34

Schmideberg, Melitta, *Children in Need* (London: George Allen and Unwin, 1948)

Schneer, David, *Through Soviet Jewish Eyes: Photography, War, and the Holocaust* (New Brunswick, NJ: Rutgers University Press, 2011)

Schneider, Wolfgang, and Pressley, Michael (eds), *Memory Development between Two and Twenty*, 2nd edn (Mahwah, NJ: Lawrence Erlbaum Associates, 1997)

Schrafstetter, Susanna, 'The Diplomacy of *Wiedergutmachung*: Memory, the Cold War, and the Western European Victims of Nazism, 1956–1964', *Holocaust and Genocide Studies*, 7:3 (2003), pp. 459–79

Schwarz, Joseph W., *The Redeemers: A Saga of the Years, 1945–1952* (New York: Farrar, Straus and Young, 1953)

Segev, Tom, *The Seventh Million: The Israelis and the Holocaust* (New York: Henry Holt, 2000)

Seidman, Naomi, 'Elie Wiesel and the Scandal of Jewish Rage', *Jewish Social Studies*, 3:1 (1996), pp. 1–19

Shafter, Toby, 'How DP Children Play', *Congress Weekly* (26 March 1948)

Shapira, Michal, *The War Inside: Psychoanalysis, Total War, and the Making of the Democratic Self in Postwar Britain* (Cambridge: Cambridge University Press, 2013)

Sharples, Caroline, and Jensen, Olaf (eds), *Britain and the Holocaust* (Basingstoke: Palgrave Macmillan, 2013)

Sheftel, Anna, and Zembrzycki, Stacey, 'We Started over Again, We Were Young: Postwar Social Worlds of Child Holocaust Survivors in Montreal', *Urban History Review*, 39:1 (2010), pp. 20–30

Shenker, Noah, *Reframing Holocaust Testimony* (Bloomington, IN: Indiana University Press, 2015)

Shephard, Ben, *The Long Road Home: The Aftermath of the Second World War* (London: Bodley Head, 2010)

Sherman, Judith H., *Say the Name: A Survivor's Tale in Prose and Poetry* (Albuquerque, NM: University of New Mexico Press, 2005)

Sherwin, Michael, 'The Law in Relation to the Wishes and Feelings of the Child', in Ronald Davie, Graham Upton, and Ved Varma (eds), *The Voice of the Child: A Handbook for Professionals* (London: Falmer Press, 1996)

Śliwowska, Wiktoria (ed.), *The Last Eyewitnesses: Children of the Holocaust Speak* (Evanston, IL: Northwestern University Press, 1993)

Snyder, Timothy, *Bloodlands: Europe Between Hitler and Stalin* (London: Vintage, 2011)

Solomon, Susan Gross, 'Patient Dossiers and Clinical Practice in 1950s French Child Psychiatry', *Revue d'histoire de l'enfance 'irrégulière'*, 18 (2016), pp. 275–96

Somers, Margaret R., 'The Narrative Construction of Identity: A Relational and Network Approach', *Theory and Society*, 23 (1994), pp. 605–49

Sonnert, Gerhard, and Holton, Gerald, *What Happened to the Children Who Fled Nazi Persecution* (New York: Palgrave, 2008)

Stargardt, Nicholas, 'Children's Art of the Holocaust', *Past and Present*, 161 (1998), pp. 191–235

——*Witnesses of War: Children's Lives under the Nazis* (London: Pimlico, 2006)

Stein, Arlene, *Reluctant Witnesses: Survivors, Their Children, and the Rise of Holocaust Consciousness* (Oxford: Oxford University Press, 2014)

Steinitz, Lucy Y., and Szonyi, David M. (eds), *Living after the Holocaust: Reflections by the Post-War Generation in America* (New York: Bloch Publishing, 1975)

Sterling, Eric (ed.), *Life in the Ghettos during the Holocaust* (Syracuse, NY: Syracuse University Press, 2005)

Stewart, John, *Child Guidance in Britain, 1918–1955: The Dangerous Age of Childhood* (London: Pickering and Chatto, 2013)

——' "The Dangerous Age of Childhood": Child Guidance and the "Normal" Child in Great Britain, 1920–1950', *Paedagogica Historica*, 47 (2011), pp. 785–803

Stone, Dan, 'The Domestication of Violence: Forging a Collective Memory of the Holocaust in Britain, 1945–6', *Patterns of Prejudice*, 33:2 (1999), pp. 13–24

——(ed.), *The Historiography of the Holocaust* (London: Palgrave Macmillan, 2004)

——'The Holocaust and its Historiography', in Dan Stone (ed.), *The Historiography of Genocide* (Basingstoke: Palgrave Macmillan, 2008), pp. 373–99

——*The Liberation of the Camps: The End of the Holocaust and Its Aftermath* (New Haven, CT: Yale University Press, 2015)

Strutz, Andrea, ' "Detour to Canada": The Fate of Juvenile Austrian-Jewish Refugees after the "Anschluss" of 1938', in Simone Gigliotti and Monica Tempian (eds), *The Young Victims of the Nazi Regime: Migration, the Holocaust, and Postwar Displacement* (London: Bloomsbury, 2016), pp. 31–50

Suleiman, Susan Rubin, 'The 1.5 Generation: Thinking about Child Survivors and the Holocaust', *American Imago*, 59:3 (2002), pp. 277–95

——'Orphans of the Shoah and Jewish Identity in Post-Holocaust France: From the Individual to the Collective', in Seán Hand and Steven T. Katz (eds), *Post-Holocaust France and the Jews, 1945–1955* (New York: New York University Press, 2015), pp. 118–38

Sutro, Nettie, *Jugend Auf Der Flucht, 1933–1948* (Zurich: Chronos Verlag, 1952)

Tannen, Deborah, *Talking Voices: Repetition, Dialogue, and Imagery in Conversational Discourse* (Cambridge: Cambridge University Press, 2007)

Taylor, Lynn, *In the Children's Best Interests: Unaccompanied Children in American-Occupied Germany, 1945–1952* (Toronto: University of Toronto Press, 2017)

Tec, Nechama, *Jewish Children Between Protectors and Murderers* (Washington, DC: USHMM, 2005)

The Child Survivors' Association of Great Britain, *We Remember: Child Survivors of the Holocaust Speak* (Leicester: Matador, 2011)

Trimble, Michael R., 'Post-Traumatic Stress Disorder: History of a Concept', in Charles R. Figley (ed.), *Trauma and its Wake: The Study and Treatment of Post-Traumatic Stress Disorder)*, vol. I (Hove: Psychology Press, 1985), pp. 5–14

Trossman, Bernard, 'Adolescent Children of Concentration Camp Survivors', *Canadian Psychiatric Association Journal*, 13:2 (April 1968), pp. 121–3

Urban, Susanne, ' "More Children are to be Interviewed": Child Survivors' Narratives in the Child Search Brach Files', in Henning Borggräfe, Akim Jah, Nina Ritz, and Steffen Jost, with Elisabeth Schwabauer (eds), *Freilegungen: Rebuilding Lives – Child Survivors and DP Children in the Aftermath of the Holocaust and Forced Labour* (Göttingen: Wallstein Verlag, 2017), pp. 70–92

——'Unaccompanied Children and the Allied Child Search', in Simone Gigliotti and Monica Tempian (eds), *The Young Victims of the Nazi Regime: Migration, the Holocaust, and Postwar Displacement* (London: Bloomsbury, 2016)

Urwin, Cathy, and Sharland, Elaine, 'From Bodies to Minds in Childcare Literature: Advice to Parents in Inter-War Britain', in Roger Cooter (ed.), *In the Name of the Child: Health and Welfare in England, 1880–1940* (New York: Routledge, 1992)

Valent, Paul, *Child Survivors of the Holocaust* (New York: Routledge, 2002)

Vegh, Claudine, *Je Ne Lui Ai Pas Dit Au Revoir: Des Enfants de déportés parlent* (Paris: Gallimard, 2005)

Vromen, Suzanne, *Hidden Children of the Holocaust: Belgian Nuns and Their Daring Rescue of Young Jews from the Nazis* (Oxford: Oxford University Press, 2010)

——'Linking Religion and Family: Memories of Children Hidden in Belgian Convents during the Holocaust', in Marie Louise Seeberg, Irene Levin, and Claudia Lenz (eds), *The Holocaust as Active Memory* (Farnham, Surrey: Ashgate, 2013), pp. 15–28

Wachsmann, Nikolaus, *KL: A History of the Nazi Concentration Camps* (London: Abacus, 2016)

Warhaftig, Zorach, and Freid, Jacob, *Uprooted: Jewish Refugees and Displaced Persons after Liberation* (New York: American Jewish Congress, 1946)

*Washington Post* staff, *The Obligation to Remember* (Washington, DC: The Washington Post, 1983)

Wells, Christine, Morrison, Catriona, and Conway, Martin, 'Adult Recollections of Childhood Memories: What Details Can Be Recalled?', *The Quarterly Journal of Experimental Psychology*, 67:7 (2013), pp. 1,249–61

Whitworth, Wendy (ed.), *Journeys: Children of the Holocaust Tell their Stories* (London: Quill Press, 2009)

Wiesel, Elie, *Night*, trans. Stella Rodway (London: Panther Books, 1960)

Wieviorka, Annette, *Déportation et génocide* (Paris: Plon, 1992)

——*The Era of the Witness*, trans. Jared Stark (Ithaca, NY: Cornell University Press, 2006)

Winnik, H. Z., 'Contribution to Symposium on Psychic Traumatization through Social Catastrophe', *International Journal of Psycho-Analysis*, 49 (1968), pp. 298–301

Winograd, Eugene, 'The Authenticity and Utility of Memories', in Robyn Fivush and Ulric Neisser (eds), *The Remembering Self: Construction and Accuracy in the Self-Narrative* (Cambridge: Cambridge University Press, 1994), pp. 243–51

Wolf, Diane, *Beyond Anne Frank: Hidden Children and Postwar Families in Holland* (Berkeley, CA: University of California Press, 2007)

Wyman, Mark, *DPs: Europe's Displaced Persons* (New York: Cornell University Press, 1998)

Young, Jackie, 'Lost and Waiting to Be Found', unpublished memoir, 2005

Young-Bruehl, Elisabeth, *Anna Freud: A Biography* (New York: Summit Books, 1989)

Zahra, Tara, ' "A Human Treasure": Europe's Displaced Children Between Nationalism and Internationalism', *Past and Present*, 210:6 (2011), pp. 332–50

——*The Lost Children: Reconstructing Europe's Families after World War II* (Cambridge, MA: Harvard University Press, 2011)

Zaretsky, Eli, *Secrets of the Soul: A Social and Cultural History of Psychoanalysis* (New York: Vintage, 2005)

Zeitoun, Sabine, *Histoire de l'OSE: De la Russie tsariste à l'Occupation en France* (Paris: L'Harmattan, 2010)

Zoff, Otto, *They Shall Inherit the Earth* (New York: The John Day Company, 1943)

Zweig, Ronald W., *German Reparations and the Jewish World: A History of the Claims Conference* (Boulder, CO: Westview, 1987)

# INDEX

adolescent survivors
  conformity within new communities
    134–5
  education and future career prospects
    139–41
  in foster families 138–9
  indemnification scheme for victims of
    Nazi persecution 145–53
  knowledge of childhood histories 136–8
  mental health issues 141–4, 166
  and self-identity 132–3
adoption
  adoptability of the children 64–5, 74–5,
    125
  class factors and 64–5, 125
  knowledge of pre-adoption lives 130–2,
    135–6, 192–3, 255–6
  relatives' opposition to 82–4
  stigma of 135–6
  *see also* Canadian Jewish Congress (CJC);
    war orphan schemes
adult carers
  care strategies of 1–2, 8, 18, 54
  children's manipulation of 54–6
  emotional needs of 114
  expectations of children's play 51–2
  and media representations of child
    survivors 46–7
  perceptions of the child survivors 7–8, 41,
    44–7, 54–5, 61
  professionalization of 43–4, 54
  reconstruction of children's identities
    16–17
  re-normalization debates 40–2, 156
  *see also* parents
adult survivors
  ability to care for children 96
  definitions of 200–2
  denial of child survivor's suffering 9–10
  difficulties in reclaiming their children 88

emotional health of 48–9, 101–2
  physical health of 101–2
  post-war conditions of 92–3
  post-war perceptions of 41, 96
  psychosomatic symptoms 159–60
  working in care homes 114–16, 119–20
agency
  of child survivors 7–8
  of child survivors during interview
    processes 244–8
  childhood innocence notion and 219–20
  children as agents of memory 185
  of the children being claimed 65, 98
  of children in family reunification
    scenarios 97
  in migration schemes 84–8, 246–7
aid organizations
  interview projects by 244–8
  model for unaccompanied children
    71–2
  professionalization of 43–4, 54
  role in family reunification 93–6
  *see also* adult carers
Aide aux Israélites Victimes de la Guerre
  (AIVG) 66, 71–5
American Friends' Service Committee 22
American Gathering of Jewish Holocaust
  Survivors 9
Auschwitz-Birkenau concentration camp
  arrivals from Theresienstadt 29, 34
  child numbers in 34
  death marches 111, 112
  evacuation transports 35, 38
  family camp of 34–5
  liberation of 35–6
  parent survivors of 104
  transfers from Bliżyn camp 34
Australia 73–4, 75, 77, 81
Australian Jewish Welfare Society (AJWS)
  75–6

318